Book **2**

Sixth Edition

The Humanistic Tradition

Medieval Europe and the World Beyond

Book

Sixth Edition

The Humanistic Tradition

Medieval Europe and the World Beyond

Gloria K. Fiero

Connect
Learn
Succeed™

Boston   Burr Ridge, IL   Dubuque, IA   New York   San Francisco   St. Louis
Bangkok   Bogotá   Caracas   Kuala Lumpur   Lisbon   London   Madrid   Mexico City
Milan   Montreal   New Delhi   Santiago   Seoul   Singapore   Sydney   Taipei   Toronto

THE HUMANISTIC TRADITION, BOOK 2
MEDIEVAL EUROPE AND THE WORLD BEYOND

Published by McGraw-Hill, an imprint of The McGraw-Hill Companies, Inc.,
1221 Avenue of the Americas, New York, NY, 10020.

This book is printed on acid-free paper.

1 2 3 4 5 6 7 8 9 0 / 0

Library of Congress Cataloging-in-Publication Data

Fiero, Gloria K.
    The humanistic tradition / Gloria K. Fiero.– 6th ed.
        p. cm.
    Includes bibliographical references and index.
    ISBN-13: 978-0-07-352397-2 (bk. 1 : alk. paper)
    ISBN-10: 0-07-352397-6 (bk. 1 : alk. paper)
        1. Civilization, Western–History–Textbooks.
        2. Humanism–History–Textbooks.
        I. Title.

    CB245.F47 2009
    909'.09821–dc22

                                                        2009027018

Permissions Acknowledgments appear on page 173,
and on this page by reference.

Publisher: *Chris Freitag*
Director of Development: *Rhona Robbin*
Associate Sponsoring Editor: *Betty Chen*
Editorial Coordinator: *Sarah Remington*
Marketing Manager: *Pamela Cooper*
Managing Editor: *David Staloch*
Senior Production Supervisor: *Tandra Jorgensen*
Typeface: *10/12 Goudy*
Printer: *Phoenix Offset, Hong Kong*

http://www.mhhe.com

 This book was designed and produced by
Laurence King Publishing Ltd., London
www.laurenceking.com

Commissioning Editor: *Kara Hattersley-Smith*
Senior Editor: *Melissa Danny*
Production Controller: *Simon Walsh*
Picture Researcher: *Emma Brown*
Designer: *Robin Farrow*

Front cover
William Duke of Normandy's Fleet Crossing
the Channel, detail from the Bayeux
Tapestry, late eleventh century. Wool
embroidery on linen, depth approx. 20 in.,
entire length 231 ft. The Art Archive /
Musée de la Tapisserie Bayeux / Gianni
Dagli Orti.

Back cover
Standing Vishnu, from southern India, Chola
period, tenth century. Bronze, with greenish
blue patination, height 33¾ in. The
Metropolitan Museum of Art, New York.
Purchase 1962. Gift of Mr. and Mrs. John D.
Rockefeller.

Frontispiece
Nave facing east, Chartres Cathedral. Nave
completed in 1220. Height of nave 122 ft.
Bob Burch/Bruce Coleman Inc.

Series Contents

Book 2 Contents

MUSIC LISTENING SELECTIONS

CD One Selections 2 to 14

Gregorian chant, "Alleluya, vidimus stellam," codified 590–604 34

Buddhist chant, Morning Prayers (based on the Lotus Scripture) at Nomanji, Japan, excerpt 41

Islamic Call to Prayer 64

Anonymous, Twisya no. 3 of the Nouba 64

Bernart de Ventadour, "Can vei la lauzeta mouver" ("When I behold the lark"), ca. 1150, excerpt 90

Medieval liturgical drama, *The Play of Daniel*, "Ad honorem tui, Christe," "Ecce sunt ante faciem tuam" 139

Hildegard of Bingen, *O Successores* (Your Successors), ca. 1150 139

Two examples of early medieval polyphony: parallel organum, "Rex caeli, Domine," excerpt; melismatic organum, "Alleluia, Justus ut palma," ca. 900–1150; excerpts 140

Pérotin, three-part organum, "Alleluya" (Nativitas), twelfth century 140

Anonymous, Motet, "En non Diu! Quant voi, Eius in Oriente," thirteenth century, excerpt 140

French dance, "Estampie," thirteenth century 141

Indian music, *Thumri*, played on the sitar by Ravi Shankar 150

Chinese music: Cantonese music drama for male solo zither, and other musical instruments, "Ngoh wai heng kong" ("I'm Mad About You") 158

Preface

Each generation leaves a creative legacy, the sum of its ideas and achievements. This legacy represents the response to our effort to ensure our individual and collective survival, our need to establish ways of living in harmony with others, and our desire to understand our place in the universe. Meeting the challenges of *survival, communality,* and *self-knowledge,* we have created and transmitted the tools of science and technology, social and political institutions, religious and philosophic systems, and various forms of personal expression—the totality of which we call *culture.* Handed down from generation to generation, this legacy constitutes the humanistic tradition, the study of which is called *humanities.*

The Humanistic Tradition originated more than two decades ago out of a desire to bring a global perspective to my humanities courses. My fellow humanities teachers and I recognized that a western-only perspective was no longer adequate to understanding the cultural foundations of our global world, yet none of the existing texts addressed our needs. At the time, the challenge was daunting—covering the history of western poetry and prose, art, music, and dance was already an ambitious undertaking for a survey course; how could we broaden the scope to include Asia, Africa, and the Americas without over-packing the course? What evolved was a thematic approach to humanities, not as a collection of disciplines, but as a discipline in itself. This thematic approach considers the interrelatedness of various forms of expression as they work to create, define, and reflect the unique culture of a given time and place. It offers a conceptual framework for students to begin a study of the humanistic tradition that will serve them throughout their lives. I am gratified that others have found this approach to be highly workable for their courses, so much so that *The Humanistic Tradition* has become a widely adopted book for the humanities course.

The Humanistic Tradition pioneered a flexible six-book format in recognition of the varying chronological range of humanities courses. Each slim volume was also convenient for students to bring to classes, the library, and other study areas. The sixth edition continues to be available in this six-book format, as well as in a two-volume set for the most common two-term course configuration.

The Sixth Edition of
The Humanistic Tradition

While the sixth edition of *The Humanistic Tradition* contains a number of new topics, images, and selections, it remains true to my original goal of offering a manageable and memorable introduction to global cultures. At the same time, I have worked to develop new features that are specifically designed to help students master the material and critically engage with the text's primary source readings, art

reproductions, and music recordings. The integration of literary, visual, and aural primary sources is a hallmark of the text, and every effort has been made to provide the most engaging translations, the clearest color images, and the liveliest recorded performances, as well as the most representative selections for every period. The book and companion supplements are designed to offer all of the resources a student and teacher will need for the course.

New Features that Promote Critical Thinking

New to the sixth edition are special features that emphasize connections between time periods, styles, and cultures, and specific issues of universal significance. These have been added to encourage critical thinking and classroom discussion.

- **Exploring Issues** focuses on controversial ideas and current debates, such as the battle over the ownership of antiquities, the role of the non-canonical Christian gospels, the use of optical devices in Renaissance art, the dating of African wood sculptures, and creationism versus evolution.
- **Making Connections** brings attention to contrasts and continuities between past and present ideas, values, and styles. Examples include feudalism East and West, Classical antiquities as models for Renaissance artists, and African culture as inspiration for African-American artists.

New Features that Facilitate Learning and Understanding

The sixth edition provides chapter introductions and summaries that enhance the student's grasp of the materials, and a number of features designed to make the materials more accessible to students:

- **Looking Ahead** offers a brief, preliminary overview that introduces students to the main theme of the chapter.
- **Looking Back** closes each chapter with summary study points that encourage students to review key ideas.
- **Iconographic "keys"** to the meaning of images have been inset alongside selected artworks.
- **Extended captions** to illustrations throughout the text provide additional information about artworks and artists.
- **Chronology boxes** in individual chapters place the arts and ideas in historical background.
- **Before We Begin** precedes the Introduction with a useful guide to understanding and studying humanities.

Organizational Improvements and Updated Content

The sixth edition responds to teachers' requests that the coverage of Mesopotamia precede Egypt and other ancient African cultures in the opening chapters. The global coverage has been refined with revised coverage of the early Americas, new content on archeological discoveries in ancient Peru, a segment on the role of the West in the Islamic Middle East, and a discussion of China's global ascendance. Chapters 36 through 38 have been updated and reorganized: Ethnicity and ethnic identity have been moved to chapter 38 (Globalism and the Contemporary World), which brings emphasis to recent developments in digital technology, environmentalism, and global terrorism. Other revisions throughout the text also respond to teacher feedback; for example, a description of the *bel canto* style in music has been added; Jan van Eyck's paintings appear in both chapters 17 and 19 (in different contexts); and T. S. Eliot's works are discussed in both chapters 32 and 35.

Among the notable writers added to the sixth edition are William Blake, Jorge Luis Borges, Seamus Heaney, and John Ashbury. New additions to the art program include works by Benozzo Gozzoli, Buckminster Fuller, Kara Walker, Jeff Wall, Damien Hirst, El Anatsui, and Norman Foster.

Beyond *The Humanistic Tradition*

Connect Humanities

Connect Humanities is a learning and assessment tool designed and developed to improve students' performance by making the learning process more efficient and more focused through the use of engaging, assignable content, which is text-specific and mapped to learning objectives, and integrated tools. Using this platform, instructors can deliver assignments easily online, and save time through an intuitive and easy to use interface and through modifiable pre-built assignments.

Connect provides instructors with the Image Bank, a way to easily browse and search for images and to download them for use in class presentations.

Visit mcgrawhillconnect.com

Traditions: Humanities Readings through the Ages

Traditions is a new database conceived as both a stand-alone product as well as a companion source to McGraw-Hill's humanities titles. The collection is broad in nature, containing both western and non-western readings from ancient and contemporary eras, hand-picked from such disciplines as literature, philosophy, and science. The flexibility of Primis Online's database allows the readings to be arranged both chronologically and by author.

Visit www.primisonline.com/traditions

Music Listening Compact Discs

Two audio compact discs have been designed exclusively for use with *The Humanistic Tradition*. CD One corresponds to the music listening selections discussed in Books 1–3 (Volume I), and CD Two contains the music in Books 4–6 (Volume II). Music logos (right) that appear in the margins of the text refer to the Music Listening Selections found on the audio compact discs. The compact discs can be packaged with any or all of the six books or two-volume versions of the text.

Online Learning Center

A complete set of web-based resources for *The Humanistic Tradition* can be found at

www.mhhe.com/fierotht6e

Materials for students include an audio pronunciation guide, a timeline, research and writing tools, links to select readings, and suggested readings and Web sites. The instructor side of the Online Learning Center includes discussion and lecture suggestions, music listening guides, key themes and topics, and study questions for student discussion and review and written assignments.

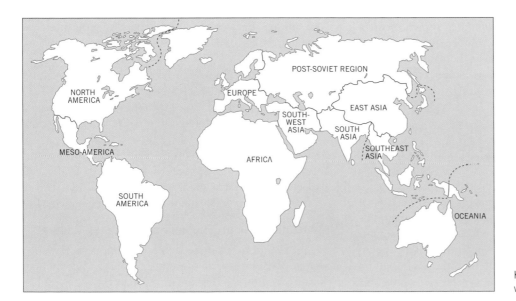

Key map indicating areas shown as white highlights on the locator maps

Acknowledgments

Personal thanks go to my discerning editor, Betty Chen (McGraw-Hill), and to the editorial and production staff of Laurence King Publishing. As with former editions, my colleague and husband, James H. Dormon, read all parts of the manuscript and made substantive editorial suggestions. This edition is dedicated to him. I am also grateful to Eric C. Shiner (curator and art historian) for his assistance in contemporary Asian art.

In the preparation of the sixth edition, I have benefited from the suggestions and comments generously offered by Donald F. Andrews (Chattanooga State Technical Community College), Samuel Barnett (University of Maryland), Bobbie Bell (Seminole Community College), Marjorie Berman (Red Rocks Community College), Terri Birch (Harper College), Pat Bivin (International Academy of Design and Technology), Casey Blanton (Daytona Beach Community College), Diane Boze (Northeastern State University), Nellie Brannan (Brevard Community College), Diane S. Brown (Valencia Community College, Osceola), Joyce Caldwell Smith (University of Tennessee at Chattanooga), Cynthia Clegg (Pepperdine University), Harry S. Coverston (University of Central Florida), Julie deGraffenried (Baylor University), Ann Dunn (University of North Carolina, Asheville), Renae Edge (Norwalk Community College), Monika Fleming (Edgecombe Community College), A. Flowers (College of Alameda), Rod Freeman (Estrella Mountain College), Arby L. Frost (Roanoke College), Samuel Garren (North Carolina A&T University), Caryl Gibbs (Rose State College), Robin Hardee (Santa Fe College), Melissa T. Hause (Belhaven College), Barbara A. Hergianto (South Florida Community College), Dale Hoover (Edison College), Ron Israel (San Diego Mesa College), Marian Jacobson (Albany College of Pharmacy), Theresa James (South Florida Community College), Judith Jamieson (Providence College), Keith W. Jensen (William Rainey Harper College), Jerry Jerman (University of Oklahoma), Patrick Kiley (Marian College), Donald Koke (Butler County College), Jayson Larremore (Oral Roberts University), Bonnie Loss (Glendale Community College), Diana Lurz (Rogers State University), Eldonna Loraine May (Wayne State University), Barbara J. Mayo (Northeast Lakeview College), Susan McClung (Hillsborough Community College), Trudy McNair (Valencia Community College), Richard Middleton-Kaplan (Harper College), Yvonne J. Milspaw (Harrisburg Area Community College), Maureen Moore (Cosumnes River College), Sean P. Murphy (College of Lake County), Judy Navas (Sonoma State University), Jack L. Nawrocik (St. Philip's College), James Norwood (University of Minnesota), Craig Payne (Indian Hills College), Randall M. Payne (South Florida Community College), Laurel S. Peterson (Norwalk Community College), Richard W. Peyton (Florida Agricultural and Mechanical University), Anne L. Pierce (Hampton University), William H. Porterfield (West Virginia State Community & Technical College), Judith Poxon (Sacramento City College), Robin Poynor (University of Florida), Verbie Lovorn Prevost (University of Tennessee at Chattanooga), Andreas W. Reif (Southern New Hampshire University), Denise M. Rogers (University of Louisiana at Lafayette), Karen Rumbley (Valencia Community College), Maria Rybakova (San Diego State University), John Scolaro (Valencia Community College), Vanessa Sheldon (College of the Desert), Mary Slater (Missouri Valley College), Linda Spain (Linn-Benton Community College), Hartley S. Spatt (SUNY Maritime College), Lisa Stokes (Seminole Community College), Alice Taylor (West Los Angeles College), Andreia Thaxton (Florida Community College at Jacksonville), Randall K. Van Schepen (Roger Williams University), Andrew Vassar (Northeastern State University), John Michael Vohlidka (Gannon University), Laura Wadenpfuhl (New Jersey City College), John R. Webb (Highland Community College), Jason Whitmarsh (Florida State College at Jacksonville), and Linda Woodward (Lone Star Montgomery College).

—Gloria K. Fiero

BEFORE WE BEGIN

Studying humanities engages us in a dialogue with *primary sources*: works original to the age in which they were produced. Whether literary, visual, or aural, a primary source is a text; the time, place, and circumstances in which it was created constitute the context; and its various underlying meanings provide the subtext. Studying humanities from the perspective of text, context, and subtext helps us understand our cultural legacy and our place in the larger world.

Text

The *text* of a primary source refers to its medium (that is, what it is made of), its form (its outward shape), and its content (the subject it describes).

Literature: Literary form varies according to the manner in which words are arranged. So, *poetry*, which shares rhythmic organization with music and dance, is distinguished from *prose*, which normally lacks regular rhythmic patterns. Poetry, by its freedom from conventional grammar, provides unique opportunities for the expression of intense emotions. Prose usually functions to convey information, to narrate, and to describe.

Philosophy, (the search for truth through reasoned analysis), and *history* (the record of the past) make use of prose to analyze and communicate ideas and information.

In literature, as in most forms of expression, content and form are usually interrelated. The subject matter or form of a literary work determines its *genre*. For instance, a long narrative poem recounting the adventures of a hero constitutes an *epic*, while a formal, dignified speech in praise of a person or thing constitutes a *eulogy*.

The Visual Arts: The visual arts employ a wide variety of media, ranging from the traditional colored pigments used in painting, to wood, clay, marble, and (more recently) plastic and neon used in sculpture, to a wide variety of digital media, including photography and film. The form or outward shape of a work of art depends on the manner in which the artist manipulates the elements of color, line, texture, and space. Unlike words, these formal elements lack denotative meaning.

The visual arts are dominantly spatial, that is, they operate and are apprehended in space. Artists manipulate form to describe or interpret the visible world (as in the genres of portraiture and landscape), or to create worlds of fantasy and imagination. They may also fabricate texts that are non-representational, that is, without identifiable subject matter.

Music and Dance: The medium of music is sound. Like literature, music is durational: it unfolds over the period of time in which it occurs. The major elements of music are melody, rhythm, harmony, and tone color—formal elements that also characterize the oral life of literature.

However, while literary and visual texts are usually descriptive, music is almost always nonrepresentational: it rarely has meaning beyond sound itself. For that reason, music is the most difficult of the arts to describe in words.

Dance, the artform that makes the human body itself the medium of expression, resembles music in that it is temporal and performance-oriented. Like music, dance exploits rhythm as a formal tool, and like painting and sculpture, it unfolds in space as well as in time.

Studying the text, we discover the ways in which the artist manipulates medium and form to achieve a characteristic manner of execution or expression that we call *style*. Comparing the styles of various texts from a single era, we discover that they usually share certain defining features and characteristics. Similarities between, for instance, ancient Greek temples and Greek tragedies, or between Chinese lyric poems and landscape paintings, reveal the unifying moral and aesthetic values of their respective cultures.

Context

The *context* describes the historical and cultural environment of a text. Understanding the relationship between text and context is one of the principal concerns of any inquiry into the humanistic tradition. To determine the context, we ask: In what time and place did our primary source originate? How did it function within the society in which it was created? Was it primarily decorative, didactic, magical, or propagandistic? Did it serve the religious or political needs of the community? Sometimes our answers to these questions are mere guesses. For instance, the paintings on the walls of Paleolithic caves were probably not "artworks" in the modern sense of the term, but, rather, magical signs associated with religious rituals performed in the interest of communal survival.

Determining the function of the text often serves to clarify the nature of its form, and vice-versa. For instance, in that the Hebrew Bible, the *Song of Roland*, and many other early literary works were spoken or sung, rather than read, such literature tends to feature repetition and rhyme, devices that facilitate memorization and oral delivery.

Subtext

The *subtext* of a primary source refers to its secondary or implied meanings. The subtext discloses conceptual messages embedded in or implied by the text. The epic poems of the ancient Greeks, for instance, which glorify prowess and physical courage, suggest an exclusively male perception of virtue. The state portraits of the seventeenth-century French king Louis XIV bear the subtext of unassailable and absolute power. In our own time, Andy Warhol's serial adaptations of Coca-Cola bottles offer wry commentary on the commercial mentality of American society. Examining the implicit message of the text helps us determine the values of the age in which it was produced, and offers insights into our own.

Chapter 8

A Flowering of Faith: Christianity and Buddhism

ca. 400 B.C.E.–300 C.E.

"Do not imagine that I have come to abolish the Law or the Prophets. I have come not to abolish but to complete them."
Gospel of Matthew

Figure 8.1 The Good Shepherd, ca. 425–450 C.E. Mosaic. While pictured as a shepherd tending his flock, Jesus is shown wearing the purple and gold robes of a Roman emperor—the subtext conflates humility and royal status. The shepherd's crook is replaced by a cruciform staff, a reference to Christ's death by crucifixion.

LOOKING AHEAD

Shortly after the reign of the Roman emperor Octavian, in the province of Judea (the Roman name for Palestine), an obscure Jewish preacher named Joshua (in Greek, Jesus) brought forth a message that became the basis for a new world religion: Christianity. This fledgling faith came to provide an alternative to the secular focus of Classical culture. It offered the apocalyptic hope of messianic deliverance and eternal life.

As Christianity began to win converts within the Roman Empire, a somewhat older set of religious teachings was spreading in the East. The message of Siddhartha Gautama, the fifth-century-B.C.E.* founder of Buddhism, was rooted in the Hinduism of ancient India. Spreading into China and Japan, Buddhism absorbed the older traditions of East Asia, while projecting a deeply personalized spiritual message. By the third century B.C.E., Buddhism had become India's state religion, and by the fifth century C.E. it was the principal religious faith of China. The similarities and differences between Buddhism and Christianity offer valuable insights into the spiritual communities of the East and West. While no in-depth analysis of either religion can be offered here, a brief look at the formative stages of these two world faiths provides some understanding of their significance within the humanistic tradition.

The Background to Christianity

 Both as a religious faith and as a historical phenomenon, Christianity emerged out of three distinctly different cultural traditions: Greco-Roman, Near Eastern (West Asian), and Hebraic. All three of these cultures have been examined in the first seven chapters of this book; however, by focusing on the religious life of each at the turn of the first millennium—just prior to the birth of Jesus—we are better able to understand the factors that contributed to the rise of the religion that would become the largest of the world's faiths.

The Greco-Roman Background

Roman religion, like Roman culture itself, was a blend of native and borrowed traditions. Ancient pagan religious rituals marked seasonal change and celebrated seedtime and harvest. Augury, the interpretation of omens (a prac-

---

* B.C.E. designates dates "Before the Christian (or common) era," while dates from the "Christian (or common) era" are either designated by C.E. where necessary to distinguish them from B.C.E. dates or are left undesignated.

tice borrowed from the Etruscans), was important to Roman religious life as a means of predicting future events. As with the Greeks, Rome's favorite deities were looked upon as protectors of the household, the marketplace, and the state: Vesta, for instance, guarded the hearth fire, and Mars, god of war, ministered to soldiers. The Romans welcomed the gods of non-Roman peoples and honored them along with the greater and lesser Roman gods. They embraced the Greek gods, who had assumed Latin names (see Table, chapter 4). Tolerance for non-Roman cults and creeds contributed to a lack of religious uniformity, as well as to wide speculation concerning the possibility of life after death. Roman poets pictured a shadowy underworld in which the souls of the dead survived (similar to the Greek Hades and the Hebrew Sheol), but Roman religion promised neither retribution in the afterlife nor the reward of eternal life.

Rome hosted a wide variety of religious beliefs and practices, along with a number of quasi-religious Hellenistic philosophies (see chapter 6). Of these, Stoicism and Neoplatonism were the most influential. Stoicism's ethical view of life and its emphasis on equality among human beings offered an idealized alternative to a social order marked by wide gaps between rich and poor, and between citizens and slaves. Neoplatonism, a school of philosophy developed in Alexandria, took as its inspiration some of the principal ideas in the writings of Plato and his followers. It anticipated a mystical union between the individual soul and "the One" or Ultimate Being—comparable with Plato's Form of Goodness. According to Plotinus, a third-century Egyptian-born Neoplatonist, union with the One could be achieved only by the soul's ascent through a series of levels or degrees of spiritual purification. Neoplatonism's view of the soul as eternal and divine, and its perception of the universe as layered in ascending degrees of perfection, would have a shaping influence on Early Christian thought.

Following the decline of the Roman Republic and in the wake of repeated diplomatic contacts with the royal courts of Persia and Egypt, Rome absorbed a number of uniquely Eastern traditions. Roman emperors came to be regarded as theocratic monarchs and assumed titles such as *dominus* ("lord") and *deus* ("god"). By the second century, Rome enjoyed a full-blown imperial cult that honored the living emperor as semidivine and deified him after his death. At the same time, widespread social, political, and economic unrest fed a rising distrust of reason and a growing impulse toward mysticism.

The Near Eastern Background

In Greece, Egypt, and throughout Southwest Asia, there had long flourished numerous religious cults whose appeal was less intellectual than that of Neoplatonism and far more personal than that of the prevailing Greco-Roman religious philosophies. The promise of personal immortality was the central feature of the "mystery cults," so called because their initiation rituals were secret (in Greek, *mysterios*). The cults of Isis in Egypt, Cybele in Phrygia,

Dionysus in Greece, and Mithra in Persia, to name but four, had a heritage dating back to Neolithic times. As we have seen in earlier chapters, ancient agricultural societies celebrated seasonal change by means of symbolic performances of the birth, death, and rebirth of gods and goddesses associated with the regeneration of crops. The mystery cults perpetuated these practices. Their initiates participated in symbolic acts of spiritual death and rebirth, including ritual baptism and a communal meal at which they might consume the flesh or blood of the deity.

The cult of Isis originated in the Egyptian myth of the descent of the goddess Isis into the underworld to find and resurrect her mate Osiris (see chapter 2). Followers identified Isis as Earth Mother and Queen of Heaven and looked to her to ensure their own salvation (Figure **8.2**). Initiation into the cult included formal processions, a ritual meal, purification of the body, and a ten-day period of fasting that culminated in the ecstatic vision of the goddess herself. During the second century, in a Latin novel entitled *The Golden Ass*, or *Metamorphoses*, the Roman writer Lucius Apuleius described the initiation rites of the cult of Isis. At the close of the solemn rites, according to Apuleius, the initiate fell prostrate before the image of the Queen of Heaven and recited the prayer that is reproduced in part in the passage that follows. The ecstatic tone of this prayer—a startling departure from the measured restraint of most Greco-Roman literature—reflects the mood of religious longing that characterized the late Classical era.

Figure 8.2 *Isis and Horus Enthroned*, Middle Egyptian, fourth century C.E. Limestone, height 35 in.

READING 8.1 From Apuleius' *Initiation into the Cult of Isis* (ca. 155)

"O holy and eternal savior of mankind, you who ever   1
bountifully nurture mortals, you apply the sweet affection of
a mother to the misfortunes of the wretched. Neither a day
nor a night nor even a tiny moment passes empty of your
blessings: you protect men on sea and land, and you drive
away the storm-winds of life and stretch forth your rescuing
hand, with which you unwind the threads of the Fates even
when they are inextricably twisted, you calm the storms of
Fortune, and you repress harmful motions of the stars. The
spirits above revere you, the spirits below pay you homage.   10
You rotate the earth, light the sun, rule the universe, and tread
Tartarus[1] beneath your heel. The stars obey you, the seasons
return at your will, deities rejoice in you, and the elements are
your slaves. At your nod breezes breathe, clouds give
nourishment, seeds sprout, and seedlings grow. Your majesty
awes the birds traveling the sky, the beasts wandering upon
the mountains, the snakes lurking in the ground, and the
monsters that swim in the deep. But my talent is too feeble to
speak your praises and my inheritance too meager to bring you
sacrifices. The fullness of my voice is inadequate to express   20
what I feel about your majesty; a thousand mouths and as
many tongues would not be enough, nor even an endless flow
of inexhaustible speech. I shall therefore take care to do the
only thing that a devout but poor man can: I shall store your
divine countenance and sacred godhead in the secret places of
my heart, forever guarding it and picturing it to myself. . . ."

Q What are the powers of Isis that are praised in this reading?

Q How does this compare to "The Hymn to the Aten" (Reading 2.1)?

While the worship of Isis, Dionysus, and Cybele was peculiar to the Mediterranean, Mithraism, the most popular of the mystery cults, originated in Persia. Mithraism looked back to one of the oldest religious philosophies of the ancient world, Zoroastrianism (see chapter 1). Over the centuries, the ancient hero-god Mithra, who had appeared as judge in the Zoroastrian Judgment ceremony, came to play a major part in this Persian belief system. Associated with the forces of Light and the Good, Mithra's slaughter of the Sacred Bull, one of many heroic "labors," was thought to render the earth fertile (Figure **8.3**). By their personal attachment to Mithra, his devotees looked forward to spiritual well-being and everlasting life. Mithraism featured strict initiation rites, periods of fasting, ritual baptism, and a communal meal of bread and wine. Mithra's followers celebrated his birth on December 25— that is, just after the sun's "rebirth" at the winter solstice. While Mithraism excluded the participation of women, it quickly became the favorite religion of Roman soldiers,

[1] In Greek mythology, a part of the underworld where the wicked are punished.

Figure 8.3 Mithraic relief, early third century C.E. Bronze.

who identified with Mithra's physical prowess and self-discipline.

From Persia, Mithraism spread throughout Europe and North Africa, where archeologists have discovered the remains of numerous Mithraic chapels. Indeed, for the first two centuries of the common era, Mithraism was the chief rival of Christianity. The similarities between Mithraism and Christianity—a man-god hero, ritual baptism, a communal meal, and the promise of deliverance from evil—suggest that some of the basic features of Christianity already existed in the religious history of the ancient world prior to the time of Jesus. It is no surprise that many educated Romans considered Christianity to be an imitation of Mithraism.

Although the mystery cults often involved costly and demanding rituals, they were successful in attracting devotees. The Romans readily accommodated the exotic gods and goddesses of these cults as long as their worship did not challenge the authority of the Roman imperial cult or threaten the security of the Roman state.

The Jewish Background

Judaism, the oldest living religion in the Western world, differed from the other religions and religious cults of this period in its strongly ethical bias, its commitment to monotheism, and its exclusivity—that is, its emphasis on a special relationship (or covenant) between God and the Chosen People, the Jews themselves. As discussed in chapter 1, the early history of the Hebrews followed a dramatic narrative of wandering, settlement, and conquest at the hands of foreign powers. Following the sixty years of exile known as the Babylonian Captivity (586–539 B.C.E.), the Hebrews returned to Jerusalem, rebuilt the Temple of Solomon, and renewed their faith in the Torah. Many, however, in the great dispersion of the Jews known as the **Diaspora**, settled elsewhere. Under the influence of the scholar and teacher, Ezra (fl. 428 B.C.E.), the books of the Bible became ever more central in shaping the Hebrew identity. With the eastward expansion of Alexander the Great, the Jews were "Hellenized," and by the second century B.C.E. a Greek translation of Hebrew Scriptures appeared. Called the *Septuagint* ("Seventy"), as it was reputed to have been translated by seventy or seventy-two scholars in a period of seventy-two days, this edition is the first known translation of a sacred book into another language. Repeated contact with Greek and Persian peoples also influenced Hebraic thought. The Book of Daniel, written in 165 B.C.E., makes the first clear reference to resurrection and the afterlife in the Hebrew Bible: "Many of those who sleep in the dust of the earth shall awake, some to everlasting life, and some to shame and everlasting contempt."

The homeland of the Jews became the Roman province of Judea in 63 B.C.E., when the Roman general Pompey (106–48 B.C.E.) captured Jerusalem and the neighboring territories. Imperial taxes and loyalty to Rome were among the traditional demands of the conquerors, but Judaism, a monotheistic faith, forbade the worship of Rome's rulers and Rome's gods. Hence the Roman presence in Jerusalem caused mutual animosity and perpetual discord, conditions that would culminate in the Roman assault on the city and the destruction of the Second Temple in 70 C.E.* (see Figure 6.22). In 135, the Romans renamed Judea "Provincial Syria Palaestina," after the Philistines ("Sea People") who had settled there in the twelfth century B.C.E. Not until 1948, when the independent state of Israel came into being, did Judaism have a primary location in the world. During the first century B.C.E., however, unrest in Judea was complicated by disunity of opinion and biblical interpretation. Even as a special group of **rabbis** (Jewish teachers) met in 90 C.E. to draw up the authoritative list of thirty-six books that would constitute the canonic Hebrew Bible,** there was no agreement concerning the meaning of many Scriptural references. What, for instance, was the destiny of the Jew in the hereafter? What was the nature and the mission of the figure called by the Hebrew prophets the **Messiah** (the "Anointed One")? The Sadducees, a learned sect of Jewish aristocrats who advocated cultural and religious solidarity among the Jews, envisioned the Messiah as a temporal leader who would consolidate Jewish ideals and lead the Jews to political

---

* Hereafter, unless otherwise designated, all dates refer to the Christian (or common) era.
** Following ancient Hebrew tradition, these were grouped into three divisions: the Law (the first five books of instruction, called the Torah), the Prophets, and the Writings—that is, wisdom literature (see chapter 1).

Figure 8.4 *Crucifixion*, west doors of Santa Sabina, Rome, ca. 430 C.E. Wood, 11 × 15¾ in.

freedom. Defending a literal interpretation of the Torah, they denied that the soul survived the death of the body. The Pharisees, the more influential group of Jewish teachers and the principal interpreters of Hebrew law, believed in the advent of a messianic redeemer who, like a shepherd looking after his flock, would lead the righteous to salvation (see Figure 8.1). In their view (one that recognized oral tradition along with Scripture), the human soul was imperishable and the wicked would suffer eternal punishment.

In addition to the Sadducees and the Pharisees, there existed in Judea a minor religious sect called the Essenes, whose members lived in monastic communities near the Dead Sea. Renouncing worldly possessions, they practiced **asceticism**—strict self-denial and self-discipline. The Essenes believed in the immortality of the soul and its ultimate release and liberation from the body. They may have been responsible for the copying and preservation of some of the oldest extant fragments of the Hebrew Bible: The Dead Sea Scrolls, found in 1947 in caves at Qumran near the Dead Sea, forecast an apocalyptic age marked by the coming of a Teacher of Righteousness. In Judea, where all of these groups, along with scores of self-proclaimed miracle workers and preachers, competed for an audience, the climate of intense religious expectation was altogether receptive to the appearance of a charismatic leader.

The Rise of Christianity

The Life of Jesus

That charismatic leader proved to be a young Jewish rabbi from the city of Nazareth. The historical Jesus is an elusive figure. His name is not mentioned in the non-Christian literature until almost the end of the first century C.E. The Christian writings that describe his life and teachings, known as the Gospels (literally "Good News"), date from at least forty years after his death. And since the authors of the Gospels—the evangelists Matthew, Mark, Luke, and John—gave most of their attention to the last months of Jesus' life, these books are not biographies in the true sense of the word. Nevertheless, the Gospels constitute a body of revelations, beginning with the miraculous birth of Jesus

and his baptism by the preacher John at the Jordan River in Galilee: "And when Jesus was baptized, he went up immediately from the water," writes Matthew, "and behold, the heavens were opened and he saw the Spirit of God descending like a dove, and alighting on him; and lo, a voice from heaven saying, 'This is my beloved Son, with whom I am well pleased'" (Matthew 3:16–17).

Written in Greek and Aramaic, the Gospels describe the life of a charismatic teacher, healer, and reformer, who proclaimed his mission to "complete" Hebrew law and fulfill the lessons of the prophets. Word of the preacher from Nazareth and stories of his miraculous acts of healing spread like wildfire throughout Judea. While the Roman authorities viewed his presence in Jerusalem as subversive, the Pharisees and the Sadducees accused him of violating Jewish law and contradicting Scripture. Many questioned his legitimacy as the biblical Messiah. Finally, the Romans condemned him as a threat to imperial stability. By the authority of the Roman governor Pontius Pilate (ruled from 26 to ca. 36), Jesus was put to death by crucifixion, the humiliating and horrific public punishment Rome dispensed to thieves and traitors (Figure **8.4**). All four of the Gospels report that Jesus rose from the dead on the third day after his death, and that he appeared to his disciples before ascending into heaven. This event, the *resurrection* of Jesus, became fundamental to the religion called Christianity, from the Greek word for Messiah, "*Christos*." In the earliest representations of Jesus, however, it is not his death on the Cross, nor his reported resurrection, but his role as redeemer and protector—as Good Shepherd—that is immortalized (see Figure 8.1).

The Message of Jesus

While the message of Jesus embraced the ethical monotheism of traditional Judaism, it gave new emphasis to the virtues of pacifism and compassion. It warned of the perils of wealth and the temptations of the secular world. In simple and direct language, embellished with homely parables (stories that illustrated a moral), Jesus urged the renunciation of material possessions, not only as a measure of freedom from temporal enslavement, but as preparation for eternal life and ultimate reward in "the kingdom of heaven." Such teachings represented a new direction in ancient thought, for, with few exceptions, such as the Stoics, the Neoplatonists, and the Essenes, Classical culture was fundamentally materialistic.

Criticizing the Judaism of his time, with its emphasis on strict observance of ritual, Jesus stressed the importance of faith and compassion that lay at the heart of the Hebrew covenant: love of god and love of one's neighbor. He embraced the spirit rather than the letter of Hebrew law, picturing its omnipotent god as stern, but also loving, merciful, and forgiving. In the Sermon on the Mount, as recorded by the **apostle** (disciple) Matthew, Jesus sets forth the injunctions of an uncompromising ethic: love your neighbor as yourself, accept persecution with humility, pass no judgment on others, and treat others as you would have them treat you. This ideal, unconditional love is linked to an equally lofty directive: "You must . . . be perfect, just as your heavenly Father is perfect" (Matthew 5:48).

> ## READING 8.2 From the Gospel of Matthew
> (ca. 80–90)
>
> ### Sermon on the Mount
> ### Chapter 5: The Beatitudes
> ¹Seeing the crowds, he went onto the mountain. And when he was seated his disciples came to him. ²Then he began to speak. This is what he taught them:
> ³How blessed are the poor in spirit:
> the kingdom of Heaven is theirs.
> ⁴Blessed are *the gentle*:
> *they shall have the earth as inheritance.*
> ⁵Blessed are those who mourn:
> they shall be comforted.
> ⁶Blessed are those who hunger and thirst for uprightness:
> they shall have their fill.
> ⁷Blessed are the merciful:
> they shall have mercy shown them.
> ⁸Blessed are the pure in heart:
> they shall see God.
> ⁹Blessed are the peacemakers:
> they shall be recognised as children of God.
> ¹⁰Blessed are those who are persecuted in the cause of
> uprightness:
> the kingdom of Heaven is theirs.
> ¹¹"Blessed are you when people abuse you and persecute you and speak all kinds of calumny against you falsely on my account. ¹²Rejoice and be glad, for your reward will be great in heaven; this is how they persecuted the prophets before you.

Salt for the earth and light for the world

¹³"You are salt for the earth. But if salt loses its taste, what can make it salty again? It is good for nothing, and can only be thrown out to be trampled under people's feet.

¹⁴"You are light for the world. A city built on a hill-top cannot be hidden. ¹⁵No one lights a lamp to put it under a tub; they put it on the lamp-stand where it shines for everyone in the house. ¹⁶In the same way your light must shine in people's sight, so that, seeing your good works, they may give praise to your Father in heaven.

The fulfilment of the Law

¹⁷"Do not imagine that I have come to abolish the Law or the Prophets. I have come not to abolish but to complete them. ¹⁸In truth I tell you, till heaven and earth disappear, not one dot, not one little stroke, is to disappear from the Law until all its purpose is achieved. ¹⁹Therefore, anyone who infringes even one of the least of these commandments and teaches others to do the same will be considered the least in the kingdom of Heaven; but the person who keeps them and teaches them will be considered great in the kingdom of Heaven.

The new standard higher than the old

²⁰"For I tell you, if your uprightness does not surpass that of the scribes and Pharisees, you will never get into the kingdom of Heaven.

²¹"You have heard how it was said to our ancestors, *You shall not kill*; and if anyone does kill he must answer for it before the court. ²²But I say this to you, anyone who is angry with a brother will answer for it before the court; anyone who calls a brother 'Fool' will answer for it before the Sanhedrin; and anyone who calls him 'Traitor' will answer for it in hell fire. ²³So then, if you are bringing your offering to the altar and there remember that your brother has something against you, ²⁴leave your offering there before the altar, go and be reconciled with your brother first, and then come back and present your offering. ²⁵Come to terms with your opponent in good time while you are still on the way to the court with him, or he may hand you over to the judge and the judge to the officer, and you will be thrown into prison. ²⁶In truth I tell you, you will not get out till you have paid the last penny.

²⁷"You have heard how it was said, *You shall not commit adultery*. ²⁸But I say this to you, if a man looks at a woman lustfully, he has already committed adultery with her in his heart. ²⁹If your right eye should be your downfall, tear it out and throw it away; for it will do you less harm to lose one part of yourself than to have your whole body thrown into hell. ³⁰And if your right hand should be your downfall, cut it off and throw it away; for it will do you less harm to lose one part of yourself than to have your whole body go to hell.

³¹"It has also been said, *Anyone who divorces his wife must give her a writ of dismissal*. ³²But I say this to you, everyone who divorces his wife, except for the case of an illicit marriage, makes her an adulteress; and anyone who marries a divorced woman commits adultery.

³³"Again, you have heard how it was said to our ancestors,

You must not break your oath, but must fulfil your oaths to the Lord. ³⁴But I say this to you, do not swear at all, either by *heaven*, since that is *God's throne*; ³⁵or by *earth*, since that is *his footstool*; or by Jerusalem, since that is *the city of the great King*. ³⁶Do not swear by your own head either, since you cannot turn a single hair white or black. ³⁷All you need say is 'Yes' if you mean yes, 'No' if you mean no; anything more than this comes from the Evil One.

³⁸"You have heard how it was said: *Eye for eye and tooth for tooth*. ³⁹But I say this to you: offer no resistance to the wicked. On the contrary, if anyone hits you on the right cheek, offer him the other as well; ⁴⁰if someone wishes to go to law with you to get your tunic, let him have your cloak as well. ⁴¹And if anyone requires you to go one mile, go two miles with him. ⁴²Give to anyone who asks you, and if anyone wants to borrow, do not turn away.

⁴³"You have heard how it was said, *You will love your neighbor* and hate your enemy. ⁴⁴But I say this to you, love your enemies and pray for those who persecute you; ⁴⁵so that you may be children of your Father in heaven, for he causes his sun to rise on the bad as well as the good, and sends down rain to fall on the upright and the wicked alike. ⁴⁶For if you love those who love you, what reward will you get? Do not even the tax collectors do as much? ⁴⁷And if you save your greetings for your brothers, are you doing anything exceptional? ⁴⁸Do not even the gentiles do as much? You must therefore be perfect, just as your heavenly Father is perfect."

Chapter 6: Almsgiving in secret

¹"Be careful not to parade your uprightness in public to attract attention; otherwise you will lose all reward from your Father in heaven. ²So when you give alms, do not have it trumpeted before you; this is what the hypocrites do in the synagogues

The New Testament

Gospels

Matthew	Luke
Mark	John

Acts of the Apostles

Letters of Paul

Romans	I Thessalonians
I Corinthians	II Thessalonians
II Corinthians	I Timothy
Galatians	II Timothy
Ephesians	Titus
Philippians	Philemon
Colossians	Hebrews

Letters of

James	II John
I Peter	III John
II Peter	Jude
I John	

The Book of Revelations

(The Apocalypse)

and in the streets to win human admiration. In truth I tell you, they have had their reward. ³But when you give alms, your left hand must not know what your right is doing; ⁴your almsgiving must be secret, and your Father who sees all that is done in secret will reward you.

Prayer in secret

⁵"And when you pray, do not imitate the hypocrites; they love to say their prayers standing up in the synagogues and at the street corners for people to see them. In truth I tell you, they have had their reward. ⁶But when you pray, *go to your private room*, shut yourself in, and so pray to your Father who is in that secret place, and your Father who sees all that is done in secret will reward you.

How to pray. The Lord's Prayer

⁷"In your prayers do not babble as the gentiles do, for they think that by using many words they will make themselves heard. ⁸Do not be like them; your Father knows what you need before you ask him. ⁹So you should pray like this:

> Our Father in heaven,
>   may your name be held holy,
> ¹⁰your kingdom come,
>   your will be done,
>   on earth as in heaven.
> ¹¹Give us today our daily bread.
> ¹²And forgive us our debts,
>   as we have forgiven those who are in debt to us.
> ¹³And do not put us to the test,
>   but save us from the Evil One.

¹⁴"Yes, if you forgive others their failings, your heavenly Father will forgive you yours; ¹⁵but if you do not forgive others, your Father will not forgive your failings either.

Fasting in secret

¹⁶"When you are fasting, do not put on a gloomy look as the hypocrites do: they go about looking unsightly to let people know they are fasting. In truth I tell you, they have had their reward. ¹⁷But when you fast, put scent on your head and wash your face, ¹⁸so that no one will know you are fasting except your Father who sees all that is done in secret; and your Father who sees all that is done in secret will reward you.

True treasures

¹⁹"Do not store up treasures for yourselves on earth, where moth and woodworm destroy them and thieves can break in and steal. ²⁰But store up treasures for yourselves in heaven, where neither moth nor woodworm destroys them and thieves cannot break in and steal. ²¹For wherever your treasure is, there will your heart be too."

Chapter 7: Do not judge

¹"Do not judge, and you will not be judged; ²because the judgements you give are the judgements you will get, and the standard you use will be the standard used for you. ³Why do you observe the splinter in your brother's eye and never notice the great log in your own? ⁴And how dare you say to your

brother, 'Let me take that splinter out of your eye,' when, look, there is a great log in your own? ⁵Hypocrite! Take the log out of your own eye first, and then you will see clearly enough to take the splinter out of your brother's eye.

Do not profane sacred things
⁶"Do not give dogs what is holy; and do not throw your pearls in front of pigs, or they may trample them and then turn on you and tear you to pieces.

Effective prayer
⁷"Ask, and it will be given to you; search, and you will find; knock, and the door will be opened to you. ⁸Everyone who asks receives; everyone who searches finds; everyone who knocks will have the door opened. ⁹Is there anyone among you who would hand his son a stone when he asked for bread? ¹⁰Or would hand him a snake when he asked for a fish? ¹¹If you, then, evil as you are, know how to give your children what is good, how much more will your Father in heaven give good things to those who ask him!

The golden rule
¹²"So always treat others as you would like them to treat you; that is the Law and the Prophets.

The two ways
¹³"Enter by the narrow gate, since the road that leads to destruction is wide and spacious, and many take it; ¹⁴but it is a narrow gate and a hard road that leads to life, and only a few find it."

Q **What moral injunctions form the core of this sermon, as recounted by Matthew?**

Q **Which might be the most difficult to fulfill?**

The Teachings of Paul

The immediate followers of Jesus were a group of apostles who anticipated a Second Coming in which all who had followed Jesus would be delivered to the Kingdom of Heaven. Despite their missionary activities, only a small percentage of the population of the Roman Empire—scholarly estimates range from ten to fifteen percent—became Christians in the first hundred years after Jesus' death. And those who did convert came mainly from communities where Jewish tradition was not strong. However, through the efforts of the best known of the apostles, Paul (d. 65), the message of Jesus gained widespread appeal. A Hellenized Jew from Tarsus in Asia Minor, Paul had been schooled in both Greek and Hebrew. Following a mystical experience in which Jesus is said to have revealed himself to Paul, he became a passionate convert to the teachings of the preacher from Nazareth. Paul is generally believed to have written ten to fourteen of the twenty-seven books of the Christian Scriptures called by Christians the "New Testament," to distinguish it from the Hebrew Bible, which they referred to as the "Old Testament." Paul's most

important contributions lie in his having universalized and systematically explained Jesus' message. While Jesus preached only to the Jews, Paul spread his teachings to the gentile (non-Jewish) communities of Greece, Asia Minor, and Rome, thus earning the title "Apostle to the Gentiles." He stressed that the words of Jesus were directed not exclusively to Jews, but to non-Jews as well. Paul explained the messianic mission of Jesus and the reason for his death. He described Jesus as a living sacrifice who died for the sins of humankind, and, specifically, for the sin that had entered the world through Adam's defiance of God in the Garden of Eden. For Paul, the death of Jesus was the act of atonement that "acquitted" humankind of Original Sin. Where Adam's sin had condemned humankind, Jesus—the New Adam—would redeem humankind. His resurrection confirmed the promise of eternal salvation. By their faith in Jesus, promised Paul, the faithful would be rewarded with everlasting life.

These concepts, which indelibly separated Christianity from both its parent faith, Judaism, and from the Classical belief in the innate goodness and freedom of human nature, are set forth in Paul's Epistle to the Church in Rome, parts of which follow. Written ten years before his death, the letter imparts the message that those who are "baptized in Christ" will "live a new life." The view of Jesus as a sacrifice for human sin accommodated ancient religious practices in which guilt for communal (or individual) transgressions was ritually displaced onto a living sacrifice. It also rehearsed a basic aspect of the mystery cults: the promise of eternal life as reward for devotion to a savior deity. However, Paul's focus on moral renewal and redemption would set Christianity apart from the mystery religions. So important was Paul's contribution to the foundations of the new faith that he has been called "the co-founder of Christianity."

READING 8.3 From Paul's Epistle to the Church in Rome (ca. 57)

Chapter 1: Thanksgiving and prayer
⁸First I give thanks to my God through Jesus Christ for all of you because your faith is talked of all over the world. ⁹God, whom I serve with my spirit in preaching the gospel of his Son, is my witness that I continually mention you in my prayers, ¹⁰asking always that by some means I may at long last be enabled to visit you, if it is God's will. ¹¹For I am longing to see you so that I can convey to you some spiritual gift that will be a lasting strength, ¹²or rather that we may be strengthened together through our mutual faith, yours and mine. ¹³I want you to be quite certain too, brothers, that I have often planned to visit you—though up to the present I have always been prevented—in the hope that I might work as fruitfully among you as I have among the gentiles elsewhere. ¹⁴I have an obligation to Greeks as well as barbarians, to the educated as well as the ignorant, ¹⁵and hence the eagerness on my part to preach the gospel to you in Rome too.

EXPLORING ISSUES

The Non-Canonical Gospels

The canon of twenty-seven writings known as the New Testament was established in 325 C.E. by the Council of Nicaea. Modern scholars agree that the four canonical Gospels—Matthew, Mark, Luke, and John—were probably written in the first century, but possibly not by first-person witnesses to the life of Jesus. From the late first and second centuries, however, come many apocryphal writings that describe the life and teaching of Jesus. Some of these non-canonical writings, such as the Gospel of Thomas, the Gospel of Mary Magdalene, and the Gospel of Judas, record detailed conversations between Jesus and his disciples. Discovered in the 1970s in an Egyptian cavern, the 26-page Gospel of Judas portrays this disciple as a favorite of Jesus. In the Gospel

of Thomas, Jesus is said to have advised his followers: ". . . the Kingdom [of Heaven] is inside you and outside you. When you know yourselves, then you will be known, and you will understand that you are children of the living Father. But if you do not know yourselves, then you live in poverty . . . ."

Whether or not the non-canonical Gospels are historically reliable, they offer valuable insights into the beliefs and concerns of Jesus' contemporaries. In an effort to unify and consolidate the young Christian faith, however, early church leaders either rejected or suppressed these writings, some of which have only recently been translated into English.

Chapter 2: The Jews are not exempt from the retribution of God

[1]So no matter who you are, if you pass judgement you have no excuse. It is yourself that you condemn when you judge others, since you behave in the same way as those you are condemning. [2]We are well aware that people who behave like that are justly condemned by God. [3]But you—when you judge those who behave like this while you are doing the same yourself—do you think you will escape God's condemnation? [4]Or are you not disregarding his abundant goodness, tolerance and patience, failing to realise that this generosity of God is meant to bring you to repentance? [5]Your stubborn refusal to repent is only storing up retribution for yourself on that Day of retribution when God's just verdicts will be made known. [6]*He will repay everyone as their deeds deserve.* [7]For those who aimed for glory and honour and immortality by persevering in doing good, there will be eternal life; [8]but for those who out of jealousy have taken for their guide not truth but injustice, there will be the fury of retribution. [9]Trouble and distress will come to every human being who does evil—Jews first, but Greeks as well; [10]glory and honour and peace will come to everyone who does good—Jews first, but Greeks as well. [11]*There is no favouritism with God.*

Chapter 5: Faith guarantees salvation

[1]So then, now that we have been justified by faith, we are at peace with God through our Lord Jesus Christ; [2]it is through him, by faith, that we have been admitted into God's favour in which we are living, and look forward exultantly to God's glory. [3]Not only that; let us exult, too, in our hardships, understanding that hardship develops perseverance, [4]and perseverance develops a tested character, something that gives us hope, [5]and a hope which will not let us down, because the love of God has been poured into our hearts by the Holy Spirit which has been given to us. [6]When we were still helpless, at the appointed time, Christ died for the godless. [7]You could hardly find anyone ready to die even for someone upright; though it is just possible that, for a really good person, someone might

undertake to die. [8]So it is proof of God's own love for us, that Christ died for us while we were still sinners. [9]How much more can we be sure, therefore, that, now that we have been justified by his death, we shall be saved through him from the retribution of God. [10]For if, while we were enemies, we were reconciled to God through the death of his Son, how much more can we be sure that, being now reconciled, we shall be saved by his life. [11]What is more, we are filled with exultant trust in God, through our Lord Jesus Christ, through whom we have already gained our reconciliation.

Adam and Jesus Christ

[12]Well then; it was through one man that sin *came into the world*, and through sin death, and thus death has spread through the whole human race because everyone has sinned. [13]Sin already existed in the world before there was any law, even though sin is not reckoned when there is no law. [14]Nonetheless death reigned over all from Adam to Moses, even over those whose sin was not the breaking of a commandment, as Adam's was. He prefigured the One who was to come. . . .

[15]There is no comparison between the free gift and the offense. If death came to many through the offense of one man, how much greater an effect the grace of God has had, coming to so many and so plentifully as the free gift through the one man Jesus Christ! [16]Again, there is no comparison between the gift and the offense of one man. One single offense brought condemnation, but now, after many offenses, have come the free gift and so acquittal! [17]It was by one man's offense that death came to reign over all, but how much greater the reign in life of those who receive the fullness of grace and the gift of saving justice, through the one man, Jesus Christ. [18]One man's offense brought condemnation on all humanity; and one man's good act has brought justification and life to all humanity. [19]Just as by one man's disobedience many were made sinners, so by one man's obedience are many to be made upright. [20]When law came on the scene,

it was to multiply the offenses. But however much sin increased, grace was always greater; ²¹so that as sin's reign brought death, so grace was to rule through saving justice that leads to eternal life through Jesus Christ our Lord.

Chapter 6: Baptism

¹What should we say then? Should we remain in sin so that grace may be given the more fully? ²Out of the question! We have died to sin; how could we go on living in it? ³You cannot have forgotten that all of us, when we were baptised into Christ Jesus, were baptised into his death. ⁴So by our baptism into his death we were buried with him, so that as Christ was raised from the dead by the Father's glorious power, we too should begin living a new life. ⁵If we have been joined to him by dying a death like his, so we shall be by a resurrection like his; ⁶realising that our former self was crucified with him, so that the self which belonged to sin should be destroyed and we should be freed from the slavery of sin. ⁷Someone who has died, of course, no longer has to answer for sin.

⁸But we believe that, if we died with Christ, then we shall live with him too. ⁹We know that Christ has been raised from the dead and will never die again. Death has no power over him any more. ¹⁰For by dying, he is dead to sin once and for all, and now the life that he lives is life with God. ¹¹In the same way, you must see yourselves as being dead to sin but alive for God in Christ Jesus.

Chapter 8: The life of the spirit

¹Thus, condemnation will never come to those who are in Christ Jesus, ²because the law of the Spirit which gives life in Christ Jesus has set you free from the law of sin and death. ³What the Law could not do because of the weakness of human nature, God did, sending his own Son in the same human nature as any sinner to be a sacrifice for sin, and condemning sin in that human nature. ⁴This was so that the Law's requirements might be fully satisfied in us as we direct our lives not by our natural inclinations but by the Spirit. ⁵Those who are living by their natural inclinations have their minds on the things human nature desires; those who live in the Spirit have their minds on spiritual things. ⁶And human nature has nothing to look forward to but death, while the Spirit looks forward to life and peace, ⁷because the outlook of disordered human nature is opposed to God, since it does not submit to God's Law, and indeed it cannot, ⁸and those who live by their natural inclinations can never be pleasing to God....

Q How does Paul explain the death of Jesus?

Q What is his position on sin and salvation?

The Spread of Christianity

A variety of historical factors contributed to the slow but growing receptivity to Christianity within the Roman Empire. The decline of the Roman Republic had left in its wake large gaps between the rich and the poor. Octavian's efforts to restore the old Roman values of duty and civic pride had failed to offset increasing impersonalism and bureaucratic corruption. Furthermore, as early as the second

century B.C.E., Germanic tribes had been migrating into the West and assaulting Rome's borders (see chapter 11). Repeatedly, these nomadic people put Rome on the defensive and added to the prevailing sense of insecurity. Amid widespread oppression and grinding poverty, Christianity promised redemption from sins, personal immortality, and a life to come from which material adversities were absent. The message of Jesus was easy to understand, free of cumbersome regulations (characteristic of Judaism) and costly rituals (characteristic of the mystery cults), and, in contrast to Mithraism, it was accessible to all—male and female, rich and poor, free and enslaved. The unique feature of the new faith, however, was its historical credibility, that is, the fact that Jesus—unlike the elusive gods of the mystery cults or the remote Yahweh—had actually lived among Judea's men and women and had practiced the morality he preached.

Nevertheless, at the outset the new religion failed to win official approval. While both Roman religion and the mystery cults were receptive to many gods, Christianity—like Judaism—professed monotheism. Christians not only refused to worship the emperor as divine but also denied the existence of the Roman gods. Even more threatening to the state was the Christian refusal to serve in the Roman army. While the Romans dealt with the Jews by destroying Jerusalem, how might they annihilate a people whose kingdom was in heaven? During the first century, Christian converts were simply expelled from the city of Rome, but during the late third century—a time of famine, plague, and war—Christians who refused to make sacrifices to the Roman gods of state suffered horrific forms of persecution: they were tortured, burned, beheaded, or thrown to wild beasts in the public amphitheaters. Christian martyrs astonished Roman audiences by going to their deaths joyously proclaiming their anticpation of a better life in the hereafter.

Not until 313 C.E., when the emperor Constantine issued the Edict of Milan, did the public persecution of Christians come to an end. The Edict, which proclaimed religious toleration in the West, not only liberated Christians from physical and political oppression, but encouraged the development of Christianity as a legitimate faith. Christian leaders were free to establish a uniform doctrine of belief, an administrative hierarchy, the guidelines for worship, and a vocabulary for religious expression (see chapter 9). By the end of the fourth century, the minor religious sect called Christianity had become the official religion of the Roman Empire.

The Rise of Buddhism

The Life of the Buddha

The reasons why similar world-historical developments occur at approximately the same time within two remotely related cultures is a mystery never solved by historians. One of the most interesting such parallels is that between the spread of Buddhism in the East and the emergence of

Christianity in the West, both of which occurred during the first century of the Christian era. Siddhartha Gautama, known as the Buddha ("Enlightened One"), lived in India some three to five centuries before Jesus—scholars still disagree as to whether his life spanned the years 560–480 or 440–360 B.C.E. Born into a princely Hindu family, Siddhartha was well-educated and protected from the experience of pain and suffering. At the age of nineteen, he married his cousin and fathered a son. Legend has it that upon leaving the palace one day, Siddhartha encountered a diseased man, a wrinkled old man, and a rotting corpse. The realization of these three "truths" of existence—sickness, old age, and death—led the twenty-nine-year-old Siddhartha to renounce his wealth, abandon his wife and child, and begin the quest for inner illumination. With shaven head, yellow robe, and begging bowl, he followed the way of the Hindu ascetic. After six years, however, he concluded that the life of self-denial was futile. Turning inward, Siddhartha sat beneath a bo (fig) tree (Figure **8.5**) and began the work that would bring him to enlightenment—the omniscient consciousness of reality. Meditation would lead Siddhartha to the full perception that the cause of human sufferings is desire, that is, attachment to material things. For the next forty years—he died at the age of eighty—the Enlightened One preached a message of humility and compassion, the pursuit of which might lead his followers to *nirvana*, the ultimate release from illusion and from the Wheel of Rebirth.

Figure 8.5 *Seated Buddha*, from the Gandharan region of northwest Pakistan, ca. 200 C.E. Gray schist, 4 ft. 3 in. × 31 in. Born into India's princely Shakya clan, the Buddha was known as Shakyamuni, "sage of the Shakyas." He is shown here wearing the simple robes of a monk; his elongated earlobes are a reference to his princely origins. The iconic Buddha-pose is a study in psychic self-containment.

The Message of the Buddha

With his earliest sermons, the Buddha set in motion the Wheel of the Law (*dharma*). His message was simple. The path to enlightenment begins with the Four Noble Truths:

1. pain is universal
2. desire causes pain
3. ceasing to desire relieves pain
4. right conduct leads to release from pain.

Right conduct takes the Middle Way, or Eightfold Path: right views, right intention, right speech, right action, right livelihood, right effort, right mindfulness, and right concentration. The Eightfold Path leads to insight and knowledge, and, ultimately, to *nirvana*. The Buddhist's goal is not, as with Christianity, the promise of personal immortality, but rather, escape from the endless cycle of birth, death, and rebirth. For the Buddhist, "salvation" lies in the extinction of the Self.

The Buddha was an eloquent teacher whose concerns, like those of Jesus, were ethical and egalitarian. Just as Jesus criticized Judaism's emphasis on ritual, so Siddhartha attacked the existing forms of Hindu worship, including animal sacrifice and the authority of the *Vedas*. In accord with Hinduism, he encouraged the annihilation of worldly desires and the renunciation of material wealth. But in contrast to the caste-oriented Hinduism of his time, the Buddha held that enlightenment could be achieved by all people, regardless of caste. Renouncing reliance on the popular gods of the *Vedas* (see chapter 3), the Buddha urged his followers to work out their own salvation.

Ultimately, Jesus and Siddhartha were reformers of older world faiths: Judaism and Hinduism. Soon after his enlightenment, Siddhartha assembled a group of disciples, five of whom founded the first Buddhist monastic order. In the years after his death, his life came to be surrounded by miraculous tales, which, along with his sermons, were preserved and recorded by his followers. For instance, legend has it that Siddhartha was born miraculously from the right side of his mother, Queen Maya; and at that very moment, the tree she touched in the royal garden burst into bloom.

The Buddha himself wrote nothing, but his disciples memorized his teachings and set them down during the first century B.C.E. in three main books, the *Pitakas* or "Baskets of the Law." These works, written in Pali and Sanskrit, were divided into instructional chapters known as **sutras** (Sanskrit for "thread"). The most famous of the works in the Buddhist canon is the sermon that the Buddha preached to his disciples at the Deer Park in Benares (modern Varanasi in northeast India). The Sermon at Benares, part of which is reproduced here, urges the abandonment of behavioral extremes and the pursuit of the Eightfold Path of right conduct. In its emphasis on modesty, moderation, and compassion, and on the renunciation of worldly pleasures, it has much in common with Jesus' Sermon on the Mount. Comparable also to Jesus' teachings (see Matthew 5:11, for instance) is the Buddha's regard for loving kindness that "commends the return of good for evil"—a concept central to the Sermon on Abuse.

READING 8.4a From the Buddha's Sermon at Benares (recorded ca. 100 B.C.E.)

"There are two extremes, O bhikkhus,[1] which the man who   1
has given up the world ought not to follow—the habitual practice,
on the one hand, of self-indulgence which is unworthy, vain and fit
only for the worldly-minded—and the habitual practice, on the
other hand, of self-mortification, which is painful, useless and
unprofitable.

"Neither abstinence from fish or flesh, nor going naked, nor
shaving the head, nor wearing matted hair, nor dressing in a
rough garment, nor covering oneself with dirt, nor sacrificing
to Agni,[2] will cleanse a man who is not free from delusions.   10

"Reading the Vedas, making offerings to priests, or
sacrifices to the gods, self-mortification by heat or cold, and
many such penances performed for the sake of immortality,
these do not cleanse the man who is not free from delusions.

"Anger, drunkenness, obstinacy, bigotry, deception, envy,
self-praise, disparaging others, superciliousness and evil
intentions constitute uncleanness; not verily the eating of
flesh.

"A middle path, O bhikkhus, avoiding the two extremes, had
been discovered by the Tathāgata[3]—a path which opens the   20
eyes, and bestows understanding, which leads to peace of
mind, to the higher wisdom, to full enlightenment, to Nirvāna!
"What is that middle path, O bhikkhus, avoiding these two
extremes, discovered by the Tathāgata—that path which
opens the eyes, and bestows understanding, which leads to
peace of mind, to the higher wisdom, to full enlightenment, to
Nirvāna?

"Let me teach you, O bhikkhus, the middle path, which
keeps aloof from both extremes. By suffering, the emaciated
devotee produces confusion and sickly thoughts in his mind.   30
Mortification is not conducive even to worldly knowledge; how
much less to a triumph over the senses!

"He who fills his lamp with water will not dispel the
darkness, and he who tries to light a fire with rotten wood will
fail. And how can any one be free from self by leading a
wretched life, if he does not succeed in quenching the fires of
lust, if he still hankers after either worldly or heavenly
⁹pleasures. But he in whom self has become extinct is free
from lust; he will desire neither worldly nor heavenly
pleasures, and the satisfaction of his natural wants will not   40
defile him. However, let him be moderate, let him eat and drink
according to the needs of the body.

"Sensuality is enervating; the self-indulgent man is a slave
to his passions, and pleasure-seeking is degrading and vulgar.

"But to satisfy the necessities of life is not evil. To keep the
body in good health is a duty, for otherwise we shall not be
able to trim the lamp of wisdom, and keep our mind strong
and clear. Water surrounds the lotus-flower, but does not wet
its petals.

"This is the middle path, O bhikkhus, that keeps aloof from   50

both extremes."

And the Blessed One spoke kindly to his disciples, pitying
them for their errors, and pointing out the uselessness of their
endeavors, and the ice of ill-will that chilled their hearts
melted away under the gentle warmth of the Master's
persuasion.

Now the Blessed One set the wheel of the most excellent
law[4] rolling, and he began to preach to the five bhikkhus,
opening to them the gate of immortality, and showing them
the bliss of Nirvāna.   60

The Buddha said:

"The spokes of the wheel are the rules of pure conduct:
justice is the uniformity of their length; wisdom is the tire;
modesty and thoughtfulness are the hub in which the
immovable axle of truth is fixed.

"He who recognizes the existence of suffering, its cause, its
remedy, and its cessation has fathomed the four noble truths.
He will walk in the right path.

"Right views will be the torch to light his way. Right
aspirations will be his guide. Right speech will be his   70
dwelling-place on the road. His gait will be straight, for it is
right behavior. His refreshments will be the right way of
earning his livelihood. Right efforts will be his steps: right
thoughts his breath; and right contemplation will give him the
peace that follows in his footprints.

"Now, this, O bhikkhus, is the noble truth concerning
suffering:

"Birth is attended with pain, decay is painful, disease is
painful, death is painful. Union with the unpleasant is painful,
painful is separation from the pleasant; and any craving that is   80
unsatisfied, that too is painful. In brief, bodily conditions
which spring from attachment are painful.

"This, then, O bhikkhus, is the noble truth concerning
suffering.

"Now this, O bhikkhus, is the noble truth concerning the
origin of suffering:

"Verily, it is that craving which causes the renewal of
existence, accompanied by sensual delight, seeking
satisfaction now here, now there, the craving for the
gratification of the passions, the craving for a future life, and   90
the craving for happiness in this life.

"This, then, O bhikkhus, is the noble truth concerning the
origin of suffering.

"Now this, O bhikkhus, is the noble truth concerning the
destruction of suffering:

"Verily, it is the destruction, in which no passion remains, of
this very thirst; it is the laying aside of, the being free from, the
dwelling no longer upon this thirst.

"This, then, O bhikkhus, is the noble truth concerning the
destruction of suffering.   100

"Now this, O bhikkhus, is the noble truth concerning the
way which leads to the destruction of sorrow. Verily! it is this
noble eightfold path; that is to say:

"Right views; right aspirations; right speech; right behavior;
right livelihood; right effort; right thoughts; and right
contemplation.

---

[1] Disciples.
[2] The Vedic god of fire, associated with sun and lightning.
[3] "The successor to his predecessors in office," another name
for the Buddha.

[4] The Wheel of the Law.

"This, then, O bhikkhus, is the noble truth concerning the destruction of sorrow.

"By the practice of loving kindness I have attained liberation of heart, and thus I am assured that I shall never return in renewed births. I have even now attained Nirvāna." **110**

And when the Blessed One had thus set the royal chariot wheel of truth rolling onward, a rapture thrilled through the universes. . . .

Q **How does the Buddhist Middle Path compare with Aristotle's Doctrine of the Mean (Reading 4.7)?**

Q **How might a Stoic (Reading 6.2) respond to the Buddha's sermon?**

READING 8.4b From the Buddha's Sermon on Abuse (recorded ca. 100 B.C.E.)

And the Blessed One observed the ways of society and **1** noticed how much misery came from malignity and foolish offenses done only to gratify vanity and self-seeking pride.

And the Buddha said: "If a man foolishly does me wrong, I will return to him the protection of my ungrudging love; the more evil comes from him, the more good shall go from me; the fragrance of goodness always comes to me, and the harmful air of evil goes to him."

A foolish man learning that the Buddha observed the principle of great love which commends the return of good for **10** evil, came and abused him. The Buddha was silent, pitying his folly.

When the man had finished his abuse, the Buddha asked him, saying: "Son, if a man declined to accept a present made to him, to whom would it belong?" And he answered: "In that case it would belong to the man who offered it."

"My son," said the Buddha, "thou has railed at me, but I decline to accept thy abuse, and request thee to keep it thyself. Will it not be a source of misery to thee? As the echo belongs to the sound, and the shadow to the substance, so **20** misery will overtake the evil-doer without fail."

The abuser made no reply, and the Buddha continued:

"A wicked man who reproaches a virtuous one is like one who looks up and spits at heaven; the spittle soils not the heaven, but comes back and defiles his own person.

"The slanderer is like one who flings dust at another when the wind is contrary; the dust does but return on him who threw it. The virtuous man cannot be hurt and the misery that the other would inflict comes back on himself."

The abuser went away ashamed, but he came again and took **30** refuge in the Buddha, the Dharma,[1] and the Sangha[2]. . . .

Q **Based on these sermons, how do the teachings of Jesus (Reading 8.2) and the Buddha compare?**

---

[1] The Law of Righteousness; the Wheel of the Law.
[2] An assemblage of those who vow to pursue the Buddhist life.

The Spread of Buddhism

During the third century B.C.E., the emperor Asoka (273–232 B.C.E.) made Buddhism the state religion of India. Asoka's role in spreading Buddhism foreshadowed Constantine's labors on behalf of Christianity; but Asoka went even further. He initiated official policies of nonviolence (*ahimsa*), promoted vegetarianism, and defended egalitarianism. He built monuments and shrines honoring the Buddha throughout India; and he sent Buddhist missionaries as far west as Greece and southeast into Ceylon (present-day Sri Lanka). In spite of Asoka's efforts to give the world a unified faith, the Buddha's teachings generated varying interpretations and numerous factions. By the first century C.E., there were as many as 500 major and minor Buddhist sects in India alone. In general, however, two principal divisions of Buddhism emerged: Hinayana ("Lesser Vehicle") Buddhism and Mahayana ("Greater Vehicle") Buddhism. Hinayana Buddhism (also known as Theravada Buddhism) emphasized the personal pursuit of *nirvana*, and its followers consider that in doing so they remain close to the teachings of the Buddha and his emphasis on self-destiny. Mahayana Buddhism, on the other hand, elevated the Buddha to the level of a divine being. It taught that the Buddha was the path to salvation, that he had come to earth in the form of a man to guide humankind. Mahayana Buddhists regarded Siddhartha Gautama as but one of the Buddha's earthly incarnations, of which there had been many in the past and would be many in the future. The gods of other religions, including those of Hindusim, were held to be incarnations of the Buddha, who had appeared in various bodily forms in his previous lives.

Mahayana Buddhism developed the concept of many different Buddhist divinities who inhabit the heavens, but also manifested themselves in earthly form in order to help believers attain enlightenment. These "Buddhas-to-be" or **bodhisattvas** (Figure **8.6**) are beings who have reached enlightenment, but who—out of compassion—have held back from entering *nirvana* until every last soul has been brought to enlightenment. *Bodhisattvas* are the heroes of Buddhism; and much like the Christian saints, they became objects of many popular Buddhist cults. The most famous *bodhisattva* is Avalokiteshvara (known in Chinese as Guanyin and in Japanese as Kannon). Although *bodhisattvas*, like the Buddha, are beings beyond sexual gender, they are generally depicted as male. However, in East Asia Avalokiteshvara came to be regarded as a goddess of mercy, hence depicted as a woman (see Figure 14.12) and worshiped much in the way that Roman Catholics and Orthodox Christians honor the Virgin Mary.

Despite Asoka's efforts, Buddhism never gained widespread popularity in India. The strength of the established Hindu tradition in India (like that of Judaism in Judea) and the resistance of the Brahmin caste to Buddhist egalitarianism ultimately hindered the success of the new faith. By the middle of the first millennium, Hinduism was at least as prevalent as Buddhism in India, and by the year

1000, Buddhism was the religion of a minority. Buddhist communities nevertheless continued to flourish in India until the Islamic invasion of northern India in the twelfth and thirteenth centuries (see chapter 14) during which time Buddhism became all but extinct. Buddhism did, however, continue to thrive in lands far from its place of birth. In China, Mahayana Buddhism gained an overwhelming following and influence. From China, the new religion spread also to Korea, Japan, and Vietnam, where its impact was similarly great. Buddhism's tolerance for other religions enhanced its popularity and universal appeal. Mahayana Buddhism brought a message of hope and salvation to millions of people in East Asia. Hinayana Buddhism dominated as the faith in Ceylon (Sri Lanka), and spread from there to Burma (Myanmar), Thailand, and Cambodia.

Buddhism in China and Japan

Buddhism entered China during the first century C.E. and rose to prominence during the last, turbulent decades of the Han era (see chapter 7). At that time, Buddhist texts were translated into Chinese; over the following centuries, Buddhism was popularized in China by the writings of the Indian poet Asvaghosha (ca. 80–ca. 150). Asvaghosha's Sanskrit descriptions of the life of the Buddha, which became available in the year 420, was the literary medium for Mahayana Buddhism. Here, as in many other parts of Asia, the Buddha was regarded not simply as a teacher or reformer, but as a divine being. Daoism and Buddhism made an early and largely amicable contact in China, where their religious traditions would contribute to the formation of a syncretic popular faith. Buddhist "paradise sects," closely resembling the mystery cults of Southwest Asia promised their adherents rebirth in an idyllic, heavenly realm presided over by a heavenly Buddha. The most popular of these came to be the "Pure Land of the West" of Amitabha Buddha.

Still another Buddhist sect, known in China as Chan ("meditation") and in Japan as Zen, rose to prominence in the later centuries of the first millennium. Chan emphasized the role of meditation and visionary insight in reaching *nirvana*. Strongly influenced by Daoist thought, this sect held that enlightenment could not be attained by rational means but, rather, through intense concentration that led to a spontaneous awakening of the mind. Among the tools of Zen masters were such mind-sharpening riddles as: "You know the sound of two hands clapping; what, then, is the sound of one hand clapping?" The Zen monk's attention to such queries forced him to move beyond reason. Legend has it that heavily caffeinated tea was introduced from India to China and Japan as an aid to prolonging meditation, by which practice one might reach a higher state of consciousness.

Figure 8.6 *Standing Bodhisattva*, from the Gandharan region of northwest Pakistan, late second century C.E. Gray schist, height approx. 3 ft. Unlike the Buddha, who wears a humble monk's robe, *bodhisattvas* like this one are adorned with richly draped robes and elaborate jewelry that reflect the worldliness they will ultimately shed.

Glossary

apostle one of the twelve disciples chosen by Jesus to preach his gospel

asceticism strict self-denial and self-discipline

bodhisattva (Sanskrit, "one whose essence is enlightenment") a being who has postponed his or her own entry into *nirvana* in order to assist others in reaching that goal;

worshiped as a deity in Mahayana Buddhism

Diaspora the dispersion of Jews following the Babylonian captivity

Messiah Anointed One, or Savior; in Greek, *Christos*

rabbi a teacher and master trained in the Jewish law

sutra (Sanskrit, "thread") an instructional chapter or discourse in any of the sacred books of Buddhism

LOOKING BACK

The Background to Christianity

- Christianity emerged out of three distinctly different cultural traditions: Greco-Roman, Near Eastern (West Asian), and Hebraic.
- Popular Near Eastern mystery cults promised rebirth and resurrection to devotees of fertility gods and goddesses.
- In the Jewish community, Sadducees, Pharisees, and Essenes held differing interpretations of the biblical Messiah.
- Amidst mutual animosity and perpetual discord between Romans and Jews in Roman-occupied Judea, scores of self-proclaimed miracle workers and preachers competed for an audience.

The Rise of Christianity

- The oldest canonical record of the life and teachings of Jesus is the Christian Gospels ("good news"), dating from at least forty years after Jesus' death.
- The message of Jesus emphasized an abiding faith in God, compassion for one's fellow human beings, and the renunciation of material wealth.
- Jesus cast his message in simple and direct language, and in parables that carried moral instruction.

The Teachings of Paul

- The apostle Paul universalized Jesus' message by preaching to non-Jewish communities, thus earning the title "Apostle to the Gentiles." He explained the death of Jesus as atonement for sin and anticipated eternal life for his followers.
- Paul is generally believed to have written ten to fourteen of the twenty-seven books of the Christian Scriptures or "New Testament."

The Spread of Christianity

- Christianity slowly won converts among populations that experienced poverty and oppression. It promised redemption from sins, personal immortality, and a life to come from which material adversities were absent.
- In contrast with the elusive gods of the mystery cults, Jesus had actually lived among men and women, and had practiced the morality he preached.

- Not until the rule of Constantine, and the Edict of Milan (313), did the public persecution of Christians come to an end. The Edict encouraged the development of Christianity as a legitimate faith.

The Rise of Buddhism

- Siddhartha Gautama was a Hindu prince whose teachings established his role as the Buddha ("the enlightened one"). He taught that the path to enlightenment begins with the four Noble Truths: pain is universal, desire causes pain, ceasing to desire relieves pain, and right conduct (the Eightfold Path) leads to release from pain.
- The Buddhist's goal is not the promise of personal immortality, but rather escape from the endless cycle of birth, death, and rebirth. For the Buddhist, "salvation" lies in the extinction of the Self.
- Like Jesus, the Buddha's concerns were profoundly ethical. Preaching the law (*dharma*) of compassion and humility, he promised that enlightenment could be achieved by all people regardless of class.
- The Buddha himself left no written records; his disciples memorized his teachings and wrote them down during the first century B.C.E. in three main books, the *Pitakas*.

The Spread of Buddhism

- During the third century B.C.E., the emperor Asoka made Buddhism the state religion of India, sending Buddhist missionaries as far west as Greece and southeast into present-day Sri Lanka.
- In spite of Asoka's efforts to establish a unified faith, the Buddha's teachings generated varying interpretations and numerous factions. By the first century C.E., at least 500 Buddhist sects flourished in India alone. Mahayana Buddhists claimed the Buddha as a divinity who would lead his followers to personal salvation.
- Buddhism entered China during the first century C.E. and rose to prominence during the last decades of the Han Era. Buddhism was popularized in China by the writings of the Indian poet Asvaghosha.
- Given the strength of Hinduism in India, Buddhism never gained widespread popularity; in China and elsewhere in Southeast Asia, however, Buddhism became the faith of millions.

Chapter

9

The Language of Faith: Symbolism and the Arts

ca.300–600 C.E.

"The earthly city loves its own strength as revealed in its men of power, the heavenly city says to its God: 'I will love thee, O Lord, my strength.'"
Augustine of Hippo

Figure 9.1 *Jesus Calling the First Apostles, Peter and Andrew*, early sixth century. Mosaic. Detail of upper register of north wall, Sant'Apollinare Nuovo, Ravenna. Adorning the wall of this Early Christian basilica, the highly stylized scene belongs to the earliest surviving mosaic cycle showing events in the life of Jesus.

LOOKING AHEAD

Christianity began its rise to world significance amidst an empire beset by increasing domestic difficulties and the assaults of barbarian nomads (see chapter 11). The last great Roman emperors, Diocletian (245–316) and Constantine (ca. 274–337), made valiant efforts to restructure the Empire and reverse military and economic decline. In order to govern Rome's sprawling territories more efficiently, Diocletian divided the Empire into western and eastern halves and appointed a co-emperor to share the burden of administration and defense. After Diocletian retired, Constantine levied new taxes and made unsuccessful efforts to revive a money economy. By means of the Edict of Milan (313), which proclaimed toleration of all religions (including the fledgling Christianity), Constantine tried to heal Rome's internal divisions. Failing to breathe new life into the waning Empire, however, in 330 he moved the seat of power from the beleaguered city of Rome to the eastern capital of the Empire, Byzantium, which he renamed Constantinople.

While the Roman Empire languished in the West, the East Roman or Byzantine Empire—the economic heart of the Roman world—prospered. Located at the crossroads of Europe and Asia, Constantinople was the hub of a vital trade network and the heir to the cultural traditions of Greece, Rome, and Asia. Byzantine emperors formed a firm alliance with church leaders and worked to create an empire that flourished until the mid-fifteenth century. The Slavic regions of Eastern Europe (including Russia) converted to Orthodox Christianity during the ninth and tenth centuries, thus extending the religious influence of the city that Constantine had designated the "New Rome." As Christians in Rome and Byzantium worked to formulate an effective language of faith, Buddhists in India, China, and Southeast Asia were developing their own vocabulary of religious expression. Buddhism inspired a glorious outpouring of art, architecture, and music that—like Early Christian art in the West—nourished the spiritual needs of millions of people throughout the East.

The Christian Identity

 Between the fourth and sixth centuries, Christianity grew from a small, dynamic sect into a full-fledged religion; and its ministerial agent, the Roman Catholic Church, came to replace the Roman Empire as the dominant authority in the West. The history of these developments sheds light on the formation of the Christian identity.

In the first centuries after the death of Jesus, there was little unity of belief and practice among those who called themselves Christians. But after the legalization of the faith in 313, the followers of Jesus moved toward resolving questions of church hierarchy, **dogma** (prescribed doctrine), and liturgy (the rituals for public worship). From Rome, church leaders in the West took the Latin language, the Roman legal system (which would become the basis for church or **canon law**), and Roman methods of architectural construction. The Church retained the Empire's administrative divisions, appointing archbishops to oversee the provinces, bishops in the dioceses, and priests in the parishes. As Rome had been the hub of the Western Empire, so it became the administrative center of the new faith. When church leaders in Constantinople and Antioch contested the administrative primacy of Rome, the bishop of Rome, Leo the Great (ca. 400–461), advanced the "Petrine Doctrine," claiming that Roman pontiffs inherited their position as the successors to Peter, the First Apostle and the principal evangelist of Rome. As Roman emperors had held supreme authority over the state, so Roman Catholic popes—the temporal representatives of Christ—would govern Western Christendom. The new spiritual order in the West was thus patterned after imperial Rome.

A functional administrative hierarchy was essential to the success of the new faith; so too was the formulation of a uniform doctrine of belief. As Christianity spread, the story of Jesus and the meaning of his message provoked various kinds of inquiry. Was Jesus human or divine? What was the status of Jesus in relation to God? Such fundamental questions drew conflicting answers. To resolve them, Church officials would convene to hammer out a systematic explanation of the life, death, and resurrection of Jesus. The first **ecumenical** (worldwide) council of churchmen was called by the emperor Constantine. It met at Nicaea (present-day Iznik), Turkey, in 325. At the Council of Nicaea, a consensus of opinion among church representatives laid the basis for Christian dogma. It was resolved—to the objection of some dissenting Eastern churchmen—that Jesus was of one substance (or essence) with God the Father. The council issued a statement of Christian belief known as the Nicene Creed. A version of the Nicene Creed issued in 381 and still used by Eastern Orthodox Christians is reproduced below. It pledges commitment to a variety of miraculous phenomena, including virgin birth, the resurrection of the dead, and a mystical Trinity comprising Jesus, God the Father, and the Holy Spirit. The principal formula of Christian belief, it stands as the turning point between Classical rationalism and Christian mysticism. Challenging reason and the evidence of the senses, it embraces faith and the intuition of truths that transcend ordinary understanding. As such, it anticipates the shift from a homocentric Classical world-view to the God-centered medieval world-view.

READING 9.1 The Nicene Creed (381)

We believe in one God the Father All-Sovereign, maker of heaven and earth, and of all things visible and invisible;   **1**

And in one Lord Jesus Christ, the only-begotten Son of God, Begotten of the Father before all the ages, Light of Light, true God of true God, begotten not made, of one substance with the Father, through whom all things were made; who for us men and for our salvation came down from the heavens, and was made flesh of the Holy Spirit and the Virgin Mary, and became man, and was crucified for us under Pontius Pilate, and suffered and was buried, and rose again on the third day   **10** according to the Scriptures, and ascended into the heavens, and sitteth on the right hand of the Father, and cometh again with glory to judge living and dead, of whose kingdom there shall be no end:

And in the Holy Spirit, the Lord and the Life-giver, that proceedeth from the Father, who with Father and Son is worshipped together and glorified together, who spake through the prophets:

In one holy Catholic and Apostolic Church:

We acknowledge one baptism unto remission of sins. We   **20** look for a resurrection of the dead, and the life of the age to come.

Q What is a "creed"?

Q How does the Nicene Creed illustrate the "leap of faith" that is basic to all religious belief?

Christian Monasticism

Even before the coming of Christ, communal asceticism (self-denial) was a way of life among those who sought an environment for study and prayer and an alternative to the decadence of urban life. Such was the case with the Essenes in the West and the Buddhist monks of Asia. The earliest Christian monastics (the word comes from the Greek *monas*, meaning "alone") pursued sanctity in the deserts of Egypt. Fasting, poverty, and celibacy were the essential features of the ascetic lifestyle instituted by the Greek bishop Saint Basil (ca. 329–379) and still followed by monastics of the Eastern Church.

In the West, the impulse to retreat from the turmoil of secular life became more intense as the last remnants of Classical civilization disappeared. In 529, the same year that Plato's Academy closed its doors in Athens, the first Western monastic community was founded at Monte Cassino in southern Italy. Named after its founder, Benedict of Nursia (ca. 480–547), the Benedictine rule (in Latin, *regula*) required that its members take vows of poverty (the renunciation of all material possessions), chastity (abstention from sexual activity), and obedience to the governing **abbot**, or father of the **abbey** (the monastic community). Benedictine monks followed a routine of work that freed them from dependence on the secular world, balanced by religious study and prayer: the daily recitation of the Divine Office, a cycle of prayers that marked eight devotional intervals in the twenty-four-hour

period. This program of *ora et labora* ("prayer and work") gave structure and meaning to the daily routine, and provided a balanced standard best expressed by the Benedictine motto, *mens sana in corpore sano* ("a sound mind in a sound body").

Monastics and church fathers alike generally regarded women as the daughters of Eve, inherently sinful and dangerous as objects of sexual temptation. The Church prohibited women from holding positions of church authority and from receiving ordination as **secular clergy** (priests). However, women were not excluded from joining the ranks of the religious. In Egypt, some 20,000 women—twice the number of men—lived in monastic communities as nuns. In the West, aristocratic women often turned their homes into Benedictine nunneries, where they provided religious education for women of all classes. Saint Benedict's sister, Scholastica (d. 543), became abbess of a monastery near Monte Cassino. A refuge for female intellectuals, the convent offered women an alternative to marriage.

From the fifth century on, members of the **regular clergy** (those who follow the rule of a monastic order) played an increasingly important role in Western intellectual history. As Greek and Roman sources of education dried up and fewer men and women learned to read and write, the task of preserving the history and literature of the past fell to the last bastions of literacy: the monasteries. Benedictine monks and nuns hand-copied and illustrated Christian as well as Classical manuscripts, and stored them in their libraries. Over the centuries, Benedictine monasteries provided local education, managed hospices, sponsored sacred music and art, and produced a continuous stream of missionaries, scholars, mystics, and Church reformers. One little-known sixth-century abbot, Dionysius Exiguus (Denis the Little, fl. 525), was responsible for establishing the calendar that is most widely used in the world to this day. In an effort to fix the Church timetable for the annual celebration of Easter, Dionysius reckoned the birth of Jesus at 754 years after the founding of Rome. Although he was inaccurate by at least three years, he applied his chronology to establish the year one as *Anno domini nostri Jesu Christi* ("the Year of Our Lord Jesus Christ"). This method of dating became the standard practice in the West when the English abbot and scholar known as the Venerable Bede (673–735) employed the Christian calendar in writing his monumental history of England.

The Latin Church Fathers

In the formulation of Christian dogma and liturgy in the West, the most important figures were four Latin scholars who lived between the fourth and sixth centuries: Jerome, Ambrose, Gregory, and Augustine. Saint Jerome (ca. 347–420), a Christian educated in Rome, translated into Latin both the Hebrew Bible and the Greek books of the "New Testament." This mammoth task resulted in the Vulgate, the Latin edition of Scripture that became the official Bible of the Roman Catholic Church. Although Jerome considered pagan culture a distraction from the spiritual life, he admired the writers of Classical antiquity and did not hesitate to plunder the spoils of Classicism—and Hebraism—to build the edifice of a new faith.

Like Jerome, Ambrose (339–397) drew on Hebrew, Greek, and Southwest Asian traditions in formulating Christian doctrine and liturgy. A Roman aristocrat who became bishop of Milan, Ambrose wrote some of the earliest Christian hymns for congregational use. Influenced by eastern Mediterranean chants and Hebrew psalms, Ambrose's hymns are characterized by a lyrical simplicity that made them models of religious expression. In the hymn that follows, divine light is the unifying theme. The reference to God as the "Light of light" distinctly recalls the cult of Mithras, as well as Plato's analogy between the Good and the Sun. Culminating in a burst of praise for the triune God, the hymn conveys a mood of buoyant optimism.

READING 9.2 Saint Ambrose's "Ancient Morning Hymn" (ca. 380)

O Splendor of God's glory bright,	1
O Thou who bringest light from light,	
O Light of light, light's living spring,	
O Day, all days illumining!	
O Thou true Sun, on us Thy glance	5
Let fall in royal radiance;	
The Spirit's sanctifying beam	
Upon our earthly senses stream.	
The Father, too, our prayers implore,	
Father of glory evermore,	10
The Father of all grace and might,	
To banish sin from our delight.	
To guide whate'er we nobly do,	
With love all envy to subdue,	
To make ill-fortune turn to fair,	15
And give us grace our wrongs to bear.	
Rejoicing may this day go hence;	
Like virgin dawn our innocence,	
Like fiery noon our faith appear,	
Nor know the gloom of twilight drear.	20
Morn in her rosy car is borne:	
Let him come forth, our perfect morn,	
The Word in God the Father one,	
The Father perfect in the Son.	
All laud to God the Father be;	25
All praise, eternal Son, to Thee;	
All glory, as is ever meet,	
To God the holy Paraclete.[1]	

Q How does this song of praise compare to "The Hymn to the Aten" (Reading 2.1) and to Psalm 8 (Reading 1.4e)?

The contribution of the Roman aristocrat Gregory the Great (ca. 540–604) was vital to the development of early church government. Elected to the papacy in 590, Gregory established the administrative machinery by which all subsequent popes would govern the Church of Rome. A born organizer, Gregory sent missionaries to convert England to Christianity; he extended the temporal authority of the Roman Church throughout Western Europe. Despite the lack of historical evidence, his name has long been associated with the codification of the body of chants that became the liturgical music of the early Church.

The most profound and influential of all the Latin church fathers was Augustine of Hippo (354–430). His treatises on the nature of the soul, free will, and the meaning of evil made him the greatest philosopher of Christian antiquity. A native of Roman Africa and an intellectual who came under the spell of both Paul and Plotinan Neoplatonism, Augustine converted to Christianity at the age of thirty-three. Before his conversion to Christianity, Augustine had enjoyed a sensual and turbulent youth, marked by womanizing, gambling, and fathering an illegitimate child. Augustine's lifelong conflict between his love of worldly pleasures, dominated by what he called his "lower self," and his love of God, exercised by the "higher part of our nature," is the focus of his fascinating and self-scrutinizing autobiography known as the *Confessions*. Here, Augustine makes a fundamental distinction between physical and spiritual satisfaction, arguing that "no bodily pleasure, however great it might be . . . [is] worthy of comparison, or even of mention, beside the happiness of the life of the saints." The dualistic model of the human being as the locus of warring elements—the "unclean body" and the "purified soul"—drew heavily on the Neoplatonist duality of Matter and Spirit and the Pauline promise that the sin of Adam might be cleansed by the sacrifice of Jesus.

In the extract below from his *Confessions*, Augustine identifies the three temptations that endanger his soul: the lust of the flesh, the lust of the eyes, and the ambition of the world. Nowhere is Augustine's motto, "Faith seeking understanding," so intimately reflected as in the self-examining prose of the *Confessions*.

READING 9.3 From Saint Augustine's *Confessions* (ca. 400)

Certainly you command me to restrain myself from the *lust of*   1
the flesh, the lust of the eyes, and the ambition of the world.
You commanded me to abstain from sleeping with a mistress,
and with regard to marriage you advised me to take a better
course than the one that was permitted me. And since you
gave me the power, it was done, even before I became a
dispenser of your Sacrament. But there still live in that
memory of mine, of which I have spoken so much, images of

---

[1] Holy Spirit.

the things which my habit has fixed there. These images come into my thoughts, and, though when I am awake they are [10] strengthless, in sleep they not only cause pleasure but go so far as to obtain assent and something very like reality. These images, though real, have such an effect on my soul, in my flesh, that false visions in my sleep obtain from me what true visions cannot when I am awake. Surely, Lord my God, I am myself when I am asleep? And yet there is a very great difference between myself and myself in that moment of time when I pass from being awake to being asleep or come back again from sleep to wakefulness. Where then is my reason which, when I am awake, resists such suggestions and [20] remains unshaken if the realities themselves were presented to it? Do reason's eyes close with the eyes of the body? Does reason go to sleep when the bodily senses sleep? If so, how does it happen that even in our sleep we do often resist and, remembering our purpose and most chastely abiding by it, give no assent to enticements of this kind? Nevertheless, there is a great difference, because, when it happens otherwise, we return on waking to a peace of conscience and, by the very remoteness of our state now and then, discover that it was not we who did something which was, to our regret, somehow [30] or other done in us.

Almighty God, surely your hand is powerful enough to cure all the sickness in my soul and, with a more abundant measure of your grace, to quench even the lustful impulses of my sleep. Lord, you will increase your gifts in me more and more, so that my soul, disentangled from the birdlime of concupiscence,[1] may follow me to you; so that it may not be in revolt against itself and may not, even in dreams, succumb to or even give the slightest assent to those degrading corruptions which by means of sensual images actually disturb [40] and pollute the flesh. . . .

I must now mention another form of temptation which is in many ways more dangerous. Apart from the concupiscence of the flesh which is present in the delight we take in all the pleasures of the senses (and the slaves of it perish as they put themselves far from you), there is also present in the soul, by means of these same bodily senses, a kind of empty longing and curiosity which aims not at taking pleasure in the flesh but at acquiring experience through the flesh, and this empty curiosity is dignified by the names of learning and science. [50] Since this is in the appetite for knowing, and since the eyes are the chief of our senses for acquiring knowledge, it is called in the divine language the lust of the eyes. For "to see" is used properly of the eyes; but we also use this word of the other senses when we are employing them for the purpose of gaining knowledge. We do not say: "Hear how it flashes" or "Smell how bright it is" or "Taste how it shines" or "Feel how it gleams"; in all these cases we use the verb "to see." But we not only say: "See how it shines," a thing which can only be perceived by the eyes; we also say "See how it sounds," [60] "See how it smells," "See how it tastes," "See how hard it is." Therefore, the general experience of the senses is, as was said before, called "the lust of the eyes," because seeing,

which belongs properly to the eyes, is used by analogy of the other senses too when they are attempting to discover any kind of knowledge.

In this it is easy to see how pleasure and curiosity have different objects in their use of the senses. Pleasure goes after what is beautiful to us, sweet to hear, to smell, to taste, to touch; but curiosity, for the sake of experiment, may go [70] after the exact opposites of these, not in order to suffer discomfort, but simply because of the lust to find out and to know. What pleasure can there be in looking at a mangled corpse, which must excite our horror? Yet if there is one near, people flock to see it, so as to grow sad and pale at the sight. They are actually frightened of seeing it in their sleep, as though anyone had forced them to see it when they were awake or as if they had been induced to look at it because it had the reputation of being a beautiful thing to see. The same is true of the other senses. There is no need to go to the [80] length of producing examples. Because of this disease of curiosity monsters and anything out of the ordinary are put on show in our theaters. From the same motive men proceed to investigate the workings of nature which is beyond our ken— things which it does no good to know and which men only want to know for the sake of knowing. So too, and with this same end of perverted science, people make enquiries by means of magic. Even in religion we find the same thing: God is tempted when signs and portents are demanded and are not desired for any salutary purpose, but simply for the experience [90] of seeing them. . . .

We are tempted, Lord, by these temptations every day; without intermission we are tempted. The tongue of man is the furnace in which we are tried every day. Here too you command us to be continent. Give what you command, and command what you will. You know how on this matter my heart groans to you and my eyes stream tears. For I cannot easily discover how far I have become cleaner from this disease, and I much fear my hidden sins which are visible to your eyes, though not to mine. For in other kinds of temptation [100] I have at least some means of finding out about myself; but in this kind it is almost impossible. With regard to the pleasures of the flesh and the unnecessary curiosity for knowledge I can see how far I have advanced in the ability to control my mind simply by observing myself when I am without these things, either from choice or when they are not available. For I can then ask myself how much or how little I mind not having them. So too with regard to riches, which are desired for the satisfaction of one or two or all of those three concupiscences; if one is not able to be quite sure in one's own mind whether [110] or not one despises them when one has them, it is possible to get rid of them so as to put oneself to the test. But how can we arrange things so as to be without praise and make the same experiment with regard to it? Are we to live a bad life, to live in such a wicked and abandoned way that everyone who knows us will detest us? Nothing could be madder than such a suggestion as that. On the contrary, if praise both goes with and ought to go with a good life and good works, we should

---

[1] Strong desire, especially sexual desire.

no more part with it than with the good life itself. Yet
unless a thing is not there I cannot tell whether it is difficult   120
or easy for me to be without it. . . .

— Q **Which temptation does Augustine seem to find
the most difficult of resist?**

— Q **How might he respond to Buddhism's Four
Noble Truths?**

Augustine's *City of God*

A living witness to the decline of the Roman Empire,
Augustine defended his faith against recurrent pagan
charges that Christianity was responsible for Rome's
downfall. In his multivolume work the *City of God*, he
distinguishes between the earthly city of humankind and
the heavenly city that is the eternal dwelling place of the
Christian soul. Augustine's earthly abode, a place where
"wise men live according to man," represents the Classical
world prior to the coming of Jesus. By contrast, the
heavenly city—the spiritual realm where human beings
live according to divine precepts—is the destiny of those
who embrace the "New Dispensation" of Christ.

Augustine's influence in shaping Christian dogma
cannot be overestimated. His rationalization of evil as the
perversion of the good created by God, and his defense
of "just war"—that is, war as reprisal for the abuse of morality—testify to the analytic subtlety of his mind. His
description of history as divinely ordered and directed
toward a predestined end became fundamental to
Christian historiography. Finally, his dualistic model of
reality—matter and spirit, body and soul, earth and heav-
en, Satan and God, state and Church—governed Western
thought for centuries to come. The conception of the visible world (matter) as an imperfect reflection of the divine
order (spirit) determined the allegorical character of
Christian culture. According to this model, matter was the
matrix in which God's message was hidden. In Scripture, as
well as in every natural and created thing, God's invisible
order might be discovered. For Augustine, the Hebrew
Bible was a symbolic prefiguration of Christian truths, and
history itself was a cloaked message of divine revelation.

The extract from the *City of God* illustrates Augustine's
dual perception of reality and suggests its importance to
the tradition of Christian allegory. Augustine's description
of Noah's ark as symbolic of the City of God, the Church,
and the body of Christ exemplifies the way in which a
single image might assume various meanings within the
language of Christian faith.

┌─ **READING 9.4** From Saint Augustine's *City of God
Against the Pagans* (413–426)

*On the character of the two cities, the earthly and the
heavenly.*
The two cities then were created by two kinds of love: the   1
earthly city by a love of self carried even to the point of
contempt for God, the heavenly city by a love of God carried

even to the point of contempt for self. Consequently, the
earthly city glories in itself while the other glories in the Lord.[1]
For the former seeks glory from men, but the latter finds its
greatest glory in God, the witness of our conscience. The
earthly city lifts up its head in its own glory; the heavenly city
says to its God: "My glory and the lifter of my head."[2] In the
one, the lust for dominion has dominion over its princes as   10
well as over the nations that it subdues; in the other, both
those put in charge and those placed under them serve one
another in love, the former by their counsel, the latter by their
obedience. The earthly city loves its own strength as revealed
in its men of power; the heavenly city says to its God: "I will
love thee, O Lord, my strength."[3]

Thus in the earthly city its wise men who live according to
man have pursued the goods either of the body or of their own
mind or of both together; or if any of them were able to know
God, "they did not honor him as God or give thanks to him, but   20
they became futile in their thinking and their senseless minds
were darkened; claiming to be wise," that is, exalting
themselves in their own wisdom under the dominion of pride,
"they became fools, and exchanged the glory of the immortal
God for images resembling mortal man or birds or beasts or
reptiles," for in the adoration of idols of this sort they were
either leaders or followers of the populace, "and worshiped
and served the creature rather than the creator, who is blessed
forever."[4] In the heavenly city, on the other hand, man's only
wisdom is the religion that guides him rightly to worship the   30
true God and awaits as its reward in the fellowship of saints,
not only human but also angelic, this goal, "that God may be
all in all."[5] . . .

*That the ark which Noah was ordered to make symbolizes
Christ and the church in every detail.*

Now God, as we know, enjoined the building of an ark upon
Noah, a man who was righteous and according to the true
testimony of Scripture, perfect in his generation,[6] that is,
perfect, not as the citizens of the City of God are to become in
that immortal state where they will be made equal with the   40
angels of God, but as they can be during their sojourn here on
earth. In this ark he was to be rescued from the devastation of
the flood with his family, that is, his wife, sons and daughters-
in-law, as well as with the animals that came to him in the ark
at God's direction. We doubtless have here a symbolic
representation of the City of God sojourning as an alien in this
world, that is, of the church which wins salvation by virtue of
the wood on which the mediator between God and men, the
man Christ Jesus,[7] was suspended.

The very measurements of the ark's length, height and   50
breadth symbolize the human body, in the reality of which it
was prophesied that Christ would come to mankind, as, in fact,
he did come. For the length of the human body from top to toe

[1] Cf. 2 Corinthians 10:17.
[2] Psalms 3:3.
[3] Psalms 18:1.
[4] Romans 1:21–23, 25.
[5] 1 Corinthians 15:28.
[6] Cf. Genesis 6:9.
[7] 1 Timothy 2:5.

is six times its breadth from one side to the other and ten times its thickness measured on a side from back to belly. Thus if you measure a man lying on his back or face down, his length from head to foot is six times his breadth from right to left or from left to right and ten times his elevation from the ground. This is why the ark was made three hundred cubits in length, fifty in breadth and thirty in height. And as for the door that it received **60** on its side, that surely is the wound that was made when the side of the crucified one was pierced by the spear.[8] This is the way by which those who come to him enter, because from this opening flowed the sacraments with which believers are initiated. Moreover, the order that it should be made of squared beams contains an allusion to the foursquare stability of saints' lives, for in whatever direction you turn a squared object, it will stand firm. In similar fashion, everything else mentioned in the construction of this ark symbolizes some aspect of the church....

Q How is allegory used in this reading?

Q Why was allegory such an important tool in shaping the "New Dispensation"?

Symbolism and Early Christian Art

Christian signs and symbols linked the visible to the invisible world. They worked by analogy, in much the same way that allegory operated in Augustine's *City of God*. Since in Christian art the symbolic significance of a representation is often more important than its literal meaning, the identification and interpretation of the subject matter (a discipline known as **iconography**) is especially important. Before Christianity was legalized in 313, visual symbols served the practical function of identifying new converts to the faith among themselves. Followers of Jesus adopted the sign of the fish because the Greek word for fish (*ichthys*) is an acrostic combination of the first letters of the Greek words "Jesus Christ, Son of God, Savior." They also used the first and last letters of the Greek alphabet, *alpha* and *omega*, to designate Christ's presence at the beginning and the end of time. Roman converts to Christianity saw in the Latin word for peace, *pax*, a symbolic reference to

Christ, since the last and first letters could also be read as *chi* and *rho*, the first two letters in the Greek word *Christos*. Indeed, *pax* was emblazoned on the banner under which the emperor Constantine was said to have defeated his enemies. Such symbols soon found their way into Early Christian art.

On a sixth-century sarcophagus (stone coffin) of the archbishop Theodorus of Ravenna (Figure **9.2**), the *chi* and *rho* and the *alpha* and *omega* have been made into an insignia that resembles both a crucifix (symbolizing Christ as Savior) and a pastoral cross (symbolizing Christ as Shepherd, Figure **9.3**). Three laurel wreaths, Roman imperial symbols of triumph, encircle the medallions on the coffin lid. On either side of the central medallion are grapevines designating the wine that represents the blood of Christ. The tiny birds that stand beneath the vines— derived from Greek funerary art—refer to the human soul. Also included in the iconographic program are two popular Southwest Asian symbols of immortality: the peacock or phoenix, a legendary bird that was thought to be reborn from its own ashes, and the rosette, an ancient symbol of Isis in her regenerative role. Taken as a whole, the archbishop's coffin is the vehicle of a sacred language signifying Christ's triumph and the Christian promise of resurrection and salvation.

In Early Christian art, music, and literature, almost every number and combination of numbers was thought to bear allegorical meaning. The number 3, for example, signified the Trinity; 4 signified the evangelists; 5 symbolized the wounds of Jesus; 12 stood for the apostles, and so on. The evangelists were usually represented by four winged creatures: the man for Matthew, the lion for Mark, the ox for Luke, and the eagle for John (see Figure 9.3 and the upper portion of Figure 9.10). Prefigured in the Book of Revelation (4:1–8), each of the four creatures came to be associated with a particular Gospel. The lion, for example, was appropriate to Mark because in his Gospel he emphasized the royal dignity of Christ; the heaven-soaring eagle suited John, who produced the most lofty and mystical of the Gospels. The halo, a zone of light used in Roman art to

Figure 9.2 Sarcophagus of Archbishop Theodorus, sixth century. Marble.

[8] Cf. John 19:34.

Figure 9.3
(a) Christian monograms;
(b) symbols of the four evangelists;
(c) Latin and Greek crosses.

Figure 9.4 *Orans* (praying figure), ca. 300. Fresco. Catacombs of Saint Priscilla, Rome. The figure is shown here wearing the Jewish prayer shawl known as the *tallis* (or *tallit*).

resembles that of secular Roman art (see chapter 6): figures are small but substantial and deftly shaded to suggest three-dimensionality. Setting and specific indications of spatial depth are omitted, however, so that human forms appear to float in ethereal space.

In the centuries following the legalization of Christianity, stories about the life of Jesus came to form two main narrative cycles: The Youth of Christ and The Passion of Christ. Not until the fifth century, however, when the manner of Jesus' death began to lose its ignoble associations, was Jesus depicted on the Cross. One of the earliest of such scenes is that carved in low relief on the wooden west doors of Santa Sabina in Rome (see Figure 8.4). Christ assumes the *orans* in a rigid and static frontal position that also signifies a crucified body. The tripartite composition of the relief includes the smaller (because less important) figures of the thieves who flanked Jesus at the crucifixion. Despite its narrative content, the image is far from being a representation of the crucifixion of Jesus. Rather, it is a symbolic statement of Christian redemption.

Early Christians had little use for the Roman approach to art as a window on the world. Roman Realism, with its scrupulous attention to time, place, and personalities, was ill-suited to convey the timeless message of a universal

Figure 9.5 *Christ as Good Shepherd*, mid-fourth century. Fresco. Catacombs of Saints Pietro and Marcellino, Rome.

signify divinity or holiness, became a favorite symbolic device in the visual representation of Jesus, the evangelists, and others whom the Church canonized as holy persons capable of interceding for sinners.

Some of the earliest evidence of Christian art comes from the **catacombs**, subterranean burial chambers outside the city of Rome. These vast networks of underground galleries and rooms include gravesites whose walls are covered with frescoes illustrating scenes from the Old and New Testaments. One figure is shown in the *orans* position—with arms upraised in an attitude of prayer—an ancient gesture (see Figure 1.2) used in the performance of ritual (Figure **9.4**). Like the story of Noah's ark, "decoded" by Augustine to reveal its hidden significance, Early Christian imagery was multilayered and pregnant with symbolic meaning. For example, the popular figure of Jesus as Good Shepherd, an adaptation of the calf- or lamb-bearing youth of Greco-Roman art (see chapter 5), symbolizes Jesus' role as savior-protector (shepherd) and sacrificial victim (lamb). Featured in catacomb frescoes (Figure **9.5**) and in freestanding sculpture (see Figure 9.6), the Good Shepherd evokes the Early Christian theme of deliverance. But while the message of the catacomb frescoes is one of salvation and deliverance, the style of these paintings faith and the miraculous events surrounding the life of a savior god. Moreover, Christian artists inherited the Jewish prohibition against "graven images." As a result, very little freestanding sculpture was produced between the second and eleventh centuries; that which was produced, such as the fourth-century *Good Shepherd* (Figure **9.6**), retains only the rudimentary features—such as the *contrapposto* stance—of High Classical statuary. On the other hand, hand-illuminated manuscripts and **diptychs** (two-leaved hinged tablets or panels) designed for private devotional use were produced in great numbers. A sixth-century ivory book cover from Murano, Italy (Figure **9.7**), is typical of the Early Christian artist's preoccupation with didactic content and surface adornment. Scenes of Jesus' miracles are wedged together in airless compartments surrounding the central image of the enthroned Jesus with Peter and Paul. A royal canopy flanked by **Latin crosses** (see Figure 9.3) crowns the holy space. In the top register,

Iconography of the Life of Jesus

THE YOUTH OF CHRIST (principal events)

1 The Annunciation
The archangel Gabriel announces to the Virgin Mary that God has chosen her to bear his son

2 The Visitation
The pregnant Mary visits her cousin, Elizabeth, who is pregnant with the future John the Baptist

3 The Nativity
Jesus is born to Mary in Bethlehem

4 The Annunciation to the Shepherds
An angel announces the birth of Jesus to humble shepherds, who hasten to Bethlehem

5 The Adoration of the Magi
Three wise men from the East follow a star to Bethlehem where they present the Christ Child with precious gifts (gold, frankincense, and myrrh)

6 The Presentation in the Temple
Mary and Joseph present Jesus to the high priest at the Temple in Jerusalem

7 The Massacre of the Innocents and the Flight to Egypt
King Herod murders all the newborn of Bethlehem; the Holy Family (Mary, Joseph, and Jesus) flee to Egypt

8 The Baptism
John the Baptist, a preacher in the wilderness of Judea, baptizes Jesus in the Jordan River

9 The Temptation
Jesus fasts for forty days and nights in the wilderness; he rejects the worldly wealth offered to him by the devil

10 The Calling of the Apostles
Near the Sea of Galilee, Jesus calls the brothers Simon (Peter) and Andrew into his service

11 The Raising of Lazarus
Jesus restores to life Lazarus, the brother of Mary and Martha

12 The Transfiguration
On Mount Tabor in Galilee, among his disciples Peter, James, and John the Evangelist, the radiantly transfigured Jesus is hailed by God as his beloved Son

THE PASSION OF CHRIST (principal events)

1 The Entry into Jerusalem
Jesus, riding on a donkey, enters Jerusalem amidst his disciples and receptive crowds

2 The Last Supper
At the Passover *seder*, Jesus reveals to his disciples his impending death and instructs them to consume the bread (his body) and the wine

3 The Agony in the Garden
In the Garden of Gethsemane on the Mount of Olives, while the disciples Peter, James, and John sleep, Jesus reconciles his soul to death

4 The Betrayal
Judas Iscariot, who has been bribed to point Jesus out to his enemies, identifies him by kissing him as he leaves the Garden of Gethsemane

5 Jesus Before Pilate
Jesus comes before the Roman governor of Judea and is charged with treason; when the crowd demands Jesus be put to death, Pilate washes his hands to signify his innocence of the deed

6 The Flagellation
Jesus is scourged by his captors, the Roman soldiers

7 The Mocking of Jesus
Pilate's soldiers dress Jesus in royal robes and put a crown of thorns on his head

8 The Road to Calvary
Jesus carries the Cross to Golgotha (Calvary) where he is to be executed affixed to a cross raised to stand upright

9 The Crucifixion
At Golgotha, Jesus is crucified between two thieves

10 The Descent from the Cross and the Lamentation
Grief-stricken followers remove the body of Jesus from the Cross; the Virgin, Mary Magdalene, and others grieve over it

11 The Entombment
Mary and the followers of Jesus place his body in a nearby tomb

12 The Resurrection
Three days after his death, Jesus rises from the tomb

Figure 9.6 *The Good Shepherd*, ca. 300. Marble, height 3 ft. (The legs are restored.) One of the most common images of Jesus in Early Christian art shows him as a youthful figure holding a lamb on his shoulders, a theme illustrating the parable of the Good Shepherd (Luke 15:4–7 and John 10:11–16).

Figure 9.7 Book cover, from Murano, Italy, sixth century. Ivory.

triumphal wreath

angels

Greek cross

the raising of Lazarus

Christ healing the blind

Christ enthroned

Saint Peter

Saint Paul

Christ exorcising demons

Christ healing at the pool of Bethesda

the three Hebrews in the fiery furnace

Jonah under the gourd tree

Jonah thrown overboard

two angels modeled on Classical **putti** (winged angelic beings) carry a **Greek cross** encircled by a triumphal wreath, while below, scenes from the life of Jonah ("reborn" from the belly of the whale) make reference to redemption and resurrection in Christ. Despite its Classical borrowings, the piece abandons Greco-Roman Realism in favor of symbolic abstraction.

Early Christian Architecture

The legalization of Christianity made possible the construction of monumental houses for public religious worship. In the West, the Early Christian church building was modeled on the Roman basilica (see Figure 6.16). As with the sacred temples of antiquity, the Christian church consisted of a hierarchy of spaces that ushered the devotee from the chaos of the everyday world to the serenity of the sacred chamber, and ultimately, to the ritual of deliverance. One entered Rome's earliest Christian basilicas, Saint Peter's and Saint Paul's, through the unroofed atrium that was surrounded on three sides by a covered walkway or **ambulatory**, and on the fourth side (directly in front of the church entrance) by a vestibule, or **narthex**. This outer zone provided a transition between temporal and spiritual realms. Having crossed the vestibule and entered through the west portal, one proceeded down the long, colonnaded central hall or **nave**, flanked on either side by two aisles; the upper wall of the nave consisted of the **gallery** and the **clerestory** (Figure **9.8**). The gallery was often decorated with mosaics or frescoes illuminated by light that entered the basilica through the clerestory windows (Figure **9.9**).

Toward the east end of the church, lying across the axis of the nave, was a rectangular area called the **transept**. The north and south arms of the transept, which might be extended to form a Latin cross, provided entrances additional to the main doorway at the west end of the church. Crossing the transept, one continued toward the triumphal arch that framed the apse, the semicircular space beyond the transept. In the apse, at an altar that stood on a raised platform, one received the sacrament of Holy Communion. As in ancient Egypt, which prized the eastern horizon as the site of the sun's daily "rebirth," so in Christian ritual the most important of the sacraments was celebrated in the east. The Christian pilgrimage from secular to sacred space thus symbolized the soul's progress from sin to salvation.

Early Christian churches served as places of worship, but they also entombed the bones of Christian martyrs, usually beneath the altar. Hence, church buildings were massive shrines, as well as settings for the performance of the liturgy. Their spacious interiors—Old Saint Peter's basilica was approximately 355 feet long and 208 feet wide—accommodated thousands of Christian pilgrims. However, the wood-trussed roofs of these churches made them especially vulnerable to fire. None of the great Early Christian structures has survived, but the heavily restored basilica of Saint Paul Outside the Walls offers some idea of the magnificence of the early church interior.

The Latin cross plan (see Figure 9.3) became the model for medieval churches in the West. The church exterior, which clearly reflected the functional divisions of the interior, was usually left plain and unadorned, while the interior was lavishly decorated with mosaics consisting of tiny pieces of colored glass or marble set in wet cement. The technique had been used by the Romans to decorate

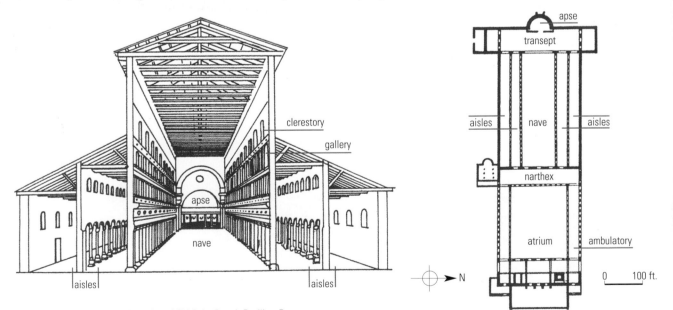

Figure 9.8 Cross section and floor plan of Old Saint Peter's Basilica, Rome, fourth century. Interior of basilica approx. 208 × 355 ft., height of nave 105 ft.

Figure 9.9 Interior of the nave of Saint Paul's Outside the Walls, Rome (after reconstruction), begun 386. The chancel arch, supported by Ionic columns and resembling the monumental triumphal arches of the Romans (see Figure 6.21), makes reference to the victory of Christ.

Figure 9.10 *Christ Teaching the Apostles in the Heavenly Jerusalem*, ca. 401–417. Mosaic. Apse of Santa Pudenziana, Rome.

public and private buildings (see Figure 6.9). In Early Christian art, however, where the mosaic medium was employed to flatten and simplify form, it became the ideal vehicle for capturing the transcendental character of the Christian message. Glass backed with gold leaf provided a supernatural spatial field in which brightly colored figures seemed to float (see Figure 9.1). As daylight or candlelight flickered across church walls embellished with mosaic, images were transformed into sparkling and ethereal apparitions.

In the fifth-century mosaic of *Christ Teaching the Apostles* from the apse of Santa Pudenziana in Rome (Figure **9.10**), the heavenly city unfolds below the hovering image of a magnificent jeweled cross flanked by winged symbols of the four evangelists. The bearded Jesus, here conceived as a Roman emperor, rules the world from atop "the throne set in heaven" as described in Revelation 4. Two female figures, personifications of the Old and New Testaments, offer wreaths of victory to Peter and Paul. Looking like an assembly of Roman senators, the apostles receive the Law, symbolized by the open book, and the **benediction** (blessing) of Jesus.

Byzantine Art and Architecture

In the churches of Byzantium, the mosaic technique reached its artistic peak. Byzantine church architects favored the Greek cross plan by which all four arms of the structure were of equal length (see Figure 9.3). At the crossing point rose a large and imposing dome. Occasionally, as with the most notable example of Byzantine architecture, Hagia Sophia ("Holy Wisdom"), the longitudinal axis of the Latin cross plan was combined

with the Greek cross plan (Figure **9.11**). The crowning architectural glory and principal church of Constantinople, Hagia Sophia (Figures **9.12**, **9.13**) was commissioned in 532 by the East Roman emperor Justinian (481–565). Its massive dome—112 feet in diameter—rises 184 feet above the pavement (40 feet higher than the Pantheon; see chapter 6). Triangular **pendentives** make the transition between the square base of the building and the superstructure (Figure **9.14**). Light filtering through the forty closely set windows at the base of the dome creates the impression that the dome is floating miraculously above the substance of the building. That light, whose symbolic value was as important to Byzantine liturgy as it was to Saint Ambrose's "Ancient Morning Hymn," illuminated the resplendent mosaics and colored marble surfaces that once filled the

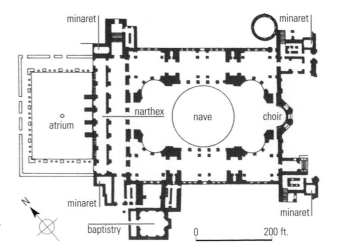

Figure 9.11 Plan of Hagia Sophia, Constantinople (Istanbul), Turkey.

Figure 9.12 Anthemius of Tralles and Isidorus of Miletus, Hagia Sophia, from the southwest, Constantinople, Turkey, 532–537. Dome height 184 ft.; diameter 112 ft. The body of the original church is now surrounded by later additions, including the minarets built after 1453 under the Ottoman Turks. When Justinian saw the completed church, he is said to have boasted, "Solomon, I have surpassed you," a reference to the achievement of the Hebrew king's Temple of Jerusalem.

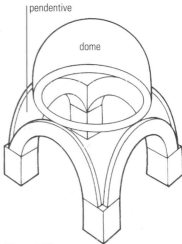

Figure 9.14
Schematic drawing of the dome of Hagia Sophia, showing pendentives.

Figure 9.13 Hagia Sophia, Constantinople.

interior of the church. After the fall of Constantinople to the Turks in 1453, the Muslims transformed Hagia Sophia into a mosque and whitewashed its mosaics (in accordance with the Islamic prohibition against images). Modern Turkish officials, however, have made the building a museum and restored some of the original mosaics.

Hagia Sophia marks the golden age of Byzantine art and architecture that took place under the leadership of the emperor Justinian. Assuming the throne in 527, Justinian envisioned Constantinople as the "New Rome." Supported by his politically shrewd consort Theodora, he sought to reunify the eastern and western portions of the old Roman Empire (Map **9.1**). Though he did not achieve this goal, he nevertheless restored the prestige of ancient Rome by commissioning one of the monumental projects of his time: the revision and codification of Roman law. The monumental *Corpus juris civilis* (*Collected Civil Law*) consisted of four parts: the *Code*, a compilation of Roman laws; the *Digest*, summaries of the opinions of jurists; the *Institutes*, a legal textbook; and the *Novels*, a collection of laws issued after 533. This testament to the primacy of law over imperial authority would have an enormous influence on legal and political history in the West, especially after the eleventh century, when it became the basis for the legal systems in most of the European states. Justinian's influence was equally important to the Byzantine economy. By directing his ambassadors to smuggle silkworm eggs out of China, Justinian initiated the silk industry that came to compete with Eastern markets.

The city that served as Justinian's western imperial outpost was Ravenna, located in northwest Italy (see Map

Figure 9.15 San Vitale, Ravenna, Italy, ca. 526–547.

Figure 9.16 San Vitale, Ravenna.

9.1). Here Justinian commissioned the construction of one of the small gems of Byzantine architecture: the church of San Vitale (Figure **9.15**). The drab exterior of this domed octagonal structure hardly prepares one for the radiant interior, the walls of which are embellished with polychrome marble, carved alabaster columns, and some of the most magnificent mosaics in the history of world art (Figure **9.16**). The mosaics on either side of the altar show Justinian and his consort Theodora, each carrying offerings to Christ (Figures **9.17**, **9.18**). The iconography of the Justinian representation illustrates the bond between Church and state that characterized Byzantine history: Justinian is flanked by twelve companions, an allusion to Christ and the apostles. On his right are his soldiers, the defenders of Christ (note the *chi* and *rho* emblazoned on the shield), while on his left are representatives of the clergy, who bear the instruments of the liturgy: the crucifix, the book, and the incense vessel. Crowned by a solar disk or halo—a device often used in Persian and late Roman art to indicate divine status—Justinian

Figure 9.17 *Emperor Justinian and His Courtiers*, ca. 547. Mosaic. San Vitale, Ravenna.

Figure 9.18 *Empress Theodora and Retinue*, ca. 547. Mosaic. San Vitale, Ravenna.

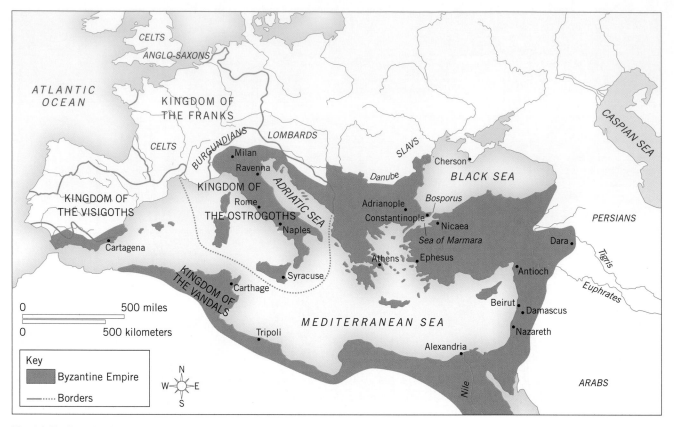

Map 9.1 The Byzantine World Under Justinian, 565. This map indicates how much of the old Roman Empire has fallen to the Germanic peoples, who, by the sixth century, had established individual kingdoms in the West.

assumes the sacred authority of Christ on earth; temporal and spiritual power are united in the person of the emperor. At the same time, Justinian and his empress reenact the ancient rite of royal donation, a theme underscored by the illustration of the Three Magi on the hem of Theodora's robe (see Figure 9.18).

The style of the mosaic contributes to the solemn formality of the event: Justinian and his courtiers stand grave and motionless, as if frozen in ceremonial attention. They are slender, elongated, and rigidly positioned—like the notes of a musical score—against a gold background that works to eliminate spatial depth. Minimally shaded, these "paper cut-out" figures with small, flapperlike feet seem to float on the surface of the picture plane, rather than stand anchored in real space. A comparison of these mosaics with, for instance, any Roman paintings or sculptural reliefs (see chapter 6) underlines the vast differences between the aesthetic aims and purposes of Classical and Christian art. Whereas the Romans engaged a realistic narrative style to honor temporal authority, the Christians cultivated an abstract language of line and color to celebrate otherworldly glory.

The sixth-century mosaic of *Jesus Calling the First Apostles, Peter and Andrew* (see Figure 9.1) found in Sant'Apollinare Nuovo in Ravenna—a Christian basilica ornamented by Roman and Byzantine artisans—provides yet another example of the surrender of narrative detail to symbolic abstraction. In the composition, setting is minimal: a gold background shuts out space and provides a

Chronology

313	Edict of Milan
326	Council of Nicaea
476	Fall of Rome
533	Justinian: *Corpus juris*

celestial screen against which formal action takes place. The figures, stiff and immovable, lack substance. There is almost no sense of muscle and bone beneath the togas of Christ and the apostles. The enlarged eyes and solemn gestures impart a powerful sense of otherworldliness.

The Byzantine Icon

Although religious imagery was essential to the growing influence of Christianity, a fundamental disagreement concerning the role of **icons** (images) in divine worship led to conflict between the Roman Catholic and Eastern Orthodox Churches. Most Christians held that visual representations of God the Father, Jesus, the Virgin, and the saints worked to inspire religious reverence. Others, however, adhering to the prohibition of "graven images" in the Hebrew Bible (Exodus 20:4–5), considered images to be no better than pagan idols. During the eighth century, the issue came to a head when the Byzantine emperor Leo III (ruled 717–741) inaugurated a policy of *iconoclasm*

Figure 9.19 *Virgin and Child with Saints and Angels*, second half of sixth century. Icon: encaustic on wood, 27 × 18⅜ in. Monastery of Saint Catherine, Mount Sinai, Egypt. Tradition held that Saint Luke had painted a portrait of the Virgin and Child that served as a model for icons such as this one. Enthroned in majesty and wearing a purple robe (in the manner of official portraits of the emperor), the Virgin points to the Christ Child as the Way to Salvation. She is flanked by Saints Theodore and George, and by angelic attendants who look toward the ray of light emanating from the hand of God.

("image-breaking") that called for the wholesale destruction of religious sculpture and the whitewashing of mosaics and wall-paintings. The Iconoclastic Controversy, which remained unresolved until the middle of the ninth century, generated a schism between the Eastern and Western Churches. Compounded by other liturgical and theological differences, that schism would become permanent in 1054 (see chapter 12). Nevertheless, both before the Iconoclastic Controversy and in the centuries following its resolution, the Greek Orthodox faith inspired the production of countless religious icons of Jesus, Mary, and the saints. These devotional images are regarded by the faithful as sacred; some are thought to provide miraculous healing or protective powers. The idea of the icon as epiphany or "appearance" is linked to the belief that the image is the tangible confirmation of the saint's miraculous appearance. The anonymity of icon painters and the formulaic quality of the image from generation to generation reflects the unique nature of the icon as an archetypal image—one that cannot be altered by the human imagination.

Executed in glowing colors and gold paint on small, portable panels, Byzantine icons usually featured the Virgin and Child (alone or surrounded by saints) seated frontally in a formal, stylized manner (Figure **9.19**; compare Figure 9.18). While such representations look back to portrayals of Mediterranean mother cult deities (see Figure 8.2), they also prefigure medieval representations of the Virgin (see Figures 13.25, 13.29).

Following the conversion of Russia to Orthodox Christianity in the tenth century, artists brought renewed splendor to the art of the icon, often embellishing the painted panel with gold leaf and semiprecious jewels, or enhancing the garments of the saint with thin sheets of hammered gold or silver. To this day, the icon assumes a special importance in the Eastern Orthodox Church and home, where it may be greeted with a kiss, a bow, and the sign of the Cross.

Early Christian Music

Early Christians distrusted the sensuous and emotional powers of music, especially instrumental music. Saint Augustine noted the "dangerous pleasure" of music and confessed that on those occasions when he was more "moved by the singing than by what was sung" he felt that he had "sinned criminally." For such reasons, the early Church was careful to exclude all forms of individual expression from liturgical music. Ancient Hebrew religious ritual, especially the practice of chanting daily prayers and singing psalms (see chapter 1), directly influenced church music. Hymns of praise such as those produced by Saint Ambrose were sung by the Christian congregation led by a cantor. But the most important music of Christian antiquity, and that which became central to the liturgy of the Church, was the music of the Mass.

The most sacred rite of the Christian liturgy, the Mass celebrated the sacrifice of Christ's body and blood as enacted at the Last Supper. The service culminated in the sacrament of Holy Communion (or Eucharist), by which Christians ritually shared the body and blood of their Redeemer. In the West, the service called High Mass featured a series of Latin chants known as either plainsong, plainchant, or Gregorian chant—the last because Gregory the Great was said to have codified and made uniform the many types of religious chant that existed in Early Christian times. The invariable or "ordinary" parts of the Mass—that is, those used throughout the year—included "Kyrie eleison" ("Lord have mercy"), "Gloria" ("Glory to God"), "Credo" (the affirmation of the Nicene Creed), "Sanctus" ("Holy, Holy, Holy"), "Benedictus" ("Blessed is He that cometh in the name of the Lord"), and "Agnus Dei" ("Lamb of God"). Eventually, the "Sanctus" and the "Benedictus" appeared as one chant, making a total of five parts to the ordinary of the Mass.

One of the oldest bodies of liturgical song still in everyday use, Gregorian chant stands among the great treasures of Western music. Like all Hebrew and Early Christian hymnody, it is monophonic, that is, regardless of the number of voices in the performing group, there is only one line of melody. Sung *a cappella* (without instrumental accompaniment), the plainsong of the Early Christian era was performed by the clergy and by choirs of monks rather than by members of the congregation. Both the Ambrosian hymns and plainsong could be performed in a responsorial style, with the chorus answering the voice of the cantor, or antiphonally, with parts of the choir or congregation singing alternating verses. In general, the rhythm of the words dictated the rhythm of the music. Plainsong might be **syllabic** (one note to one syllable), or it might involve **melismatic** embellishments (many notes to one syllable). Since no method for notating music existed before the ninth century, choristers depended on memory and on **neumes**—marks entered above the words of the text to indicate the rise and fall of the voice. The duration and exact pitch of each note, however, had to be committed to memory.

Lacking fixed meter or climax, the free rhythms of Gregorian chant echoed through Early Christian churches, whose cavernous interiors must have contributed to producing effects that were otherworldly and hypnotic. These effects, conveyed only to a limited degree by modern recordings, are best appreciated when Gregorian chant is performed in large, acoustically resonant basilicas such as the remodeled Saint Peter's in Rome.

See Music Listening Selections at end of chapter.

The Buddhist Identity

Buddhism, as it spread through India and China, followed a very different path from that of Christianity. Under the leadership of Asoka (see chapter 8), councils of Buddhist monks tried to organize the Master's teachings into a uniform, official canon; but they did not succeed in creating a single, monolithic interpretation of the Buddha's teachings—one adhered to by the entire Buddhist community, or even a majority thereof. Despite the unifying influence of the Buddha's sermons as collected in the *Pitakas*, Buddhism established no church hierarchy or uniform liturgy—a standardized ritual for public worship—comparable to that of the Roman and Orthodox communities of Christianity. The Buddhist identity was embellished, however, by a large body of folklore and legend, along with stories of the Master's previous lives, known as *jatakas* ("birth-stories"). The heart of Buddhist Scripture, however, is a body of discourses informed by the Master's sermons. Devoted to uncovering "the truth of life," these teachings deal with such subjects as the nature of the Self, the cultivation of infinite consciousness, and the development of proper breathing. The essential element of the Buddhist "creed" calls for adherence to the Law of Righteousness (*dharma*) and the Eightfold Path. In its purist (Hinayana) form, it urges Buddhists to work out their own salvation. In its later (Mahayana) development, it seeks divine help in the quest for enlightenment. Within every Buddhist sect, however, can be found the monastic community—a place for religious retreat and spiritual practice similar to that of the early Benedictine community. The ancient Buddhist monastic complex centered on a hall used for teaching and meditation. An adjacent shrine or pagoda might hold relics or ashes of the Buddha.

While the majority of Buddhists belong to the laity, the Buddhist monk became the model of religious life. To this day, religious "services" consist only of the chanting of Buddhist texts (mainly the Buddha's sermons), the recitation of hymns and **mantras** (sacred word and sound formulas), meditation, and confession. Despite the deification of the Buddha among Mahayana Buddhists and the popular adulation of *bodhisattvas* who might aid humans to achieve *nirvana*, Buddhism never abandoned its profoundly contemplative character.

Buddhist Art and Architecture in India

Buddhist texts relate that upon his death, the body of the Buddha was cremated and his ashes divided and enshrined in eight burial mounds or **stupas**. When the emperor Asoka made Buddhism the state religion of India in the third century B.C.E., he further divided the ashes, distributing them among some 60,000 shrines. These came to house the relics of the Buddha (and his disciples) and mark the places at which he had taught. The most typical of Buddhist structures, the *stupa* is a beehivelike mound of earth encased by brick or stone. Derived from the prehistoric

burial mound, it symbolizes at once the World Mountain, the Dome of Heaven, and the hallowed Womb of the Universe. A hemisphere set atop a square base, the *stupa* is also the three-dimensional realization of the cosmic **mandala**—a diagrammatic map of the universe used as a visual aid to meditation. Separating the shrine from the secular world are stone balustrades. Four gates mark the cardinal points of the compass; the walls and gates are carved with symbols of the Buddha and his teachings. As Buddhist pilgrims pass through the east gate and circle the *stupa* clockwise, tracing the path of the sun, they make the sacred journey that awakens the mind to the rhythms of the universe. The spiritual journey of the Early Christian pilgrim is linear (from narthex to apse), marking the movement from sin to salvation, while the Buddhist journey is circular, symbolizing the cycle of regeneration and the quest for *nirvana*.

Begun in the third century B.C.E., the Great Stupa at Sanchi in central India was one of Asoka's foremost achievements (Figure **9.20**). Elevated on a 20-foot drum and surrounded by a circular stone railing and four stone portals (**toranas**, Figure **9.21**), the shrine is 105 feet in diameter and rises to a height of 50 feet. It is surmounted by a series of **chatras**, umbrellalike shapes that signify the sacred bo tree under which the Buddha reached *nirvana*. The *chatras* also symbolize the levels of human consciousness through which the soul ascends in

Figure 9.21 *Yakshi* (female fertility spirit) bracket figure, east *torana*, Great Stupa, Sanchi, India. Sandstone, height approx. 5 ft. The individual figures on these profusely ornamented entrance gates convey a sense of rhythmic vitality that is typical of early Buddhist art.

Figure 9.22 Interior of carved *chaitya* cave, Karli, India, ca. 50. The Buddhist cave-temple was carved from solid rock; however, similar prayer halls were erected as freestanding structures.

seeking enlightenment. Occasionally, *stupas* were enclosed in massive, rock-cut caves or placed at the end of arcaded halls adjacent to monastic dwellings (Figures **9.22**, **9.23**). Known as **chaitya** halls, these sacred spaces were not intended for the kind of congregational worship associated with the Early Christian Mass; rather, they were sanctuaries for individual meditation and prayer. Nevertheless, the *chaitya* hall bears a striking resemblance to the Early Christian basilica. Like the basilica, a long colonnaded hall leads the devotee from the veranda at the entrance to the semicircular apse in which the *stupa* is situated. The ceilings of both the Early Christian church and the *chaitya* hall were made of wood, but the latter was usually barrel vaulted, its curved rafters carrying the eye downward toward an ornate frieze or rows of elephants—ancient symbols of royal authority and spiritual strength associated with the Buddha.

Buddhism's prohibition of idolatry influenced art in the first centuries after the Master's death, during which time artists avoided portraying the Buddha in human form. Like the Early Christians, who devised a body of sacred signs to represent the Christos (see Figure 9.3), Buddhists adopted a variety of symbols for the Buddha, such as the fig tree under which he meditated, his footprints, elephants, and, most important, the wheel (signifying both the sun and the Wheel of the Law). These devices, along with scenes from the Buddha's former lives and images of Vedic nature deities, make up the densely ornamented surface of the 34-foot-high stone gateways that mark the entrances to the Great Stupa at Sanchi (see Figure 9.21). Notably different from the Augustinian antagonism of flesh and spirit, and Christianity's general abhorrence of carnal pleasure, Buddhism (like Hinduism) regarded sexuality and spirituality as variant forms of a single, fundamental cosmic force. Hence, Buddhist art—in contrast with Christian art—did not condemn the representation of the nude body. Indeed, Sanchi's voluptuous fertility goddesses, whose globular breasts and tubelike limbs swell with life, celebrate female sexuality as candidly as any Classically carved Venus.

Figure 9.23 Elevation and ground plan of *chaitya* cave, Karli.

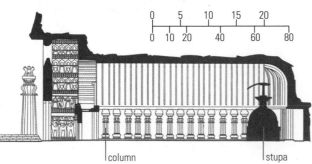

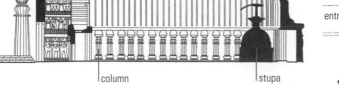

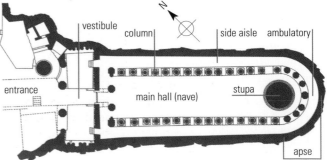

Figure 9.24 *Enlightenment*, detail of frieze showing four scenes from the life of the Buddha: *Birth*, *Enlightenment*, *First Preaching*, and *Nirvana*, from the Gandharan region of northwest Pakistan, Kushan dynasty, late second–early third century. Dark gray-blue slate, height 26⅜ in., width 114⅛ in., thickness 31⁹⁄₁₆ in.

abhaya mudra
reassurance
and protection

bhumisparsha
mudra calling
the earth to
witness

vitarka mudra
intellectual
debate

dharmachakra mudra
teaching; the Wheel of the Law

dhyana mudra
meditation

Figure 9.25 *Mudras*. The circles formed by the thumb and index fingers (lower left) represent the turning of the Wheel of the Law.

Mahayana Buddhism, however, glorified the Buddha as a savior, and thus, by the second century C.E., the image of the Buddha himself became important in popular worship. Contacts between northwest India (Gandhara) and the West influenced the emergence of a distinctly human Buddha icon inspired by Hellenistic and Roman representations of the god Apollo. Gandharan artists created classically draped and idealized freestanding figures of the Buddha and the *bodhisattvas* (see Figures 8.5, 8.6). They also carved elaborate stone reliefs depicting the life of the Buddha. One well-preserved frieze shows scenes from this narrative: the birth of the Buddha—shown miraculously emerging from the hip of his mother Queen Maya; the demonic assault on the Buddha as he achieves enlightenment beneath the Bodhi tree, his right hand touching the earth in the **mudra** (symbolic gesture) that calls the earth to witness his enlightenment (Figures **9.24**, **9.25**); the Buddha preaching the *Sermon at Benares*; and the death of the Buddha. In its union of realistic narrative and abstract symbols, the frieze has much in common with Early Christian devotional images (see Figure 9.7).

Between the fourth and sixth centuries, under the sway of the Gupta Empire, India experienced a golden age in the arts as well as in the sciences. Gupta rulers commissioned Sanskrit prose and poetry that ranged from adventure stories and plays to sacred and philosophical works. Gupta mathematicians were the first to use a special sign for the numeric zero and Hindu physicians made significant advances in medicine. (As we shall see in chapter 10, the Arabs transmitted many of these innovations to the West.)

In the hands of Gupta sculptors, the image of the Buddha assumed its classic form: a figure seated cross-legged in the position of yoga meditation (Figure **9.26**). The Buddha's oval head, framed by an elaborately ornamented halo, features a mounded protuberance (symbolizing spiritual wisdom), elongated earlobes (a reference to Siddhartha's princely origins), and a third "eye"—a symbol

Figure 9.26 *Teaching Buddha*, from Sarnath, India, Gupta period, fifth century. Sandstone, height 5 ft. 2 in.

of spiritual vision—between the eyebrows (see Figure 8.5). His masklike face, with downcast eyes and gentle smile, denotes the still state of inner repose. His hands form a *mudra* that indicates the Wheel of the Law, the subject of the Buddha's first sermon (see Figure 9.25). Wheels, symbolizing the Wheel of the Law, are engraved on the palms of his hands and the soles of his feet. The lotus, a favorite Buddhist symbol of enlightenment (and an ancient symbol of procreativity), appears on the seat of the throne and in the decorative motifs on the halo. Finally, in the relief on the base of the throne is the narrative depiction of the Buddha preaching: six disciples flank the Wheel of the Law, while two rampant deer (foreground) signify the site of the sermon, the Deer Park in Benares (see Reading 8.4a). More stylized than their Gandharan predecessors, Gupta figures are typically full-bodied and smoothly modeled with details reduced to decorative linear patterns.

The Gupta period also produced some of the earliest surviving examples of Indian painting. Hundreds of frescoes found on the walls of some thirty rock-cut sanctuaries at Ajanta in Central India show scenes from the lives and incarnations of the Buddha (as told in Mahayana literature), as well as stories from Indian history and legend. In the Ajanta frescoes, musicians, dancers, and lightly clad *bodhisattvas* (Figure 9.27) rival the sensual elegance of the carved goddesses at Sanchi. The Ajanta frescoes are among the best-preserved and most magnificent of Indian paintings. They rank with the frescoes of the catacombs and the mosaic cycles of Early Christian and Byzantine churches, though in their naturalistic treatment of form and in their mythic subject matter (which includes depictions of erotic love), they have no equivalent in the medieval West. They underline the fact that, in Buddhist thought, the divine and the human, the spirit and the body, are considered complementary.

Figure 9.27 Palace scene, Cave 17, Ajanta, India, Gupta period, fifth century. Wall painting. Buddhist frescoes are found in numerous caves throughout Southeast Asia. At Bamiyan in Afghanistan, researchers recently detected the early use of oil-based paints, dating from between the mid-seventh and tenth centuries.

Buddhist Art and Architecture in China

Between the first and third centuries, Buddhist missionaries introduced many of the basic conventions of Indian art and architecture into China. The Chinese adopted the *stupa* as a temple-shrine and place of private worship, transforming its moundlike base and umbrella-like structure into a **pagoda**, or multitiered tower with many roofs. These temple-towers are characterized by sweeping curves and upturned corners similar to those used in ancient watchtowers and multistoried houses (see chapter 7). At the same time, they recreate the image of the spreading pine tree, a beneficent sign in Chinese culture. Favoring timber as the principal building medium, Chinese architects devised complex vaulting systems for the construction of pagodas, of which no early examples have survived.

The earliest dated Buddhist building in China is the twelve-sided brick pagoda on Mount Song in Henan, which served as a shrine for the nearby Buddhist monastery (Figure **9.28**). Constructed in the early sixth century, this pagoda has a hollow interior that may once have held a large statue of the Buddha. Pagodas, whether built in brick or painted wood, became popular throughout Southeast Asia and provided a model for all religious shrines—Daoist and Confucian—as well as for Hindu temples in medieval India.

In addition, the Chinese produced rock-cut sanctuaries modeled on India's monastic shrines. These contain colossal images of the Buddha and his *bodhisattvas*. Once sheltered by a sandstone cave front that collapsed centuries ago, the gigantic Buddha and standing *bodhisattva* at Yungang Cave 20 reveal sharply cut, masklike faces and calligraphic folds of clinging draperies (Figure **9.29**). The Chinese preference for abstract patterns and flowing, rhythmic lines also dominates the relief carvings in the limestone rock walls of late fifth- and sixth-century Buddhist caves at Longmen (Figure **9.30**). Once painted with bright colors, the reliefs showing the emperor Xuanwu and his consort bearing ritual gifts to the shrine of the Buddha may be compared with the almost contemporaneous mosaics of Justinian and Theodora in San Vitale, Ravenna (see Figures 9.17, 9.18). Both the Ravenna mosaics and the Longmen reliefs are permanent memorials of wordly rulers in the act of religious devotion. Lacking the ceremonial formality of its Byzantine counterpart, the image of *The Empress as Donor with Attendants* achieves an ornamental elegance that is as typical of Chinese relief sculpture as it is of Chinese calligraphy and painting.

By the sixth century, the Maitreya Buddha—the Buddha of the Future—had become the favorite devotional image of Mahayana Buddhism. A messianic successor of the historic Buddha, Maitreya was said to be a *bodhisattva* who would come to earth to deliver his followers to a special place in paradise. In an elegant bronze altarpiece (Figure **9.31**), the Maitreya Buddha raises his right hand in the gesture of reassurance. Standing above a group of *bodhisattvas* and monks, he is framed by a perforated, flame-shaped halo from which sprout winged angelic creatures, each playing a musical instrument. Comparison of this devotional object with one from the Christian West—such as the ivory book cover from Murano (see Figure 9.7)—reveals certain formal similarities: the sacred personages (Jesus and the Buddha) are pictured centrally and physically larger than the accompanying figures, thus indicating their greater importance. Both make use of special symbols, such as the halo and the throne, to indicate divine status; and both favor iconic stylization and abstraction. Such devices, employed by artists East and West, contributed to the language of faith that served Buddhism and Christianity.

Figure 9.28 Pagoda of the Song Yue Temple, Mount Song, Henan, China, 523.

Figure 9.29 *Large Seated Buddha with Standing Bodhisattva*, Cave 20, Yungang, Shanxi, China, Northern Wei dynasty, ca. 460–470. Stone, height 44 ft. Similar colossal rock-cut Buddhas were carved in cliffs along caravan routes into Southeast Asia. Splendidly painted and gilded, they were visible to approaching pilgrims and travelers from miles away. In 2001, iconoclastic radical Muslims known as the Taliban destroyed two of the most notable of these shrines at Bamiyan in Afghanistan. Efforts are currently underway to reconstruct the destroyed statues.

Figure 9.30 *The Empress as Donor with Attendants*, from the Binyang cave chapel, Longmen, Henan, China, Northern Wei dynasty, ca. 522. Fine gray limestone with traces of color, 6 ft. 4 in. × 9 ft. 1 in.

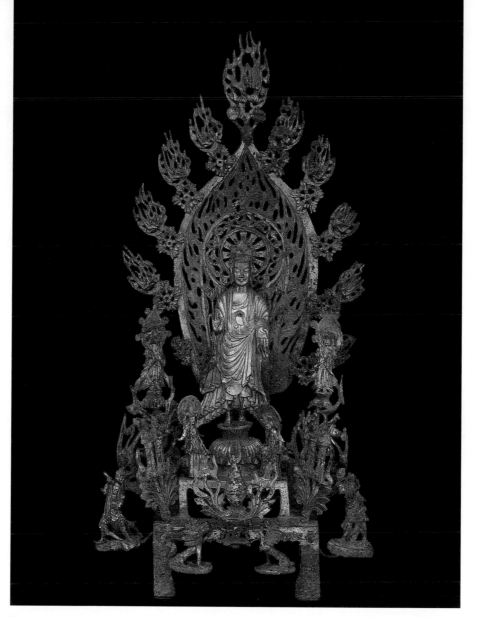

Figure 9.31 Altar with Maitreya Buddha, Northern Wei dynasty, 524. Gilt bronze, height 30¼ in. Two *bodhisattvas* flank the central figure, while two more, along with two donors, surround an incense burner below. Infused with ornamental, calligraphic vitality, the shrine was commissioned by a father to commemorate the death of his son.

Buddhist Music

Scholars did not begin to survey Buddhist music until the early twentieth century. It seems clear, however, that Buddhist religious practices were based in India's ancient musical traditions, specifically those that involved the intoning of sacred Hindu texts. The recitation of *mantras* and the chanting of Sanskrit prayers were central acts of meditation among Buddhist monks throughout Asia, and the performance of such texts assumed a trancelike quality similar to that of Western plainsong. Buddhist chant was monophonic and lacked a fixed beat; but, unlike Western church music, it was usually accompanied by percussion instruments (such as drums, bells, cymbals, and gongs) that imparted a rich rhythmic texture. Complex drumming techniques were among the most notable of Indian musical contributions.

As in India, Buddhist chant in China and Japan was performed in the monasteries. It featured the intoning of statements and responses interrupted by the sounding of percussion instruments such as bells or drums. As the chant proceeded, the pace of recitation increased, causing an overlapping of voices and instruments that produced a hypnotic web of sound.

Sliding, nasal tones characterized the performance of Chinese music. Such tones were achieved by both the voice and by the instruments peculiar to Chinese culture. One of China's oldest and most popular instruments was the zither, a five- or seven-stringed instrument that is generally plucked with a plectrum and the fingertips (see chapter 7). Associated with ancient religious and ceremonial music, the zither was quickly adopted by Buddhist monks. The vibrato or hum produced by plucking the strings of the zither is audible long after the instrument is touched, a phenomenon that Buddhists found comparable to the pervasive resonance of chant (and to the human breath seeking union with the One).

♪ See Music Listening Selections at end of chapter.

The Christian Identity

- Rome became the administrative center of the newly unified Christian faith in the West. As Roman emperors had held supreme authority over the state, so Roman Catholic popes—the temporal representatives of Christ—would govern Western Christendom.
- At the Council of Nicaea a consensus of opinion among church representatives laid the basis for Christian dogma, resolving that Jesus was of one substance with God the Father.
- The Benedictine order, the first monastic community in the West, was founded in southern Italy. It required vows of poverty, chastity, and obedience to the governing abbot; it established a routine of work that freed monks from dependence on the secular world.
- The four Latin church fathers, Jerome, Ambrose, Gregory, and Augustine, were responsible for the formulation of Christian dogma and liturgy. Augustine's writings were crucial to the development of the allegorical tradition.

Symbolism and Early Christian Art

- Christian signs and symbols linked the visible to the invisible world. The language of Symbolism came to convey the Christian message of deliverance. Accordingly, a more abstract, ethereal style replaced the worldly Realism of Greco-Roman art.
- In the catacombs outside the city of Rome, vast networks of underground galleries enclose gravesites whose walls are covered with frescoes illustrating scenes from the Old and New Testaments.
- The legalization of Christianity made possible the construction of monumental houses for public religious worship. Early Christian churches in the West were modeled on the Roman basilica, but engaged a Latin cross plan.
- Byzantine church architects favored the Greek cross plan by which all four arms of the structure were of equal length. At the crossing point rose a large and imposing dome, such as the one crowning Hagia Sophia.
- In the churches of Constantinople and in Ravenna, Italy, the East Roman emperor Justinian commissioned some of Early Christianity's finest mosaics. As with the painted devotional icons popular in Byzantium, these mosaics abandon literal representation in favor of formal abstraction and religious symbolism.

Early Christian Music

- Ancient Hebrew religious ritual, especially the practice of chanting daily prayers and singing psalms, directly influenced church music.
- The sacred rite of the Christian liturgy, the Mass, celebrates the sacrifice of Christ. The service features a series of Latin chants known as plainsong or Gregorian chant.
- Early Christian music features a single line of melody that lacks fixed meter. Since no method for notating music existed before the ninth century, choristers depended on memory or on textual marks known as neumes.

The Buddhist Identity

- Buddhism established no single, monolithic interpretation of the Buddha's teachings, and therefore no church hierarchy or uniform liturgy comparable to that of the Roman and Orthodox Christian communities. The Buddhist identity was embellished by a large body of folklore and legend.
- The Buddhist monk became the model of religious life for the laity; the monastic community centered on a hall used for teaching and meditation.
- The most typical of early Buddhist structures in India, the *stupa*, was a mound-shaped shrine honoring the Buddha. A three-dimensional realization of the cosmic *mandala*—a diagrammatic map of the universe used as a visual aid to meditation—it was circled by Buddhist pilgrims. The rock-cut caves and halls that occasionally enclosed *stupas* provided sanctuaries for individual contemplation.
- Buddhism's prohibition of idolatry influenced art in the first centuries after the Master's death: artists avoided portraying the Buddha in human form, adopting instead a variety of symbols, the most important of which was the Wheel (of the Law).
- Buddhist missionaries introduced the basic conventions of Indian art and architecture into China. The Chinese adopted the *stupa* as a temple-shrine and place of private worship, transforming its moundlike base and umbrellalike structure into a pagoda.
- Buddhist religious practices were based in India's ancient musical traditions, specifically those that involved the intoning of sacred Hindu texts. The recitation of *mantras* and the chanting of prayers were central acts of meditation among Buddhist monks throughout Asia.

Music Listening Selections

CD One Selection 2 Gregorian chant, "Alleluya, vidimus stellam," codified 590–604.

CD One Selection 3 Buddhist chant, Morning prayers (based on the Lotus Scripture) at Nomanji, Japan, excerpt.

Glossary

abbey a monastery or convent

abbot (Latin, "father") the superior of an abbey or monastery for men; the female equivalent in a convent of nuns is called an "abbess"

a cappella choral singing without instrumental accompaniment

ambulatory a covered walkway, outdoors or indoors (see Figures 9.8, 13.3)

benediction the invocation of a blessing; in art, indicated by the raised right hand with fore and middle fingers extended

canon law the ecclesiastical law that governs the Christian Church

catacomb a subterranean complex consisting of burial chambers and galleries with recesses for tombs

chaitya a sacred space, often applied to arcaded assembly halls that enclose a *stupa*

chatra an umbrellalike shape that signifies the sacred tree under which the Buddha reached *nirvana*

clerestory (also "clerstory") the upper part of the nave, whose walls contain openings for light (see Figure 9.8)

diptych a two-leaved hinged tablet; a two-paneled altarpiece

dogma a prescribed body of doctrines concerning faith or morals, formally stated and authoritatively proclaimed by the Church

ecumenical worldwide in extent; representing the whole body of churches

gallery the area between the clerestory and the nave arcade, usually adorned with mosaics in Early Christian churches (see Figure 9.8)

Greek cross a cross in which all four arms are of equal length

icon (Greek, "likeness") the image of a saint or other religious figure

iconography the study, identification, and interpretation of subject matter in art; also the visual imagery that conveys specific concepts and ideas

Latin cross a cross in which the vertical member is longer than the horizontal member it intersects

mandala a diagrammatic map of the universe used as a visual aid to meditation and as a ground plan for Hindu and Buddhist temple-shrines

mantra a sacred formula of invocation or incantation common to Hinduism and Buddhism

melismatic with many notes of music to one syllable

mudra (Sanskrit, "sign") a symbolic gesture commonly used in Buddhist art

narthex a porch or vestibule at the main entrance of a church (see Figure 9.8)

nave the central aisle of a church between the altar and the apse, usually demarcated from the side aisles by columns or piers (see Figure 9.8)

neume a mark or symbol indicating the direction of the voice in the early notation of Gregorian chant

orans a gesture involving the raising of the arms in an attitude of prayer

pagoda an East Asian shrine in the shape of a tower, usually with roofs curving upward at the division of each of several stories

pendentive a concave piece of masonry that makes the transition between the angle of two walls and the base of the dome above (see Figure 9.14)

putto (Italian, "child," plural *putti*) a nude, male child, usually winged; related to the Classical Cupid (see chapter 6) and to Greco-Roman images of the angelic psyche or soul

regular clergy (Latin, *regula*, meaning "rule") those who have taken vows to obey the rules of a monastic order; as opposed to secular clergy (see below)

secular clergy (Latin, *seculum*, meaning "in the world") those ordained to serve the Christian Church in the world

stupa a hemispherical mound that serves as a Buddhist shrine

syllabic with one note of music per syllable

torana a gateway that marks one of the four cardinal points in the stone fence surrounding a *stupa*

transept the part of a basilican-plan church that runs perpendicular to the nave (see Figure 9.8)

Chapter

10

The Islamic World: Religion and Culture

ca. 570–1300

"Whoever goes aright, for his own soul does he go aright; and whoever goes astray, to its detriment only does he go astray . . ."
The Qur'an

Figure 10.1 The *mihrab* of the Great Mosque at Córdoba, eleventh century. Gold and glass mosaic on marble. Lavishly ornamented with gold and mosaic glass, the horseshoe arch opens onto the *mihrab*, the niche that marks the direction of Muslim prayer (towards Mecca).

LOOKING AHEAD

Islam, the world's youngest major religion, was born in the seventh century among the people of the Arabian peninsula. The faith of the followers of Muhammad, it became the unifying force in the rise of the first global civilization to flourish following the fall of Rome. Bridging Europe and East Asia, Islam forged the historical link between Classical and early modern civilization. As early as the mid-eighth century, an international Islamic community stretched from Spain (Al-Andalus) across North Africa into India (Map **10.1**).

Just as rising Christianity had absorbed the cultural legacy of the Mediterranean and the Roman world, so, in its expansion, Islam embraced the cultures of Arabia, the Near East, and Persia. Between the eighth and fourteenth centuries, the new faith brought religious unity and cultural cohesiveness to people of a wide variety of languages and customs. Muslim communities in Spain, North Africa, and the Near East cultivated rich traditions in the arts, the sciences, and technology. Muslim scholars in the cities of Baghdad (in present-day Iraq) and Córdoba (in southern Spain) copied Greek manuscripts, creating an invaluable preserve of Classical literature; and Islamic intermediaries carried into the West many of the greatest innovations of Asian culture. These achievements had far-reaching effects on global culture, on the subsequent rise of the European West and, more broadly, on the global humanistic tradition.

The religion of Islam is practiced today by some one billion people, more than two-thirds of whom live outside of Southwest Asia. In the United States, home to over six million Muslims, Islam is the fastest growing religion. These facts suggest that, despite a decline in Islamic culture after 1350, Islam remains one of the most powerful forces in world history.

The Religion of Islam

Muhammad and Islam

Centuries before the time of Christ, nomadic Arabs known as Bedouins lived in the desert peninsula of Arabia east of Egypt. At the mercy of this arid land, they traded along the caravan routes of Southwest Asia. Bedouin Arabs were an animistic, tribal people who worshiped some 300 different nature deities. Statues of these gods, along with the sacred Black Stone (probably an ancient meteorite), were housed in the **Kaaba**, a cubical sanctuary located in the city of Mecca (in modern Saudi Arabia). Until the

Map 10.1 The Expansion of Islam, 622–ca. 750.

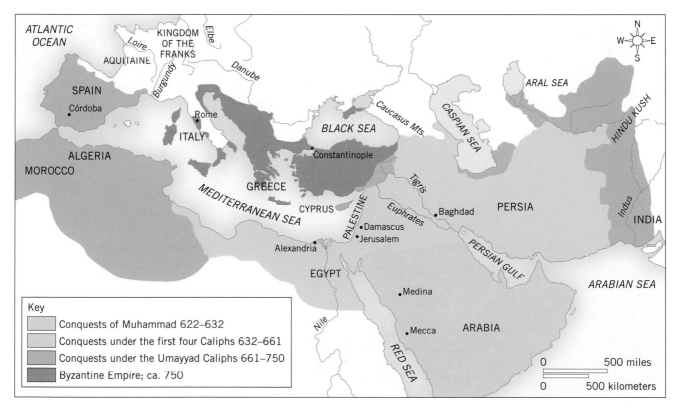

Key
- Conquests of Muhammad 622–632
- Conquests under the first four Caliphs 632–661
- Conquests under the Umayyad Caliphs 661–750
- Byzantine Empire; ca. 750

The Five Pillars

1 Confession   of faith: "There is no god but Allah, and Muhammad is his Messenger"

2 Recitation   of prayers five times a day, facing Mecca

3 Almsgiving   the practice of making charitable contributions to the Islamic community

4 Fasting   from dawn to sunset during the sacred month of Ramadan (during which Muhammad received his calling)

5 Pilgrimage (*hajj*) to the holy city of Mecca at least once in a Muslim's lifetime (Figure **10.2**)

sixth century C.E., the Arabs remained polytheistic and disunited, but the birth of the prophet Muhammad in 570 in Mecca changed these circumstances dramatically.

Orphaned at the age of six, Muhammad received little formal education. He traveled with his uncle on caravan journeys that brought him into contact with communities of Jews, Christians, and pagans. At the age of twenty-five he married Khadijah, a wealthy widow fifteen years his senior, and assisted in running her flourishing caravan trade. Long periods of retreat and solitary meditation in the desert, however, led to a transformation in Muhammad's life: according to Muslim teachings, the Angel Gabriel appeared to Muhammad and commanded him to receive the revelation of the one and only Allah (the Arabic word for "God"). Now forty-one years old, Muhammad declared himself the final messenger in a history of religious revelation that had begun with Abraham and continued through Moses and Jesus.

While Muhammad preached no new doctrines, he emphasized the bond between Allah and his followers, and the importance of the community (*umma*) of the faithful, whose unswerving love of God would govern every aspect of their lives and conduct. His message reinforced many of the basic precepts of Christianity and Judaism. Some of Allah's revelations to Muhammad, such as the immortality of the soul, the anticipation of a final judgment, and the certainty of Heaven and Hell, were staples of Early Christianity. Others, such as an uncompromising monotheism, a strict set of ethical and social injunctions, and special dietary laws, were fundamental to Hebraic teaching.

Figure 10.2 The *Kaaba*, Mecca, Saudi Arabia. According to Muslim tradition, the *Kaaba* was built by Abraham and his son Ishmael; it is also said to mark the sacred spot where, at God's command, Abraham had prepared to sacrifice his son, Isaac. Muslims are expected to make the *hajj* to the *Kaaba* at least once during their lifetime. Some two million pilgrims throng to Mecca annually to take part in the ritual procession that circles the shrine seven times.

At the outset, Muhammad's message attracted few followers. Since his attack on idolatry threatened Mecca's prominence as a prosperous pilgrimage site, the polytheistic Meccan elite actively resisted the new faith. Tribal loyalties among Meccans ran deep, and armed conflict was common. In 622, after twelve years of indecisive warfare with the Meccan opposition, the Prophet abandoned his native city. Along with some seventy Muslim families, he emigrated to Medina—a journey known as the *hijra* ("migration"). Eight more years marked by sporadic warfare were to elapse before the population of Medina was converted. When Muhammad returned to Mecca with a following of 10,000 men, the city opened its gates to him. Muhammad conquered Mecca and destroyed the idols in the *Kaaba*, with the exception of the Black Stone. Thereafter, Muhammad assumed spiritual and political authority—establishing a theocracy that bound religious and secular realms in a manner not unlike that of the early Hebrew kings. By the time Muhammad died in 632, the entire Arabian peninsula was united in its commitment to Islam. Since the history of Muhammad's successful missionary activity began with the *hijra* of 622, that date marks the first years of the Muslim calendar.

Submission to God

Muhammad's followers—called Muslims ("those who submit to Allah")—honor him as the last of the prophets, human rather than divine in nature. They acknowledge Allah as the one true god, identical with the god of the Jews and the Christians. Fulfilling the Judeo-Christian tradition of deliverance, Islam (literally, "submission to God's will") claims to complete God's revelation to humankind.

The declaration of faith in Allah and his Messenger is the first of the so-called Five Pillars of Muslim practice.

The Qur'an

Muhammad himself wrote nothing, but his disciples memorized his teachings and recorded them some ten years after his death. Written in Arabic, the Qur'an (literally, "recitation") is the holy book of Islam (Figure **10.3**). The Muslim guide to spiritual and secular life, the Qur'an consists of 114 chapters (*suras*), each of which opens with the **bismillah** (invocation), "In the name of God, the Lord of Mercy, the Giver of Mercy." As the supreme authority and fundamental source of Muslim ritual, ethics, and laws, the Qur'an provides guidelines for worship and specific moral and social injunctions for everyday conduct. It condemns drinking wine, eating pork, and all forms of gambling. Islam limits **polygyny** (marriage to several women at the same time) to no more than four wives, provided that a man can support and protect all of them. Although the Qur'an defends the equality of men and women before God (see Sura 4.3–7), it describes men as being "a degree higher than women" (in that they are the providers) and endorses the pre-Islamic tradition requiring women to veil their bodies from public view (Sura 24.31; see Figure 10.4). A husband has unrestricted rights of divorce and can end a marriage by renouncing his wife publicly. Nevertheless, Muhammad's teachings raised the status of women by condemning female infanticide, according women property rights, and ensuring their financial support in an age when such protections were not commonly guaranteed.

Muslim Scripture reveals the nature of God and the inevitability of judgment and resurrection. It teaches that

Figure 10.3 Kufic calligraphy from the Qur'an, from Persia, ninth–tenth centuries. Ink and gold leaf on vellum, 8½ × 21 in. Qur'ans, like the holy books of Judaism and early Christianity, were usually handwritten on sheepskin (parchment) or calfskin (vellum) and hand-decorated or "illuminated"—that is, ornamented with gold leaf or gold paint and brightly colored pigments. Arabic script, like Hebrew script, is read from right to left. Kufic calligraphy is notable for its angularity and its horizontal extensions.

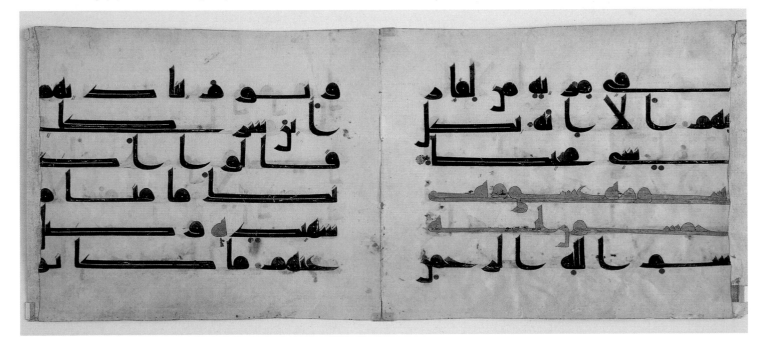

human beings are born in the purity of God's design, free from Original Sin. To the righteous, those who practice submission, humility, and reverence for God, it promises a hereafter resembling a garden of paradise, filled with cool rivers and luscious fruit trees. To the wicked and to **infidels** (nonbelievers), it promises the terrifying punishments of Hell—as hot and dusty as the desert itself.

Muslims consider the Qur'an the eternal and absolute word of God. Chanted or recited, rather than read silently, it is often committed to memory by the devout. The Qur'an is the primary text for the study of the Arabic language. It is considered untranslatable, not only because its contents are deemed holy, but because it is impossible to capture in other languages the musical nuances of the original Arabic.

READING 10.1 From the Qur'an

Chapter 5 The Feast
In the name of God, the Lord of Mercy, the Giver of Mercy

. . . .

6. You who believe, when you are about to pray, wash your faces and your hands up to the elbows, wipe your heads, wash your feet up to the ankles and, if required, wash your whole body. If any of you is sick or on a journey, or has just relieved himself, or had intimate contact with a woman, and can find no water, then take some clean sand and wipe your face and hands with it. God does not wish to place any burden on you: He only wishes to cleanse you and perfect His blessing on you, so that you may be thankful.

7. So remember God's blessing on you and the pledge with which you were bound when you said, "We hear and we obey." Be mindful of God: God has full knowledge of the secrets of the heart.

8. You who believe, be steadfast in your devotion to God and bear witness impartially: do not let hatred of others lead you away from justice, but adhere to justice, for that is closer to awareness of God. Be mindful of God: God is well aware of all that you do.

9. God has promised forgiveness and a rich reward to those who have faith and do good works;

10. those who reject faith and deny Our revelations will inhabit the blazing Fire.

11. You who believe, remember God's blessing on you when a certain people were about to raise their hands against you and He restrained them. Be mindful of God: let the believers put their trust in Him.

. . . .

19. People of the Book[1], Our Messenger comes to you now, after a break in the sequence of messengers, to make things clear for you in case you should say, "No one has come to give us good news or to warn us." So someone has come to you to give you good news and warn you: God has the power to do all things.

. . . .

65. If only the People of the Book would believe and be mindful of God, We would take away their sins and bring them into the Gardens of Delight.

66. If they had upheld the Torah and the Gospel and what was sent down to them from their Lord, they would have been given abundance from above and from below: some of them are on the right course, but many of them do evil.

67. Messenger, proclaim everything that has been sent down to you from the Lord—if you do not, then you will not have communicated His message—and God will protect you from people. God does not guide those who defy Him.

68. Say, "People of the Book, you have no true basis [for your religion] unless you uphold the Torah, the Gospel, and that which has been sent down to you from your Lord," but what has been sent down to you [Prophet] from your Lord is sure to increase many of them in their insolence and defiance: do not worry about those who defy [God].

69. The [Muslim] believers, the Jews, the Sabians[2], and the Christians—those who believe in God and the Last Day and do good deeds—will have nothing to fear or to regret.

70. We took a pledge from the Children of Israel, and sent messengers to them. Whenever a messenger brought them anything they did not like, they accused some of lying and put others to death;

71. they thought no harm could come to them and so became blind and deaf [to God]. God turned to them in mercy but many of them again became blind and deaf: God is fully aware of their actions.

72. Those who say, "God is the Messiah, son of Mary," although the Messiah himself said, "Children of Israel, worship God, my Lord and your Lord," have defied [what he said]: if anyone associates others with God, God will forbid him from the Garden, and Hell will be his home. No one will help such evildoers.

73. Those people who say that God is the third of three[3] are defying [the truth]: there is only One God. If they persist in what they are saying, a painful punishment will afflict those of them who defy [the truth].

74. Why do they not turn to God and ask His forgiveness, when God is most forgiving, most merciful?

75. The Messiah, son of Mary, was only a messenger; other messengers had come and gone before him; his mother was a virtuous woman; both ate food [like other mortals]. See how clear We make these signs for them; see how deluded they are.

76. Say, "How can you worship something other than God, that has no power to do you harm or good? God alone is the All Hearing and All Knowing."

77. Say, "People of the Book, do not overstep the bounds of truth in your religion and do not follow the whims of those who went astray before you—they led many others astray themselves, and continue to stray from the right path."

. . . .

Chapter 17 The Israelites
In the name of God, the Lord of Mercy, the giver of Mercy.

. . . .

---

[1] Jews and Christians.

[2] Semitic merchants from the Saba, a kingdom in southern Arabia.
[3] The Trinity.

9. This Qur'an does indeed show the straightest way. It gives the faithful who do right the good news that they will have a great reward and

10. warns that We have prepared an agonizing punishment for those who do not believe in the world to come.

11. Yet man prays for harm, just as he prays for good: man is ever hasty.

12. We made the night and the day as two signs, then darkened the night and made the day for seeing, for you to seek your Lord's bounty and to know how to count the years and calculate. We have explained everything in detail.

13. We have bound each human being's destiny to his neck. On the Day of Resurrection, We shall bring out a record for each of them, which you will find spread wide open,

14. "Read your record. Today your own soul is enough to calculate your account."

15. Whoever accepts guidance does so for his own good; whoever strays does so at his own peril. No soul will bear another's burden, nor do We punish until We have sent a messenger.

16. When We decide to destroy a town, We command those corrupted by wealth [to reform], but they [persist in their] disobedience; Our sentence is passed, and We destroy them utterly.

17. How many generations We have destroyed since Noah! Your Lord knows and observes the sins of His servants well enough.

18. If anyone desires [only] the fleeting life, We speed up whatever We will in it, for whoever We wish; then We have prepared Hell for him in which to burn, disgraced and rejected.

19. But if anyone desires the life to come and strives after it as he should, as a true believer, his striving will be thanked.

20. To both the latter and the former, We give some of your Lord's bounty. [Prophet], your Lord's bounty is not restricted—

21. see how We have given some more than others—but the Hereafter holds greater ranks and greater favors.

22. Set up no other god beside God, or you will end up disgraced and forsaken.

23. Your Lord has commanded that you should worship none but Him, and that you be kind to your parents. If either or both of them reach old age with you, say no word that shows impatience with them, and do not be harsh with them, but speak to them respectfully

24. and, out of mercy, lower your wing in humility toward them and say, "Lord, have mercy on them, just as they cared for me when I was little."

25. Your Lord knows best what is in your heart. If you are good, He is most forgiving to those who return to Him.

26. Give relatives their due, and the needy, and travelers—do not squander your wealth wastefully:

27. those who squander are the brothers of Satan, and Satan is most ungrateful to his Lord—

28. but if, while seeking some bounty that you expect from your Lord, you turn them down, then at least speak some word of comfort to them.

29. Do not be tight-fisted, nor so open-handed that you end up blamed and overwhelmed with regret.

30. Your Lord gives abundantly to whoever He will, and sparingly to whoever He will: He knows and observes His servants thoroughly.

31. Do not kill your children for fear of poverty—We shall provide for them and for you—killing them is a great sin.

32. And do not go anywhere near adultery: it is an outrage, and an evil path.

33. Do not take life—which God has made sacred—except by right. If anyone is killed wrongfully, We have given authority to the defender of his rights, but he should not be excessive in taking life, for he is already aided [by God].

34. Do not go near the orphan's property, except with the best intentions, until he reaches the age of maturity. Honor your pledges: you will be questioned about your pledges.

35. Give full measure when you measure, and weigh with accurate scales: that is better and fairer in the end.

36. Do not follow blindly what you do not know to be true: ears, eyes, and heart, you will be questioned about all these.

37. Do not strut arrogantly about the earth: you cannot break it open, nor match the mountains in height.

38. The evil of all these is hateful to your Lord.

. . . .

Chapter 47 Muhammad
In the name of God, the Lord of Mercy, the Giver of Mercy

1. God will bring to nothing the deeds of those who disbelieve and bar others from the way of God,

2. but He will overlook the bad deeds of those who have faith, do good deeds, and believe in what has been sent down to Muhammad—the truth from their Lord—and He will put them into a good state.

3. This is because the disbelievers follow falsehood, while the believers follow the truth from their Lord. In this way God shows people their true type.

4. When you meet the disbelievers in battle, strike them in the neck, and once they are defeated, bind any captives firmly—later you can release them by grace or by ransom—until the toils of war have ended. That [is the way]. God could have defeated them Himself if He had willed, but His purpose is to test some of you by means of others. He will not let the deeds of those who are killed for His cause come to nothing;

5. He will guide them and put them into a good state;

6. He will admit them into the Garden He has already made known to them.

7. You who believe! If you help God, He will help you and make you stand firm.

8. As for the disbelievers, how wretched will be their state! God has brought their deeds to nothing.

9. It is because they hate what God has sent down that He has caused their deeds to go to waste.

10. Have they not traveled the earth and seen how those before them met their end? God destroyed them utterly: a similar fate awaits the disbelievers.

11. That is because God protects the believers while the disbelievers have no one to protect them:

12. God will admit those who believe and do good deeds to Gardens graced with flowing streams; the disbelievers may take their fill of pleasure in this world, and eat as cattle do, but the Fire will be their home.

13. We have destroyed many a town stronger than your own [Prophet]—the town which [chose to] expel you—and they had no one to help them.

. . . .

Chapter 76 Man

In the name of God, the Lord of Mercy, the Giver of Mercy

1. Was there not a period of time when man was nothing to speak of?[4]

2. We created man from a drop of mingled fluid to put him to the test; We gave him hearing and sight;

3. We guided him to the right path, whether he was grateful or not.

4. We have prepared chains, iron collars, and blazing Fire for the disbelievers, but

5. the righteous will have a drink mixed with *kafur*,[5]

6. a spring for God's servants, which flows abundantly at their wish.

7. They fulfill their vows; they fear a day of widespread woes;

8. they give food to the poor, the orphan, and the captive, though they love it themselves,

9. saying, "We feed you for the sake of God alone: We seek neither recompense nor thanks from you.

10. We fear the Day of our Lord—a woefully grim Day."

11. So God will save them from the woes of that Day, give them radiance and gladness,

12. and reward them, for their steadfastness, with a Garden and silken robes.

13. They will sit on couches, feeling neither scorching heat nor biting cold,

14. with shady [branches] spread above them and clusters of fruit hanging close at hand.

15. They will be served with silver plates

16. and gleaming silver goblets according to their fancy,

17. and they will be given a drink infused with ginger

18. from a spring called Salsabil.[6]

19. Everlasting youths will attend them—if you could see them, you would think they were scattered pearls,

20. and if you were to look around, you would see a vast, blissful kingdom—

21. and they will wear garments of green silk and brocade. They will be adorned with silver bracelets. Their Lord will give them a pure drink.

22. [It will be said], "This is your reward. Your endeavors are appreciated."

23. We Ourself have sent down this Qur'an to you [Prophet] in gradual revelation.

24. Await your Lord's Judgment with patience; do not yield to any of these sinners and disbelievers;

25. remember the name of your Lord at dawn and in the evening;

26. bow down before Him, and glorify Him at length by night.

27. These people love the fleeting life. They put aside [all thoughts of] a Heavy Day.

28. Yet We created them; We strengthened their constitution; if We please, We can replace such people completely.

29. This is a reminder. Let whoever wishes, take the way to his Lord.

---

[4] Literally, "Has there not come over man a period of time when he was not mentioned?" This refers to the time before a person is born, the point being that he was nothing, then God created him, just as he will bring him to life again for judgment.

[5] A fragrant herb.

[6] Literally, "Seek the Way"; the word also means "sweet" and "rapid-flowing."

30. But you will only wish to do so if God wills—God is all knowing, all wise—

31. He admits whoever He will into His Mercy and has prepared a painful punishment for the disbelievers.

Q How does the Qur'an describe the "People of the Book?"

Q How does the Muslim view of reward and punishment compare with that of other world faiths?

The Spread of Islam

Islam's success in becoming a world faith is explained in part by the fact that, at the outset, religious, political, and military goals were allied. However, other factors were crucial to the success of Islam. The new faith offered rules of conduct that were easy to understand and to follow—a timely alternative, perhaps, to the complexities of Jewish ritual and Christian theology. In contrast with Christianity and Judaism, Islam remained free of dogma and liturgy and unencumbered by a priestly hierarchy. Orthodox Muslims regarded the Trinity and the Christian cult of saints as polytheistic; they denied the divinity of Jesus, admiring him as a prophet, like Moses or Muhammad himself. On the other hand, like Jews and Christians ("People of the Book"), the Muslim community was united by a message of piety and faith. The core Islamic texts, the Qur'an and the *Hadith* (a compilation of Muhammad's sayings and deeds compiled a century after his death), provide the all-embracing code of ethical conduct known as the **sharia** ("the path to follow"). Spiritual supervision is shared by prayer leaders (**imams**), scholars trained in Muslim law (**mullahs**), and public officials (**qadi**) who judge matters related to the *sharia*. *Mullahs* also function as teachers in Islamic schools (**madrasas**), affiliated with the Muslim place of worship known as the **mosque**.

Islam unified the tribal population of Arabia in a common religious and ethnic bond that propelled Muslims out of their desert confines into East Asia, Africa, and the West. The young religion assumed a sense of historical mission much like that which drove the ancient Romans. In fact, the militant expansion of Islam was the evangelical counterpart of **jihad**, fervent religious struggle. Often translated as "holy war," the word signifies all aspects of the Muslim drive toward moral and religious perfection, including the defense and spread of Islam. In Muslim thought and practice, the term denotes both "the lesser *jihad*" (war) and "the greater *jihad*" (self-control: the struggle to contain lust, anger, and other forms of indulgence). Militant Muslims would have agreed with Augustine that a "just cause" made warfare acceptable in the eyes of God (see chapter 9). Indeed, Christian soldiers anticipated heavenly rewards if they died fighting for Christ, while Muslims looked forward to Paradise if they died in the service of Allah.

Generally speaking, early Muslim expansion succeeded not so much by the militant coercion of foreign populations as it did by the economic opportunities Muslims

EXPLORING ISSUES

Translating the Qur'an

The Qur'an is said to be untranslatable; even non-Arabic-speaking Muslims often learn it in its original language. Nevertheless, this holy book has been translated numerous times—into English and many other languages. Most translations adhere as closely as possible to the classical Arabic used at the time of Muhammad; others attempt to modernize the Arabic. As with all efforts to translate great literature from its original language, clarity and accuracy of meaning are major goals. In the case of works that are said to be divinely revealed, accurate translation is even more crucial (see Translating the Hebrew Bible, Chapter 1). The choice of a single word or phrase may modify the meaning of the text.

The following translations are of the same excerpt from the Qur'an, which appears in a chapter that deals with family relations and the rights and obligations of men and women in achieving proper behavior. Similar to both ancient Jewish and early Christian cultures, Muslim society was patriarchal. Sura 4:34 offers instruction as to how Muslim men should deal with disobedient wives. The differences between the two translations illustrate the problematic relationship between translation and interpretation.

1) "Men are the protectors and maintainers of women, because Allah has given the one more (strength) than the other, and because they support them from their means. Therefore the righteous women are devoutly obedient, and guard in (the husband's) absence, what Allah would have them guard. As to those women on whose part ye fear disloyalty and ill-conduct, admonish them (first), (next), refuse to share their beds, (and last) beat them (lightly); but if they return to obedience, seek not against them Means (of annoyance): For Allah is Most High, great (above you all)."

Translated by Abdullah Yusuf Ali (1934)

2) "Men are supporters of wives because God has given some of them an advantage over others and because they spend of their wealth. So the ones who are in accord with morality are the ones who are morally obligated, the ones who guard the unseen of what God has kept safe. But those whose resistance you fear, then admonish them and abandon them in their sleeping place then go away from them; and if they obey you, surely look not for any way against them; truly God is Lofty, Great."

Translated by Laleh Bakhtiar (2006)

---

offered conquered people. Unlike Christianity and Buddhism, Islam neither renounced nor condemned material wealth. Jews and Christians living in Muslim lands were taxed but not persecuted. Converts to Islam were exempt from paying a poll-tax levied on all non-Muslim subjects. Into the towns that would soon become cultural oases, Muslims brought expertise in navigation, trade, and commercial exchange. They fostered favorable associations between Arab merchants and members of the ruling elite (in Africa, for instance) and rewarded converts with access to positions of power and authority. While many subject people embraced Islam out of genuine spiritual conviction, others found clear commercial and social advantages in conversion to the faith of Muhammad.

Muhammad never designated a successor; hence, after his death, bitter controversies arose concerning Muslim leadership. Rival claims to authority produced major divisions within the faith and armed conflicts that still exist today; the Sunni (from *sunna*, "the tradition of the Prophet") consider themselves the orthodox of Islam. Representing approximately 90 percent of the modern Muslim world population, they hold that religious rulers should be chosen by the faithful. By contrast, the Shiites or Shiah-i-Ali ("partisans of Ali") (the majority population in present-day Iran and Iraq) claim descent through Muhammad's cousin and son-in-law Ali. They hold that

only his direct descendants should rule. Following Muhammad's death, the **caliphs**, theocratic successors to Muhammad, were appointed by his followers. The first four caliphs, who ruled until 661, assumed political and religious authority, and their success in carrying Islam outside of Arabia (see Map 10.1) resulted in the establishment of a Muslim empire. Damascus fell to Islam in 634, Persia in 636, Jerusalem in 638, and Egypt in 640. Within another seventy years, under the leadership of the Umayyad caliphs (661–750), all of North Africa and Spain lay under Muslim rule.

Muslim expansion played a key role in defining the geographic borders of Western Europe. The control of the Mediterranean by Muslim forces snuffed out the waning Western sea trade, isolating the Christian West (see chapter 11). The Muslim advance upon the West encountered only two significant obstacles: the first was Constantinople, where Byzantine forces equipped with "Greek fire" (an incendiary compound catapulted from ships) deterred repeated Arab attacks. The second was in southwest France near Tours, where, in 732, Frankish soldiers led by Charles Martel (the grandfather of Charlemagne) turned back the Muslims, barring the progress of Islam into Europe. Nevertheless, in less than a century, Islam had won more converts than Christianity had gained in its first 300 years.

Islam in Africa

Islam's success in Africa was remarkable. As early as the seventh century, on the edges of the Sahara Desert and in North Africa, the Muslim merchants came to dominate commerce in salt, gold, and slaves (Figure 10.4). The volume of slave raids within the native Berber population west of the Nile River was so large as to spark open revolt. Nevertheless, Muslim traders soon commanded the trans-Saharan network that linked West Africa to Cairo and continued through Asia via the Silk Road to China (see chapters 7, 14).

Islam quickly became Africa's fastest growing religion, mingling with various aspects of local belief systems as it attracted a following primarily among the ruling elite of the continent's burgeoning kingdoms: in West Africa, Ghana, Mali, and Songhai (see chapter 18). The kings of Mali incorporated Islamic rituals into native African ceremonies; adopted the Arabic language for administrative purposes; hired Muslim scribes and jurists; and underwrote the construction of mosques and universities, the greatest of which was located at Timbuktu. In East Africa, as elsewhere, Swahili rulers who converted to Islam did not actively impose the religion on their subjects, so that only the larger African towns and centers of trade became oases of Islamic culture.

Figure 10.4 *The Slave Market at Zabīd, Yemen,* from the *Maqāmāt of al-Harīrī,* 1237. The woman shown here is veiled with the *hajib* that covers her neck and bosom, as well as part of her face. Local customs concerning dress varied locally, with some Muslim communities calling for women to wear the *chador* that covers the body from head to toe. The latter practice is not prescribed in the Qur'an.

Islam in the Middle East

Between 661 and 750, Damascus (in present-day Syria) served as the political center of the Muslim world. However, as Islam spread eastward under the leadership of a new Muslim dynasty—the Abbasids—the capital shifted to Baghdad (in modern Iraq). In Baghdad, a multi-ethnic city of more than 300,000 people, a golden age would come to flower. Between the eighth and tenth centuries, the city became an international trade center and expansive commercial activity enriched the growing urban population. Arab merchants imported leopards and rubies from India; silk, paper, and porcelain from China; horses and camels from Arabia; and topaz and cotton cloth from Egypt. The court of the caliph Harun al-Rashid (ruled 786–809) attracted musicians, dancers, writers, and poets. Harun's sons opened a House of Wisdom (*Dar al-Hikmet*) in which scholars prepared Arabic translations of Greek, Persian, Syriac, and Sanskrit manuscripts. In the ninth century, no city in the world could match the breadth of educational instruction or boast a library as large as that of Baghdad. Al-Yaqubi, a late ninth-century traveler, called Baghdad "the navel of the earth" and "the greatest city, which has no peer in the east or the west of the world in extent, size, prosperity, abundance of water, or health of climate. . . ." He continued:

> To [Baghdad] they come from all countries, far and near, and people from every side have preferred Baghdad to their own homelands. There is no country, the peoples of which have not their own quarter and their own trading and financial arrangements. In it

there is gathered that which does not exist in any other city in the world. On its flanks flow two great rivers, the Tigris and the Euphrates, and thus goods and foodstuffs come to it by land and water with the greatest ease, so that every kind of merchandise is completely available, from east and west, from Muslim and non-Muslim lands. Goods are brought from India, Sind [modern Pakistan], China, Tibet, the lands of the Turks, . . . the Ethiopians, and others to such an extent that [products] are more plentiful in Baghdad than in the countries from which they come. They can be procured so readily and so certainly that it is as if all the good things of the world are sent there, all the treasures of the earth assembled there, and all the blessings of creation perfected there. . . . The people excel in knowledge, understanding, letters, manners, insight, discernment, skill in commerce and crafts, cleverness in every argument, proficiency in every calling, and mastery of every craft. There is none more learned than their scholars, better informed than their traditionists, more cogent than their theologians, more perspicuous than their grammarians, more accurate than their [calligraphers], more skillful than their physicians, more melodious than their singers, more delicate than their craftsmen, more literate than their scribes, more lucid than their logicians, more devoted than their worshipers, more pious than their ascetics, more juridical than their [magistrates], more eloquent than their preachers, more poetic than their poets, and more reckless than their rakes.

Although this description may reflect the sentiments of an overly enthusiastic tourist, it is accurate to say that, between the eighth and tenth centuries, the cosmopolitan cities of the Muslim world boasted levels of wealth and culture that far exceeded those of Western Christendom. Even after invading Turkish nomads gained control of Baghdad during the eleventh century, the city retained cultural primacy within the civilized world—although Córdoba, with a library of some 400,000 volumes, came to rival Baghdad as a cultural and educational center. The destruction of Baghdad in 1258 at the hands of the Mongols ushered in centuries of slow cultural decline. However, Mongols and Turks, themselves converts to Islam, carried Islamic culture into India and China. In Egypt, an independent Islamic government ruled until the sixteenth century. The Tunisian historian Ibn Khaldun, visiting fourteenth-century Egypt, called Cairo "the mother of the world, the great center of Islam and the mainspring of the sciences and the crafts." Until the mid-fourteenth century, Muslims continued to dominate a system of world trade that stretched from Western Europe to China. Thereafter, the glories of medieval Muslim culture began to wane, to be revived only in the lavish court of the sixteenth-century Ottoman Turks and by the Moguls of seventeenth-century India (see chapter 21). The same cannot be said of the religion of Islam: over the centuries of Islamic expansion, millions of people found Islam

Science and Technology

765	the medical hospital constructed at Baghdad becomes a prototype for those built elsewhere
820	publication of *Al-jabr wa I mugābalah,* an Arabic adaptation of Hindu numerals to solve equations (called "algebra" in Europe)
ca. 830	geographers at Baghdad's House of Wisdom estimate the earth's circumference by directly measuring one degree of latitude on the earth's surface
850	the Arabs refine the astrolabe (from Greek prototypes)
910	the Arab physician Rhazes writes the first medical account of smallpox
950	al-Farabi publishes a treatise, the *Catalogue of the Sciences,* on applied mathematics

responsive to their immediate spiritual needs, and in most of the Asiatic and African regions conquered prior to the late seventh century (see Map 10.1), it is still the dominant faith. To date, Islam has experienced less change and remains closer to its original form than any other world religion.

Islamic Culture

From its beginnings, Islam held the status of a state-sponsored religion. Where Church and state were interdependent in both Byzantium and the Christian West, in Muslim lands they were inseparable. Theocratic rule brought a strong element of unity to Islamic culture, which is otherwise notable for its ethnic diversity, the product of its assimilation of many different peoples. The principal languages of the Islamic world, for instance, are Arabic, Persian, and Turkish, but dozens of other languages, including Berber, Swahili, Kurdish, Tamil, Malay, and Javanese, are spoken by Muslims. As Islam expanded, it absorbed many different styles from the arts of non-Arab peoples. "Islamic," then, is a term used to describe the culture of geographically diverse regions—Arab and non-Arab—dominated by Islam.

Chronology

570	birth of Muhammad
661–750	Umayyad caliphate
750–1258	Abbasid caliphate
1258	Mongols conquer Baghdad

Scholarship in the Islamic World

Following Muhammad's dictum to "seek knowledge," Islam was enthusiastically receptive to the intellectual achievements of other cultures and aggressive in its will to understand the workings of the natural world. At a time when few Westerners could read or write Latin and even fewer could decipher Greek, Arab scholars preserved hundreds of ancient Greek manuscripts—the works of Plato, Aristotle, Archimedes, Hippocrates, Galen, Ptolemy, and others—copying and editing them in Arabic translations. An important factor in this burst of literary creativity was the availability of paper, which originated in China as early as the second century and came into use in Baghdad during the ninth century. In the copying of Classical manuscripts, in the codification of religious teachings (that had heretofore been passed orally), and in the production of new types of literature, such as scientific treatises, cookbooks, poems and tales (see Readings 10.2–4), paper provided a major advance over parchment and papyrus, expensive materials from whose surfaces ink could easily be erased.

Between the ninth and twelfth centuries, Muslims absorbed and preserved much of the medical, botanical, and astrological lore of the Hellenized Mediterranean. This fund of scientific and technological knowledge, along with Arabic translations of Aristotle's works in logic and natural philosophy, and Muslim commentaries on Aristotle, filtered into the urban centers of Europe. There, in the twelfth century, they stimulated a rebirth of learning and contributed to the rise of Western universities (see chapter 12). Muslim philosophers compared the theories of Aristotle and the Neoplatonists with the precepts of Islam, seeking a unity of truth that would become the object of inquiry among Italian Renaissance humanists.

Crucial to the advancement of learning was the Muslim transmission of Hindu numbers, which replaced cumbersome Roman numerals with so-called "Arabic numbers" such as those used to paginate this book. Muslims also provided the West with such technological wonders as block printing (after the eighth century) and gunpowder (after the thirteenth century), both of which originated in China. Muslims thus borrowed and diffused the knowledge of Greek, Chinese, and Indian culture as energetically as they circulated commercial goods.

But the scholars of the Islamic world were not merely copyists; they made original contributions in mathematics, medicine, optics, chemistry, geography, philosophy, and astronomy. In the field of medicine, Islamic physicians wrote treatises on smallpox, measles, and diseases transmitted by animals (such as rabies), on the cauterization of wounds, and on the preparation of medicinal drugs (Figure 10.5). The single most important medieval health handbook, the *Tacuinum Sanitatis*, originated among Arab physicians who examined the effects of various foods, drinks, and clothing on human well-being. Translated into Latin in the eleventh century, this manuscript came into widespread popular use throughout the West. The vast *Canon of Medicine* compiled by the Persian physician and philosopher Ibn Sina (Avicenna, 980–1037) was a systematic repository of medical knowledge in use well into the sixteenth century. Muslim chemists invented the process of distillation and produced a volatile liquid (and forbidden intoxicant) called *alkuhl* (alcohol).

At a time when most Europeans knew little of the earth's physical size or shape, geographers in Baghdad estimated with some accuracy the earth's circumference, as well as its shape and curvature. Muslim astronomers made advances in spherical geometry and trigonometry that aided religious observance, which required an accurate lunar calendar and the means of determining the direction of Mecca from any given location. By refining the astrolabe, an ancient instrument for measuring the altitude of heavenly bodies above the horizon (Figure 10.6), Muslims were able to determine the time of day, hence estimate the correct hours for worship.

Islamic Poetry

In the Islamic literary tradition—a tradition dominated by two highly lyrical languages, Arabic and Persian—poetry played an infinitely more important role than prose. As within the cultures of ancient Greece, Africa, and China, poetry and music were intimately related, and local bards or wandering minstrels were the "keepers" of a

Figure 10.5 *Preparing Medicine from Honey*, from an Arabic manuscript of *Materia Medica* by Dioscorides, thirteenth century. Colors and gilt on paper, 12⅜ × 9 in.

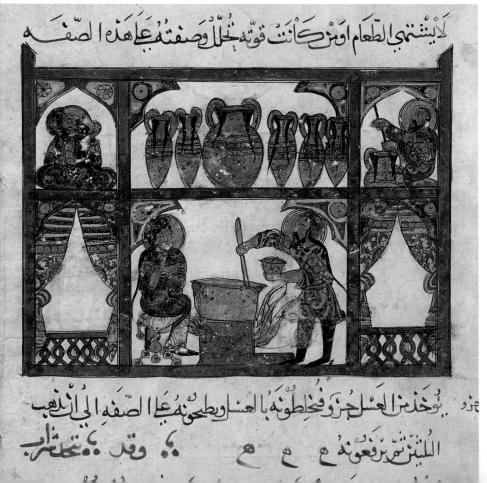

Figure 10.6 Abd al-Karim al-Misri, Astrolabe, from Cairo, 1235–1236. Brass, height 15½ in.

popular oral verse tradition. The Bedouin minstrels of pre-Islamic culture celebrated in song themes of romantic love, tribal warfare, and nomadic life. Bedouin songs, like the Arabic language itself, are rich in rhyme, and a single rhyme often dominates an entire poem. No English translation can capture the musical qualities of Arabic verse, and only some translations succeed in preserving its colorful descriptive imagery. Such is the case with the sixth-century ode by Tarafa in Reading 10.2, which uses vivid similes to convey a memorable portrait of the camel that has captured his heart.

Following the rise of Islam, no literature was prized more highly than the Arabic lyrics that constituted the Qur'an.

Science and Technology

1005	a comprehensive science library is founded in Cairo
1030	Ibn al-Haytham (Alhazen) publishes the first major work on optics since Hellenistic times
1035	publication of Ibn Sina's *Canon of Medicine*, an Arab compilation of Greek and Arab medical principles
1075	Arab astronomers posit the elliptical orbits of the planets
ca. 1150	al-Idrisi prepares a geographical survey of the world with maps for climatic sections

However, the pre-Islamic affection for secular verse persisted: the dominant themes in Islamic poetry included laments over injustice, elegies for the departed, and celebrations of the physical delights of nature. Romantic love—both heterosexual and homosexual, and often strongly erotic—was a favorite subject, especially among those who came under the influence of Persian literature. The eighth-century "Romance of Antar," a eulogy in honor of a beautiful and bewitching female, attributed to al-Asmai, reflects the sensual power of the finest Islamic lyrics. The poet's "ailment" of unrequited love, or "lovesickness," was a popular conceit in Arabic verse and one that became central to the code of courtly love in the medieval West. With their frank examination of physical desire and their reverence for female beauty, the poems of al-Asmai (740–828), Ibn Zaydun (1003–1071), and Ibn Abra—the latter two representative of Moorish* Islam—influenced the various genres of literature in Western Europe. This includes *troubadour* poetry, the medieval romance (see chapter 11), and the sonnets and songs of the Renaissance poet Petrarch (see chapter 16).

READING 10.2 Secular Islamic Poems (ca. 800–1300)

From Tarafa's "Praise for His Camel"

. . . .

Yet I have means to fly from grief, when such pursues me, on a lean high beast, which paces swiftly by day and by night,	1
A camel sure of foot, firm and thin as the planks of a bier, whom I guide surely over the trodden ways, ways etched in earth as texture is in cloth;	5
A she-camel, rival of the best, swift as an ostrich. When she trots her hind feet fall in the marks of her forefeet on the beaten road.	
With her white feathery tail she lashes backward and forward. Sometimes the lash falls on her rider, sometimes on her own dried udder, where no milk is, flaccid as an old bottle of leather.	10
Firm and polished are her haunches as two worn jambs of a castle gate.	15
The bones of her spine are supple and well-attached, and her neck rises solidly.	
When she raises her long neck it is like the rudder of a boat going up the Tigris.	
She carries her strong thighs well apart, as a carrier of water holds apart his buckets.	20
Red is the hair under her chin. Strong she is of back, long of stride; easily she moves her forelegs.	
The marks of the girths on her sides are as the marks of water-courses over smooth rock.	25

* The term "Moor" describes a Northwest African Muslim of mixed Arab and Berber descent. The Moors invaded and occupied Spain in the eighth century and maintained a strong presence there until they were expelled from Granada, their last stronghold, in 1492.

Sometimes the marks unite and sometimes are distinct,
    like the gores in fine linen, well-cut and stitched.
Her long skull is like an anvil, and where the bones unite
    their edges are sharp as the teeth of a file.
Her cheek is smooth as paper of Syria, and her upper lip   **30**
    like leather of Yemen, exactly and smoothly cut.
The two polished mirrors of her eyes gleam in the caverns
    of their sockets as water gleams in rocky pools.

Her ears are sharp to hear the low voices of the night, and
    not inattentive to the loud call,   **35**
Pricked ears, that show her breeding, like those of a lone
    wild bull in the groves of Haumel.
Her upper lip is divided and her nose pierced. When she
    stretches them along the ground her pace increases.
I touch her with my whip and she quickens her step, even   **40**
    though it be the time when the mirage shimmers on
    the burning sands.
She walks with graceful gait, as the dancing girl walks,
    showing her master the skirts of her trailing garment.

From Al-Asmai's "Romance of Antar"

. . . .

The lovely virgin has struck my heart with the arrow of a   **1**
    glance, for which there is no cure.
Sometimes she wishes for a feast in the sand-hills, like a
    fawn whose eyes are full of magic.
My disease preys on me; it is in my entrails: I conceal it;   **5**
    but its very concealment discloses it.
She moves: I should say it was the branch of the tamarisk[1]
    that waves its branches to the southern breeze.
She approaches: I should say her face was truly the sun
    when its luster dazzles the beholders.   **10**
She walks away: I should say her face was truly the sun
    when its luster dazzles the beholders.
She gazes: I should say it was the full moon of the night
    when Orion[2] girds it with stars.
She smiles: and the pearls of her teeth sparkle, in which   **15**
    there is the cure for the sickness of lovers.
She prostrates herself in reverence towards her God;
    and the greatest of men bow down to her beauties.
O Abla! when I most despair, love for thee and all its
    weaknesses are my only hope!   **20**

Ibn Zaydun's "Two Fragments"

I

The world is strange
For lack of you;
Times change their common hue—
The day is black, but very night
With you was shining white.

II

Two secrets in the heart of night

---

[1] A small tree or shrub from the Mediterranean region.
[2] A constellation of bright stars represented by the figure of a hunter
    with belt and sword.

We were until the light
Of busybody day
Gave both of us away.

Ibn Abra's "The Beauty-Spot"

A mole on Ahmad's cheek
Draws all men's eyes to seek
The love they swear reposes
In a garden there.
That breathing bed of roses
In a Nubian's care.

Q   **What are the principal themes in these poems?**

Q   **What similes and metaphors make these
poems distinctive?**

Sufi Poetry

One of the richest sources of literary inspiration in Islamic
history was the movement known as Sufism. As early as the
eighth century, some followers of Muhammad began to pursue a meditative, world-renouncing religious life that
resembled the spiritual ideals of Christian and Buddhist
ascetics and Neoplatonic mystics. The Sufi, so-called for
the coarse wool (*suf*) garments they wore, were committed
to purification of the soul and mystical union with God
through meditation, fasting, and prayer. As the movement
grew, Sufism placed increasing emphasis on visionary experience and the practice of intensifying physical sensation
through music, poetry, and dance. Religious rituals involving whirling dances (associated with Persian sufis, known
as "dervishes") functioned to transport the pious to a state
of ecstasy (Figure **10.7**). The union of the senses and the
spirit sought by the members of this ascetic brotherhood is
also evident in Sufi poetry.

    Sufi poetry, as represented in the works of the great
Persian mystic and poet Jalal al-Din Rumi (ca. 1207–
1273), draws on the intuitive, nonrational dimensions of
the religious experience. In the first of the following three
poems, a number of seeming contradictions work to characterize the unique nature of the spiritual master. The body
of Sufi instructions outlined in the second poem might be
equally appropriate to the Buddhist or the Christian mystic. In the third piece, "The One True Light," from *Love is
a Stranger*, Rumi rehearses an ancient parable that illumi-
nates the unity of God: seeing beyond the dim gropings of
the ordinary intellect, the mystic perceives that religions
are many, but God is One.

READING 10.3 Rumi's Poems (ca. 1250)
The Man of God

The man of God is drunken while sober.   **1**
The man of God is full without meat.
The man of God is perplexed and bewildered.
The man of God neither sleeps nor eats.
The man of God is a king clothed in rags.   **5**
The man of God is a treasure in the streets.

Figure 10.7 *Dancing Dervishes*, from a manuscript of the *Diwan* (*Book of Poems*) of Hafiz, Herat School, Persia, ca. 1490. Colors and gilt on paper, 11¾ × 7⅜ in.

The man of God is neither of sky nor land.
The man of God is neither of earth nor sea.
The man of God is an ocean without end.
The man of God drops pearls at your feet.   10
The man of God has a hundred moons at night.
The man of God has a hundred suns' light.
The man of God's knowledge is complete.
The man of God doesn't read with his sight.
The man of God is beyond form and disbelief.   15
The man of God sees good and bad alike.
The man of God is far beyond non-being.
The man of God is seen riding high.

The man of God is hidden, Shamsuddin.
The man of God you must seek and find.   20

Empty the Glass of Your Desire

Join yourself to friends   1
and know the joy of the soul.
Enter the neighborhood of ruin
with those who drink to the dregs.

Empty the glass of your desire   5
so that you won't be disgraced.
Stop looking for something out there

and begin seeing within.
Open your arms if you want an embrace.
Break the earthen idols and release the radiance.
Why get involved with a hag like this world?
You know what it will cost.   10

And three pitiful meals a day
is all that weapons and violence can earn.
At night when the Beloved comes
will you be nodding on opium?   15

If you close your mouth to food,
you can know a sweeter taste.
Our Host is no tyrant. We gather in a circle.
Sit down with us beyond the wheel of time.   20

Here is the deal: give one life
and receive a hundred.
Stop growling like dogs,
and know the shepherd's care.

You keep complaining about others   25
and all they owe you?
Well, forget about them;
just be in His presence.

When the earth is this wide,
why are you asleep in a prison?   30
Think of nothing but the source of thought.
Feed the soul; let the body fast.

Avoid knotted ideas;
untie yourself in a higher world.
Limit your talk   35
for the sake of timeless communion.

Abandon life and the world,
and find the life of the world.

The One True Light

The lamps are different, but the Light is the same: it
  comes from Beyond.   1
If thou keep looking at the lamp, thou art lost: for thence
  arises the appearance of number and plurality.
Fix thy gaze upon the Light, and thou art delivered from
  the dualism inherent in the finite body.
O thou who art the kernel of Existence, the disagreement
  between Moslem, Zoroastrian and Jew depends on the
  standpoint.

Some Hindus brought an elephant, which they exhibited
  in a dark shed.
As seeing it with the eye was impossible, every one felt it
  with the palm of his hand.
The hand of one fell on its trunk: he said, "This animal
  is like a water-pipe."
Another touched its ear: to him the creature seemed like
  a fan.
Another handled its leg and described the elephant as
  having the shape of a pillar.
Another stroked its back. "Truly," said he, "this elephant
  resembles a throne."

Had each of them held a lighted candle, there would
  have been no contradiction in their words.   10

Q **What aspects of these poems reflect religious mysticism?**

Q **Do they also put forth practical insights or advice?**

Islamic Prose Literature

Islam prized poetry over prose, but both forms drew on enduring oral tradition and on the verbal treasures of many regions. Unique to Arabic literature was rhyming prose, which brought a musical quality to everyday speech. One of the most popular forms of prose literary entertainment was a collection of eighth-century animal fables, which instructed as they amused. Another, which narrated the adventures of a rogue or vagabond characters, anticipated by five centuries the picaresque novel in the West (see chapter 19).

The rich diversity of Islamic culture is nowhere better revealed, however, than in the collection of prose tales known as *The Thousand and One Nights*. This literary classic, gradually assembled between the eighth and tenth centuries, brought together in the Arabic tongue various tales from Persian, Arabic, and Indian sources. It typifies the narrative technique of the **frame tale**, whereby a main story is composed for the purpose of including a group of shorter stories. The frame derives from an Indian fairy tale: Shahrasad (in English, Scheherazade) marries a king who fears female infidelity so greatly that he kills each new wife on the morning after the wedding night. In order to forestall her own death, Scheherazade entertains the king by telling stories, each of which she carefully brings to a climax just before dawn, so that, in order to learn the ending, the king must allow her to live. Scheherazade—or, more exactly, her storytelling—has a humanizing effect upon the king, who, after a thousand nights, comes to prize his clever wife. *The Thousand and One Nights*, which exists in many versions, actually contains only some 250 tales, many of which have become favorites with readers throughout the world: the adventures of Ali Baba, Aladdin, Sinbad, and other post-medieval stories are filled with fantasy, exotic characters, and spicy romance. The manner in which each tale loops into the next, linking story to story and parts of each story to each other, resembles the regulating principles of design in Islamic art, which include repetition, infinite extension, and the looping together of motifs to form a meandering, overall pattern (Figure **10.8**).

The story of Prince Behram and the Princess Al-Datma, reproduced below, addresses some of the major themes in Islamic literary culture: the power of female beauty, survival through cunning, and the "battle" of the sexes. While the story provides insight into Islamic notions of etiquette, it confirms the subordinate role of women in this, as in Western, society (see Reading 11.3). Nevertheless, ingenuity (exercised by both of the major characters in their

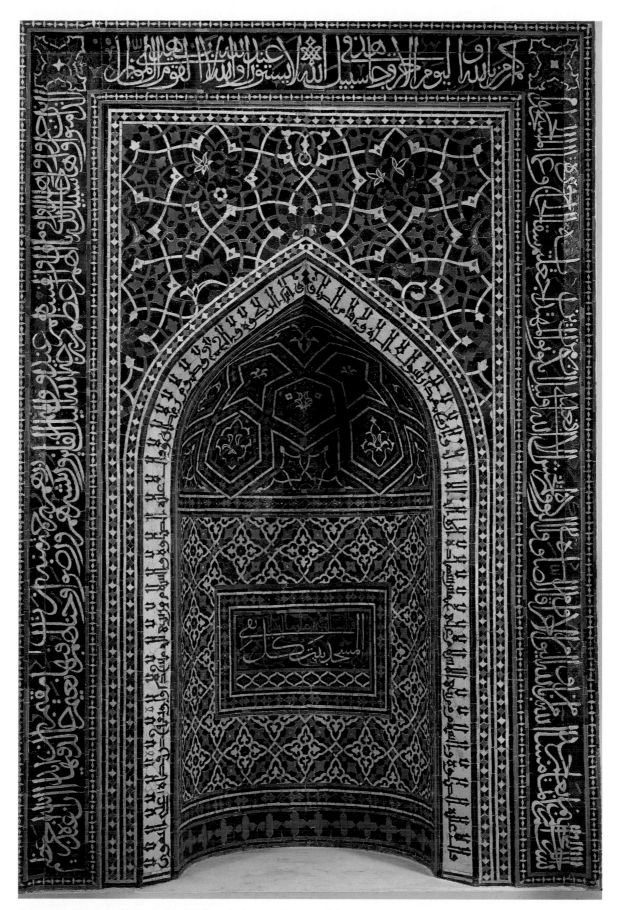

Figure 10.8 Niche (*mihrab*) showing Islamic calligraphy, from Iran. The rectangle in the center of the niche bears the evocation to Allah with which every chapter of the Qur'an begins: "In the name of Allah, the Lord of Mercy, the Giver of Mercy." Geometric designs, abstract floral motifs, and calligraphic text combine to ornament the surface.

efforts to achieve what they most desire) plays a saving role in both the tale told by Scheherazade and in the destiny of the storyteller herself, whose beauty, wit, and verbal powers prove to be a civilizing force.

READING 10.4 From *The Thousand and One Nights* (ca. 850)

"Prince Behram and the Princess Al-Datma"

There was once a king's daughter called Al-Datma who, in her   1
time, had no equal in beauty and grace. In addition to her lovely looks, she was brilliant and feisty and took great pleasure in ravishing the wits of the male sex. In fact, she used to boast, "There is nobody who can match me in anything." And the fact is that she was most accomplished in horsemanship and martial exercises, and all those things a cavalier should know.

Given her qualities, numerous princes sought her hand in marriage, but she rejected them all. Instead, she proclaimed,   10
"No man shall marry me unless he defeats me with his lance and sword in fair battle. He who succeeds I will gladly wed. But if I overcome him, I will take his horse, clothes, and arms and brand his head with the following words: 'This is the freedom of Al-Datma.'"

Now the sons of kings flocked to her from every quarter far and near, but she prevailed and put them to shame, stripping them of their arms and branding them with fire. Soon, a son of the king of Persia named Behram ibn Taji heard about her and journeyed from afar to her father's court. He brought men and   20
horses with him and a great deal of wealth and royal treasures. When he drew near the city, he sent her father a rich present, and the king came out to meet him and bestowed great honors on him. Then the king's son sent a message to him through his vizier and requested his daughter's hand in marriage. However, the king answered, "With regard to my daughter Al-Datma, I have no power over her, for she has sworn by her soul to marry no one but him who defeats her in the listed field."

"I journeyed here from my father's court with no other   30
purpose but this," the prince declared. "I came here to woo her and to form an alliance with you."

"Then you shall meet her tomorrow," said the king.

So the next day he sent for his daughter, who got ready for battle by donning her armor of war. Since the people of the kingdom had heard about the coming joust, they flocked from all sides to the field. Soon the princess rode into the lists, armed head to toe with her visor down, and the Persian king's son came out to meet her, equipped in the fairest of fashions.

Then they charged at each other and fought a long time,   40
wheeling and sparring, advancing and retreating, and the princess realized that he had more courage and skill than she had ever encountered before. Indeed, she began to fear that he might put her to shame before the bystanders and defeat her. Consequently, she decided to trick him, and raising her visor, she showed her face, which appeared more radiant than the full moon, and when he saw it, he was bewildered by her beauty. His strength failed, and his spirit faltered. When she perceived this moment of weakness, she attacked and knocked him from his saddle. Consequently, he became like a   50
sparrow in the clutches of an eagle. Amazed and confused, he

did not know what was happening to him when she took his steed, clothes, and armor. Then, after branding him with fire, she let him go his way.

When he recovered from his stupor, he spent several days without food, drink, or sleep. Indeed, love had gripped his heart. Finally, he decided to send a letter to his father via a messenger, informing him that he could not return home until he had won the princess or died for want of her. When his sire received the letter, he was extremely distressed about his son   60
and wanted to rescue him by sending troops and soldiers. However, his ministers dissuaded him from this action and advised him to be patient. So he prayed to Almighty Allah for guidance.

In the meantime, the prince thought of different ways to attain his goal, and soon he decided to disguise himself as a decrepit old man. So he put a white beard over his own black one and went to the garden where the princess used to walk most of the days. Here he sought out the gardener and said to him, "I'm a stranger from a country far away, and from my   70
youth onward I've been a gardener, and nobody is more skilled than I am in the grafting of trees and cultivating fruit, flowers, and vines."

When the gardener heard this, he was extremely pleased and led him into the garden, where he let him do his work. So the prince began to tend the garden and improved the Persian waterwheels and the irrigation channels. One day, as he was occupied with some work, he saw some slaves enter the garden leading mules and carrying carpets and vessels, and he asked them what they were doing there.   80

"The princess wants to spend an enjoyable afternoon here," they answered.

When he heard these words, he rushed to his lodging and fetched some jewels and ornaments he had brought with him from home. After returning to the garden, he sat down and spread some of the valuable items before him while shaking and pretending to be a very old man.

And Scheherazade noticed that dawn was approaching and stopped telling her story. When the next night arrived, however, she received the king's permission to continue her tale and said,   90

In fact, the prince made it seem as if he were extremely decrepit and senile. After an hour or so a company of damsels and eunuchs entered the garden with the princess, who looked just like the radiant moon among the stars. They ran about the garden, plucking fruits and enjoying themselves, until they caught sight of the prince disguised as an old man sitting under one of the trees. The man's hands and feet were trembling from old age, and he had spread a great many precious jewels and regal ornaments before him. Of course, they were astounded by this and asked him what he was   100
doing there with the jewels.

"I want to use these trinkets," he said, "to buy me a wife from among the lot of you."

They all laughed at him and said, "If one of us marries you, what will you do with her?"

"I'll give her one kiss," he replied, "and then divorce her."

"If that's the case," said the princess, "I'll give this damsel to you for your wife."

So he rose, leaned on his staff, staggered toward the damsel, and gave her a kiss. Right after that he gave her the jewels and ornaments, whereupon she rejoiced and they all went on their way laughing at him. 110

The next day they came again to the garden, and they found him seated in the same place with more jewels and ornaments than before spread before him.

"Oh sheikh," they asked him, "what are you going to do with all this jewelry?"

"I want to wed one of you again," he answered, "just as I did yesterday."

So the princess said, "I'll marry you to this damsel." 120

And the prince went up to her, kissed her, and gave her the jewels, and they all went their way.

After seeing how generous the old man was to her slave girls, the princess said to herself, "I have more right to these fine things than my slaves, and there's surely no danger involved in this game." So when morning arrived, she went down by herself into the garden dressed as one of her own damsels, and she appeared all alone before the prince and said to him, "Old man, the king's daughter has sent me to you so that you can marry me." 130

When he looked at her, he knew who she was. So he answered, "With all my heart and love," and he gave her the finest and costliest of jewels and ornaments. Then he rose to kiss her, and since she was not on her guard and thought she had nothing to fear, he grabbed hold of her with his strong hands and threw her down on the ground, where he deprived her of her maidenhead. Then he pulled the beard from his face and said, "Do you recognize me?"

"Who are you?"

"I am Behram, the King of Persia's son," he replied. "I've 140 changed myself and have become a stranger to my people, all for your sake. And I have lavished my treasures for your love."

She rose from him in silence and did not say a word to him. Indeed, she was dazed by what had happened and felt that it was best to be silent, especially since she did not want to be shamed. All the while she was thinking to herself, "If I kill myself, it will be senseless, and if I have him put to death, there's nothing that I'd really gain. The best thing for me to do is to elope with him to his own country."

So, after leaving him in the garden, she gathered together 150 her money and treasures and sent him a message informing him what she intended to do and telling him to get ready to depart with his possessions and whatever else he needed. Then they set a rendezvous for their departure.

At the appointed time they mounted racehorses and set out under cover of darkness, and by the next morning they had traveled a great distance. They kept traveling at a fast pace until they drew near his father's capital in Persia, and when his father heard about his son's coming, he rode out to meet him with his troops and was full of joy. 160

After a few days went by, the king of Persia sent a splendid present to the princess's father along with a letter to the effect that his daughter was with him and requested her wedding outfit. Al-Datma's father greeted the messenger with a happy heart (for he thought he had lost his daughter and had been grieving for her). In response to the king's letter, he

summoned the kazi[1] and the witnesses and drew up a marriage contract between his daughter and the prince of Persia. In addition, he bestowed robes of honor on the envoys from the king of Persia and sent his daughter her marriage 170 equipage. After the official wedding took place, Prince Behram lived with her until death came and sundered their union.

No sooner had Scheherazade concluded her tale than she said, "And yet, oh king, this tale is no more wondrous than the tale of the three apples."

— **Q** Does this tale have a "moral"? If so, what does it teach?

Islamic Art and Architecture

Five times a day, at the call of **muezzins** (criers) usually located atop **minarets** (tall, slender towers; see Figure 9.12), Muslims are summoned to interrupt their activities to kneel and pray facing Mecca. Such prayer is required whether believers are in the heart of the desert or in their homes. The official Muslim place of worship, however, is the mosque: a large, columned hall whose square or rectangular shape derives from the simple urban house made of sun-dried bricks. The design of the mosque is not, as with the Early Christian church, determined by the needs of religious liturgy. Rather, the mosque is first and foremost a place of prayer. Every mosque is oriented toward Mecca, and that direction (**qibla**) is marked by a niche (**mihrab**) located in the wall (see Figure 10.1). Occasionally, the niche holds a lamp that symbolizes Allah as the light of the heavens and the earth (Sura 24.35). To the right of the *mihrab* is a small, elevated platform (**minbar**) at which the Qur'an may be read.

The Great Mosque in Córdoba, Spain, begun in 784 and enlarged over a period of 300 years, is one of the noblest examples of early Islamic architecture. Its interior consists of more than 500 double-tiered columns that originally supported a wooden roof. The floor plan of the Great Mosque (now a Catholic cathedral), with its seemingly infinite rows of columns (Figure **10.9**), represents a sharp contrast with the design of the Early Christian basilica, which moves the worshiper in a linear fashion from portal to altar. At Córdoba, horseshoe-shaped arches consisting of contrasting wedges of white marble and red sandstone crown a forest of ornamental pillars (Figure **10.10**). Such arches seem to "flower" like palm fronds from their column "stems." In some parts of the structure, multilobed arches are set in "piggyback" fashion, creating further ornamental rhythms. The dome of the *mihrab*, constructed on eight intersecting arches and lavishly decorated with mosaics, is clear evidence of Muslim proficiency in mathematics, engineering, and artistic virtuosity.

Islam was self-consciously resistant to image-making. Like the Jews, Muslims condemned the worship of pagan idols and considered making likenesses of living creatures an act of pride that "competed" with the Creator God.

[1] Chief justice.

Therefore, in Islamic religious art, there is almost no three-dimensional sculpture, and, with the exception of occasional scenes of the Muslim Paradise, no pictorial representations of the kind found in Christian art. Islamic art also differs from Christian art in its self-conscious avoidance of symbols. But such self-imposed limitations did not prevent Muslims from creating one of the richest bodies of visual ornamentation in the history of world art. Three types of motifs dominate the Islamic decorative repertory: *geometric*, *floral*, and *calligraphic*. Geometric designs, drawn largely from a Classical repertory, were developed in complex and variegated patterns. Abstract, interlocking shapes often enclose floral motifs that feature the **arabesque**, a type of ornamentation based on plant and flower forms inspired by Byzantine and Persian art (see Figure 10.8). Calligraphy, that is "beautiful writing," completes the vocabulary of ornamentation. In Islamic art, where the written word takes precedence, calligraphy assumes a sacramental character. Most calligraphic inscriptions were drawn from the Qur'an. In carved, painted, and enameled surfaces, the Word of Allah, written in elegant **Kufic**, the earliest form of Arabic script (originating in the Iraqi town of Kufa) plays an essential part in both embellishment and revelation. Whether calligraphic, floral, or geometric, Islamic motifs are repeated in seemingly infinite, rhythmic extension, bound only by the borders of the frame. This device may be viewed as the visual equivalent of the frame tale, in which many individual stories are incorporated into the whole. "Meander and frame"—an expression of the universal theme of variety and unity in nature—is a fundamental principle of the Islamic decorative tradition and (as noted earlier) of Islamic aesthetics. The aesthetic of infinite extension sees Truth as intuitive and all-pervasive, rather than (as in Western Christian thought) as apocalyptic and self-fulfilling.

The bold use of color is one of the key features of Islamic art and architecture. Complex surface designs executed in mosaics and polychrome patterned glazed tiles transform the exteriors of mosques and palaces into shimmering veils of light and color. At the Dome of the Rock (Figure **10.11**), the earliest surviving Islamic sanctuary, Qur'anic inscriptions in gold mosaic cubes on a blue ground wind around the spectacular octagon. Constructed on a 35-acre plateau in east Jerusalem, the sanctuary (also known as the Mosque of Omar) is capped by a **gilded** dome. While much of the exterior has been refaced with glazed pottery tiles, the interior still shelters the original dazzling mosaics. Both in its harmonious proportions and its lavishly ornamented surfaces, the structure is a landmark of the Muslim faith. It is believed to crown the site of the creation of Adam and mark the spot from which Muhammad ascended to Heaven. It is also said to be the site of the biblical Temple of Solomon. Hence, the Dome of the Rock is a sacred shrine whose historical significance—like that of Jerusalem itself—is shared, but also bitterly contested, by Jews, Muslims, and Christians.

A lavish combination of geometric, floral, and calligraphic designs distinguishes Islamic frescoes, carpets,

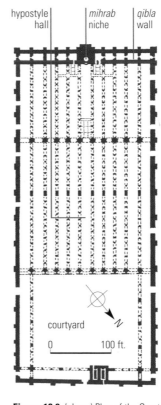

hypostyle hall | *mihrab* niche | *qibla* wall

courtyard

0   100 ft.

Figure 10.9 (above) Plan of the Great Mosque, Córdoba. The additions of 832–848 and 961 are shown, but not the final enlargement of 987.

Figure 10.10 (below) Columns in the Moorish part of the Great Mosque, Córdoba, 784–987. White marble and red sandstone.

Figure 10.11 Dome of the Rock, Jerusalem, Israel, ca. 687–691. Lying below the Dome is the sacred rock that some identify as the foundation stone of Solomon's Temple. Islamic maps identified this spot in the city of Jerusalem as the "center of the world."

ivories, manuscripts, textiles, and ceramics. Occasionally, however, calligraphy alone provides ornamentation. Along the rim of a tenth-century earthenware bowl, for instance, elegant Kufic script imparts Muhammad's injunction: "Planning before work protects one from regret; prosperity and peace" (Figure **10.12**). Here, as on the pages of an early **illuminated manuscript** of the Qur'an (see Figure 10.3), fluid calligraphic strokes (with red and yellow dots to indicate vowels) provide the sole "decoration."

While figural subjects are avoided in religious art, they abound in secular manuscripts, and especially in those produced after 1200 (see Figure 10.4). Travel tales, fables, romances, chronicles, and medical treatises (see Figure 10.5) are freely illustrated with human and animal activities. In one miniature from an illustrated manuscript of Sufi poetry, dervishes (some of whom have succumbed to vertigo), musicians, and witnesses congregate in a tapestrylike landscape filled with flowers and blooming trees (see Figure 10.7).

Islamic art and architecture often feature the garden and garden motifs as symbolic of the Muslim Paradise, (which is mentioned in the Qur'an no fewer than 130 times). Like the biblical Garden of Eden and the Babylonian Dilmun (see Reading 1.2), the paradisal garden is a place of spiritual and physical refreshment. Watered by cool rivers and filled with luscious fruit trees, the Garden of the Afterlife takes its earthly form in Islamic architecture. Luxuriant palaces throughout the Muslim world—real-life settings for the fictional Scheherazade—as well as royal tombs like the Taj Mahal (see chapter 21) normally feature gardens and park pavilions with fountains and water pools. At the oldest well-preserved Islamic palace in the world, the Alhambra in Granada, Spain, rectangular courtyards are cooled by clear, reflecting pools of water and bubbling, central fountains from which flow (in the cardinal directions) the four "paradisal rivers" (Figure **10.13**). This fourteenth-century palace—the stronghold of Muslim culture in the West until 1492—makes use of polychrome **stucco** reliefs, glazed tiles, lacy arabesque designs, and lush gardens simulating Heaven on earth.

Figure 10.12 Islamic bowl with inscription. Glazed earthenware, height 7 in., diameter 18 in.

Figure 10.13 Court of the Lions, the Alhambra, Granada, Spain, fourteenth century.

Music in the Islamic World

For the devout Muslim, there was no religious music other than the sound of the chanted Qur'an and the *muezzin's* call to prayer. Muslims regarded music as a forbidden pleasure and condemned its "killing charm" (as *The Thousand and One Nights* describes it). Nevertheless, the therapeutic uses of music were recognized by Arab physicians and its sensual powers were celebrated by Sufi mystics. During Islam's golden age, secular music flourished in the courts of Córdoba and Baghdad, and, even earlier, Arab song mingled with the music of Persia, Syria, Egypt, and Byzantium.

The music of the Islamic world originated in the songs of the desert nomads—songs featuring the solo voice and unmeasured rhythms. (The meter of one type of caravan song, however, is said to resemble the rhythm of the camel's lurching stride.) As in ancient Greece, India, and China, the music of Arabia consisted of a single melodic line, either unaccompanied or with occasional instrumental accompaniment. It was, as well, modal (each mode bearing association with a specific quality of emotion). Two additional characteristics of Arab music (to this day) are its use of microtones (the intervals that lie between the semitones of the Western twelve-note system) and its preference for improvisation (the performer's original, spur-of-the-moment variations on the melody or rhythm of a given piece). Both of these features, which also occur in modern jazz, work to give Arab music its unique sound. The melodic line of the Arab song weaves and wanders, looping and repeating themes in a kind of aural arabesque; the voice slides and intones in subtle and hypnotic stretches. In its linear ornamentation and in its repetitive rhythmic phrasing, Arab music has much in common with literary and visual forms of Islamic expression. This vocal pattern, resembling Hebrew, Christian, or Buddhist chant, is not unlike the sound of the *muezzin* calling Muslims to prayer.

Instrumental music took second place to the voice everywhere in the Islamic world, except in Persia, where a strong pre-Islamic instrumental tradition flourished. Lyres, flutes, and drums—all light, portable instruments—were used to accompany the songs of Bedouin camel drivers, while bells and tambourines might provide percussion for dancing. At the end of the sixth century, the Arabs developed the lute (in Arabic, *ud*, meaning "wood"), a half-pear-shaped wooden string instrument that was used to accompany vocal performance (Figures **10.14**, **10.15**). The forerunner of the guitar, the lute has a right-angled neck and is played with a small quill.

Some time after the eighth century, Muslim musicians in Spain began to compose larger orchestral pieces divided into five or more distinct movements, to be performed by string and wind instruments, percussion, and voices. It is

See Music Listening Selections at end of chapter.

possible that the Western tradition of orchestral music, along with the development of such instruments as oboes, trumpets, viols, and kettledrums, originated among Arab musicians during the centuries of Muslim rule in Spain. Indeed, the renowned ninth-century musician Ziryab (known for his dark complexion as "the Blackbird") traveled from Baghdad through North Africa to Córdoba to become the founder of the first conservatory of music and patriarch of Arabo-Andalusian musical art. Music composition and theory reached a peak between the ninth and eleventh centuries, when noted Islamic scholars wrote almost two hundred treatises on musical performance and theory. They classified the aesthetic, ethical, and medicinal functions of the modes, recommending specific types of music to relieve specific illnesses. One Arab writer, al-Isfahani (897–967), compiled the *Great Book of Songs*, a twenty-one-volume encyclopedia that remains the most important source of information about Arab music and poetry from its beginnings to the tenth century. The wide range of love songs, many with motifs of complaint and yearning, would have a distinct influence on both the secular and the religious music of the Western Middle Ages and the Renaissance.

Figure 10.14 Lute with nine strings. Spanish miniature from the *Cantigas de Santa Maria*, 1221–1289.

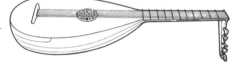

Figure 10.15 Drawing of a lute.

LOOKING BACK

 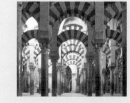 

The Religion of Islam

- In seventh-century Arabia, Islam emerged as the third of the monotheistic world faiths. Divine revelation came by way of the angel Gabriel, who instructed Muhammad to declare himself the Prophet of Allah, the last in a line of prophets beginning with the biblical Abraham.
- Muhammad's migration (*hijra*) from Mecca to Medina in 622 marks the first year of the Muslim calendar. After his return to Mecca, Muhammad assumed spiritual and political authority, establishing a theocracy that bound religious and secular realms. By the time he died in 632, the entire Arabian peninsula was united in its commitment to Islam.
- The Five Pillars of religious practice govern the everyday life of Muslims ("those who submit to Allah"). The faithful can expect the reward of eternal life, while those who disbelieve or stray from Allah's law are doomed to the punishments of Hell.
- The Qur'an, a record of Muhammad's recitations set down by his disciples ten years after the Prophet's death, is the Holy Book of Islam. The Muslim guide to spiritual and secular life, the Qur'an consists of 114 chapters that offer guidance on Muslim rituals, ethics, and laws.

The Spread of Islam

- Islam's success in becoming a world faith is in large part due to the fact that, from the outset, religious, political, and military goals were allied. The new faith also offered rules of conduct, and ritual practices that resembled those of Christianity and Judaism.
- Early Muslim expansion succeeded not so much by the militant coercion of foreign populations as it did by the economic opportunities Muslims offered conquered people.
- In that Muhammad did not designate a successor, disputes concerning the leadership of Islam followed his death. Here began the splintering of Islam into Shiite and Sunni partisans.
- The first four deputies (caliphs) carried Islam outside of Arabia, initiating the rise of a Muslim empire. The Umayyad caliphs took the faith west, across North Africa into Spain. After 750,

- the Abbasid caliphate established its authority across the Middle East.
- Between the eighth and thirteenth centuries, the great centers of Muslim urban life—Baghdad in Iraq, Córdoba in Spain, and Cairo in Egypt—surpassed the cities of Western Europe in learning and the arts. Their cultural primacy was shattered at the hands of the Mongols, who destroyed Baghdad in 1258.
- Until the mid-fourteenth century, Muslims dominated a system of world trade that stretched from Western Europe to China.

Islamic Culture

- The Muslims created the first global culture—a culture united by a single system of belief, but embracing a wide variety of regions, languages, and customs.
- Muslim scholars produced original work in the fields of mathematics, optics, philosophy, geography, and medicine. They translated into Arabic the valuable corpus of Greek writings, which they transmitted to the West along with the technological and scientific inventions of Asian civilizations.

- Themes of unrequited love were popular in Arab lyric verse. The poetry of the Islamic mystics known as the Sufi drew on the intuitive and mystical dimensions of religious experience. Lyrical repetition and infinite extension are notable features of the classic collection of prose tales: *The Thousand and One Nights.*
- The Great Mosque in Córdoba and the Dome of the Rock in Jerusalem are two examples of Islamic architectural ingenuity: the first for its inventive disposition of horseshoe-shaped arches, the second for its domed, octagonal plan and its dazzling mosaics.
- Resistant to image-making, Islamic religious art is dominated by geometric, floral, and calligraphic motifs, often interlaced in patterns of infinite extension. Secular manuscripts, such as herbals and chronicles, feature lively scenes of everyday activities.
- Islamic music, confined to secular rather than religious purposes, is rich in song and unique in the invention of early instrumental ensembles. Treatises on composition and theory, and encyclopedic collections of Arab music and poetry, date from the ninth to eleventh centuries.

Music Listening Selection

CD One Selection 4 Islamic Call to Prayer.

CD One Selection 5 Anonymous, Twisya No. 3 of the Nouba.

Glossary

arabesque a type of ornament featuring intertwined leaf and flower forms

bismillah the invocation that precedes the chapters of the Qur'an and many Muslim prayers: "In the name of God [Allah], God of Mercy, the Giver of Mercy"

caliph (Arabic, "deputy") the official successor to Muhammad and theocratic ruler of an Islamic state

frame tale a narrative technique by which a main story incorporates a group of shorter stories

gilded (or **gilt**) gold-surfaced; covered with a thin layer of gold, gold paint, or gold foil

hajj pilgrimage to Mecca,

the fifth Pillar of the Faith in Islam

hijra (Arabic, "migration" or "flight") Muhammad's journey from Mecca to Medina in the year 622

illuminated manuscript a handwritten and ornamented book, parts of which (the script, illustrations, or decorative devices) may be embellished with gold or silver paint or with gold foil, hence "illuminated"

imam a Muslim prayer leader

infidel a nonbeliever

jihad (Arabic, "struggle" [to follow God's will]) the struggle to lead a virtuous life and to further the universal mission of Islam through

teaching, preaching, and, when necessary, warfare

Kaaba (Arabic, "cube") a religious sanctuary in Mecca; a square shrine containing the sacred Black Stone thought to have been delivered to Abraham by the Angel Gabriel

Kufic the earliest form of Arabic script; it originated in the Iraqi town of Kufa

madrasa an Islamic school affiliated with a mosque

mihrab a special niche in the wall of a mosque that indicates the direction of Mecca

minaret a tall, slender tower usually attached to a mosque and surrounded by a balcony from which the *muezzin* summons Muslims to prayer

minbar a stepped pulpit in a mosque

mosque the Muslim house of worship

muezzin a "crier" who calls the hours of Muslim prayer five times a day

mullah a Muslim trained in Islamic law and doctrine

polygyny the marriage of one man to several women at the same time

qadi a Muslim judge

qibla the direction that should be faced when a Muslim prays

sharia the body of Muslim law based on the Qur'an and the *Hadith*

stucco fine plaster or cement used to coat or decorate walls

Chapter

11

Patterns of Medieval Life

ca. 500–1300

"When they mount chargers, take up their swords and shields,
Not death itself could drive them from the field.
They are good men; their words are fierce and proud."
Song of Roland

Figure 11.1 *William Duke of Normandy's Fleet Crossing the Channel*, detail from the Bayeux Tapestry, late eleventh century. Wool embroidery on linen, depth approx. 20 in., entire length 231 ft. The ship pictured here is typical of the wooden vessels that carried the Vikings across the North and Mediterranean Seas. Some 70 feet in length, they were propelled by sails and oars.

LOOKING AHEAD

Scholars once described the five centuries following the fall of Rome as a "dark age" whose cultural achievements fell far short of those of ancient Greece and Rome. Our present understanding suggests otherwise: the Early Middle Ages (ca. 500–1000) was one of the most creative periods in Western history. During this time, three distinct traditions—Classical, Germanic, and Christian—came together to produce a vigorous new culture. While Germanic invasions (Map **11.1**) contributed to the decline and decentralization of the Roman Empire, Germanic practices slowly blended with those of ancient Rome and rising Christianity. In the territories that would come to be called "Europe," the political and military system known as feudalism would shape the social and cultural patterns of early medieval life.

Ushering in the new mobility of Europe's High Middle Ages (ca. 1000–1300), the Christian Crusades altered these patterns. The Crusades encouraged the rise of towns and trade dominated by a rising middle class whose values differed from those of the feu-

dal nobility. The patterns of medieval secular life reflect the shift from a feudal society to a more centralized and urbanized one: a society distinguished by complex social interactions between lord and vassal, farmer and merchant, male and female.

The Germanic Tribes

The Germanic peoples were a tribal folk who followed a migratory existence. Dependent on their flocks and herds, they lived in pre-urban village communities throughout Asia and frequently raided and plundered nearby lands for material gain, yet they settled no territorial state. As early as the first century B.C.E., a loose confederacy of Germanic tribes began to threaten Roman territories, but it was not until the fourth century C.E. that these tribes, driven westward by the fierce Central Asian nomads known as Huns, pressed into the Roman Empire. Lacking the hallmarks of civilization—urban settlements, monumental architecture, and the art of writing—the Germanic tribes struck the Romans as inferiors, as outsiders, hence, as "barbarians." Ethnically distinct from the Huns, the Germanic folk, including East Goths (Ostrogoths), West Goths (Visigoths), Franks, Vandals, Burgundians, Angles, and Saxons, belonged to one and the same language family, dialects of which differed from tribe to tribe. The Ostrogoths occupied the steppe region between the Black

Map 11.1 The Early Christian World and the Barbarian Invasions, ca. 500. The map indicates the routes of the Germanic tribes as they invaded the Roman Empire. Note that many of the tribes came into Italy in the early to mid-fifth century; the Visigoths attacked Rome in 410; the Vandals sacked the city in 455.

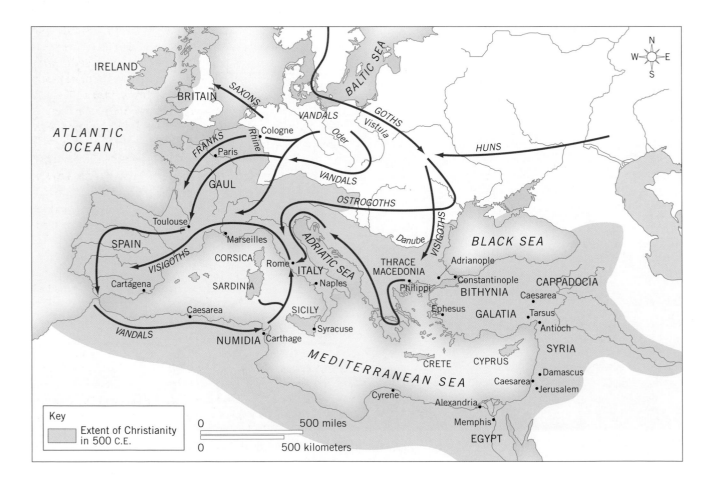

and Baltic Seas, while the Visigoths settled in territories closer to the Danube River (see Map 11.1). As the tribes pressed westward, an uneasy alliance was forged: the Romans allowed the barbarians to settle on the borders of the Empire, but in exchange the Germanic warriors were obliged to protect Rome against other invaders. Antagonism between Rome and the West Goths led to a military showdown. At the Battle of Adrianople (130 miles northwest of Constantinople, near modern Edirne in Turkey) in 378, the Visigoths defeated the "invincible" Roman army, killing the East Roman emperor Valens and dispersing his army. Almost immediately thereafter, the Visigoths swept across the Roman border, raiding the cities of the declining West, including Rome itself in 410.

The Battle of Adrianople opened the door to a sequence of barbarian invasions. During the fifth century, the Empire fell prey to the assaults of many Germanic tribes, including the Vandals, whose willful, malicious destruction of Rome in 455 produced the English word "vandalize." In 476, a Germanic commander named Odoacer deposed the reigning Roman emperor in the West, an event that is traditionally taken to mark the official end of the Roman Empire. Although the Germanic tribes leveled the final assaults on an already declining empire, they did not utterly destroy Rome's vast resources, nor did they ignore the culture of the late Roman world. The Ostrogoths embraced Christianity and sponsored literary and architectural enterprises modeled on those of Rome and Byzantium, while the Franks and the Burgundians chose to commit their legal traditions to writing, styling their codes of law on Roman models.

Germanic culture differed dramatically from that of Rome: in the agrarian and essentially self-sufficient communities of these nomadic peoples, fighting was a way of life and a highly respected skill. Armed with javelins and shields, Germanic warriors fought fiercely on foot and on horseback. Superb horsemen, the Germanic cavalry would come to borrow from the Mongols spurs and foot stirrups—devices (originating in China) that firmly secured the rider in his saddle and improved his driving force. In addition to introducing to the West superior methods of fighting on horseback, the Germanic tribes imposed their own long-standing traditions on medieval Europe. Every Germanic chieftain retained a band of warriors that followed him into battle, and every warrior anticipated sharing with his chieftain the spoils of victory. At the end of the first century, the Roman historian Tacitus (see chapter 6) wrote an account of the habits and customs of the Germanic peoples. He observes:

> All [men] are bound, to defend their leader . . . and to make even their own actions subservient to his renown. If he dies in the field, he who survives him survives to live in infamy. . . . This is the bond of union, the most sacred obligation. The chief fights for victory; the followers for their chief. . . . The chief must show his liberality, and the follower expects it. He demands, at one time this warlike horse, at another, that victorious lance drenched with the blood of the enemy.

The bond of **fealty**, or loyalty, between the Germanic warrior and his chieftain and the practice of rewarding the warrior would become fundamental to the medieval practice of feudalism.

Germanic Law

Germanic law was not legislated by the state, as in Roman tradition, but was, rather, a collection of customs passed orally from generation to generation. The Germanic dependence on custom would have a lasting influence on the development of law, and especially **common law**, in parts of the West. Among the Germanic peoples, tribal chiefs were responsible for governing, but general assemblies met to make important decisions: fully armed, clan warriors demonstrated their assent to propositions "in a military manner," according to Tacitus—by brandishing their javelins. Since warlike behavior was commonplace, tribal law was severe, uncompromising, and directed toward publicly shaming the guilty. Tacitus records that punishment for an adulterous wife was "instant, and inflicted by the husband. He cuts off the hair of his guilty wife, and having assembled her relations, expels her naked from his house, pursuing her with stripes through the village. To public loss of honor no favor is shown. She may possess beauty, youth and riches; but a husband she can never obtain."

As in most ancient societies—Hammurabi's Babylon, for instance—penalties for crimes varied according to the social standing of the guilty party. Among the Germanic tribes, however, a person's guilt or innocence might be determined by an ordeal involving fire or water; such trials reflected the faith Germanic peoples placed in the will of nature deities. Some of the names of these gods came to designate days of the week; for example, the English word "Wednesday" derives from "Woden's day" and "Thursday" from "Thor's day."

Germanic Literature

Germanic traditions, including those of personal valor and heroism associated with a warring culture, are reflected in the epic poems of the Early Middle Ages. The three most famous of these, *Beowulf*, *The Song of the Nibelungen*, and the *Song of Roland*, were transmitted orally for hundreds of years before they were written down some time between the tenth and thirteenth centuries. *Beowulf*,

---

Science and Technology

568	Germanic tribes introduce stirrups (from China) into Europe
600	a heavy iron plow is used in Northern Europe
770	iron horseshoes are used widely in Western Europe

which originated among the Anglo-Saxons around 700, was recorded in Old English—the Germanic language spoken in the British Isles between the fifth and eleventh centuries. *The Song of the Nibelungen*, a product of the Burgundian tribes, was recorded in Old German; and the Frankish *Song of Roland*, in Old French. Celebrating the deeds of warrior-heroes, these three epic poems have much in common with the *Iliad*, the *Mahabharata*, and other orally transmitted adventure poems.

The 3000-line epic known as *Beowulf* is the first monumental literary composition in a European vernacular language. The tale of a daring Scandinavian prince, *Beowulf* brings to life the heroic world of the Germanic people with whom it originated. In unrhymed Old English verse embellished with numerous two-term metaphors known as **kennings** ("whale-path" for "sea," "ring-giver" for "king"), the poem recounts three major adventures: Beowulf's encounter with the monster Grendel, his destruction of Grendel's hideous and vengeful mother, and (some five decades later) his effort to destroy the fire-breathing dragon which threatens his people. These stories—the stuff of legend, folk tale, and fantasy—immortalize the mythic origins of the Anglo-Saxons. Composed in the newly Christianized England of the eighth century, the poem was not written down for another two centuries. Only a full reading of *Beowulf* conveys its significance as a work of art. However, the passage that follows—from a modern translation by Burton Raffel—offers an idea of the poem's vigorous style and narrative. The excerpt (lines 2510–2601 of the work), which describes Beowulf's assault on the fire-dragon, opens with a "battle-vow" that broadcasts the boastful courage of the epic hero. Those who wish to know the outcome of this gory contest must read further in the poem.

READING 11.1 From *Beowulf*

And Beowulf uttered his final boast: 1
    "I've never known fear; as a youth I fought
In endless battles. I am old, now,
But I will fight again, seek fame still,
If the dragon hiding in his tower dares   5
To face me."
    Then he said farewell to his followers,
Each in his turn, for the last time:
    "I'd use no sword, no weapon, if this beast
Could be killed without it, crushed to death
Like Grendel, gripped in my hands and torn   10
Limb from limb. But his breath will be burning
Hot, poison will pour from his tongue.
I feel no shame, with shield and sword
And armor, against this monster: when he comes to me
I mean to stand, not run from his shooting   15
Flames, stand till fate decides
Which of us wins. My heart is firm,
My hands calm: I need no hot
Words. Wait for me close by, my friends.
We shall see, soon, who will survive   20

This bloody battle, stand when the fighting
Is done. No one else could do
What I mean to, here, no man but me
Could hope to defeat this monster. No one
Could try. And this dragon's treasure, his gold   25
And everything hidden in that tower, will be mine
Or war will sweep me to a bitter death!"
    Then Beowulf rose, still brave, still strong,
And with his shield at his side, and a mail shirt on his breast,
Strode calmly, confidently, toward the tower, under   30
The rocky cliffs: no coward could have walked there!
And then he who'd endured dozens of desperate
Battles, who'd stood boldly while swords and shields
Clashed, the best of kings, saw
Huge stone arches and felt the heat   35
Of the dragon's breath, flooding down
Through the hidden entrance, too hot for anyone
To stand, a streaming current of fire
And smoke that blocked all passage. And the Geats'[1]
Lord and leader, angry, lowered   40
His sword and roared out a battle cry,
A call so loud and clear that it reached through
The hoary rock, hung in the dragon's
Ear. The beast rose, angry,
Knowing a man had come—and then nothing   45
But war could have followed. Its breath came first,
A steaming cloud pouring from the stone,
Then the earth itself shook. Beowulf
Swung his shield into place, held it
In front of him, facing the entrance. The dragon   50
Coiled and uncoiled, its heart urging it
Into battle. Beowulf's ancient sword
Was waiting, unsheathed, his sharp and gleaming
Blade. The beast came closer; both of them
Were ready, each set on slaughter. The Geats'   55
Great prince stood firm, unmoving, prepared
Behind his high shield, waiting in his shining
Armor. The monster came quickly toward him,
Pouring out fire and smoke, hurrying
To its fate. Flames beat at the iron   60
Shield, and for a time it held, protected
Beowulf as he'd planned; then it began to melt,
And for the first time in his life that famous prince
Fought with fate against him, with glory
Denied him. He knew it, but he raised his sword   65
And struck at the dragon's scaly hide.
The ancient blade broke, bit into
The monster's skin, drew blood, but cracked
And failed him before it went deep enough, helped him
Less than he needed. The dragon leaped   70
With pain, thrashed and beat at him, spouting
Murderous flames, spreading them everywhere.
And the Geats' ring-giver did not boast of glorious
Victories in other wars: his weapon
Had failed him, deserted him, now when he needed it   75

[1] The Scandinavian tribe led by Beowulf.

Most, that excellent sword. Edgetho's
Famous son stared at death,
Unwilling to leave this world, to exchange it
For a dwelling in some distant place—a journey
Into darkness that all men must make, as death   80
Ends their few brief hours on earth.
   Quickly, the dragon came at him, encouraged
As Beowulf fell back; its breath flared,
And he suffered, wrapped around in swirling
Flames—a king, before, but now   85
A beaten warrior. None of his comrades
Came to him, helped him, his brave and noble
Followers; they ran for their lives, fled
Deep in a wood. And only one of them
Remained, stood there, miserable, remembering,   90
As a good man must, what kinship should mean. . . .

Q **How does the poet bring color and excitement
to Beowulf's assault on the fire-dragon?**

Germanic Art

The artistic production of nomadic peoples consists largely of easily transported objects such as carpets, jewelry, and
weapons. Germanic folk often buried the most lavish of
these items with their deceased chieftains in boats that
were cast out to sea (as described in *Beowulf*). In 1939,
archeologists at Sutton Hoo in eastern England excavated
a seventh-century Anglo-Saxon grave that contained
weapons, coins, utensils, jewelry, and a small lyre. These
treasures were packed, along with the corpse of their chieftain, into an 89-foot-long ship that served as a tomb.

Among the remarkable metalwork items found at
Sutton Hoo were gold buckles, shoulder clasps, and the lid
of a purse designed to hang from the chieftain's waistbelt
(Figure **11.2**). These objects are adorned with semiprecious stones and *cloisonné*—enamelwork produced by
pouring molten colored glass between thin gold partitions
(Figure **11.3**). The purse lid is ornamented with a series of
motifs: interlaced fighting animals, two frontal male figures

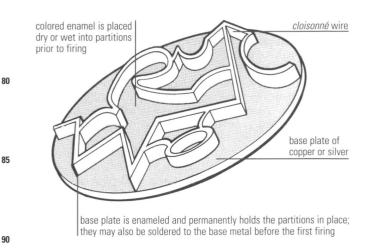

colored enamel is placed
dry or wet into partitions
prior to firing

cloisonné wire

base plate of
copper or silver

base plate is enameled and permanently holds the partitions in place;
they may also be soldered to the base metal before the first firing

Figure 11.3 *Cloisonné* enameling process.

between pairs of rampant beasts (compare Figure 1.3), and
two curved-beaked predators attacking wild birds. These
motifs explore the interface between man and beast in
what was primarily a hunting society. A 5-pound gold belt
buckle is richly ornamented with a dense pattern of interlaced snakes incised with a black sulfurous substance called
niello (see Figure 11.4).

The high quality of so-called "barbarian" art, as evi-
denced at Sutton Hoo and elsewhere, shows that technical
sophistication and artistic originality were by no means the
monopoly of "civilized" societies. It also demonstrates the
continuous diffusion and exchange of styles across Asia
and into Europe. The **zoomorphic** (animal-shaped) motifs
found on the artifacts at Sutton Hoo, along with many of
the metalwork techniques used in their fabrication, are evidence of contact between the Germanic tribes and the
nomadic populations of Central Asia, who perpetuated the
decorative traditions of ancient Persian, Scythian, and
Chinese craftspeople.

As the Germanic tribes poured into Europe, their art
and their culture commingled with that of the people with
whom they came into contact. A classic example is the

Figure 11.2 Sutton Hoo purse cover,
East Anglia, England, ca. 630. Gold
with garnets and *cloisonné* enamel,
8 in. long. The Germanic tribes
carried west techniques and motifs
popular in the arts of the nomadic
peoples of Mesopotamia and the
Russian steppes. Compare the
frontal male figures flanked by
animals on the purse lid with the
image of Gilgamesh standing
between two human-headed bulls
(see Figure 1.3).

MAKING CONNECTIONS

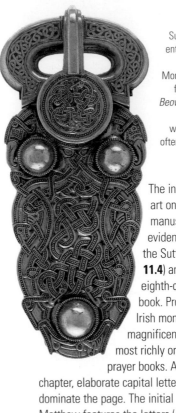

Figure 11.4 Buckle, from Sutton Hoo, first half of seventh century. Gold and niello, length 5¼ in., weight 5 lb. Monsters and serpents, which figure in the Germanic epic *Beowulf*, were associated with the dark forces of nature, while knots and braids were often seen as magical devices.

The influence of Anglo-Saxon art on early medieval manuscript illumination is evident in the comparison of the Sutton Hoo buckle (Figure **11.4**) and the Book of Kells, an eighth-century Latin Gospel book. Produced by monks at the Irish monastery of Kells, this magnificent manuscript is the most richly ornamented of all Celtic prayer books. At the beginning of each chapter, elaborate capital letters make up designs that dominate the page. The initial page of the Gospel of Matthew features the letters (*chi, rho, iota*) of the Greek word *Christos*, which opens the Gospel (Figure **11.5**). Like a sheet of metal engraved with the decorative devices of Anglo-Saxon weapons and jewelry, the parchment page is covered with a profusion of spirals, knots, scrolls, interlaced snakes, and, here and there, human and animal forms. As early as the eleventh century, this manuscript was known as "the chief relic of the Western world."

Figure 11.5 Monogram XPI, first page of Matthew's Gospel, Book of Kells, ca. 800 C.E. Manuscript illumination, 13 × 9½ in. Because of its similarities to the techniques and devices of Germanic metalwork, this and other folios in the Book of Kells have inspired historians to dub its artist "the Goldsmith."

fusion of Celtic and Anglo-Saxon styles. The Celts were a non-Germanic, Iron Age folk that had migrated throughout Europe between the fifth and third centuries B.C.E., settling in the British Isles before the time of Christ. A great flowering of Celtic art and literature occurred in Ireland and England following the conversion of the Celts to Christianity in the fifth century C.E. The instrument of this conversion was the fabled Saint Patrick (ca. 385–461), the British monk who is said to have baptized more than 120,000 people and founded 300 churches in Ireland. In the centuries thereafter, Anglo-Irish monasteries produced a number of extraordinary illuminated manuscripts, whose decorative style is closely related to the dynamic linear ornamentation of the Sutton Hoo artifacts.

The syncretic union of Germanic, Asiatic, and Mediterranean techniques and motifs influenced both the illumination of Christian manuscripts and the production of Christian liturgical objects, such as the **paten** (Eucharistic plate) and the **chalice** (Eucharistic cup). Used in the celebration of the Mass, these objects usually commanded the finest and most costly materials; and, like the manuscripts that accompanied the sacred rites, they received inordinate care in execution. The Ardagh Chalice, made of silver, gilded bronze, gold wire, glass, and enamel, displays the technical virtuosity of early eighth-century metalworkers in Ireland (Figure **11.6**). On the surface of the vessel, a band of interlace designs is offset by raised roundels worked in enamel and gold thread. Clearly, in the liturgical objects and illuminated manuscripts of the Early Middle Ages, the abstract, ornamental Germanic style provided Christian art with an aesthetic alternative to Classical modes of representation.

Charlemagne and the Carolingian Renaissance

From the time he came to the throne in 768 until his death in 814, the Frankish chieftain Charles the Great (in French, "Charlemagne") pursued the dream of restoring the Roman Empire under Christian leadership. A great warrior and an able administrator, the fair-haired heir to the Frankish kingdom conquered vast areas of land (Map 11.2). His holy wars resulted in the forcible conversion of the Saxons east of the Rhine River, the Lombards of northern Italy, and the Slavic peoples along the Danube. Charlemagne's campaigns also pushed the Muslims back beyond the Pyrenees into Spain.

In the year 800, Pope Leo III crowned Charlemagne "Emperor of the Romans," thus establishing a firm relationship between Church and state. But, equally significantly, Charlemagne's role in creating a Roman Christian or "Holy" Roman Empire cast him as the prototype of Christian kingship. For the more than thirty years during which he waged wars in the name of Christ, Charlemagne sought to control conquered lands by placing them in the hands of local administrators—on whom he bestowed the titles "count"

Figure 11.6 Ardagh Chalice, from Ireland, early eighth century. Silver, gilt bronze, gold wire, glass, and enamel.

Map 11.2 The Empire of Charlemagne, 814. It required thirty-two campaigns to subdue the Saxons living between the Rhine and Elbe Rivers. The eastern frontier brought Slavs, Avars, and other Asiatic peoples under Charlemagne's rule in an area that later became Austria. The Spanish March (or Mark) established a frontier against the Muslims.

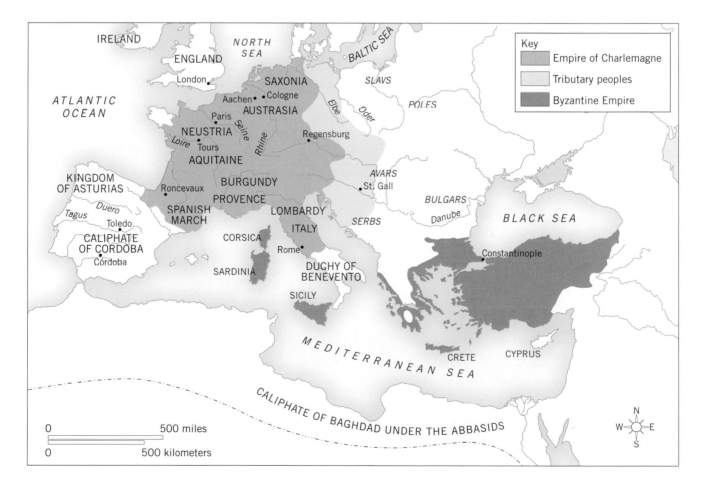

and "duke"—and by periodically sending out royal envoys to carry his edicts abroad. He revived trade with the East, stabilized the currency of the realm, and even pursued diplomatic ties with Baghdad, whose caliph, Harun al-Rashid, graced Charlemagne's court with the gift of an elephant.

Charlemagne's imperial mission was animated by a passionate interest in education and the arts. Having visited San Vitale in Ravenna (see Figures 9.15, 9.16), he had its architectural plan and decorative program imitated in the Palatine Chapel at Aachen (Figure **11.7**). The topmost tier, crowned by a mosaic dome, represented Heaven and the bottom tier the earth, where priest and congregation met for worship; enthroned in the gallery between, which was connected by a passageway to the royal palace, Charlemagne

assumed his symbolic role as mediator between God and ordinary mortals. Alert to the legacy of his forebears, he revived the bronze-casting techniques of Roman sculptors, though on a small scale (Figure **11.8**). Despite the fact that he himself could barely read and write—his sword hand was, according to his biographers, so callused that he had great difficulty forming letters—he sponsored a revival of learning and literacy. To initiate this **renaissance** or "rebirth," Charlemagne invited to his court missionaries and scholars from all over Europe. He established schools at Aachen (Aix-la-Chapelle), in town centers throughout the Empire, and in Benedictine monasteries such as that at Saint-Gall in Switzerland (see Figure 11.12). In Carolingian ***scriptoria*** (monastic writing rooms), monks and nuns copied

Figure 11.7 Odo of Metz, Palatine Chapel of Charlemagne, Aachen, Germany, 792–805.

Figure 11.8 Equestrian statuette of Charlemagne, from Metz, ninth century. Bronze with traces of gilt, height 9½ in. Although this sculpture is less than 10 inches high, it shares the monumental presence of its Classical predecessor, the equestrian statue of Marcus Aurelius (see Figure 6.23).

Figure 11.9
Comparison of Merovingian (pre-Carolingian) book script and Caroline (Carolingian) minuscule.

Figure 11.10 *The Ascension*, from the Sacramentary of Archbishop Drogo of Metz, ca. 842.

religious manuscripts, along with texts on medicine, drama, and other secular subjects. The scale of the Carolingian renaissance is evident in that eighty percent of the oldest surviving Classical Latin manuscripts exist in Carolingian copies.

Carolingian copyists rejected the Roman script, which lacked punctuation and spaces between words, in favor of a neat, uniform writing style known as the minuscule (Figure **11.9**), the ancestor of modern typography. The decorative programs of many Carolingian manuscripts reflect the union of late Roman Realism and Germanic stylization. The former is revealed in the pictorial narrative that fills (or "historiates") the capital letter in Figure **11.10**, while the latter is seen in the ribbonlike pattern of the initial itself. But the Carolingian Renaissance was not limited to the copying of manuscripts. Among the most magnificent artifacts of the period were liturgical and devotional objects, often made of ivory or precious metals. Dating from the decades after Charlemagne's death, the

book cover for the Lindau Gospels testifies to the superior technical abilities of Carolingian metalsmiths (Figure **11.11**). The surface of the back cover, worked in silver gilt, inlaid with *cloisonné* enamel, and encrusted with precious gems, consists of an ornate Greek cross that dominates a field of writhing, interlaced creatures similar to those found in Anglo-Saxon metalwork (see Figure 11.4) and Anglo-Irish manuscripts. At the corners of the inner rectangle of the book cover are four tiny scenes showing the evangelists at their writing desks. These realistically conceived representations contrast sharply with the more stylized figural images that appear in the arms of the cross.

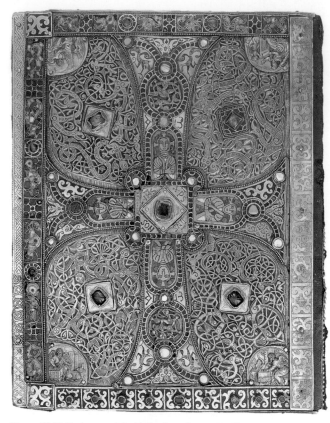

Figure 11.11 Back cover of the Lindau Gospels, ca. 870. Silver gilt with *cloisonné* enamel and precious stones, 13⅜ × 10⅜ in.

The integration of Germanic, Roman, and Byzantine stylistic traditions evident in the cover of the Lindau Gospels typifies the Carolingian Renaissance, the glories of which would not be matched for at least three centuries.

The Abbey Church

During the Carolingian Renaissance, Charlemagne authorized the construction of numerous Benedictine monasteries, or abbeys. Central to each abbey was a church that served as a place of worship and as a shrine that housed sacred relics. Though built on a smaller scale than that of Early Christian churches, most abbey churches were simple basilicas with square towers added at the west entrance and at the crossing of the nave and transept.

In the construction of the abbey church, as in the arrangement of the monastic complex as a whole, Carolingian architects pursued a strict geometry governed by Classical principles of symmetry and order. The plan for an ideal monastery (Figure **11.12**) found in a manuscript in the library of the monastery of Saint-Gall, Switzerland, reflects these concerns: each part of the complex, from **refectory** (dining hall) to cemetery, is fixed on the gridlike plan according to its practical function. Monks gained access to the church, for example, by means of both the adjacent dormitory and the cloister. At the abbey church of Saint-Gall, where a second transept provided longitudinal symmetry, the monks added chapels along the aisles and transepts to house relics of saints and martyrs whose bones had been exhumed from the Roman catacombs.

Early Medieval Culture

Feudal Society

When Charlemagne died in the year 814, the short-lived unity he had brought to Western Europe died with him. Although he had turned the Frankish kingdom into an empire, he failed to establish any legal and administrative machinery comparable with that of imperial Rome. There was no standing army, no system of taxation, and no single code of law to unify the widely diverse population. Following his death, the fragile stability of the Carolingian Empire was shattered by Scandinavian seafarers known as Vikings. Charlemagne's sons and grandsons could not repel the raids of these fierce invaders, who ravaged the northern coasts of the Empire; at the same time, neither were his heirs able to arrest the repeated forays of the Muslims along the Mediterranean coast. Lacking effective leadership, the Carolingian Empire disintegrated.

In the mid-ninth century, Charlemagne's three grandsons divided the Empire among themselves, separating French- from German-speaking territories. Increasingly, however, administration and protection fell to members of the local ruling aristocracy—heirs of the counts and dukes whom Charlemagne had appointed to administer portions of the realm, or simply those who had taken land by force. The fragmentation of the Empire and the insecurity generated by the Viking invasions caused people at all social

Figure 11.12 Plan for an ideal Benedictine monastery, ninth century. 13½ × 10¼ in.

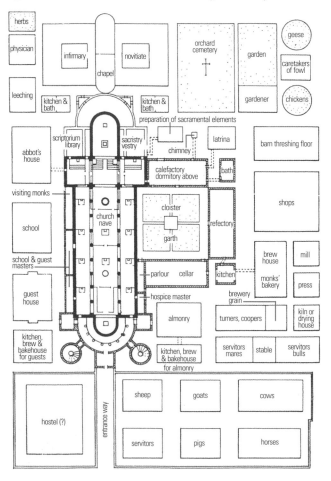

levels to attach themselves to members of a military nobility who were capable of providing protection. These circumstances enhanced the growth of a unique system of political and military organization known as **feudalism**.

Derived from Roman and Germanic traditions of rewarding warriors with the spoils of war, feudalism involved the exchange of land for military service. In return for the grant of land, known as a **fief** or *feudum* (the Germanic word for "property"), a **vassal** owed his **lord** a certain number of fighting days (usually forty) per year. The contract between lord and vassal also involved a number of other obligations, including the lord's provision of a court of justice, the vassal's contribution of ransom if his lord were captured, and the reciprocation of hospitality between the two. In an age of instability, feudalism provided a rudimentary form of local government while answering the need for security against armed attack.

Those engaged in the feudal contract constituted roughly the upper 10 percent of European society. The feudal nobility, which bore the twin responsibilities of military defense and political leadership, was a closed class of men and women whose superior status was inherited at birth. A male member of the nobility was first and foremost a mounted man-at-arms—a *chevalier* (from the French *cheval*, for "horse") or knight (from the Germanic *Knecht*, a youthful servant or soldier). The medieval knight was a cavalry warrior equipped with stirrups, protected by **chain mail** (flexible armor made of interlinked metal rings), and armed with such weapons as broadsword and shield.

The knight's conduct and manners in all aspects of life were guided by a strict code of behavior called **chivalry**. Chivalry demanded that the knight be courageous in battle, loyal to his lord and fellow warriors, and reverent toward women. Feudal life was marked by ceremonies and symbols almost as extensive as those of the Christian Church. For instance, a vassal received his fief by an elaborate procedure known as **investiture**, in which oaths of fealty were formally exchanged (Figure **11.13**). In warfare, adversaries usually fixed the time and place of combat in advance. Medieval warfare was both a profession and a pastime, as knights entertained themselves with **jousts** (personal combat between men on horseback) or war games that imitated the trials of combat (Figure **11.14**).

Women played an active role in the chivalric society of the Middle Ages. In many parts of Europe they inherited land,

Figure 11.13 MATTHEW PARIS, *Vassal Paying Homage to his Lord,* from the Westminster Psalter, ca. 1250. The feudal status (or aristocratic lineage) of the medieval European soldier was usually indicated by heraldic devices painted on his shield or helmet, embroidered on his tunic (worn here over his protective chain mail), or displayed on flags.

which they usually defended by means of hired soldiers. A woman controlled her fief until she married, and regained it upon becoming a widow. Men and women took great pride in their aristocratic lineage and advertised the family name by means of heraldic devices emblazoned on tunics, pennants, and shields (see Figure 11.13).

Figure 11.14 French plaque from a casket, fourteenth century. Ivory, 3⅛ × ⅝ in.

The Literature of the Feudal Nobility

The ideals of the fighting nobility in a feudal age are best captured in the oldest and greatest French epic poem, the *Song of Roland*. It is based on an event that took place in 778—the ambush of Charlemagne's rear guard, led by Charlemagne's nephew Roland, as they returned from an expedition against the Muslims in Spain. This 4000-line **chanson de geste** ("song of heroic deeds") was transmitted orally for three centuries and not written down until the early 1100s. Generation after generation of **jongleurs** (professional entertainers) wandered from court to court, chanting the story (and possibly embellishing it with episodes of folklore) to the accompaniment of a lyre. Although the music for the poem has not survived, it is likely that it consisted of a single and highly improvised line of melody. The tune was probably syllabic (setting one note to each syllable) and—like folk song—dependent on simple repetition.

As with other works in the oral tradition (the *Epic of Gilgamesh* and the *Iliad*, for instance), the *Song of Roland* is grandiose in its dimensions and profound in its lyric power. Its rugged Old French verse describes a culture that prized the performance of heroic deeds that brought honor to the warrior, his lord, and his religion. The strong bond of loyalty between vassal and chieftain that characterized the Germanic way of life resonates in Roland's declaration of unswerving devotion to his temporal overlord, Charlemagne.

The *Song of Roland* brings to life such aspects of early medieval culture as the practice of naming one's battle gear and weapons (often considered sacred), the dependence on cavalry, the glorification of blood-and-thunder heroism, and the strong sense of comradeship among men-at-arms. Women play almost no part in the epic. The feudal contract did not exclude members of the clergy; hence Archbishop Turpin fights with lance and spear, despite the fact that church law forbade members of the clergy to shed another man's blood. (Some members of the clergy got around this law by arming themselves with a **mace**—a spike-headed club that could knock one's armored opponent off his horse or do damage short of bloodshed.) Roland's willingness to die for his religious beliefs, fired by the archbishop's promise of admission into paradise for those who fall fighting the infidels (in this case, the Muslims), suggests that the militant fervor of Muslims was matched by that of early medieval Christians. Indeed, the *Song of Roland* captures the powerful antagonism between Christians and Muslims that dominated all of medieval history and culminated in the Christian Crusades described later in this chapter.

The descriptive language of the *Song of Roland* is stark, unembellished, and vivid: "he feels his brain gush out," reports the poet in verse 168. Such directness and simplicity lend immediacy to the action. Characters are stereotypical ("Roland's a hero, and Oliver is wise," verse 87), and groups of people are characterized with epic expansiveness: *all* Christians are good and *all* Muslims are bad. The figure of Roland epitomizes the ideals of physical courage, religious devotion, and personal loyalty. Yet, in his refusal to call for assistance from Charlemagne and his troops, who have already retreated across the Pyrenees, he exhibits a foolhardiness—perhaps a "tragic flaw"—that leads him and his warriors to their deaths.

READING 11.2 From the *Song of Roland*

81

Count Oliver has climbed up on a hill;	1
From there he sees the Spanish lands below,	
And Saracens[1] assembled in great force.	
Their helmets gleam with gold and precious stones,	
Their shields are shining, their hauberks[2] burnished gold,	5
Their long sharp spears with battle flags unfurled.	
He tries to see how many men there are:	
Even battalions are more than he can count.	
And in his heart Oliver is dismayed;	
Quick as he can, he comes down from the height,	10
And tells the Franks what they will have to fight.	

82

Oliver says, "Here come the Saracens—	
A greater number no man has ever seen!	
The first host carries a hundred thousand shields,	
Their helms are laced, their hauberks shining white,	15
From straight wood handles rise ranks of burnished spears.	
You'll have a battle like none on earth before!	
Frenchmen, my lords, now God give you the strength	
To stand your ground, and keep us from defeat."	
They say, "God's curse on those who quit the field!	20
We're yours till death—not one of us will yield." AOI[3]	

83

Oliver says, "The pagan might is great—	
It seems to me, our Franks are very few!	
Roland, my friend, it's time to sound your horn;	
King Charles[4] will hear, and bring his army back."	25
Roland replies, "You must think I've gone mad!	
In all sweet France I'd forfeit my good name!	
No! I will strike great blows with Durendal,[5]	
Crimson the blade up to the hilt of gold.	
To those foul pagans I promise bitter woe—	30
They all are doomed to die at Roncevaux!"[6] AOI	

---

[1] Another name for Muslims.
[2] Long coats of chain mail.
[3] The letters AOI have no known meaning but probably signify a musical appendage or refrain that occurred at the end of each stanza.
[4] Charlemagne.
[5] Roland's sword.
[6] "The gate of Spain," a narrow pass in the Pyrenees where the battle takes place.

84

"Roland, my friend, let the Oliphant[7] sound!
King Charles will hear it, his host will all turn back,
His valiant barons will help us in this fight."
Roland replies, "Almighty God forbid   35
That I bring shame upon my family,
And cause sweet France to fall into disgrace!
I'll strike that horde with my good Durendal;
My sword is ready, girded here at my side,
And soon you'll see its keen blade dripping blood.   40
The Saracens will curse the evil day
They challenged us, for we will make them pay."   AOI

85

"Roland, my friend I pray you, sound your horn!
King Charlemagne, crossing the mountain pass,
Won't fail, I swear it, to bring back all his Franks."   45
"May God forbid!" Count Roland answers then.
"No man on earth shall have the right to say
That I for pagans sounded the Oliphant!
I will not bring my family to shame.
I'll fight this battle; my Durendal shall strike   50
A thousand blows and seven hundred more;
You'll see bright blood flow from the blade's keen steel.
We have good men; their prowess will prevail,
And not one Spaniard shall live to tell the tale."

86

Oliver says, "Never would you be blamed;   55
I've seen the pagans, the Saracens of Spain.
They fill the valleys, cover the mountain peaks;
On every hill, and every wide-spread plain,
Vast hosts assemble from that alien race;
Our company numbers but very few."   60
Roland replies, "The better, then, we'll fight!
If it please God and His angelic host,
I won't betray the glory of sweet France!
Better to die than learn to live with shame—
Charles loves us more as our keen swords win fame."   65

87

Roland's a hero, and Oliver is wise;
Both are so brave men marvel at their deeds.
When they mount chargers, take up their swords and shields,
Not death itself could drive them from the field.
They are good men; their words are fierce and proud.   70
With wrathful speed the pagans ride to war.
Oliver says, "Roland, you see them now.
They're very close, the king too far away.
You were too proud to sound the Oliphant:
If Charles were with us, we would not come to grief.   75
Look up above us, close to the Gate of Spain:
There stands the guards—who would not pity them!

To fight this battle means not to fight again."
Roland replies, "Don't speak so foolishly!
Cursed be the heart that cowers in the breast!   80
We'll hold our ground; if they will meet us here,
Our foes will find us ready with sword and spear."   AOI

88

When Roland sees the fight will soon begin,
Lions and leopards are not so fierce as he.
Calling the Franks, he says to Oliver: 85
"Noble companion, my friend, don't talk that way!
The Emperor Charles, who left us in command
Of twenty thousand he chose to guard the pass,
Made very sure no coward's in their ranks.
In his lord's service a man must suffer pain,   90
Bitterest cold and burning heat endure;
He must be willing to lose his flesh and blood.
Strike with your lance, and I'll wield Durendal—
The king himself presented it to me—
And if I die, whoever takes my sword   95
Can say its master has nobly served his lord."

89

Archbishop Turpin comes forward then to speak.
He spurs his horse and gallops up a hill,
Summons the Franks, and preaches in these words:
"My noble lords, Charlemagne left us here,   100
And may our deaths do honor to the king!
Now you must help defend our holy Faith!
Before your eyes you see the Saracens.
Confess your sins, ask God to pardon you;
I'll grant you absolution to save your souls.   105
Your deaths would be a holy martyrdom,
And you'll have places in highest Paradise."
The French dismount; they kneel upon the ground.
Then the archbishop, blessing them in God's name,
Told them, for penance, to strike when battle came. 110

. . . .

91

At Roncevaux Count Roland passes by,
Riding his charger, swift-running Veillantif [8]
He's armed for battle, splendid in shining mail.
As he parades, he brandishes his lance.
Turning the point straight up against the sky,   115
And from the spearhead a banner flies, pure white,
With long gold fringes that beat against his hands.
Fair to behold, he laughs, serene and gay.
Now close behind him comes Oliver, his friend,
With all the Frenchmen cheering their mighty lord.   120
Fiercely his eyes confront the Saracens;
Humbly and gently he gazes at the Franks,
Speaking to them with gallant courtesy:
"Barons, my lords, softly now, keep the pace!

---

[7] A horn made from an elephant's tusk.

[8] Roland's horse.

Here come the pagans looking for martyrdom. 125
We'll have such plunder before the day is out,
As no French king has ever won before!"
And at this moment the armies join in war. AOI

. . . .

161

The pagans flee, furious and enraged,
Trying their best to get away in Spain. 130
Count Roland lacks the means to chase them now,
For he has lost his war-horse Veillantif;
Against his will he has to go on foot.
He went to give Archbishop Turpin help,
Unlaced his helmet, removed it from his head, 135
And then took off the hauberk of light mail;
The under-tunic he cut into long strips
With which he stanched the largest of his wounds.
Then lifting Turpin, carried him in his arms
To soft green grass, and gently laid him down. 140
In a low voice Roland made this request:
"My noble lord, I pray you, give me leave,
For our companions, the men we held so dear,
Must not be left abandoned now in death.
I want to go and seek out every one, 145
Carry them here, and place them at your feet."
Said the archbishop, "I grant it willingly.
The field belongs, thank God, to you and me."

162

Alone, Count Roland walks through the battlefield,
Searching the valleys, searching the mountain heights. 150
He found the bodies of Ivon and Ivoire,
And then he found the Gascon Engelier.
Gerin he found, and Gerier his friend,
He found Aton and then Count Bérengier,
Proud Anseïs he found, and then Samson, 155
Gérard the Old, the Count of Roussillon.
He took these barons, and carried every one
Back to the place where the archbishop was,
And then he put them in ranks at Turpin's knees.
Seeing them, Turpin cannot restrain his tears; 160
Raising his hand, he blesses all the dead.
And then he says, "You've come to grief, my lords!
Now in His glory, may God receive your souls,
Among bright flowers set you in Paradise!
It's my turn now; death keeps me in such pain, 165
Never again will I see Charlemagne."

163

Roland goes back to search the field once more,
And his companion he finds there, Oliver.
Lifting him in his arms he holds him close,
Brings him to Turpin as quickly as he can, 170
Beside the others places him on a shield;
Turpin absolves him, signing him with the cross,
And then they yield to pity and to grief.

Count Roland says, "Brother in arms, fair friend,
You were the son of Renier, the duke 175
Who held the land where Runers valley lies.
For breaking lances, for shattering thick shields,
Bringing the proud to terror and defeat,
For giving counsel, defending what is right,
In all the world there is no better knight." 180

164

When Roland sees that all his peers are dead,
And Oliver whom he so dearly loved,
He feels such sorrow that he begins to weep;
Drained of all color, his face turns ashen pale,
His grief is more than any man could bear, 185
He falls down, fainting whether he will or no.
Says the archbishop, "Baron, you've come to woe."

. . . .

168

Now Roland knows that death is very near.
His ears give way, he feels his brain gush out.
He prays that God will summon all his peers; 190
Then, for himself, he prays to Gabriel.
Taking the horn, to keep it from all shame,
With Durendal clasped in his other hand,
He goes on, farther than a good cross-bow shot,
West into Spain, crossing a fallow field. 195
Up on a hilltop, under two lofty trees.
Four marble blocks are standing on the grass.
But when he comes there, Count Roland faints once more,
He falls down backward; now he is at death's door.

. . . .

174

Count Roland feels the very grip of death 200
Which from his head is reaching for his heart.
He hurries then to go beneath a pine;
In the green grass he lies down on his face,
Placing beneath him the sword and Oliphant;
He turns his head to look toward pagan Spain. 205
He does these things in order to be sure
King Charles will say, and with him all the Franks,
The noble count conquered until he died.
He makes confession, for all his sins laments.
Offers his glove to God in penitence. AOI 210

Q **What aspects of European feudalism are brought to life in the Song of Roland?**

The Norman Conquest and the Arts

As early as the eighth century the seafarers known as Vikings (but also as Norsemen, Northmen, and later, Normans) had moved beyond the bounds of their Scandinavian homelands. They constructed long wooden ships equipped with sailing gear that allowed them to tack into the wind. Expert shipbuilders, sailors, and navigators, they soon came to control the North Atlantic. The western Vikings were the first to colonize Iceland, and they set up a colony in Greenland before the year 1000. The eastern Vikings sailed across the North Sea to establish trading centers at Kiev and Novgorod. Known among Arab traders of this area as "*rus*," they gave their name to Russia. They traded animal hides, amber, and other valued items, including captive Eastern Europeans—Slavs—from which the English word "slave" derives.

The Vikings began their raids on England with an attack on the Lindisfarne monastery in 793, and by the end of the ninth century, they had settled throughout Northern Europe. Within 100 years, they made Normandy one of the strongest fiefs in France. In 1066, under the leadership of William of Normandy, some 5000 men crossed the English Channel; at the Battle of Hastings, William defeated the Anglo-Saxon duke Harold and seized the throne of England. The Norman Conquest had enormous consequences for the histories of England and France, for it marked the transfer of power in England from Anglo-Saxons to Normans who, already vassals of the king of France, were now also the ruling lords of England.

The Normans brought feudalism to England. To raise money, William ordered a detailed census of all property in the realm—the *Domesday Book*—which laid the basis for the collection of taxes. King William controlled all aspects of government with the aid of the *Curia Regis*—the royal court and council consisting of his feudal barons. Under the Norman kings, England would become one of Europe's leading medieval states.

The Normans led the way in the construction of stone castles and churches. Atop hills and at such vulnerable sites as Dover on the southeast coast of England, Norman kings erected austere castle-fortresses (Figure **11.15**). The castle featured a **keep** (square tower) containing a dungeon, a main hall, and a chapel, and incorporated a central open space with workshops and storehouses (Figure **11.16**). The enclosing stone walls were usually surmounted by turrets with **crenellations** that provided archers with protection in defensive combat. A **moat** (a trench usually filled with water) often surrounded the castle walls to deter enemy invasion. The brilliance of the Normans' achievements in architecture, apparent in their fortresses and churches (see chapter 13), lies in the use of stone to replace earlier timber fortifications and in the clarity with which the form of the building reflects its function.

The Bayeux Tapestry

One of the most famous Norman artifacts is the Bayeux Tapestry. Not an actual tapestry, but an embroidery, it is an

Figure 11.15 Dover Castle, Kent, England, twelfth century. While William's first stone fortification was the Tower of London, he constructed an earthwork castle at Dover, a defensive site that earlier held a Roman lighthouse and an Anglo-Saxon fortress. During the twelfth century Henry II rebuilt the castle in stone.

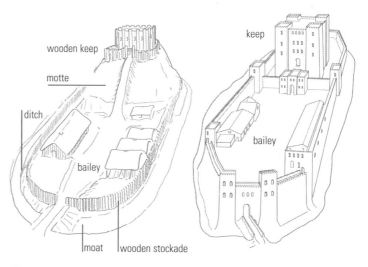

Figure 11.16 Development of the Norman castle.

unusual visual record of the conquest of England by William of Normandy. Named for the city in northwestern France where it was made and where it is still displayed today, it documents the history and folklore of the Normans with the same energetic spirit that animates the *Song of Roland*. Sewn into the bleached linen cloth, some 20 inches high and 231 feet long, are lively representations of the incidents leading up to and including the Battle of Hastings (see Figure 11.1 and Figure **11.17**). Above and alongside the images are Latin captions that serve to identify characters, places, and events. The seventy-nine scenes in this wall-hanging progress in the manner of a parchment scroll or a cartoon comic strip (they also call to mind the

Figure 11.17 *The Battle Rages*, detail from the Bayeux Tapestry, late eleventh century. Wool embroidery on linen, depth approx. 20 in., entire length 231 ft. The Latin script embroidered above the action reads, "Here the English and French have fallen together in battle." At the far right, Bishop Odo (on a black stallion) rallies the Norman cavalry with a swinging mace. The bottom register is filled with fallen soldiers, shields, weapons, and a bodiless head.

style of ancient Assyrian narrative reliefs, pictured in chapter 1). Rendered in only eight colors of wool yarn, the ambitious narrative includes 626 figures, 190 horses, and over 500 other animals. Since embroidery was almost exclusively a female occupation, it is likely that the Bayeux Tapestry was the work of women—although women are depicted only four times in the entire piece.

The *Song of Roland* and the Bayeux Tapestry have much in common: both are epic in theme and robust in style. Both consist of sweeping narratives whose episodes are irregular rather than uniform in length. Like the stereotypical (and almost exclusively male) characters in the *chanson*, the figures of the tapestry are delineated by means of expressive gestures and simplified physical features; the Normans, for instance, are distinguished by the shaved backs of their heads. Weapons and armor in both epic and embroidery are described with loving detail. Indeed, in the Bayeux Tapestry, scenes of combat provide a veritable encyclopedia of medieval battle gear: kite-shaped shields, conical iron helmets, hauberks, short bows, double-edged swords, battle axes, and lances. Both the *Song of Roland* and the Bayeux Tapestry offer a vivid record of feudal life in all its heroic splendor.

The Lives of Medieval Serfs

Although the feudal class monopolized land and power within medieval society, this elite group represented only a tiny percentage of the total population. The majority of people—more than 90 percent—were unfree peasants or **serfs** who, along with freemen, farmed the soil. Medieval serfs lived quite differently from their landlords. Bound to large farms or manors they, like the farmers of the old Roman *latifundia* (see chapter 6), provided food in exchange for military protection furnished by the nobility. They owned no property. They were forbidden to leave the land, though, on the positive side, they could not be evicted.

Their bondage to the soil assured them the protection of feudal lords who, in an age lacking effective central authority, were the sole sources of political authority.

During the Middle Ages, the reciprocal obligations of serfs and lords and the serf's continuing tenure on the land became firmly fixed. At least until the eleventh century, the interdependence between the two classes was generally beneficial to both; serfs needed protection, and feudal lords, whose position as gentlemen-warriors excluded them from menial toil, needed food. For upper and lower classes alike, the individual's place in medieval society was inherited and bound by tradition.

A medieval fief usually included one or more manors. The average manor community comprised fifteen to twenty families, while a large manor of 5000 acres might contain some fifty families. The lord usually appointed the local priest, provided a court of justice, and governed the manor from a fortified residence or castle. Between the eighth and tenth centuries, such residences were simple wooden structures but, by the twelfth century, elaborate stone manor houses with crenellated walls and towers became commonplace. On long winter nights, the lord's castle might be the scene of reveling and entertainment by *jongleurs* singing epic tales like the *Song of Roland* (see Reading 11.2).

The typical medieval manor consisted of farmlands, woodland, and pasture, and included a common mill, winepress, and oven (Figure **11.18**). Serfs cultivated the major crops of oats and rye on strips of arable land. In addition to the food they produced from fields reserved for the lord, they owed the lord a percentage—usually a third—of their own agricultural yield. They also performed services in the form of labor. In the medieval world, manor was isolated from manor, and a subsistence economy similar to that of the Neolithic village prevailed. The annual round of peasant labor, beset by a continuing war with the elements, was

harsh and demanding. Nevertheless, during the Early Middle Ages, serfs made considerable progress in farm technology and agricultural practices. They developed the heavy-wheeled plow and the tandem harness, utilized wind and water mills, recovered land by dredging swamps and clearing forests, and offset soil exhaustion by devising systems of crop rotation. The "three-field system," for example, left one-third of the land fallow to allow it to recover its fertility. Such innovations eventually contributed to the production of a food surplus, which in turn stimulated the revival of trade.

Medieval serfs were subject to perennial toil and constant privations, including those of famine and disease. Most could neither read nor write. Unfortunately, art and literature leave us little insight into the lives and values of the lower classes of medieval society. Occasionally, however, in the sculptures

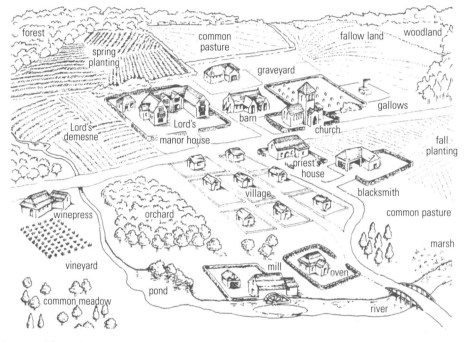

Figure 11.18 The medieval manor.

of laboring peasants found on medieval cathedrals, in stained glass windows (see Figure 13.30), and in medieval manuscripts, we find visual representations of lower-class life. As illustrations from the Luttrell Psalter indicate, peasant women worked alongside men in raising crops: sowing, reaping, gleaning, threshing, and assisting even in the most backbreaking of farming tasks (Figure **11.19**). Medieval women were associated with the professions that involved food preparation (milking, raising vegetables, brewing, and baking) and the making of cloth (sheep-shearing, carting, spinning, and weaving). The distaff, the pole on which fibers were wound prior to spinning, came to be a symbol of women's work and (universally) of womankind. But lower-class women also shared their husbands' domestic tasks and day to day responsibilities that few noblewomen shared with their upper-class partners.

Science and Technology

800	rigging (gear that controls ships' sails to take advantage of the wind) is invented by the Vikings
900	horse collars come into use in Europe
1050	crossbows are first used in France
ca. 1150	the first windmills appear in Europe

Figure 11.19 *Women and Men Reaping*, from the Luttrell Psalter, ca. 1340.

High Medieval Culture

The Christian Crusades

During the eleventh century, numerous circumstances contributed to a change in the character of medieval life. The Normans effectively pushed the Muslims out of the Mediterranean Sea and, as the Normans and other marauders began to settle down, Europeans enjoyed a greater degree of security. At the same time, rising agricultural productivity and surplus encouraged trade and travel. The Crusades of the eleventh to thirteenth centuries

Map 11.3 The Christian Crusades, 1096–1204. Over a period of some 200 years there were seven major crusades and various smaller expeditions. The four most significant crusades are shown here: the first departed from central France and proceeded overland, while the fourth, a maritime venture, began in Venice.

were a symptom of the increased freedom and new mobility of Western Europeans during the High Middle Ages. They were also the product of idealism and religious zeal. The Byzantine emperor had pressed the Catholic Church to aid in delivering the East from the Muslim Turks, who were threatening the Byzantine Empire and denying Christian pilgrims access to the Holy Land.

In 1095, Pope Urban II preached a fiery sermon that called on Christians to rescue Jerusalem from the "accursed race" who had invaded Christian lands. Thousands of laymen and clergy "took up the Cross" and marched across Europe to the Byzantine East (Map **11.3**). Well before reaching their destination, a combination of avarice and religious fervor inspired some of the Crusaders to plunder the cities along the Rhine, robbing and murdering all "enemies" of Christ, including the entire Jewish populations of Cologne and Mainz. While the First Crusade succeeded in recapturing

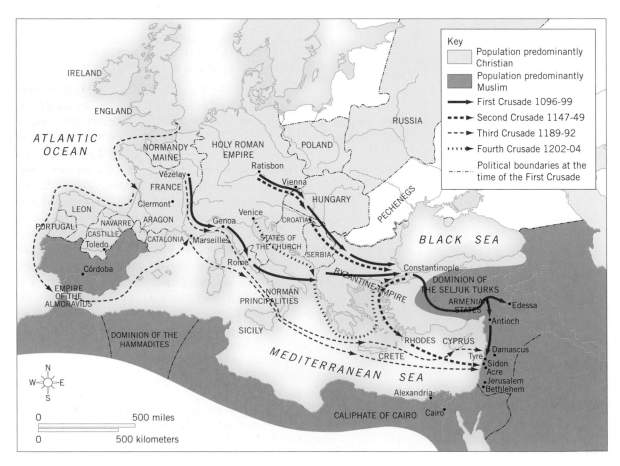

some important cities, including Jerusalem, the Crusades that followed were generally unsuccessful (Figure **11.20**).

It soon became apparent that the material benefits of the Crusades outweighed the spiritual ones, especially in that the campaigns provided economic and military advantages for the younger sons of the nobility. While the eldest son of an upper-class family inherited his father's fief under the principle of **primogeniture**, his younger brothers were left to seek their own fortunes. The Crusades stirred the ambitions of these disenfranchised young men who had been schooled in warfare. Equally ambitious were the Italian city-states, Genoa, Pisa, and Venice. Eager to expand their commercial activities, they encouraged the Crusaders to become middlemen in trade between Italy and the East. In the course of the Fourth Crusade, when the Crusaders could not pay the Venetians for the fleet of ships that was contracted to carry them east, profit-seekers persuaded them to take over (on behalf of Venice) trading ports in the Aegean; from there, the Crusaders went on to plunder and sack Constantinople. Moral inhibitions failed to restrain greed and, in 1204, the Fourth Crusade deteriorated into a contest for personal profit. A disastrous postscript to the Fourth Crusade was the Children's Crusade of 1212, in which thousands of children, aged between ten and fourteen, set out to recapture Jerusalem. Almost all died or were taken into slavery before reaching the Holy Land.

Aside from such economic advantages as those enjoyed by individual Crusaders and the Italian city-states, the gains made by the seven major Crusades were slight. By 1291, all recaptured lands, including the city of Jerusalem, were lost again to the Muslims. Indeed, in over 200 years of fighting and seven major Crusades, the Crusaders did not secure any territory permanently, nor did they stop the westward advance of the Turks. Constantinople finally fell in 1453 to a later wave of Muslim Turks.

Despite their failure as religious ventures, the Crusades had enormous consequences for the West: the revival of trade between East and West enhanced European

commercial life, encouraging the rise of towns and bringing great wealth to the Italian cities of Venice, Genoa, and Pisa. Then, too, in the absence or at the death of crusading noblemen, feudal lords (including emperors and kings) seized every opportunity to establish greater authority over the lands within their domains, thus consolidating and centralizing political power in the embryonic nation-states of England and France. Finally, renewed contact with Byzantium promoted an atmosphere of commercial and cultural exchange that had not existed since Roman times. Luxury goods, such as saffron, citrus, silks, and damasks, entered Western Europe, as did sacred relics associated with the lives of Jesus, Mary, and the Christian saints. And, to the delight of the literate, Arabic translations of Greek manuscripts poured into France, along with all genres of Islamic literature (see chapter 10).

The Medieval Romance and the Code of Courtly Love

The Crusades inspired the writing of chronicles that were an admixture of historical fact, Christian lore, and stirring fiction. As such histories had broad appeal in an age of increasing upper-class literacy, they came to be written in the everyday language of the layperson—the vernacular—rather than in Latin. The Crusades also contributed to the birth of the **medieval romance**, a fictitious tale of love and adventure that became the most popular form of literary entertainment in the West between the years 1200 and 1500. Medieval romances first appeared in twelfth-century France in the form of rhymed verse, but later ones were written in prose. While romances were probably recited before a small, courtly audience rather than read individually, the development of the form coincided with the rise of a European "textual culture," that is, a culture dependent on written language rather than on oral tradition. In this textual culture, vernacular languages gained importance for

Figure 11.20 *French knights under Louis IX besieging Damietta, Egypt,* Seventh Crusade, 1249. After the Muslims recaptured Jerusalem in 1244, King Louis IX of France (better known as "Saint Louis") led the last major Crusade, capturing the Egyptian seaport of Damietta in 1249. But the following year the Egyptians trapped the Crusaders by opening sluice gates for reservoirs on the Nile and surrounding them with floodwater. To secure their escape Louis had to surrender Damietta and pay a large ransom.

intimate kinds of literature, while Latin remained the official language of Church and state.

The "spice" of the typical medieval romance was an illicit relationship or forbidden liaison between a man and woman of the upper class. During the Middle Ages, marriage among members of the nobility was usually an alliance formed in the interest of securing land. Indeed, noble families might arrange marriages for offspring who were still in the cradle. In such circumstances, romantic love was more likely to flourish outside marriage. An adulterous affair between Lancelot, a knight of King Arthur's court, and Guinevere, the king's wife, is central to the popular twelfth-century verse romance *Lancelot*. Written in vernacular French by Chrétien de Troyes (d. ca. 1183), *Lancelot* belongs to a cycle of stories associated with a semilegendary sixth-century Welsh chieftain named Arthur. Chrétien's poem (a portion of which appears in prose translation in the following pages) stands at the beginning of a long tradition of Arthurian romance literature. Filled with bloody combat, supernatural events, and romantic alliances, medieval romances introduced a new and complex picture of human conduct and courtship associated with the so-called "code of courtly love."

Courtly love, as the name suggests, was a phenomenon cultivated in the courts of the medieval nobility. Characterized by the longing of a nobleman for a (usually unattainable) woman, the courtly love tradition, with its "rules" of wooing and winning a lady, laid the basis for concepts of romantic love in Western literature and life. Popularized in twelfth-century manuals of conduct for European aristocrats, the code held that love (whether requited or not) had a purifying and ennobling influence on the lover. To love was to suffer; witness, in the excerpt that follows, Queen Guinevere's distress upon hearing the false report of Lancelot's death. Courtly love was also associated with a variety of distressing physical symptoms, such as an inability to eat or sleep. The tenets of courtly love required that a knight prove his love for his lady by performing daring and often impossible deeds; he must even be willing to die for her. In these features, the medieval romance is far removed from the rugged, bellicose spirit of earlier literary works like the *Song of Roland*. Indeed, *Lancelot* dramatizes the feminization of the chivalric ideal. The *Song of Roland* pictures early medieval culture in terms of heroic idealism and personal loyalty between men. The Arthurian romance, however, redefined these qualities in the direction of sentiment and sensuality. Lancelot fights not for his country, nor even for his lord, but to win the affections of his mistress. His prowess is not exercised, as with Roland, on a field of battle, but as individual combat undertaken in the courtyard of his host. While Roland is motivated by the ideal of glory in battle, Lancelot is driven by his love for Guinevere.

The courtly love tradition contributed to shaping modern Western concepts of gender and courtship. It also worked to define the romantic perception of women as objects, particularly objects of reward for the performance of brave deeds. For although courtly love elevated the woman (and her prototype, the Virgin Mary) as worthy of adoration, it defined her exclusively in terms of the interests of men. Nevertheless, the medieval romance, which flattered and exalted the aristocratic lady as an object of desire, was directed toward a primarily female audience. A product of the aristocratic (and male) imagination, the lady of the medieval romance had no counterpart in the lower classes of society, where women worked side by side with men in the fields (see Figure 11.19) and in a variety of trades. Despite its artificiality, however, the theme of courtly love and the romance itself had a significant influence on Western literary tradition. In that tradition, even into modern times, writers have tended to treat love more as a mode of spiritual purification or as an emotional affliction than as a condition of true affection and sympathy between the sexes.

READING 11.3 From Chrétien de Troyes' *Lancelot* (ca. 1170)

[Gawain and Lancelot, knights of King Arthur's court, set out in quest of Queen Guinevere. In the forest, they meet a damsel, who tells them of the Queen's whereabouts.]

Then the damsel relates to them the following story: "In truth,   1
my lords, Meleagant, a tall and powerful knight, son of the
King of Gorre, has taken her off into the kingdom whence no
foreigner returns, but where he must perforce remain in
servitude and banishment." Then they ask her: "Damsel,
where is this country? Where can we find the way thither?"
She replies: "That you shall quickly learn; but you may be sure
that you will meet with many obstacles and difficult passages,
for it is not easy to enter there except with the permission of
the king, whose name is Bademagu; however, it is possible to   10
enter by two very perilous paths and by two very difficult
passage-ways. One is called 'the water-bridge,' because the
bridge is under water, and there is the same amount of water
beneath it as above it, so that the bridge is exactly in the
middle; and it is only a foot and a half in width and in
thickness. This choice is certainly to be avoided, and yet it is
the less dangerous of the two. . . . The other bridge is still
more impracticable and much more perilous, never having
been crossed by man. It is just like a sharp sword, and
therefore all the people call it 'the sword-bridge.' Now I have   20
told you all the truth I know. . . ."

[They reach the sword-bridge.]

Figure 11.21 *Lancelot Crossing the Swordbridge and Guinevere in the Tower*, from the *Romance of Lancelot*, ca. 1300. 13½ × 10 in.

At the end of this very difficult bridge they dismount from their steeds and gaze at the wicked-looking stream, which is as swift and raging, as black and turgid, as fierce and terrible as if it were the devil's stream; and it is so dangerous and bottomless that anything falling into it would be as completely lost as if it fell into the salt sea. And the bridge, which spans it, is different from any other bridge; for there never was such a one as this. If any one asks of me the truth, there never was such a bad bridge, nor one whose flooring was so bad. The **30** bridge across the cold stream consisted of a polished, gleaming sword; but the sword was stout and stiff, and was as long as two lances. At each end there was a tree-trunk in which the sword was firmly fixed. No one need fear to fall because of its breaking or bending, for its excellence was such that it could support a great weight . . . . [Lancelot] prepares, as best he may, to cross the stream, and he does a very marvelous thing in removing the armor from his feet and hands. He will be in a sorry state when he reaches the other side [Figure **11.21**]. He is going to support himself with his **40** bare hands and feet upon the sword, which was sharper than a scythe, for he had not kept on his feet either sole or upper[1] or hose. But he felt no fear of wounds upon his hands or feet; he preferred to maim himself rather than to fall from the bridge and be plunged in the water from which he could never escape. In accordance with this determination, he passes over with great pain and agony, being wounded in the hands, knees, and feet. But even this suffering is sweet to him: for Love, who conducts and leads him on, assuages and relieves the pain. Creeping on his hands, feet, and knees, he proceeds **50** until he reaches the other side. . . .

[Lancelot confronts the Queen's captors: King Bademagu's son, Meleagant, refuses to make peace with Lancelot and promptly challenges him to battle.]

. . . Very early, before prime[2] had yet been sounded, both of the knights fully armed were led to the place, mounted upon two horses equally protected. Meleagant was very graceful, alert, and shapely; the hauberk with its fine meshes, the helmet, and the shield hanging from his neck—all these became him well. . . . Then the combatants without delay make all the people stand aside; then they clash the shields

with their elbows, and thrust their arms into the straps, and spur at each other so violently that each sends his lance two **60** arms' length through his opponent's shield, causing the lance to split and splinter like a flying spark. And the horses meet head on, clashing breast to breast, and the shields and helmets crash with such a noise that it seems like a mighty thunder-clap; not a breast-strap, girth, rein or surcingle[3] remains unbroken, and the saddle-bows, though strong, are broken to pieces. The combatants felt no shame in falling to earth, in view of their mishaps, but they quickly spring to their feet, and without waste of threatening words rush at each other more fiercely than two wild boars, and deal great blows **70** with their swords of steel like men whose hate is violent. Repeatedly they trim the helmets and shining hauberks so fiercely that after the sword the blood spurts out. They furnished an excellent battle, indeed, as they stunned and wounded each other with their heavy, wicked blows. Many fierce, hard, long bouts they sustained with equal honor, so that the onlookers could discern no advantage on either side. But it was inevitable that he who had crossed the bridge should be much weakened by his wounded hands. The people who sided with him were much dismayed, for they notice that **80** his strokes are growing weaker, and they fear he will get the worst of it; it seemed to them that he was weakening, while Meleagant was triumphing, and they began to murmur all around. But up at the window of the tower there was a wise maiden who thought within herself that the knight had not undertaken the battle either on her account or for the sake of the common herd who had gathered about the list, but that his only incentive had been the Queen; and she thought that, if he knew that she was at the window seeing and watching him, his strength and courage would increase. . . . Then she came **90** to the Queen and said: "Lady, for God's sake and your own as well as ours, I beseech you to tell me, if you know, the name of

---

[1] Parts of the shoe or boot.

[2] The second of the Canonical Hours, around 6 a.m. The devout recited special devotional prayers at each of the Canonical Hours: lauds, prime, terce, sext, none, vespers, and compline.

[3] A band passing around a horse's body to bind the saddle.

yonder knight, to the end that it may be of some help to him." "Damsel," the Queen replies, "you have asked me a question in which I see no hate or evil, but rather good intent; the name of the knight, I know, is Lancelot of the Lake." "God, how happy and glad at heart I am!" the damsel says. Then she leans forward and calls to him by name so loudly that all the people hear: "Lancelot, turn about and see who is here taking note of thee!" 100

When Lancelot heard his name, he was not slow to turn around: he turns and sees seated up there at the window of the tower her whom he desired most in the world to see. From the moment he caught sight of her, he did not turn or take his eyes and face from her, defending himself with backhand blows. . . . Lancelot's strength and courage grow, partly because he has love's aid, and partly because he never hated any one so much as him with whom he is engaged. Love and mortal hate, so fierce that never before was such hate seen, make him so fiery and bold that Meleagant ceases to treat it 110 as a jest and begins to stand in awe of him, for he had never met or known so doughty a knight, nor had any knight ever wounded or injured him as this one does. . . .

[Lancelot spares Meleagant but thereafter is taken prisoner. Rumor reaches the Queen that Lancelot is dead.]

The news of this spread until it reached the Queen, who was sitting at meat. She almost killed herself on hearing the false report about Lancelot, but she supposes it to be true, and therefore she is in such dismay that she almost loses the power to speak; but, because of those present, she forces herself to say: "In truth, I am sorry for his death, and it is no wonder that I grieve, for he came into this country for my 120 sake, and therefore I should mourn for him." Then she says to herself, so that the others should not hear, that no one need ask her to drink or eat, if it is true that he is dead, in whose life she found her own. Then grieving she rises from the table, and makes her lament, but so that no one hears or notices her. She is so beside herself that she repeatedly grasps her throat with the desire to kill herself; but first she confesses to herself, and repents with self-reproach, blaming and censuring herself, for the wrong she had done him, who, as she knew, had always been hers, and would still be hers, if he were 130 alive. . . . "Alas how much better I should feel, and how much comfort I should take, if only once before he died I had held him in my arms! What? Yes, certainly, quite unclad, in order the better to enjoy him. If he is dead, I am very wicked not to destroy myself. Why? Can it harm my lover for me to live on after he is dead, if I take no pleasure in anything but in the woe I bear for him? In giving myself up to grief after his death, the very woes I court would be sweet to me, if he were only still alive. It is wrong for a woman to wish to die rather than to suffer for her lover's sake. It is certainly sweet for me to 140 mourn him long. I would rather be beaten alive than die and be at rest."

[Once freed, Lancelot makes his way to the castle and Guinevere agrees to meet with him secretly.]

Lancelot . . . was so impatient for the night to come that his restlessness made the day seem longer than a hundred

ordinary days or than an entire year. If night had only come, he would gladly have gone to the trysting place. Dark and somber night at last won its struggle with the day, and wrapped it up in its covering, and laid it away beneath its cloak. When he saw the light of day obscured, he pretended to be tired and worn, and said that, in view of his protracted vigils, he needed 150 rest. You, who have ever done the same, may well understand and guess that he pretends to be tired and goes to bed in order to deceive the people of the house; but he cared nothing about his bed, nor would he have sought rest there for anything, for he could not have done so and would not have dared, and furthermore he would not have cared to possess the courage or the power to do so. Soon he softly rose, and was pleased to find that no moon or star was shining, and that in the house there was no candle, lamp or lantern burning. Thus he went out and looked about, but there was no one on 160 the watch for him, for all thought that he would sleep in his bed all night. Without escort or company he quickly went out into the garden, meeting no one on the way, and he was so fortunate as to find that a part of the garden-wall had recently fallen down. Through this break he passes quickly and proceeds to the window, where he stands, taking good care not to cough or sneeze, until the Queen arrives clad in a very white chemise. She wore no cloak or coat, but had thrown over her a short cape of scarlet cloth and shrew-mouse fur. As soon as Lancelot saw the Queen leaning on the window-sill 170 behind the great iron bars, he honored her with a gentle salute. She promptly returned his greeting, for he was desirous of her, and she of him. Their talk and conversation are not of vulgar, tiresome affairs. They draw close to one another, until each holds the other's hand. But they are so distressed at not being able to come together more completely, that they curse the iron bars. Then Lancelot asserts that, with the Queen's consent, he will come inside to be with her, and that the bars cannot keep him out. And the Queen replies: "Do you not see how the bars are stiff to bend 180 and hard to break? You could never so twist, pull or drag at them as to dislodge one of them." "Lady," says he, "have no fear of that. It would take more than these bars to keep me out. . . ."

Then the Queen retires, and he prepares to loosen the window. Seizing the bars, he pulls and wrenches them until he makes them bend and drags them from their places. But the iron was so sharp that the end of his little finger was cut to the nerve, and the first joint of the next finger was torn; but he who is intent upon something else paid no heed to any of his 190 wounds or to the blood which trickled down. Though the window is not low, Lancelot gets through it quickly and easily . . . then he comes to the bed of the Queen, whom he adores and before whom he kneels, holding her more dear than the relic of any saint. And the Queen extends her arms to him and, embracing him, presses him tightly against her bosom, drawing him into the bed beside her and showing him every possible satisfaction: her love and her heart go out to him. It is love that prompts her to treat him so; and if she feels great love for him, he feels a hundred thousand times as much for 200 her. For there is no love at all in other hearts compared with what there is in his; in his heart love was so completely embodied that it was niggardly toward all other hearts. Now Lancelot possesses all he wants, when the Queen voluntarily seeks his company and love, and when he holds her in his arms, and she holds him in hers. Their sport is so agreeable and sweet, as they kiss and fondle each other, that in truth such a marvellous joy comes over them as was never heard or known. But their joy will not be revealed by me, for in a story it has no place. Yet, the most choice and delightful **210** satisfaction was precisely that of which our story must not speak. That night Lancelot's joy and pleasure was very great. But, to his sorrow, day comes when he must leave his mistress' side. It cost him such pain to leave her that he suffered a real martyr's agony. His heart now stays where the Queen remains; he has not the power to lead it away, for it finds such pleasure in the Queen that it has no desire to leave her: so his body goes, and his heart remains; . . .

Q **How do Roland (Reading 11.2) and Lancelot compare as medieval heroes? And what "brave deeds" does each undertake to achieve his goal?**

Lancelot's worship of Guinevere (cc. 205–206) and his repeated references to her "saintliness" illustrate the confusion of sensual and spiritual passions that characterized the culture of the High Middle Ages. The fact that Lancelot uses the terminology of religious worship to flatter an unfaithful wife suggests the paradoxical nature of the so-called "religion of love" associated with courtly romance. However one explains this phenomenon, *Lancelot* remains representative of the climate of shifting values and the degeneration of feudal ideals, especially those of honor and loyalty among gentleman-warriors.

The Poetry of the *Troubadours*

During the Early Middle Ages, few men and women could read or write. But by the eleventh century, literacy was spreading beyond the cathedral schools and monasteries. The popularity of such forms of vernacular literature as lyric poetry, the chronicle, and the romance gives evidence of increasing lay literacy among upper-class men and women. To entertain the French nobility, *trouvères* (in the north) and *troubadours* (in the south) composed and performed poems devoted to courtly love, chivalry, religion, and politics. The most famous collection of such lyric poems, the *Carmina Burana*, came from twelfth-century France. In German-speaking courts, *Minnesingers* provided a similar kind of entertainment, while *Meistersingers*, masters of the guilds of poets and musicians, flourished somewhat later in German towns.

Unlike the minstrels of old, *troubadours* were usually men and women of noble birth. Their poems, like the *chansons* of the Early Middle Ages, were monophonic and syllabic, but they were more expressive in content and more delicate in style, betraying their indebtedness to Arab poetic forms.

Often, *troubadours* (or the professional musicians who recited their poems) accompanied themselves on a lyre or a lute (see Figure 10.14). Many of the 2600 extant *troubadour* poems exalt the passionate affection of a gentleman for a lady, or, as in those written by the twenty identifiable *trobairitzes* (female *troubadours*), the reverse (Figure 11.22).

Influenced by Islamic verse such as that found in chapter 10, *troubadour* poems generally manifest a positive, even joyous, response to physical nature and the world of the senses. An eleventh-century poem by William IX, duke of Aquitaine and one of the first *troubadours*, compares the anticipation of sexual fulfillment with the coming of spring. It opens with these high-spirited words:

> In the sweetness of the new season
> when woods burst forth and birds
> sing, each in its own voice
> to the lyrics of a new song,
> *then* should one seize
> the pleasures one most desires.

In a more melancholic vein, the mid-twelfth-century poet Bernart de Ventadour explored the popular theme of

Figure 11.22 *Konrad von Altstetten Smitten by Spring and His Beloved*, from the Manesse Codex, Zürich, ca. 1300. Manuscript illumination, 14 × 9⅞ in. This richly illuminated manuscript is the single largest collection of medieval German love songs. The poems of over 140 *Minnesingers* are represented here, along with colorful illustrations and the heraldic devices of the poets.

unrequited love in the poem "When I behold the lark." Occasionally, *troubadour* verse gives evidence of hostility between upper and lower social classes. Such is the case with the second of the poems printed here, in which the *troubadour* Peire Cardenal levels a fierce attack on social inequity and upper-class greed. The third voice represented below is that of a woman: the countess of Dia (often called "Beatriz") was a twelfth-century *trobairitz*; her surviving four songs are filled with personal laments for lost love ("I've been in great anguish") and impassioned enticements of physical pleasure.

READING 11.4 *Troubadour* Poems (ca. 1050–1200)

Bernart de Ventadour's "When I behold the lark"

When I behold the lark arise	1
with wings of gold for heaven's height,	
to drop at last from flooded skies,	
lost in its fullness of delight,	
such sweetness spreads upon the day	5
I envy those who share the glee.	
My heart's so filled with love's dismay	
I wait its breaking suddenly.	
I thought in love's ways I was wise,	
yet little do I know aright.	10
I praised a woman as love's prize	
and she gives nothing to requite.	
My heart, my life she took in theft,	
she took the world away from me,	
and now my plundered self is left	15
only desire and misery.	
Her rule I'm forced to recognize	
since all my broken joys took flight.	
I looked within her lifted eyes,	
that mirror sweet with treacherous might:	20
O mirror, here I weep and dream	
of depths once glimpsed and now denied.	
I'm lost in you as in the stream	
comely Narcissus looked and died.	
Now trust in indignation dies	25
and womanhood I henceforth slight.	
I find that all her worths are lies.	
I thought her something made of light.	
And no one comes to plead for me	
with her who darkens all my days.	30
Woman I doubt and now I see	
that she like all the rest betrays.	
Aye, pity women all despise.	
Come face the truth and do not fight.	
The smallest kindness she denies,	35
yet who but she should soothe my plight?	
So gentle and so fair is she,	
it's hard for others to believe.	

♪ See Music Listening Selections at end of chapter.

She, who could save, in cruelty	
watches her wasting lover grieve.	40
My love has failed and powerless lies;	
devotion bears for me no right.	
She laughs to hear my deepest sighs—	
then silently I'll leave her sight.	
I cast my love of her away.	45
She struck and I accept the blow.	
She will not speak and I must stray	
in exile. Where, I do not know.	
Tristan, I've made an end, I say.	
I'm going—where, I do not know.	50
My song is dying, and away	
all love and joy I cast, and go.	

Peire Cardenal's "Lonely the rich need never be"

Lonely the rich need never be,	1
they have such constant company.	
For Wickedness in front we see,	
behind, all round, and far and wide.	
The giant called Cupidity	5
is always hulking at their side.	
Injustice waves the flag, and he	
is led along by Pride . . .	
If a poor man has snitched a bit of rag,	
he goes with downcast head and frightened eye.	10
But when the rich thief fills his greedy bag,	
he marches on with head still held as high.	
The poor man's hanged, he stole a rotten bridle.	
The man who hanged him stole the horse. O fie.	
To hang poor thieves the rich thieves still aren't idle.	15
That kind of justice arrow-swift will fly . . .	
The rich are charitable? Yes,	
as Cain who slew his brother Abel.	
They're thieves, no wolves as merciless.	
They're liars, like a whoreshop-babel.	20
O stick their ribs, O stick their souls!	
No truth comes bubbling from the holes,	
but lies. Their greedy hearts, abhorrent,	
are rabid as a mountain-torrent . . .	
With loving-kindness how they quicken,	25
what hoards of charity they spread.	
If all the stones were loaves of bread,	
if all the streams with wine should thicken,	
the hills turn bacon or boiled chicken,	
they'd give no extra crumb. That's flat,	30
Some people are like that.	

The Countess of Dia's "I've been in great anguish"

I've been in great anguish	1
over a noble knight I once had,	
and I want everyone to know, for all time,	
that I loved him—too much!	
Now I see I'm betrayed	5

because I didn't yield my love to him.

For that I've suffered greatly,
both in my bed and when I'm fully clad.

How I'd yearn to have my knight
in my naked arms for one night!　　　　　　　　10
He would feel a frenzy of delight
only to have me for his pillow.
I'm more in love with him
than Blancheflor ever was with Floris.[1]
To him I'd give my heart, my love,　　　　　　15
my mind, my eyes, my life.

Beautiful, gracious, sweet friend,
when shall I hold you in my power?
If I could lie with you for one night,
and give you a kiss of love,　　　　　　　　20
you can be sure I would desire greatly
to grant you a husband's place,
as long as you promised
to do everything I wished!

Q On what specific topics and themes are these songs focused?

Q What do these themes reveal about the culture that produced the troubadours?

The Origins of Constitutional Monarchy

The new social consciousness voiced by Peire Cardenal was a reflection of political and economic change, especially in England. In the year 1215, the barons of the realm forced the English king John (1167–1216) to sign the landmark document known as the Magna Carta ("great charter"). The document forbade the king to levy additional feudal taxes without the consent of his royal council. It also guaranteed other privileges, such as trial by jury. Although it was essentially a feudal agreement between English noblemen and their king, it became one of the most significant documents in the history of political freedom: by asserting the primacy of the law over the will of the ruler, the Magna Carta established the principle that paved the way for the development of constitutional monarchy.

Some fifty years after the signing of the Magna Carta, the English nobility, demanding equal authority in ruling England, imprisoned King Henry III (1207–1272) and invited representatives of a new class of people "midway" between serfs and lords—the middle class—to participate in the actions of the Great Council (Parliament). The Council was the first example of representative government among the rising nation-states of the West.

---

[1] The lovers in a popular medieval romance.

The Rise of Medieval Towns

Medieval kings looked for financial support from the middle class, and especially from the taxes provided by commercial activity. Increased agricultural production and the reopening of trade routes encouraged urban development, a process that usually began with the establishment of the local market. By the end of the eleventh century, merchants—often the disenfranchised younger sons of the nobility—were engaging in commercial enterprises that required local trade markets. Usually located near highways or rivers, outside the walls of a fortified castle (*bourg* in French, *burg* in German, *borough* in English), the market (*faubourg*) became part of manorial life. The permanent market eventually grew into the medieval town—an urban center that attracted farmers and artisans who might buy freedom from their lord or simply run away from the manor. "City air makes a man free" was the cry of those who had discovered the urban alternative to manorial life.

In the newly established towns, the middle class pursued profit from commercial exchange. Merchants and craftspeople in like occupations formed **guilds** for the mutual protection of buyers and sellers. The guilds regulated prices, fixed wages, established standards of quality in the production of goods, and provided training for newcomers in each profession. During the eleventh and twelfth centuries, urban dwellers purchased charters of self-government from lords in whose fiefs their towns were situated. Such charters allowed townspeople (*bourgeois* in French; *Burghers* in German) to establish municipal governments and regulate their own economic activities. Such commercial centers as Milan, Florence, and Venice became completely self-governing city-states similar to those of ancient Greece and Rome. The self-governing Flemish cities of Bruges and Antwerp exported fine linen and wool to England and to towns along the Baltic Sea. The spirit of urban growth was manifested in the construction of defensive stone walls that protected the citizens, as at Carcassonne in southwestern France (Figure **11.23**), and in the building of cathedrals and guildhalls that flanked the open marketplace. Although by the twelfth century town dwellers constituted less than 15 percent of the total European population, the middle class continued to expand and ultimately it came to dominate Western society.

Middle-class values differed considerably from those of the feudal nobility. Whereas warfare and chivalry

Figure 11.23 The walled city of Carcassonne, France, twelfth–thirteenth centuries.

preoccupied the nobility, financial prosperity and profit were the principal concerns of the middle class. In European cities, there evolved a lively vernacular literature expressive of middle-class concerns. It included humorous narrative tales (*fabliaux*) and poems (*dits*) describing urban occupations, domestic conflict, and street and tavern life (Figure **11.24**). These popular genres, which feature such stereotypes as the miserly husband and the lecherous monk, slyly reflect many of the social tensions and sexual prejudices of the day. A favorite theme of medieval *fabliaux* and *dits* was the antifemale diatribe, a denunciation of women as bitter as Juvenal's (see chapter 6), and one that was rooted in a long tradition of misogyny (the hatred of women). While medieval romances generally cast the female in a positive light, *fabliaux* and *dits* often described women as sinful and seductive. The hostile attitude toward womankind, intensified perhaps by women's increasing participation in some of the commercial activities traditionally dominated by men, is readily apparent in both urban legislation and in the popular literature of the late thirteenth century. The following verse, based on a widely circulated proverb, voices a popular male complaint:

> He who takes a wife trades peace for strife,
> Long weariness, despair, oppress his life,
> A heavy load, a barrel full of chatter,
> Uncorkable, her gossip makes a clatter,
> Now, ever since I took a wife,
> Calamity has marred my life.

Figure 11.24 *Young Lady Shopping for Belts and Purses,* from the Manesse Codex, Zürich, ca. 1315–1333.

LOOKING BACK

The Germanic Tribes

- The westward migrations of the Germanic tribes threatened the stability of the already waning Roman Empire. Nevertheless, these peoples introduced customs and values that came to shape the character of the European Middle Ages.
- Germanic languages, laws, and forms of artistic expression fused with those of the late Roman and newly Christianized world to fix the patterns of early medieval life. Germanic bonds of fealty and cavalry warfare gave rise to the medieval practice of feudalism, while Germanic custom would have lasting influence on the development of law in the West.
- The Anglo-Saxon epic *Beowulf* and the art of Sutton Hoo are landmarks of Germanic cultural achievement. Metalwork techniques and the decorative zoomorphic style influenced the evolution of early medieval religious art and artifacts.

Charlemagne and the Carolingian Renaissance

- Charlemagne's hope of restoring the Roman Empire under Christian leadership led to the conquest of vast areas of land; his holy wars resulted in the forcible conversion of the Saxons east of the Rhine River, the Lombards of northern Italy, and the Slavic peoples along the Danube.
- By the ninth century, the Holy Roman Empire had become the cultural oasis of the West. Under Charlemagne's influence, much of Europe converted to Christianity, while members of his court worked to encourage education and the arts.
- Charlemagne cast himself as the prototype of Christian kingship. He controlled conquered lands by placing them in the hands of local administrators. He revived trade with the East, stabilized currency, and pursued diplomatic ties with Baghdad.
- The Carolingian Renaissance saw the rebirth of monumental

architecture, bronze casting, and manuscript illumination. The Carolingian abbey church became the focal point of monastic life as well as the repository of sacred relics that drew pilgrims from neighboring areas. In the construction of the abbey church, as in the arrangement of the monastic complex as a whole, Classical principles of symmetry and order prevailed.

Early Medieval Culture

- In the turbulent century following the fragmentation of the Carolingian Empire, feudalism, the exchange of land for military service, gave noblemen the power to rule locally while providing protection from outside attack.
- The artistic monuments of the Early Middle Ages—the *Song of Roland*, the Norman castle, and the Bayeux Tapestry—all describe a heroic age that glorified feudal combat, male prowess, and the conquest of land.
- Manorialism, the economic basis for medieval society, offered the lower classes physical protection in exchange for food production.

High Medieval Culture

- The Christian Crusades altered the patterns of economic and cultural life, even as they marked the revival of European mobility. While no territorial gains were made in the Muslim East, the Crusades encouraged the rise of towns and trade dominated by a new middle class, whose ambitions were materialistic and profit-oriented.
- Changing patterns of secular life between the years 700 and 1300 reflect the shift from a feudal society to an urban one. The values of merchants and craftspeople differed from those of the feudal nobility, for whom land had provided the basis of wealth and chivalry dictated manners and morals.
- In the courtly literature of the High Middle Ages, sentiment and sensuousness replaced the heroic idealism and chivalric chastity of the early medieval era. Romantic love, a medieval invention, dominated both the vernacular romance and *troubadour* poetry. Vernacular tales and poems often satirized inequality between classes and antagonism between the sexes.

Music Listening Selections

CD One Selection 6 Bernart de Ventadour, "Can vei la lauzeta mouver" ("When I behold the lark"), ca. 1150, excerpt.

Glossary

chain mail a flexible medieval armor made of interlinked metal rings

chalice a goblet; in Christian liturgy, the Eucharistic cup

chanson de geste (French, "song of heroic deeds") an epic poem of the Early Middle Ages

chivalry a code of behavior practiced by upper-class men and women of medieval society

cloisonné (French, *cloison*, meaning "fence") an enameling technique produced by pouring molten colored glass between thin metal strips secured to a metal surface; any object ornamented in this manner (see Figure 11.3)

common law the body of unwritten law developed primarily from judicial decisions based on custom and precedent; the basis of the English legal system and that of all states in the United States with the exception of Louisiana

crenellations tooth-shaped battlements surmounting a wall and used for defensive combat

fealty loyalty; the fidelity of the warrior to his chieftain

feudalism the system of political organization prevailing in Europe between the ninth and fifteenth centuries and having as its basis the exchange of land for military defense

fief in feudal society, land or property given to a warrior in return for military service

guild an association of merchants or craftspeople organized according to occupation

investiture the procedure by which a feudal lord granted a vassal control over a fief

jongleur a professional entertainer who wandered from court to court in medieval Europe

joust a form of personal combat, usually with lances on horseback, between men-at-arms

keep a square tower, the strongest and most secure part of the medieval castle (see Figure 11.16)

kenning a two-term metaphor used in Old English verse

lord any member of the feudal nobility who invested a vassal with a fief

mace a heavy, spike-headed club used as a weapon in medieval combat

medieval romance a tale of adventure that deals with knights, kings, and ladies acting under the impulse of love, religious faith, or the desire for adventure

moat a wide trench, usually filled with water, surrounding a fortified place such as a castle (see Figure 11.16)

niello a black sulfurous substance used as a decorative inlay for incised metal surfaces; the art or process of decorating metal in this manner

paten a shallow dish; in Christian liturgy, the Eucharistic plate

primogeniture the principle by which a fief was passed from father to eldest son

refectory dining hall

renaissance (French, "rebirth") a revival of the learning of former and especially Classical culture

scriptorium a monastic writing room

serf an unfree peasant

vassal any member of the feudal nobility who vowed to serve a lord in exchange for control of a fief

zoomorphic animal-shaped; having the form of an animal

Chapter

12

Christianity and the Medieval Mind

ca. 1000–1300

"All earthly things is but vanity:
Beauty, Strength, and Discretion, do man forsake,
Foolish friends and kinsmen, that fair spake,
All fleeth save Good Deeds . . ."
Everyman

Figure 12.1 *God as Architect of the Universe,* from the Bible Moralisée, thirteenth century.

LOOKING AHEAD

There is much about the medieval world—its knights in shining armor, its walled castles, and its bloody crusades—that provides the stuff of modern fantasy. In reality, however, the Middle Ages had a powerful influence on the evolution of basic Western values, beliefs, and practices. The geographic contours of modern European states, as well as their political and linguistic traditions, emerged during this era. As Europe's population rose from 27 million in 700 to 73 million in 1300, the High Middle Ages saw the rise of new urban institutions, including the medieval university. At the same time, the Roman Catholic Church reached its peak as the dominant political, religious, and cultural authority. Its doctrines and its liturgy gave coherence and meaning to everyday life. Its earthly ministers, the priesthood, shepherded Christians through the rites of passage that marked the soul's pilgrimage to salvation. Its view of the terrestrial world as divinely ordered by an all-knowing God (see Figure 12.1) dominated all aspects of medieval expression.

The Christian Way of Life and Death

With the exception of the purest forms of Hinduism and Buddhism, which anticipate the extinction of the Self, most world religions have met the fear of death with an ideology (a body of doctrine supported by myth and symbols) that promises the survival of some aspect of the Self in a life hereafter. The nature of that hereafter usually depends on the moral status of the believer—that is, his or her conduct on earth.

Christianity made the promise of personal salvation central to the medieval world-view. It provided a unique system by which medieval Christians might achieve final victory over death. Through the **sacraments**, a set of sacred rites that impart **grace** (the free and unearned favor of God), medieval Christians were assured of the soul's redemption from sin and, ultimately, of eternal life in the world to come. The seven sacraments—the number fixed by the Fourth Lateran Council of 1215—touched every significant phase of human life: at birth, baptism purified the recipient of Original Sin; confirmation admitted the baptized to full church privileges; ordination invested those entering the clergy with priestly authority; matrimony blessed the union of man and woman; penance acknowledged repentance of sins and offered absolution; Eucharist—the central and most important of the sacraments—joined human beings to God by means of the body and blood of Jesus; and finally, just prior to death, extreme unction provided final absolution from sins.

By way of the sacraments, the Church participated in virtually every major aspect of the individual's life, enforcing a set of values that determined the collective spirituality of Christendom. Since only church officials could administer the sacraments, the clergy held a "monopoly" on personal salvation. Medieval Christians thus looked to representatives of the Mother Church as shepherds guiding the members of their flock on their long and hazardous journey from cradle to grave. Their conduct on earth determined whether their souls went to Heaven, Hell, or Purgatory (the place of purification from sins). But only by way of the clergy might they receive the gifts of grace that made salvation possible.

By the twelfth century, Christian concepts of sin and salvation had become ever more complex: church councils identified Purgatory as an intermediate realm occupied by the soul after death (and before the Last Judgment). In Purgatory punishment was imposed for the unexpiated but repented sins committed in mortal life. While ordinary Christians might suffer punishment in Purgatory, they might also benefit from prayers and good works offered on their behalf. The role of the priesthood in providing such forms of remission from sin would give the medieval Church unassailable power and authority.

The Literature of Mysticism

Most of the religious literature of the Middle Ages was didactic—that is, it served to teach and instruct. Visionary literature, however, functioned in two other ways. It reflected an individual's intuitive and direct knowledge of God (thus constituting a form of autobiography); and it conjured vivid images of the supernatural (thus providing a vocabulary by which the unknowable might actually be known). The leading mystic of the twelfth century, Hildegard of Bingen (1098–1179), was an extraordinary individual. Entering a Benedictine convent at the age of eight, she went on to become its abbess. A scholar of both Latin and her native German, she wrote three visionary tracts, treatises on natural science, medicine, and the treatment of disease, an allegorical dialogue between the vices and the virtues, and a cycle of seventy-seven songs arranged for devotional performance (see chapter 13). While some regard Hildegard as the *first* of the female visionaries, she actually follows a long line of mystics and seers whose history begins in antiquity (most famously represented by the Delphic priestesses and the Roman sibyls). One of the first great Christian mystics, however, Hildegard produced original works on such topics as the nature of the universe, the meaning of Scripture, and the destiny of the Christian soul. The Church confirmed the divine source of her visions and, along with most of her contemporaries, acknowledged her prophetic powers. In the following selection from *Scivias*, short for *Scito vias domini* (*Know the Ways of the Lord*), her encounter with the "voice from heaven" is followed by two of her most compelling visions. The miniature accompanying one of these visions (Figure **12.2**)—like all of those that illustrate her manuscripts—was supervised by Hildegard herself.

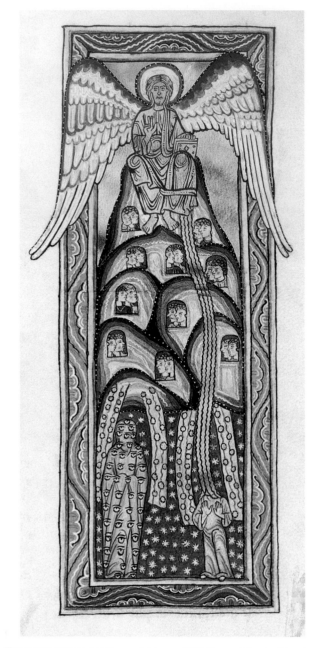

Figure 12.2 Hildegard of Bingen, *Scivias*, ca. 1146. The revelation is pictured as a burst of "fiery light" that flows from the angelic figure of Jesus at the top of the illustration to the small image of Hildegard (bottom right). The voice from heaven orders Hildegard: "Speak," in a manner similar to the command ("Recite") of the angel Gabriel to Muhammad (see chapter 10).

READING 12.1 From Hildegard of Bingen's *Know the Ways of the Lord* (ca. 1146)

1. A Solemn Declaration Concerning the True Vision Flowing from God: *Scivias*. Protestificatio

Lo! In the forty-third year of my temporal course, when I clung   1
to a celestial vision with great fear and tremulous effort, I saw
a great splendor. In it came a voice from heaven, saying:
   "O frail mortal, both ash of ashes, and rottenness of
rottenness, speak and write down what you see and hear. But
because you are fearful of speaking, simple at expounding,
and unlearned in writing—speak and write, not according to

the speech of man or according to the intelligence of human
invention, or following the aim of human composition, but
according to what you see and hear from the heavens above in   10
the wonders of God! Offer explanations of them, just as one
who hears and understands the words of an instructor
willingly makes them public, revealing and teaching them
according to the sense of the instructor's discourse. You,
therefore, O mortal, speak also the things you see and hear.
Write them, not according to yourself or to some other person,
but according to the will of the Knower, Seer, and Ordainer of
all things in the secrets of their mysteries."
   And again I heard the voice from heaven saying to me:
"Speak these wonders and write the things taught in this   20
manner—and speak!"
   It happened in the year 1141 of the Incarnation of the Son
of God, Jesus Christ, when I was forty-two years and seven
months old, that a fiery light of the greatest radiance coming
from the open heavens flooded through my entire brain. It
kindled my whole breast like a flame that does not scorch but
warms in the same way the sun warms anything on which it
sheds its rays.
   Suddenly I understood the meaning of books, that is, the
Psalms and the Gospels; and I knew other catholic books of   30
the Old as well as the New Testaments—not the significance
of the words of the text, or the division of the syllables, nor did
I consider an examination of the cases and tenses.
   Indeed, from the age of girlhood, from the time that I was
fifteen until the present, I had perceived in myself, just as until
this moment, a power of mysterious, secret, and marvelous
visions of a miraculous sort. However, I revealed these things
to no one, except to a few religious persons who were living
under the same vows as I was. But meanwhile, until this time
when God in his grace has willed these things to be revealed,   40
I have repressed them in quiet silence.
   But I have not perceived these visions in dreams, or asleep,
or in a delirium, or with my bodily eyes, or with my external
mortal ears, or in secreted places, but I received them awake
and looking attentively about me with an unclouded mind, in
open places, according to God's will. However this may be, it
is difficult for carnal man to fathom. . . .

2. The Iron-Colored Mountain and the Radiant One: *Scivias*. Book I, Vision 1

I saw what seemed to be a huge mountain having the color of
iron. On its height was sitting One of such great radiance that
it stunned my vision. On both sides of him extended a gentle   50
shadow like a wing of marvelous width and length. And in front
of him at the foot of the same mountain stood a figure
full of eyes everywhere. Because of those eyes, I was not able
to distinguish any human form.
   In front of this figure there was another figure, whose age
was that of a boy, and he was clothed in a pale tunic and
white shoes. I was not able to look at his face, because above
his head so much radiance descended from the One sitting on
the mountain. From the One sitting on the mountain a great
many living sparks cascaded, which flew around those figures   60
with great sweetness. In this same mountain, moreover, there

seemed to be a number of little windows, in which men's heads appeared, some pale and some white.

And see! The One sitting on the mountain shouted in an extremely loud, strong voice, saying: "O frail mortal, you who are of the dust of the earth's dust, and ash of ash, cry out and speak of the way into incorruptible salvation! Do this in order that those people may be taught who see the innermost meaning of Scripture, but who do not wish to tell it or preach it because they are lukewarm and dull in preserving God's 70 justice. Unlock for them the mystical barriers. For they, being timid, are hiding themselves in a remote and barren field. You, therefore, pour yourself forth in a fountain of abundance! Flow with mystical learning, so that those who want you to be scorned because of the guilt of Eve may be inundated by the flood of your refreshment!

"For you do not receive this keenness of insight from man, but from that supernal and awesome judge on high. There amidst brilliant light, this radiance will brightly shine forth among the luminous ones. Arise, therefore, and shout and 80 speak! These things are revealed to you through the strongest power of divine aid. For he who potently and benignly rules his creatures imbues with the radiance of heavenly enlightenment all those who fear him and serve him with sweet love in a spirit of humility. And he leads those who persevere in the path of justice to the joys of everlasting vision!"

3. The Fall of Lucifer, the Formation of Hell, and the Fall of Adam and Eve: *Scivias*. Book I, Vision 2

Then I saw what seemed to be a great number of living torches, full of brilliance. Catching a fiery gleam, they received a most radiant splendor from it. And see! A lake appeared here, of great length and depth, with a mouth like a well, 90 breathing forth a stinking fiery smoke. From the mouth of the lake a loathsome fog also arose until it touched a thing like a blood vessel that had a deceptive appearance.

And in a certain region of brightness, the fog blew through the blood vessel to a pure white cloud, which had emerged from the beautiful form of a man, and the cloud contained within itself many, many stars. Then the loathsome fog blew and drove the cloud and the man's form out of the region of brightness.

Once this had happened, the most luminous splendor 100 encircled that region. The elements of the world, which previously had held firmly together in great tranquility, now, turning into great turmoil, displayed fearful terrors. . . .

Now "that lake of great length and depth" which appeared to you is Hell. In its length are contained vices, and in its deep abyss is damnation, as you see. Also, "it has a mouth like a well, breathing forth a stinking, fiery smoke" means that drowning souls are swallowed in its voracious greed. For although the lake shows them sweetness and delights, it leads them, through perverse deceit, to a perdition of 110 torments. There the heat of the fire breathes forth with an outpouring of the most loathsome smoke, and with a boiling, death-dealing stench. For these abominable torments were prepared for the Devil and his followers, who turned away from the highest good, which they wanted neither to know nor to

understand. For this reason they were cast down from every good thing, not because they did not know them but because they were contemptuous of them in their lofty pride. . . .

Q **What role does revelation play in Hildegard's visions?**

Q **Which of her visionary images do you find most vivid?**

Sermon Literature

While the writings of Hildegard of Bingen addressed individual, literate Christians, medieval sermons, delivered orally from the pulpit of the church, were directed to the largely illiterate Christian community. Both visionary tracts and sermon literature, however, described grace and salvation in vivid terms. The classic medieval sermon, *On the Misery of the Human Condition*, was written by one of Christendom's most influential popes, Innocent III (d. 1216). This sermon is a compelling description of the natural sinfulness of humankind and a scathing condemnation of the "vile and filthy [human] condition." Such motifs, like those found in Hildegard's visions, proceeded from prevailing views of the human condition: weighed down by the burden of the flesh, the body is subject to corruption, disease, and carnal desire. As the temple of the soul, the body will be resurrected on Judgment Day, but not before it suffers the trials of mortality. Warning of the "nearness of death," Innocent's sermon functioned as a **memento mori**, a device by which listeners in a predominantly oral culture might "remember death" and thus prepare themselves for its inevitable arrival. Innocent's

Figure 12.3 Detail of *transi* (effigy of the dead) of François de la Sarra, ca. 1390. La Sarraz, Switzerland.

portrayal of the decay of the human body reflects the medieval disdain for the world of matter, a major theme in most medieval didactic literature. During the Late Middle Ages, especially after the onslaught of the bubonic plague (see chapter 15), the motif of the body as "food for worms"—one of Innocent's most vivid images—became particularly popular in gruesomely forthright tomb sculptures (Figure **12.3**).

Innocent's vivid account of the Christian Hell transforms the concept of corruption into an image of eternal punishment for unabsolved sinners—a favorite subject matter for medieval artists (Figure **12.4**). The contrast that Innocent draws between physical death and spiritual life has its visual counterpart in the representations of the Last Judgment depicted in medieval manuscripts and on Romanesque and Gothic church portals (see Figure 13.8).

READING 12.2 From Pope Innocent III's *On the Misery of the Human Condition*
(ca. 1200)

Of the Miserable Entrance upon the Human Condition

. . . Man was formed of dust, slime, and ashes: what is even   1
more vile, of the filthiest seed. He was conceived from the itch
of the flesh, in the heat of passion and the stench of lust, and
worse yet, with the stain of sin. He was born to toil, dread,

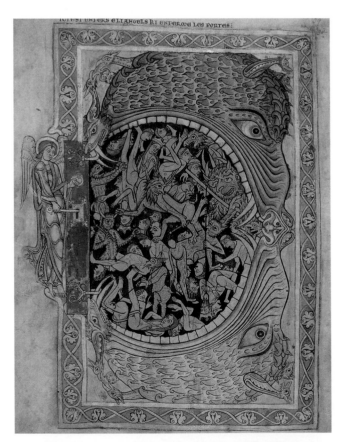

Figure 12.4 *The Mouth of Hell*, from the Psalter of Henry of Blois, Bishop of Winchester, twelfth century. An angel locks the gate that opens into the mouth of a fanged dragon; among the souls being tormented by demons are three royal figures (wearing gold crowns). Note the protruding serpentine creatures—survivals of Anglo-Saxon and Viking art.

and trouble; and more wretched still, was born only to die. He commits depraved acts by which he offends God, his neighbor, and himself; shameful acts by which he defiles his name, his person, and his conscience; and vain acts by which he ignores all things important, useful, and necessary. He will become fuel for those fires which are forever hot and burn forever   10
bright; food for the worm which forever nibbles and digests; a mass of rottenness which will forever stink and reek. . . .

On the Nearness of Death

A man's last day is always the first in importance, but his first day is never considered his last. Yet it is fitting to live always on this principle, that one should act as if in the moment of death. For it is written: "Remember that death is not slow."[1] Time passes, death draws near. In the eyes of the dying man a thousand years are as yesterday, which is past. The future is forever being born, the present forever dying and what is past is utterly dead. We are forever dying while we are alive; we   20
only cease to die when we cease to live. Therefore it is better to die to life than to live waiting for death, for mortal life is but a living death. . . .

On the Putrefaction of the Dead Body

. . . Man is conceived of blood made rotten by the heat of lust; and in the end worms, like mourners, stand about his corpse. In life he produced lice and tapeworms; in death he will produce worms and flies. In life he produced dung and vomit; in death he produces rottenness and stench. In life he fattened one man; in death he fattens a multitude of worms. What then is more foul than a human corpse? What is more horrible than   30
a dead man? He whose embrace was pure delight in life will be a gruesome sight in death.

Of what advantage, then, are riches, food, and honors? For riches will not free us from death, neither food protect us from the worm nor honors from the stench. That man who but now sat in glory upon a throne is now looked down on in the grave; the dandy who once glittered in his palace lies now naked and vile in his tomb; and he who supped once on delicacies in his hall is now in his sepulcher food for worms. . . .

That Nothing Can Help the Damned

. . . O strict judgment!—not only of actions, but "of every idle   40
word that men shall speak, they shall render an account";[2] payment with the usurer's interest will be exacted to the last penny. "Who hath showed you to flee from the wrath to come?"[3]

"The Son of Man shall send his angels and they shall gather out of his kingdom all scandals, and them that work iniquity, and they will bind them as bundles to be burnt, and shall cast them into the furnace of fire. There shall be weeping and gnashing of teeth,"[4] there shall be groaning and wailing, shrieking and flailing of arms and screaming, screeching, and   50

[1] Ecclesiastes 14:12.
[2] Matthew 12:36.
[3] Luke 3:7.
[4] Matthew 13:41–42.

shouting; there shall be fear and trembling, toil and trouble, holocaust and dreadful stench, and everywhere darkness and anguish; there shall be asperity, cruelty, calamity, poverty, distress, and utter wretchedness; they will feel an oblivion of loneliness and namelessness; there shall be twistings and piercings, bitterness, terror, hunger and thirst, cold and hot, brimstone and fire burning, forever and ever world without end. . . .

Q How does Innocent describe the nature and the destiny of humankind?

Q How does this sermon compare with the Sermon on the Mount (Reading 8.2)?

The Medieval Morality Play

While medieval churches rang with sermons like those preached by Innocent III, town squares (often immediately adjacent to a cathedral) became open-air theaters for the dramatization of Christian history and legend. To these urban spaces, townspeople flocked to see dramatic performances that might last from sunrise to sunset. The **mystery play** dramatized biblical history from the fall of Lucifer to the Last Judgment, while the **miracle play** enacted stories from the Life of Christ, the Virgin, or the saints. The **morality play**, the third type of medieval drama, dealt with the struggle between good and evil and the destiny of the soul in the hereafter. The first medieval morality play, Hildegard of Bingen's *Ordo virtutum (Play of the Virtues)* was a twelfth-century allegorical dialogue between vice and virtue. All of these types of plays were performed by members of the local guilds, and mystery plays were usually produced on **pageants** (roofed wagon-stages) that were rolled into the town square. Medieval plays were a popular form of entertainment, as well as a source of religious and moral instruction.

Medieval drama, like Greek drama, had its roots in religious performance. The Catholic Mass, the principal rite of Christian worship, admitted all of the trappings of theater: colorful costumes, symbolic props, solemn processions, dramatic gestures, and ceremonial music. It is likely that the gradual dramatization of church liturgy (see chapter 13) influenced the genesis of mystery and miracle plays. The morality play, however, had clear precedents in allegorical poetry and sermon literature. Allegory—a literary device we have encountered in Plato's *Republic* (Reading 4.6) and in Augustine's *City of God* (Reading 9.4)—uses symbolic figures to capture the essence of a person, thing, or idea. The characters in the morality play are personifications of abstract qualities and universal conditions. In the play *Everyman*, for instance, the main character represents *all* Christian souls, Fellowship stands for friends, Goods for worldly possessions, and so forth.

Although *Everyman* has survived only in fifteenth-century Dutch and English editions, plays similar to it originated considerably earlier. The most popular of all medieval morality plays, *Everyman* symbolically recreates the pilgrimage of the Christian soul to its ultimate destiny.

The play opens with the Messenger, who expounds on the transitory nature of human life. The subsequent conversation between Death and God, somewhat reminiscent of that between Satan and God in the Book of Job (see chapter 1), shows God to be an angry, petulant figure who finds human beings "drowned in sin." If left to their own devices, he opines, "they will become much worse than beasts." As the action unfolds, Everyman realizes that Death has come for him. Frightened and unprepared, he soon discovers that his best friends, his kin, his worldly possessions—indeed, all that he so treasured in life—will not accompany him to the grave. Knowledge, Five-Wits, Beauty, and Discretion may point the way to redemption, but they cannot save him. His only ally is Good-Deeds, which, with the assistance of the Catholic priesthood, will help him win salvation. Everyman is essentially a moral allegory that dramatizes the pilgrimage of the Christian soul from earthly existence to Last Judgment. Like Innocent's sermon, it teaches that life is transient, that worldly pleasures are ultimately valueless, and that sin can be mitigated solely by salvation earned through grace as dispensed by the Church.

READING 12.3 From *Everyman* (ca. 1500)

Characters

Messenger	Cousin	Strength
God (Adonai)	Goods	Discretion
Death	Good-Deeds	Five-Wits
Everyman	Knowledge	Angel
Fellowship	Confession	Doctor
Kindred	Beauty	

HERE BEGINNETH A TREATISE HOW THE HIGH FATHER OF HEAVEN SENDETH DEATH TO SUMMON EVERY CREATURE TO COME AND GIVE ACCOUNT OF THEIR LIVES IN THIS WORLD AND IS IN MANNER OF A MORAL PLAY.

Messenger: I pray you all give your audience,   1
And hear this matter with reverence,
By figure a moral play—
The Summoning of Everyman called it is,
That of our lives and ending shows
How transitory we be all day.[1]
This matter is wondrous precious,
But the intent of it is more gracious,
And sweet to bear away.
The story saith—Man, in the beginning,   10
Look well, and take good heed to the ending,
Be you never so gay!
Ye think sin in the beginning full sweet,
Which in the end causeth thy soul to weep, º
When the body lieth in clay.
Here shall you see how *Fellowship* and *Jollity*,
Both *Strength*, *Pleasure*, and *Beauty*,

[1] Always.

Will fade from thee as flower in May.
For ye shall hear, how our heaven king
Calleth *Everyman* to a general reckoning: 20
Give audience, and hear what he doth say.

God: I perceive here in my majesty,
How that all creatures be to me unkind,[2]
Living without dread in worldly prosperity:
Of ghostly[3] sight the people be so blind,
Drowned in sin, they know me not for their God:
In worldly riches is all their mind,
They fear not my right wiseness, the sharp rod:
My law that I shewed, when I for them died,
They forget clean, and shedding of my blood red: 30
I hanged between two, it cannot be denied:
To get them life I suffered to be dead:
I healed their feet, with thorns hurt was my head:
I could do no more than I did truly,
And now I see the people do clean forsake me,
They use the seven deadly sins damnable;
As pride, covetise, wrath, and lechery,
Now in the world be made commendable;
And thus they leave of angels the heavenly company;
Everyman liveth so after his own pleasure, 40
And yet of their life they be nothing sure:
I see the more that I them forbear
The worse they be from year to year;
All that liveth appaireth[4] fast,
Therefore I will in all the haste
Having a reckoning of Everyman's person
For and[5] I leave the people thus alone
In their life and wicked tempests,
Verily they will become much worse than beasts;
For now one would by envy another up eat; 50
Charity they all do clean forget.
I hoped well that Everyman
In my glory should make his mansion,
And thereto I had them all elect;
But now I see, like traitors deject,
They thank me not for the pleasure that I to them meant
Nor yet for their being that I them have lent;
I proffered the people great multitude of mercy,
And few there be that asketh it heartily;
They be so combered with worldly riches, 60
That needs of them I must do justice,
On Everyman living without fear.
Where art thou, Death, thou mighty messenger?

Death: Almighty God, I am here at your will,
Your commandment to fulfil.

God: Go thou to Everyman,
And show him in my name
A pilgrimage he must on him take,
Which he in no wise may escape:
And that he bring with him a sure reckoning 70

Without delay or any tarrying.

Death: Lord, I will in the world go run over all,
And cruelly outsearch both great and small;
Every man will I beset that liveth beastly
Out of God's laws, and dreadeth not folly:
He that loveth riches I will strike with my dart,
His sight to blind, and from heaven to depart,
Except that alms be his good friend,
In hell for to dwell, world without end.
Lo, yonder I see Everyman walking; 80
Full little he thinketh on my coming;
His mind is on fleshly lusts and his treasure,
And great pain it shall cause him to endure
Before the Lord Heaven King.
Everyman, stand still; whither art thou going
Thus gaily? Hast my Maker forgot?

Everyman: Why askst thou?
Wouldest thou wete?[6]

Death: Yea, sir, I will show you;
In great haste I am sent to thee 90
From God out of his majesty.

Everyman: What, sent to me?

Death: Yea, certainly.
Though thou have forget him here,
He thinketh on thee in the heavenly sphere,
As, or we depart, thou shalt know.

Everyman: What desireth God of me?

Death: That shall I show thee;
A reckoning he will needs have
Without any longer respite. 100

Everyman: To give a reckoning longer leisure I crave;
This blind matter troubleth my wit.

Death: On thee thou must take a long journey:
Therefore thy book of count with thee thou bring:
For turn again thou can not by no way.
And look thou be sure of thy reckoning:
For before God thou shalt answer, and show
Thy many bad deeds and good but a few;
How thou hast spent thy life, and in what wise,
Before the chief lord of paradise. 110
Have ado that we were in that way,
For, wete thou well, thou shalt make none attournay.[7]

Everyman: Full unready I am such reckoning to give.
I know thee not: what messenger art thou?

Death: I am Death, that no man dreadeth.
For every man I rest[8] and no man spareth;
For it is God's commandment
That all to me should be obedient.

Everyman: O Death, thou comest when I had thee least
in mind,
In thy power it lieth me to save, 120
Yet of my good[s] will I give thee, if ye will be kind,
Yea, a thousand pound shalt thou have,
And defer this matter till another day.

---

[2] Ungrateful.
[3] Spiritual.
[4] Decays.
[5] If.

[6] Know.
[7] Mediator.
[8] Arrest.

Death: Everyman, it may not be by no way;
I set not by gold, silver, nor riches,
Ne by pope, emperor, king, duke, ne princes,
For and I would receive gifts great,
All the world I might get;
But my custom is clean contrary.
I give thee no respite: come hence, and not tarry. 130
    Everyman: Alas, shall I have no longer respite?
I may say Death giveth no warning:
To think on thee, it maketh my heart sick,
For all unready is my book of reckoning.
But twelve year and I might have abiding,
My counting book I would make so clear,
That my reckoning I should not need to fear.
Wherefore, Death, I pray thee, for God's mercy.
Spare me till I be provided of remedy.
    Death: Thee availeth not to cry, weep, and pray: 140
But haste thee lightly that you were gone the journey.
And prove thy friends if thou can.
For, wete thou well, the tide abideth no man,
And in the world each living creature
For Adam's sin must die of nature.
    Everyman: Death, if I should this pilgrimage take,
And my reckoning surely make,
Show me, for saint charity,
Should I not come again shortly?
    Death: No, Everyman; and thou be once there, 150
Thou mayst never more come here,
Trust me verily.
    Everyman: O gracious God, in the high seat celestial,
Have mercy on me in this most need;
Shall I have no company from this vale terrestrial
Of mine acquaintance that way me to lead?
    Death: Yea, if any be so hardy,
That would go with thee and bear thee company.
Hie thee that you were gone[9] to God's magnificence,
Thy reckoning to give before his presence. 160
What, weenest[10] thou thy life is given thee,
And thy worldly goods also?
    Everyman: I had wend[11] so, verily.
    Death: Nay, nay; it was but lent thee;
For as soon as thou art go,
another awhile shall have it, and then go therefrom
Even as thou has done.
Everyman, thou art mad; thou hast thy wits five,
And here on earth will not amend thy life,
For suddenly I do come. 170
    Everyman: O wretched caitiff, whither shall I flee,
That I might scape this endless sorrow!
Now, gentle Death, spare me till to-morrow,
That I may amend me
With good advisement.
    Death: Nay, thereto I will not consent,
Nor no man will I respite,

But to the heart suddenly I shall smite
Without any advisement.
And now out of thy sight I will me nie; 180
See thou make thee ready shortly,
For thou mayst say this is the day
That no man living may scape away.
    Everyman: Alas, I may well weep with sighs deep,
Now have I no manner of company
To help me in my journey, and me to keep;
And also my writing is full unready.
How shall I do now for to excuse me?
I would to God I had never be gete![12]
To my soul a full great profit it had be; 190
For now I fear pains huge and great.
The time passeth; Lord, help that all wrought;
For though I mourn it availeth nought.
The day passeth, and is almost a-go;
I wot not well what for to do.
To whom were I best my complaint to make?
What, and I to Fellowship thereof spake,
And showed him of this sudden chance?
For in him is all mine affiance;[13]
We have in the world so many a day 200
Be on good friends in sport and play.
I see him yonder, certainly;
I trust that he will bear me company;
Therefore to him will I speak to ease my sorrow.
Well met, good Fellowship, and good morrow!
    Fellowship: Everyman, good morrow by this day.
Sir, why lookest thou so piteously?
If any thing be amiss, I pray thee, me say,
That I may help to remedy.
    Everyman: Yea, good Fellowship, yea. 210
I am in great jeopardy.
    Fellowship: My true friend, show to me your mind;
I will not forsake thee, unto my life's end,
In the way of good company.
    Everyman: That was well spoken, and lovingly.
    Fellowship: Sir, I must needs know your heaviness;
I have pity to see you in any distress;
If any have ye wronged he shall revenged be,
Though I on the ground be slain for thee—
Thou that I know before that I should die. 220
    Everyman: Verily, Fellowship, gramercy.[14]
    Fellowship: Tush! by thy thanks I set not a straw;
Show me your grief, and say no more.
    Everyman: If I my heart should to you break,
And then you to turn your mind from me,
And would not me comfort, when you hear me speak,
Then should I ten times sorrier be.
    Fellowship: Sir, I say as I will do in deed.
    Everyman: Then be you a good friend at need:
I have found you true here before. 230
    Fellowship: And so ye shall evermore;

---

[9] Hurry and go.
[10] Do you suppose.
[11] Supposed.

[12] Been born.
[13] Trust.
[14] Many thanks.

For, in faith, and thou go to Hell,
I will not forsake thee by the way!
    Everyman: Ye speak like a good friend: I believe you well;
I shall deserve[15] it, and I may.
    Fellowship: I speak of no deserving, by this day.
For he that will say and nothing do
Is not worthy with good company to go;
Therefore show me the grief of your mind,
As to your friend most loving and kind.   240
    Everyman: I shall show you how it is;
Commanded I am to go a journey,
A long way, hard and dangerous,
And give a strait count without delay
Before the high judge Adonai.[16]
Wherefore I pray you, bear me company,
As ye have promised, in this journey.
    Fellowship: That is matter indeed! Promise is duty,
But, and I should take such a voyage on me,
I know it well, it should be to my pain: 250
Also it make me afeard, certain.
But let us take counsel here as well as we can,
For your words would fear[17] a strong man.
    Everyman: Why, ye said, if I had need,
Ye would me never forsake, quick nor dead,
Though it were to Hell truly.
    Fellowship: So I said, certainly,
But such pleasures be set aside, thee sooth to say:
And also, if we took such a journey,
When should we come again?   260
    Everyman: Nay, never again till the day of doom.
    Fellowship: In faith, then will not I come there!
Who hath you these tidings brought?
    Everyman: Indeed, Death was with me here.
    Fellowship: Now, by God that all hath bought,
If Death were the messenger,
For no man that is living today
I will not go that loath journey—
Not for the father that begat me!
    Everyman: Ye promised other wise, pardie.[18]   270
    Fellowship: I wot well I say so truly
And yet if thou wilt eat, and drink, and make good cheer,
Or haunt to women, the lusty company,
I would not forsake you, while the day is clear,
Trust me verily!
    Everyman: Yea, thereto ye would be ready;
To go to mirth, solace, and play
Your mind will sooner apply
Than to bear me company in my long journey.
    Fellowship: Now, in good faith, I will not that way.   280
But and thou wilt murder, or any man kill,
In that I will help thee with a good will!
    Everyman: O that is a simple advice indeed!

Gentle fellow: help me in my necessity;
We have loved long, and now I need,
And now, gentle Fellowship, remember me.
    Fellowship: Whether ye have loved me or no,
By Saint John, I will not with thee go.

   . . . .

[Everyman next turns to members of his family, but both Kindred and Cousin refuse to accompany him to the grave. He then seeks out Goods, his worldly possessions.]

    Goods: Who calleth me? Everyman? What haste thou
        hast!
I lie here in corners, trussed and piled so high,
And in chests I am locked so fast,
Also sacked in bags, thou mayst see with thine eye,
I cannot stir; in packs low I lie,
What would ye have, lightly me say.[19]
    Everyman: Come hither, Good, in all the haste thou
        may,
For of counsel I must desire thee.
    Goods: Sir, and ye in the world have trouble or adversity.   400
That can I help you to remedy shortly.
    Everyman: It is another disease that grieveth me;
In this world it is not, I tell thee so.
I am sent for another way to go,
To give a straight account general
Before the highest Jupiter of all;
And all my life I have had joy and pleasure in thee.
Therefore I pray thee go with me,
For, peradventure, thou mayst before God Almighty
My reckoning help to clean and purify;   410
For it is said ever among,
That money maketh all right that is wrong.
    Goods: Nay, Everyman, I sing another song.
I follow no man in such voyages;
For and I went with thee
Thou shouldst fare much the worse for me;
For because on me thou did set thy mind,
Thy reckoning I have made blotted and blind
That thine account thou cannot make truly;
And that has thou for the love of me.   420
    Everyman: That would grieve me full sore,
When I should come to that fearful answer.
Up, let us go thither together.
    Goods: Nay, no so, I am too brittle, I may not endure:
I will follow no man one foot, be ye sure.
    Everyman: Alas, I have thee loved, and had great
pleasure
All my life-days on good and treasure.
    Goods: That is to thy damnation without lesing,[20]
For my love is contrary to the love everlasting
But if thou had me loved moderately during,   430
As, to the poor give part of me,

---

[15] Repay.
[16] God.
[17] Terrify.
[18] By God.

[19] Quickly tell me.
[20] Loosing, releasing.

Then shouldst thou not in this dolour[21] be,
Nor in this great sorrow and care.

. . . .

[Knowledge guides Everyman to Confession, Discretion, Strength,
Beauty, and Five-Wits, who direct him to
receive the sacrament of extreme unction.]

Knowledge: Everyman, hearken what I say;
Go to priesthood, I you advise,
And receive of him in any wise
The holy sacrament and ointment together;
Then shortly see ye turn again hither;
We will all abide you here.

   Five-Wits: Yea, Everyman, hie[22] you that ye ready were, There is
no emperor, king, duke, ne baron,
That of God hath commission,
As hath the least priest in the world being;   **530**
For of the blessed sacraments pure and benign,
He beareth the keys and thereof hath the cure
For man's redemption, it is ever sure;
Which God for our soul's medicine
Gave us out of his heart with great pine;[23]
Here in this transitory life, for thee and me
The blessed sacraments seven there be.
Baptism, confirmation, with priesthood good,
And the sacrament of God's precious flesh and blood,
Marriage, the holy extreme unction, and penance;   **540**
These seven be good to have in remembrance,
Gracious sacraments of high divinity.

. . . .

[All but Good-Deeds then abandon Everyman.]

Everyman: Methinketh, alas, that I must be gone
To make my reckoning and my debts pay,
For I see my time is nigh spent away.
Take example, all ye that this do hear or see,
How they that I loved best do forsake me,   **600**
Except my Good-Deeds that bideth truly.
   Good-Deeds: All earthly things is but vanity:
Beauty, Strength, and Discretion, do man forsake,
Foolish friends and kinsmen, that fair spake,
All fleeth save Good-Deeds, and that am I.
   Everyman: Have mercy on me, God most mighty;
And stand by me, thou Mother and Maid, holy Mary.
   Good-Deeds: Fear not, I will speak for thee.
   Everyman: Here I cry God mercy.
   Good-Deeds: Short our end, and minish[24] our pain;   **610**
Let us go and never come again.
   Everyman: Into thy hands, Lord, my soul I commend; Receive it,
Lord, that it be not lost;
As thou me boughtest, so me defend,
And save me from the fiend's boast,

That I may appear with that blessed host
That shall be saved at the day of doom.
In mannus tuas—of might's most
For ever—*commendo spiritum meum.*[25]
   Knowledge: Now hath he suffered that we all shall   **620**
   endure:
The Good-Deeds shall make all sure.
Now hath he made ending;
Methinketh that I hear angels sing
And make great joy and melody,
Where Everyman's soul received shall be.
   Angel: Come, excellent elect spouse to Jesu:[26]
Hereabove thou shalt go
Because of thy singular virtue:
Now the soul is taken the body fro;
Thy reckoning is crystal-clear.   **630**
Now shalt thou into the heavenly sphere,
Unto the which all ye shall come
That liveth well before the day of doom.
   Doctor: This moral men may have in mind;
Ye hearers, take it of worth, old and young,
And forsake pride, for he deceiveth you in the end,
And remember Beauty, Five-Wits, Strength, and
   Discretion,
They all at the last do Everyman forsake,
Save his Good-Deeds, there doth he take.
But beware, and they be small   **640**
Before God, he hath not help at all.
None excuse may be there for Everyman:
Alas, how shall he do then?
For after death amends may no man make,
For then mercy and pity do him forsake.
If his reckoning be not clear when he do come,
God will say—*ite maledicti in ignem aeternum.*[27]
And he that hath his account whole and sound,
High in heaven he shall be crowned;
Unto which place God brings us all thither   **650**
That we may live body and soul together.
Thereto help the Trinity,
Amen, say ye, for saint Charity
THUS ENDETH THIS MORAL PLAY OF EVERYMAN.

Q What key aspects of the medieval
mind are represented in this play?

Dante's *Divine Comedy*

The medieval view of life on earth as a vale of tears was balanced by a triumphant belief in the divine promise of deliverance and eternal bliss. By far the most profound statement of these ideas is the epic poem known as the *Commedia Divina* or *Divine Comedy*. Begun ca. 1308 by the Florentine poet Dante Alighieri (1265–1321), the *Commedia* records, on the literal level, an adventure-packed

---

[21] Distress.
[22] Hasten.
[23] Suffering.
[24] Diminish.

[25] Into your hands I commend my spirit.
[26] Bride of Christ, a term symbolizing the soul's union with God.
[27] Be damned to the eternal fire.

journey through the realm of the dead (Figure **12.5**). On a symbolic level, the poem describes the spiritual pilgrimage of the Christian soul from sin (Hell), through purification (Purgatory), and ultimately, to salvation (Paradise) (Figure **12.6**). The *Divine Comedy* is the quintessential expression of the medieval mind in that it gives dramatic form to the fundamental precepts of the Christian way of life and death. The structure of the poem reflects the medieval view of nature as the mirror of God's plan, while the text of the poem provides an invaluable picture of the context: the ethical, political, and theological concerns of Dante's time.

Every aspect of Dante's *Commedia* carries symbolic meaning. For instance, Dante is accompanied through Hell by the Roman poet Virgil, who stands for human reason. Dante deeply admired Virgil's great epic, the *Aeneid*, and was familiar with the hero's journey to the underworld included in the sixth book of the poem. As Dante's guide, Virgil may travel only as far as the top of Mount Purgatory, for while human reason serves as the pilgrim's initial guide to salvation, it cannot penetrate the divine mysteries of the Christian faith. In Paradise, Dante is escorted by Beatrice, the symbol of Divine Wisdom, modeled on a Florentine woman who had, throughout the poet's life, been the object of his physical desire and spiritual devotion. Dante structured the *Commedia* according to a strict moral hierarchy. The three parts of the poem correspond to the Aristotelian divisions of the human psyche: reason, will, and love. They also represent

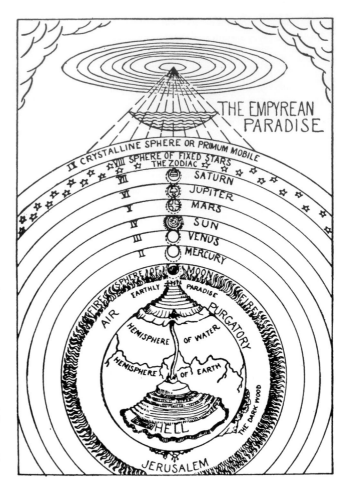

Figure 12.6 Plan of Dante's Universe.

Figure 12.5 DOMENICO DI MICHELINO, *Dante and His Poem*, 1465. Fresco, 10 ft. 6 in. × 9 ft. 7 in. Florence Cathedral, Italy. Dante, with an open copy of the *Commedia*, points to Hell with his right hand. The Mount of Purgatory with its seven terraces is behind him. Florence's cathedral (with its newly finished dome) represents Paradise on the poet's left.

the potential moral conditions of the Christian soul: perversity, repentance, and grace.

Sacred numerology—especially the number 3, symbolic of the Trinity—permeates the design of the *Commedia*. The poem is divided into three canticles (books); and each canticle has thirty-three **cantos**, to which Dante added one introductory canto to total a sublime one hundred (the number symbolizing plenitude and perfection). Each canto consists of stanzas composed in *terza rima*—interlocking lines that rhyme a/b/a, b/c/b, c/d/c. There are three guides to escort Dante, three divisions of Hell and Purgatory, three main rivers in Hell. Three squared (9) are the regions of sinners in Hell, the circles of penitents in Purgatory, and the spheres of Heaven.

The elaborate numerology of the *Commedia* is matched by multileveled symbolism that draws into synthesis theological, scientific, and historical information based in ancient and medieval sources. Given this wealth of symbolism, it is remarkable that the language of the poem is so sharply realistic. For, while the characters in the *Commedia*, like those in *Everyman*, serve an allegorical function, they are, at the same time, convincing flesh-and-blood creatures. The inhabitants of Dante's universe are real people, some drawn from history and legend, others from his own era—citizens of the bustling urban centers of Italy through which Dante had wandered for nineteen years after his exile from his native Florence for political offenses. By framing the poem on both a literal level and an allegorical one, Dante reinforces the medieval (and essentially Augustinian) bond between the City of Man and the City of God. At the same time, he animates a favorite theme of medieval sermons: the warning that actions in this life bring inevitable consequences in the next.

Well versed in both Classical and Christian literature, Dante had written Latin treatises on political theory and on the origins and development of language. But for the poem that constituted his epic masterpiece, he rejected the Latin of churchmen and scholars and wrote in his native Italian, the language of everyday speech. Dante called his poem a comedy because the piece begins with affliction (Hell) and ends with joy (Heaven). Later admirers added the adjective "divine" to the title, not simply to describe its religious character, but also to praise its sublime lyrics and its artful composition.

The most lively of the canticles, and the one that best manifests Dante's talent for creating realistic images with words, is the "Inferno," the first book of the *Commedia*. With grim moral logic, sinners are assigned to one of the nine rings in Hell (Figure **12.7**), where they are punished according to the nature of their sins: the violent are immersed for eternity in boiling blood and the gluttons wallow like pigs in their own excrement. By the law of symbolic retribution, the sinners are punished not *for* but *by* their sins. Those condemned for sins of passion—the least grave of sins—inhabit the conical rings at the top of Hell, while those who have committed sins of the will lie farther down. Those guilty of sins of the intellect are imprisoned still lower, deep within the pit ruled by Satan (Figure **12.8**). Thus, Dante's Hell pictures a moral hierarchy in which the damned suffer the destiny they have earned.

In the last canto of the "Inferno," Dante visits the ninth circle of Hell, the very bottom of the infernal pit. Lodged in ice up to his chest, a three-faced Satan beats his six batlike wings to create a chilling wind—the setting provides sharp contrast with the flaming regions of Upper Hell. Surrounding Satan, whom Dante calls "the Emperor of the Universe of Pain," those guilty of treachery—the most foul of all sins, according to Dante—are imprisoned in the ice, "like straws in glass." Satan, weeping tears "mixed with bloody froth and pus," chews with "rake-like teeth" on the bodies of the three most infamous traitors of Christian and Classical history respectively: Judas, Brutus, and Cassius. The dark and brooding despair that pervades the "Inferno"

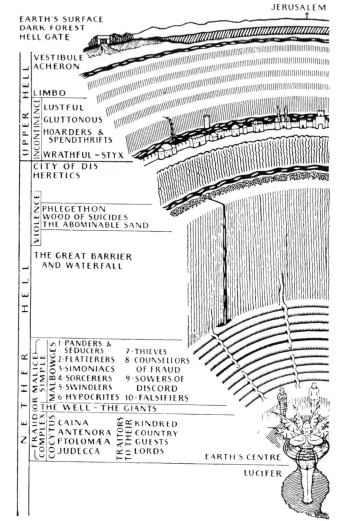

Figure 12.7 Plan of Dante's "Inferno."

reflects the medieval view of Hell as the condition of the soul farthest from the light of God. Nevertheless, the last canto of the "Inferno" ends with Dante and Virgil climbing from the frozen pit "into the shining world," a motif of ascent that pervades the second and third canticles.

Satan's domain stands in grim contrast to the blissful experience of God enjoyed by those in Paradise. Light, the least material of natural elements, is a prime image in Dante's evocation of Heaven, and light imagery—as central to the *Commedia* as it is to Saint Ambrose's hymn (see Reading 9.2)—pervades Dante's vision of God's mystery and majesty. The last eight stanzas of Canto 33 of "Paradiso" (reproduced below) are the culminating phase of that vision. In the perfect shape of the circle, as in a cathedral rose window, Dante sees the image of humankind absorbed into the substance of God. And as that wheel of love turns, the poet discovers the redemptive radiance of God.

It is impossible to recreate the grandeur of the *Commedia* by means of two cantos, especially since, translated into English, a great deal of the richness of the original Tuscan dialect is lost. Nevertheless, some of the majesty of Dante's poem may be conveyed by the excerpts reproduced here.

Figure 12.8 *Satan Eating and Excreting the Souls of the Damned in Hell.*

READING 12.4 From Dante's *Divine Comedy*

(ca. 1308–1321)

The Dark Wood of Error ("Inferno," Canto 1)

Midway in our life's journey, I went astray
   from the straight road and woke to find myself
   alone in a dark wood. How shall I say   3

what wood that was! I never saw so drear,
   so rank, so arduous a wilderness!
   Its very memory gives a shape to fear.   6

Death could scarce be more bitter than that place!
   But since it came to good, I will recount
   all that I found revealed there by God's grace.   9

How I came to it I cannot rightly say,
   so drugged and loose with sleep had I become
   when I first wandered there from the True Way.   12

But at the far end of the valley of evil
   whose maze had sapped my very heart with fear!
   I found myself before a little hill   15

and lifted up my eyes. Its shoulders glowed
   already with the sweet rays of that planet
   whose virtue leads men straight on every road,   18

and the shining strengthened me against the fright
   whose agony had wracked the lake of my heart
   through all the terrors of that piteous night.   21

Just as a swimmer, who with his last breath
   flounders ashore from perilous seas, might turn
   to memorize the wide water of his death—   24

so did I turn, my soul still fugitive
   from death's surviving image, to stare down
   that pass that none had ever left alive.   27

And there I lay to rest from my heart's race
   till calm and breath returned to me. Then rose
   and pushed up that dead slope at such a pace   30

each footfall rose above the last. And lo!
   almost at the beginning of the rise
   I faced a spotted Leopard, all tremor and flow   33

and gaudy pelt. And it would not pass, but stood
   so blocking my every turn that time and again
   I was on the verge of turning back to the wood.   36

This fell at the first widening of the dawn
   as the sun was climbing Aries with those stars
   that rode with him to light the new creation.   39

Thus the holy hour and the sweet season
   of commemoration did much to arm my fear
   of that bright murderous beast with their good omen.   42

Yet not so much but what I shook with dread
   at sight of a great Lion that broke upon me
   raging with hunger, its enormous head   45

held high as if to strike a mortal terror
   into the very air. And down his track,
   a She-Wolf drove upon me, a starved horror   48

ravening and wasted beyond all belief.
   She seemed a rack for avarice, gaunt and craving.
   Oh many the souls she has brought to endless grief!   51

She brought such heaviness upon my spirit
    at sight of her savagery and desperation,
    I died from every hope of that high summit.   **54**

And like a miser—eager in acquisition
    but desperate in self-reproach when Fortune's wheel
    turns to the hour of his loss—all tears and attrition   **57**

I wavered back; and still the beast pursued,
    forcing herself against me bit by bit
    till I slid back into the sunless wood.   **60**

And as I fell to my soul's ruin, a presence
    gathered before me on the discolored air,
    the figure of one who seemed hoarse from long silence.   **63**

At sight of him in that friendless waste I cried:
    "Have pity on me, whatever thing you are,
    whether shade or living man." And it replied: **66**

"Not man, though man I once was, and my blood
    was Lombard, both my parents Mantuan.
    I was born, though late, *sub Julio*, and bred   **69**

in Rome under Augustus in the noon
    of the false and lying gods. I was a poet
    and sang of old Anchises' noble son   **72**

who came to Rome after the burning of Troy.
    But you—why do *you* return to these distresses
    instead of climbing that shining Mount of Joy   **75**

which is the seat and first cause of man's bliss?"
    "And are you then that Virgil and that fountain
    of purest speech?" My voice grew tremulous: **78**

"Glory and light of poets! now may that zeal
    and love's apprenticeship that I poured out
    on your heroic verses serve me well!   **81**

For you are my true master and first author,
    the sole maker from whom I drew the breath
    of that sweet style whose measures have brought me honor.   **84**

See there, immortal sage, the beast I flee.
    For my soul's salvation, I beg you, guard me from her,
    for she has struck a mortal tremor through me."   **87**

And he replied, seeing my soul in tears:
    "He must go by another way who would escape
    this wilderness, for that mad beast that fleers*   **90**

before you there, suffers no man to pass.
    She tracks down all, kills all, and knows no glut,
    but, feeding, she grows hungrier than she was.   **93**

She mates with any beast, and will mate with more
    before the Greyhound comes to hunt her down.
    He will not feed on lands nor loot, but honor   **96**

and love and wisdom will make straight his way.
    He will rise between Feltro and Feltro, and in him
    shall be the resurrection and new day   **99**

---

* sneers

of that sad Italy for which Nisus died,
    and Turnus, and Euryalus, and the maid Camilla.
    He shall hunt her through every nation of sick pride   **102**

till she is driven back forever to Hell
    whence Envy first released her on the world.
    Therefore, for your own good, I think it well   **105**

you follow me and I will be your guide
    and lead you forth through an eternal place.
    There you shall see the ancient spirits tried   **108**

in endless pain, and hear their lamentation
    as each bemoans the second death of souls.
    Next you shall see upon a burning mountain   **111**

souls in fire and yet content in fire,
    knowing that whensoever it may be
    they yet will mount into the blessed choir.   **114**

To which, if it is still your wish to climb,
    a worthier spirit shall be sent to guide you.
    With her shall I leave you, for the King of Time,   **117**

who reigns on high, forbids me to come there
    since, living, I rebelled against his law.
    He rules the waters and the land and air   **120**

and there holds court, his city and his throne.
    Oh blessed are they he chooses!" And I to him:
    "Poet, by that God to you unknown,   **123**

lead me this way. Beyond this present ill
    and worse to dread, lead me to Peter's gate
    and be my guide through the sad halls of Hell."   **126**

And he then: "Follow." And he moved ahead
in silence, and I followed where he led.

Notes to "Inferno" (Canto 1)

line 1 *midway in our life's journey*: The biblical life span is three-score years and ten. The action opens in Dante's thirty-fifth year, i.e., 1300.

line 17 *that planet*: The sun. Ptolemaic astronomers considered it a planet. It is also symbolic of God as He who lights man's way.

line 31 *each footfall rose above the last*: The literal rendering would be: "So that the fixed foot was ever the lower." "Fixed" has often been translated "right" and an ingenious reasoning can support that reading, but a simpler explanation offers itself and seems more competent: Dante is saying that he climbed with such zeal and haste that every footfall carried him above the last despite the steepness of the climb. At a slow pace, on the other hand, the rear foot might be brought up only as far as the forward foot. This device of selecting a minute but exactly centered detail to convey the whole of a larger action is one of the central characteristics of Dante's style.

lines 33, 44, 48 *Leopard, Lion, She-Wolf*: These three beasts are undoubtedly taken from Jeremiah 5.6. Many additional and incidental interpretations have been advanced for them, but the central interpretation must remain as noted. They foreshadow the three divisions of Hell (incontinence, violence, and fraud) that Virgil explains at length in Canto 11, 16–111. I am not at all sure but what the She-Wolf is better interpreted as Fraud and the Leopard as Incontinence. Good arguments can be offered either way.

lines 38–39 *Aries . . . that rode with him to light the new creation*: The medieval tradition had it that the sun was in Aries at the time of the Creation. The significance of the astronomical and religious conjunction is an important part of Dante's intended allegory. It is just before dawn of Good Friday 1300 when he awakens in the Dark Wood. Thus his new life begins under Aries, the sign of creation, at dawn (rebirth), and in the Easter season (resurrection). Moreover the moon is full and the sun is in the equinox, conditions that did not fall together on any Friday of 1300. Dante is obviously constructing poetically the perfect Easter as a symbol of his new awakening.

line 69 *sub Julio*: In the reign of Julius Caesar.

lines 95–98 *the Greyhound . . .Feltro and Feltro*: Almost certainly refers to Can Grande della Scala (1290–1329), a great Italian leader born in Verona, which lies between the towns of Feltre and Montefeltro.

lines 100–101 *Nisus, Turnus, Euryalus, Camilla*: All were killed in the war between the Trojans and the Latians when, according to legend, Aeneas led the survivors of Troy into Italy. Nisus and Euryalus (*Aeneid* IX) were Trojan comrades-in-arms who died together. Camilla (*Aeneid* XI) was the daughter of the Latian king and one of the warrior women. She was killed in a horse charge against the Trojans after displaying great gallantry. Turnus (*Aeneid* XII) was killed by Aeneas in a duel.

line 110 *the second death*: Damnation. "This is the second death, even the lake of fire." (Revelation 20.14)

lines 118–119 *forbids me to come there since, living, etc*.: Salvation is only through Christ in Dante's theology. Virgil lived and died before the establishment of Christ's teachings in Rome, and therefore cannot enter Heaven.

line 125 *Peter's gate*: The gate of Purgatory. (See "Purgatorio" 9, 76 ff.) The gate is guarded by an angel with a gleaming sword. The angel is Peter's vicar (Peter, the first pope, symbolized all popes; i.e., Christ's vicar on earth) and is entrusted with the two great keys.

Some commentators argue that this is the gate of Paradise, but Dante mentions no gate beyond this one in his ascent to Heaven. It should be remembered, too, that those who pass the gate of Purgatory have effectively entered Heaven.

The three great gates that figure in the entire journey are: the gate of Hell (Canto 3, 1–11), the gate of Dis (Canto 8, 79–113, and Canto 9, 86–87), and the gate of Purgatory, as above.

The Ninth Circle of Hell ("Inferno," Canto 34)

"On march the banners of the King of Hell,"
   my Master said. "Toward us. Look straight ahead:
     can you make him out at the core of the frozen shell?"   **3**

Like a whirling windmill seen afar at twilight,
   or when a mist has risen from the ground—
     just such an engine rose upon my sight   **6**

stirring up such a wild and bitter wind
   I cowered for shelter at my Master's back
     there being no other windbreak I could find.   **9**

I stood now where the souls of the last class
   (with fear my verses tell it) were covered wholly:
     they shone below the ice like straws in glass.   **12**

Some lie stretched out; others are fixed in place
   upright, some on their heads, some on their
     soles; another, like a bow, bends foot to face.   **15**

When we had gone so far across the ice

that it pleased my Guide to show me the foul creature
   which once had worn the grace of Paradise,   **18**

he made me stop, and, stepping aside, he said:
   "Now see the face of Dis! This is the place
     where you must arm your soul against all dread."   **21**

Do not ask, Reader, how my blood ran cold
   and my voice choked up with fear. I cannot write it:
     this is a terror that cannot be told.   **24**

I did not die, and yet I lost life's breath:
   imagine for yourself what I became,
     deprived at once of both my life and death.   **27**

The Emperor of the Universe of Pain
   jutted his upper chest above the ice;
     and I am closer in size to the great mountain   **30**

the Titans make around the central pit,
   than they to his arms. Now starting from this part,
     imagine the whole that corresponds to it.   **33**

If he was once as beautiful as now
   he is hideous, and still turned on his Maker,
     well may he be the source of every woe!   **36**

With what a sense of awe I saw his head
   towering above me! for it had three faces:
     one was in front, and it was fiery red,   **39**

the other two, as weirdly wonderful,
   merged with it from the middle of each shoulder
     to the point where all converged at the top of the skull;   **42**

the right was something between white and bile;
   the left was about the color that one finds
     on those who live along the banks of the Nile.   **45**

Under each head two wings rose terribly,
   their span proportioned to so gross a bird:
     I never saw such sails upon the sea.   **48**

They were not feathers—their texture and their form
   were like a bat's wings—and he beat them so
     that three winds blew from him in one great storm: **51**

it is these winds that freeze all Cocytus. [The final pit of Hell.]
   He wept from his six eyes, and down three chins
     the tears ran mixed with bloody froth and pus.   **54**

In every mouth he worked a broken sinner
   between his rake-like teeth. Thus he kept three
     in eternal pain at his eternal dinner.   **57**

For the one in front the biting seemed to play
   no part at all compared to the ripping: at times
     the whole skin of his back was flayed away.   **60**

"That soul that suffers most," explained the Guide,
   "is Judas Iscariot, he who kicks his legs
     on the fiery chin and has his head inside.   **63**

Of the other two, who have their heads thrust forward
   the one who dangles down from the black face
     is Brutus: note how he writhes without a word.   **66**

And there, with the huge and sinewy arms, is the soul
  of Cassius. But the night is coming on
  and we must go, for we have seen the whole."   69

Then, as he bade, I clasped his neck, and he,
  watching for a moment when the wings
  were opened wide, reached over dexterously   72

and seized the shaggy coat of the king demon;
  then grappling matted hair and frozen crusts
  from one tuft to another, clambered down.   75

When we had reached the joint where the great thigh
  merges into the swelling of the haunch,
  my Guide and Master, straining terribly,   78

turned his head to where his feet had been
  and began to grip the hair as if he were climbing;
  so that I thought we moved toward Hell again.   81

"Hold fast!" my Guide said, and his breath came shrill
  with labor and exhaustion. "There is no way
  but by such stairs to rise above such evil."   84

At last he climbed out through an opening
  in the central rock, and he seated me on the rim;
  then joined me with a nimble backward spring.   87

I looked up, thinking to see Lucifer
  as I had left him, and I saw instead
  his legs projecting high into the air.   90

Now let all those whose dull minds are still vexed
  by failure to understand what point it was
  I had passed through, judge if I was perplexed.   93

"Get up. Up on your feet," my Master said.
  "The sun already mounts to middle tierce,
  and a long road and hard climbing lie ahead."   96

It was no hall of state we had found there,
  but a natural animal pit hollowed from rock
  with a broken floor and a close and sunless air.   99

"Before I tear myself from the Abyss,"
  I said when I had risen, "O my Master,
  explain to me my error in all this: 102

where is the ice? and Lucifer—how has he
  been turned from top to bottom: and how can the sun
  have gone from night to day so suddenly?"   105

And he to me: "You imagine you are still
  on the other side of the center where I grasped
  the shaggy flank of the Great Worm of Evil   108

which bores through the world—you *were* while I climbed down,
  but when I turned myself about, you passed
  the point to which all gravities are drawn.   111

You are under the other hemisphere where you stand;
  the sky above us is the half opposed
  to that which canopies the great dry land.   114

Under the mid-point of that other sky
  the Man who was born sinless and who lived

beyond all blemish, came to suffer and die.   117

You have your feet upon a little sphere
  which forms the other face of the Judecca. [Named
    for Judas Iscariot.]
  There it is evening when it is morning here.   120

And this gross Fiend and Image of all Evil
  who made a stairway for us with his hide
  is pinched and prisoned in the ice-pack still.   123

On this side he plunged down from heaven's height,
  and the land that spread here once hid in the sea
  and fled North to our hemisphere for fright;   126

and it may be that moved by that same fear,
  the one peak that still rises on this side
  fled upward leaving this great cavern here."   129

Down there, beginning at the further bound
  of Beelzebub's dim tomb, there is a space
  not known by sight, but only by the sound   132

of a little stream descending through the hollow
  it has eroded from the massive stone
  in its endlessly entwining lazy flow.   135

My Guide and I crossed over and began
  to mount that little known and lightless road
  to ascend into the shining world again.   138

He first, I second, without thought of rest
  we climbed the dark until we reached the point
  where a round opening brought in sight the blest   141

and beauteous shining of the Heavenly cars.
And we walked out once more beneath the Stars.

Notes to "Inferno" (Canto 34)

line 1 *On march the banners of the King*: The hymn ("Vexilla regis prodeunt") was written in the sixth century by Venantius Fortunatus, Bishop of Poitiers. The original celebrates the Holy Cross, and is part of the service for Good Friday to be sung at the moment of uncovering the cross.

line 17 *the foul creature*: Satan.

line 38 *three faces*: Numerous interpretations of these three faces exist. What is essential to all explanations is that they be seen as perversions of the qualities of the Trinity.

line 54 *bloody froth and pus*: The gore of the sinners he chews which is mixed with his slaver.

line 62 *Judas*: His punishment is patterned closely on that of the Simoniacs whom Dante describes in Canto 19.

line 67 *huge and sinewy arms*: The Cassius who betrayed Caesar was more generally described in terms of Shakespeare's "lean and hungry look." Another Cassius is described by Cicero (*Catiline* III) as huge and sinewy. Dante probably confused the two.

line 68 *the night is coming on*: It is now Saturday evening.

line 82 *his breath came shrill*: Cf. Canto 23, 85, where the fact that Dante breathes indicates to the Hypocrites that he is alive. Virgil's breathing is certainly a contradiction.

line 95 *middle tierce*: In the canonical day tierce is the period from about six to nine a.m. Middle tierce, therefore, is seven-thirty. In going through the center point, they have gone from night to day. They have moved ahead twelve hours.

line 128 *the one peak*: The Mount of Purgatory.

line 129 *this great cavern*: The natural animal pit of line 98. It is also "Beelzebub's dim tomb," line 131.

line 133 *a little stream*: Lethe. In Classical mythology, the river of forgetfulness, from which souls drank before being born. In Dante's symbolism it flows down from Purgatory, where it has washed away the memory of sin from the souls who are undergoing purification. That memory it delivers to Hell, which draws all sin to itself.

line 143 *Stars*: As part of his total symbolism Dante ends each of the three divisions of the *Commedia* with this word. Every conclusion of the upward soul is toward the stars, God's shining symbols of hope and virtue. It is just before dawn of Easter Sunday that the Poets emerge—a further symbolism.

From The Vision of God ("Paradiso," Canto 33)

O Light Eternal fixed in Itself alone,
    by Itself alone understood, which from Itself
    loves and glows, self-knowing and self-known;   **126**

that second aureole which shone forth in Thee,
    conceived as a reflection of the first—
    or which appeared so to my scrutiny—   **129**

seemed in Itself of Its own coloration
    to be painted with man's image. I fixed my eyes
    on that alone in rapturous contemplation.   **132**

Like a geometer wholly dedicated
    to squaring the circle, but who cannot find,
    think as he may, the principle indicated—   **135**

so did I study the supernal face.
    I yearned to know just how our image merges
    into that circle, and how it there finds place;   **138**

but mine were not the wings for such a flight.
    Yet, as I wished, the truth I wished for came
    cleaving my mind in a great flash of light.   **141**

Here my powers rest from their high fantasy,
    but already I could feel my being turned—
    instinct and intellect balanced equally   **144**

as in a wheel whose motion nothing jars—
by the Love that moves the Sun and the other stars.

Notes to "Paradiso" (Canto 33)

lines 130–144 *seemed in Itself of Its own coloration . . . instinct and intellect balanced equally*: The central metaphor of the entire Comedy is the image of God and the final triumphant in Godding of the elected soul returning to its Maker. On the mystery of that image, the metaphoric symphony of the *Comedy* comes to rest.

    In the second aspect of Triple-unity, in the circle reflected from the first, Dante thinks he sees the image of mankind woven into the very substance and coloration of God. He turns the entire attention of his soul to that mystery, as a geometer might seek to shut out every other thought and dedicate himself to squaring the circle. In *Il Convivio II*, 14, Dante asserted that the circle could not be squared, but that impossibility had not yet been firmly demonstrated in Dante's time and mathematicians still worked at the problem. Note, however, that Dante assumes the impossibility of

squaring the circle as a weak mortal example of mortal impossibility. How much more impossible, he implies, to resolve the mystery of God, study as man will.

    The mystery remains beyond Dante's mortal power. Yet, there in Heaven, in a moment of grace, God revealed the truth to him in a flash of light—revealed it, that is, to the God-enlarged power of Dante's emparadised soul. On Dante's return to the mortal life, the details of that revelation vanished from his mind but the force of the revelation survives in its power on Dante's feelings.

    So ends the vision of the *Comedy* and yet the vision endures, for ever since that revelation, Dante tells us, he feels his soul turning ever as one with the perfect motion of God's love.

    Q   **Why is Dante's Commedia considered a medieval epic?**

    Q   **Whom does Dante find in the ninth circle of Hell? Why are they there?**

The Medieval Church

During the High Middle Ages, the Catholic Church exercised great power and authority not only as a religious force, but also as a political institution. The papacy asserted the Church of Rome as the sole authority in Christendom, a position strongly opposed by the patriarchs of the Greek Orthodox Church in Constantinople. This disagreement, complicated by long-standing doctrinal and liturgical differences, led, in 1054, to a permanent breach between the Eastern and Western churches. In the West, the papacy took strong measures to ensure the independence of the Church from secular interference, especially by the emerging European states. In 1022, the Church formed the College of Cardinals as the sole body responsible for the election of popes. Medieval pontiffs functioned much like secular monarchs, governing a huge and complex bureaucracy that incorporated financial, judicial, and disciplinary branches. The Curia, the papal council and highest church court, headed a vast network of ecclesiastical courts, while the Camera (the papal treasury) handled financial matters. The medieval Church was enormously wealthy. Over the centuries, Christians had donated and bequeathed to Christendom so many thousands of acres of land that, by the end of the twelfth century, the Catholic Church was the largest single landholder in Western Europe.

    Among lay Christians of every rank the Church commanded religious obedience. It enforced religious conformity by means of such spiritual penalties as **excommunication** (exclusion from the sacraments) and **interdict**, the excommunication of an entire city or state—used to dissuade secular rulers from opposing papal policy. In spite of these spiritual weapons, **heresy** (denial of the revealed truths of the Christian faith) spread rapidly within the increasingly cosmopolitan centers of twelfth-century Europe. Such anticlerical groups as the Waldensians (followers of the French thirteenth-century reformer Peter Waldo) denounced the growing worldliness of the Church. Waldo proposed that lay Christians administer the sacraments and that the Bible—sole source of religious authority—should be translated into the vernacular.

Condemning such views as threats to civil and religious order, the Church launched antiheretical crusades that were almost as violent as those advanced against the Muslims. Further, in 1233, the pope established the Inquisition, a special court designed to stamp out heresy. The Inquisition brought to trial individuals whom local townspeople denounced as heretics. Deprived of legal counsel, the accused were usually tried in secret. Inquisitors might use physical torture to obtain confession, for the Church considered injury to the body preferable to the eternal damnation of the soul. If the Inquisition failed to restore accused heretics to the faith, it might impose such penalties as exile or excommunication, or it might turn over the defendants to the state to be hanged or burned at the stake—the latter being the preferred punishment for female heretics. With the same energy that the Church persecuted heretics, it acted as a civilizing agent. It preserved order by enforcing periods in which warfare was prohibited. It assumed moral and financial responsibility for the poor, the sick, and the homeless; and it provided for the organization of hospitals, refuges, orphanages, and other charitable institutions.

The power and prestige of the Church were enhanced by the outstanding talents of some popes as diplomats, canon lawyers, and administrators. Under the leadership of the lawyer-pope Innocent III, the papacy emerged as the most powerful political institution in Western Europe. Pope Innocent enlarged the body of canon law and refined the bureaucratic machinery of the Church. He used his authority to influence secular rulers and frequently intervened in the political, financial, and personal affairs of heads of state.

The Franciscans

At the Fourth Lateran Council (1215), Innocent III endorsed the establishment of a new monastic order that would revive the humane candor and devotional simplicity of the Sermon on the Mount. The Franciscans took their name from their founder, Giovanni Bernardone (1181–1226), whose father had nicknamed him "Francesco." The son of a wealthy Italian cloth merchant, Francis renounced a life of luxury and dedicated himself to preaching and serving the poor. In imitation of the apostles, he practiced absolute poverty and begged for his food and lodging as he traveled from town to town. Unlike Saint Benedict (see chapter 9) and other cloistered followers of Christ, Francis chose to evangelize among the citizens of the rapidly rising Italian city-states. His mendicant (begging) lifestyle made him an icon of humility; and his attention to the poor and the sickly revived the compassionate ideals of Early Christianity and of Jesus himself. Some of the legends written after the death of Francis reported that the body of the saint bore the stigmata, the marks of crucifixion. Others described Francis as a missionary to all of God's creations, hence, the popular depiction of the saint sermonizing to the beasts and the birds (Figure 12.9). In the song of praise written by Francis two years before his death, his reverence for nature is displayed with a forthright simplicity that resembles both the hymns of Ambrose (Reading 9.2) and the ritual prayers chanted by Native Americans in praise of nature (see Reading 18.5).

READING 12.5 Saint Francis' *The Canticle of Brother Sun* (1224)

Most High, all-powerful, good Lord,   1
Yours are the praises, the glory, the honor, and all blessing.
To You alone, Most High, do they belong,
and no man is worthy to mention Your name.
Praised be You, my Lord, with all your creatures,
especially Sir Brother Sun,
Who is the day and through whom You give us light.
And he is beautiful and radiant with great splendor;
and bears a likeness of You, Most High One.
Praised be You, my Lord, through Sister Moon and the stars,   10
in heaven You formed them clear and precious and beautiful.
Praised be You, my Lord, through Brother Wind,
and through the air, cloudy and serene, and every kind of weather
through which You give sustenance to Your creatures.
Praised be You, my Lord, through Sister Water,
which is very useful and humble and precious and chaste.
Praised be You, my Lord, through Brother Fire,
through whom You light the night
and he is beautiful and playful and robust and strong.

Figure 12.9 GIOTTO, *Sermon to the Birds*, ca. 1290. Fresco. Upper Church of San Francesco, Assisi, Italy.

Praised be You, my Lord, through our Sister Mother Earth,   **20**
who sustains and governs us,
and who produces varied fruits with colored flowers and herbs.
Praised be You, my Lord, through those who give pardon for Your love
and bear infirmity and tribulation.
Blessed are those who endure in peace
for by You, Most High, they shall be crowned.
Praised be You, my Lord, through our Sister Bodily Death,
from whom no living man can escape.
Woe to those who die in mortal sin.
Blessed are those whom death will find in Your most holy will,   **30**
for the second death shall do them no harm.
Praise and bless my Lord and give Him thanks
and serve Him with great humility.

Q **What is the relationship between God and nature in this song of praise?**

The Franciscans were not the sole exemplars of the wave of humanitarianism that swept through the Christian West during the thirteenth century: in 1216 the followers of the well-educated Spanish priest Saint Dominic (ca. 1170–1221) founded a second mendicant order devoted to teaching and preaching. Deeply committed to the study of theology, the Dominicans educated many renowned scholars, including Thomas Aquinas, discussed later in this chapter. The Franciscan and Dominican friars ("brothers") earned longlasting respect and acclaim for educating the young, fighting heresy, and ministering to the sick and needy.

Saint Francis and Saint Dominic drew many into their folds, but their female followers had a difficult time establishing orders in their name. The Fourth Lateran Council had confirmed church restrictions prohibiting nuns from hearing confession, preaching, and singing the Gospel—measures that limited the freedoms and privileges of Benedictine nuns and other holy women. The new orders

denied female participation, since neither Francis nor Dominic considered the apostolic life suitable for women. Nevertheless, one of the followers of Saint Francis, Clare Affreduccio (1193–1253), a young noblewoman from Assisi, renounced a life of aristocratic privilege to establish a community of women modeled on the practice of poverty and humility. Initially denied papal approval for a monastic order, Clare's rule was endorsed only days before she died. Clare was the first woman to write a rule for a religious order; the Order of Poor Ladies came to be called the Order of Saint Clare, or "Poor Clares."

The Medieval University

Of the many medieval contributions to modern Western society, one of the most significant is the university. Education in medieval Europe was almost exclusively a religious enterprise, and monastic schools had monopolized learning for many centuries. By the twelfth century, however, spurred by the resurgence of economic activity, the rise of towns, and the influx of heretofore unavailable Classical texts, education shifted from monastic and parish settings to cathedral schools located in the new urban centers of Western Europe. Growing out of these schools, groups of students and teachers formed guilds for higher learning; the Latin word *universitas* describes a guild of learners and teachers.

In medieval Europe, as in our own day, universities were arenas for intellectual inquiry and debate. At Bologna, Paris, Oxford, and Cambridge, to name but four among some eighty universities founded during the Middle Ages, the best minds of Europe grappled with the compelling ideas of their day, often testing those ideas against the teachings of the Church. The universities offered a basic Liberal Arts curriculum divided into two parts: the *trivium*, consisting of grammar, logic, and rhetoric; and the *quadrivium*, which included arithmetic, geometry, astronomy, and music. Programs in professional disciplines, such as

EXPLORING ISSUES

The Conflict Between Church and State

As secular rulers grew in power among the burgeoning nation-states of medieval Europe, the early medieval alliance between church and state slowly deteriorated. The attempts of kings and emperors to win the allegiance of their subjects—especially those in the newly formed towns—and to enlarge their financial resources often interfered with papal ambitions and Church decrees. When, for example, King Philip IV ("the Fair") of France (1268–1314) attempted to tax the clergy as citizens of the French realm, Pope Boniface VIII (ca. 1234–1303) protested, threatening to excommunicate and depose the king. In the dispute that followed, Pope Boniface issued the edict *Unam sanctam* ("One [and] Holy [Church]"), the boldest assertion of spiritual authority ever

published. The edict rested upon the centuries-old papal claim that the Church held primacy over the state, since, while the Church governed the souls of all Christians, the state governed only their bodies. In the ensuing struggle between popes and kings, the latter would emerge victorious. By the end of the fourteenth century, as European rulers freed themselves of papal interference in temporal affairs, the separation of church and state—each acting as sole authority in its own domain—would become established practice in the West. Nevertheless, *Unam sanctam* remained the classic justification for Church supremacy in both temporal and spiritual realms.

medicine, theology, and law, were also available. Textbooks—that is, handwritten manuscripts—were expensive and difficult to obtain, therefore teaching took the form of oral instruction, and students took copious notes based on class lectures (Figure **12.10**). Exams for the bachelor of arts (B.A.) degree, usually taken upon completion of a three- to five-year course of study, were oral. Beyond the B.A. degree, one might pursue additional study leading to mastery of a specialized field. The master of arts (M.A.) degree qualified the student to teach theology or practice law or medicine. Still another four years of study were usually required for the doctoral candidate, whose efforts culminated in his defense of a thesis before a board of learned masters. (Tradition required the successful candidate to honor his examiners with a banquet.)

Among the first universities was that founded at Bologna in northern Italy in 1159. Bologna was a center for the study of law. Its curriculum was run by students who hired professors to teach courses in law and other fields. University students brought pressure on townsfolk to maintain reasonable prices for food and lodging. They controlled the salaries and teaching schedules of their professors, requiring a teacher to obtain permission from his students for even a single day's absence and docking his pay if he was tardy. In contrast to the student-run university at Bologna, the university in Paris was a guild of teachers organized primarily for instruction in theology. This institution, which grew out of the cathedral school of Notre Dame, became independent of church control by way of a royal charter issued in the year 1200. Its respected degree in theology drew an international student body that made Paris the intellectual melting pot of the medieval West.

Until the thirteenth century, upper-class men and women received basically the same kinds of formal education. But with the rise of the university women were excluded from receiving a higher education, much as they were forbidden from entering the priesthood. Ranging between the ages of seventeen and forty, students often held minor orders in the Church. The intellectual enterprise of the most famous of the theologically trained schoolmen (or *Scholastics*, as they came to be called), inspired an important movement in medieval intellectual life known as Scholasticism.

Medieval Scholasticism

Before the twelfth century, intellectuals (as well as ordinary men and women) considered Scripture and the writings of the church fathers the major repositories of knowledge. Faith in these established sources superseded rational inquiry and preempted the empirical examination of the physical world. Indeed, most intellectuals upheld the Augustinian credo that faith preceded reason. They maintained that since both faith and reason derived from God, the two could never stand in contradiction. When, in the late twelfth century, Arab transcriptions of the writings of Aristotle and Arab commentaries on his works filtered into the West from Muslim Spain and Southwest Asia, a new intellectual challenge confronted churchmen and scholars. How were they to reconcile Aristotle's rational and dispassionate views on physical reality with the supernatural truths of the Christian faith? The Church's initial reaction was to ban Aristotle's works

Figure 12.10 *University Lecture by Henry of Germany*, from a medieval German edition of Aristotle's *Ethics*, second half of fourteenth century. Manuscript illumination, parchment, 7 × 8¾ in. In this all-male classroom, most of the students follow the lecturer attentively, but some appear bored, others distracted, and at least one has fallen asleep.

(with the exception of the *Logic*, which had long been available in the West), but by the early thirteenth century, all of the writings of the venerated Greek philosopher were in the hands of medieval scholars. For the next hundred years, the scholastics engaged in an effort to reconcile the two primary modes of knowledge: faith and reason, the first as defended by theology, the second as exalted in Greek philosophy.

Even before the full body of Aristotle's works was available, a brilliant logician and popular teacher at the University of Paris, Peter Abelard (1079–ca. 1144), had inaugurated a rationalist approach to church dogma—one that emphasized the freedom to doubt and to question authority. In his treatise *Sic et Non* (*Yes and No*), written several years before the high tide of Aristotelian influence, Abelard puts into practice one of the principal devices of the Scholastic method—that of balancing opposing points of view. *Sic et Non* presents 150 conflicting opinions on important religious matters from such sources as the Old Testament, the Greek philosophers, the Latin church fathers, and the decrees of the Church. Abelard's methodical compilation of Hebrew, Classical, and Christian thought is an expression of the Scholastic inclination to collect and reconcile vast amounts of information. This impulse toward synthesis also inspired the many *compendia* (collections), *specula* ("mirrors" of knowledge), and *summa* (comprehensive treatises) that were written during the twelfth and thirteenth centuries.

The impulse toward Scholastic synthesis was shared by scholars elsewhere. In Spain, home to a large Jewish population, the brilliant rabbi and physician, Moses Maimonides (1135–1205), assembled the rabbinical history of Hebrew law to produce a fourteen-volume summary known as the *Torah Mishnah*. While this work was written in Hebrew, Maimonides' more famous *Guide to the Perplexed* was written in Arabic. This effort to harmonize faith and reason drew on both the works of Aristotle (as rendered in Arabic translations) and the teachings of rabbinical Judaism. The *Guide* examines such traditional matters as free will and the existence of evil, but argues that the truths of revelation are beyond rational demonstration.

Thomas Aquinas

Maimonides' *Guide* would influence the writings of the greatest of the Scholastics, Thomas Aquinas (1225–1274). A Dominican theologian and teacher, Aquinas lectured and wrote on a wide variety of theological and biblical subjects, but his major contribution was the *Summa Theologica*, a vast compendium of virtually all of the major theological issues of the High Middle Ages. In this unfinished work, which exceeds Abelard's *Sic et Non* in both size and conception, Aquinas poses 631 questions on topics ranging from the nature of God to the ethics of money lending. The comprehensiveness of Aquinas' program is suggested by the following list of queries drawn arbitrarily from the *Summa*:

> Whether God exists
> Whether God is the highest good
> Whether God is infinite
> Whether God wills evil
> Whether there is a trinity in God
> Whether it belongs to God alone to create
> Whether good can be the cause of evil
> Whether angels assume bodies
> Whether woman should have been made in the first production of things
> Whether woman should have been made from man
> Whether the soul is composed of matter and form
> Whether man has free choice
> Whether paradise is a corporeal place
> Whether there is eternal law
> Whether man can merit eternal life without grace
> Whether it is lawful to sell a thing for more than it is worth

In dealing with each question, Aquinas follows Abelard's method of marshaling opinions that seem to oppose or contradict each other. But where Abelard merely mediates, Aquinas offers carefully reasoned answers; he brings to bear all the intellectual ammunition of his time in an effort to prove that the truths of reason (those proceeding from the senses and from the exercise of logic) are compatible with the truths of revelation (those that have been divinely revealed). Aquinas begins by posing an initial question—for instance, "Whether woman should have been made in the first production of things"; then he offers objections or negations of the proposition, followed by positive responses drawn from a variety of authoritative sources—mainly Scripture and the works of the early church fathers (see chapter 9). The exposition of these "seeming opposites" is followed by Aquinas' own opinion, a synthesis that invariably reconciles the contradictions. Finally, Aquinas provides "reply objections" answering the original objections one by one. So, for example, Objection 3, which argues that woman should not have been created because she constituted an "occasion for sin" is countered by Reply Objection 3, which asserts God's power to "direct any evil (even that of womankind) to a good end."

In the following excerpt, Aquinas deals with the question of whether and to what purpose God created women, whom most medieval churchmen regarded as the "daughters of Eve" and hence the source of humankind's depravity. Following Aristotle, Aquinas concludes that, though inferior to man in "the discernment of reason," woman was created as man's helpmate in reproducing the species. Significantly, however, Aquinas denies Aristotle's claim that woman is a defective male and, elsewhere in the *Summa*, he holds that women should retain property rights and their own earnings. Even this brief examination of the *Summa Theologica* reveals its majestic intellectual sweep, its hierarchic rigor, and its power of synthesis—three of the principal characteristics of medieval cultural expression.

READING 12.6 From Aquinas' *Summa Theologica* (1274)

Whether Woman Should Have Been Made in the First Production of Things?

We proceed thus to the First Article:

Objection 1. It would seem that woman should not have been made in the first production of things. For the Philosopher[1] says that the *female is a misbegotten male*. But nothing misbegotten or defective should have been in the first production of things. Therefore woman should not have been made at that first production.

Objection 2. Further, subjection and limitation were a result of sin, for to the woman was it said after sin (*Gen.* iii. 16): *Thou shalt be under the man's power*; and Gregory[2] says that, *Where there is no sin, there is no inequality*. But woman is naturally of less strength and dignity than man, *for the agent is always more honorable than the patient*, as Augustine says. Therefore woman should not have been made in the first production of things before sin.

Objection 3. Further, occasions of sin should be cut off. But God foresaw that woman would be an occasion of sin to man. Therefore He should not have made woman.

On the contrary, It is written (*Gen.* ii. 18): *It is not good for man to be alone; let us make him a helper like to himself.*

I answer that, It was necessary for woman to be made, as the Scripture says, as a *helper* to man; not, indeed, as a helpmate in other works, as some say, since man can be more efficiently helped by another man in other works: but as a helper in the work of generation. . . . Among perfect animals, the active power of generation belongs to the male sex, and the passive power to the female. And as among animals there is a vital operation nobler than generation, to which their life is principally directed, so it happens that the male sex is not found in continual union with the female in perfect animals, but only at the time of coition; so that we may consider that by coition the male and female are one, as in plants they are always united, even though in some cases one of them preponderates, and in some the other. But man is further ordered to a still nobler work of life, and that is intellectual operation. Therefore there was greater reason for the

distinction of these two powers in man; so that the female should be produced separately from the male, and yet that they should be carnally united for generation. Therefore directly after the formation of woman, it was said: *And they shall be two in one flesh* (*Gen.* ii. 24).

Reply Objection 1. As regards the individual nature, woman is defective and misbegotten, for the active power in the male seed tends to the production of a perfect likeness according to the masculine sex; while the production of woman comes from defect in the active power, or from some material indisposition, or even from some external influence, such as that of a south wind, which is moist, as the Philosopher observes. On the other hand, as regards universal human nature, woman is not misbegotten, but is included in nature's intention as directed to the work of generation. Now the universal intention of nature depends on God, Who is the universal Author of nature. Therefore, in producing nature, God formed not only the male but also the female.

Reply Objection 2. Subjection is twofold. One is servile, by virtue of which a superior makes use of a subject for his own benefit; and this kind of subjection began after sin. There is another kind of subjection, which is called economic or civil, whereby the superior makes use of his subjects for their own benefit and good; and this kind of subjection existed even before sin. For the good of order would have been wanting in the human family if some were not governed by others wiser than themselves. So by such a kind of subjection woman is naturally subject to man, because in man the discernment of reason predominates. Nor is inequality among men excluded by the state of innocence, as we shall prove.

Reply Objection 3. If God had deprived the world of all those things which proved an occasion of sin, the universe would have been imperfect. Nor was it fitting for the common good to be destroyed in order that individual evil might be avoided; especially as God is so powerful that He can direct any evil to a good end. . . .

Q **What does this reading reveal about the potential conflict between reason and authority?**

The Scholastics aimed at producing a synthesis of Christian and Classical learning, but the motivation for and the substance of their efforts were still largely religious. Despite their attention to Aristotle's writings and their respect for his methods of inquiry, medieval Scholastics created no system of knowledge that completely dispensed with supernatural assumptions. Nevertheless, the Scholastics were the humanists of the medieval world; they held that the human being, the noblest and most rational of God's creatures, was the link between the created universe and divine intelligence. They believed that human reason was the handmaiden of faith, and that reason—though incapable of transcending revelation—was essential to the understanding of God's divine plan.

---

[1] Aristotle.
[2] Gregory the Great (see chapter 9).

LOOKING BACK

The Christian Way of Life and Death

- The Christian immortality ideology taught that life on earth was transient and that, depending on their conduct on earth, Christian souls would reap reward or punishment in an eternal hereafter. These concepts colored all aspects of medieval expression.
- By way of the sacraments, the Church participated in virtually every major aspect of the individual's life, enforcing a set of values that determined the collective spirituality of Christendom. Only the clergy could dispense the means by which the medieval Christian achieved personal salvation.
- The visionary tracts of Hildegard of Bingen brought the Scripture to life in dazzling allegorical prose. Medieval sermons and morality plays warned Christians of the perpetual struggle between good and evil and reminded them of the need to prepare for death.
- The morality play, *Everyman*, is a medieval allegory. It teaches that life is transient, that worldly goods are ultimately valueless, that only one's good works accompany one to the grave, and, finally, that in the soul's pilgrimage to salvation, the Church is the sole guide.
- The medieval mind perceived the visible world as a reflection of invisible truths, which, in God's universal scheme, followed a predesigned and unchanging order. The late medieval work that best reflects these ideas is Dante's *Commedia*. Written in the medieval Italian vernacular, this tripartite epic poem describes the Christian pilgrimage through Hell, Purgatory, and Paradise.

The Medieval Church

- The Catholic Church was the dominant political, religious, and cultural force of the European Middle Ages. Wealthy and powerful, it governed vast lands, a complex bureaucracy, and a large body of secular and regular clergymen.
- By means of excommunication, interdict, and the Inquisition, the Church challenged a rising tide of heresy. Despite increasingly powerful secular rulers among the European states, the Church maintained a position of political dominance in the West.
- At the Fourth Lateran Council (1215), Pope Innocent III authorized the Franciscan order, the first of the mendicant orders that worked to revive Early Christian ideals of poverty, compassion, and humility.
- With the rise of universities in twelfth-century Bologna, Paris, and elsewhere, intellectual life flourished. The leading teachers at the university of Paris, Abelard and Aquinas, were proponents of Scholasticism, a movement aimed at reconciling faith and reason.
- The effort to collect and reconcile vast amounts of information, in part a response to the influx of medieval Arabic transcriptions of Aristotle, complemented the move toward intellectual synthesis. Among Scholastics, matters concerning the eternal destiny of the soul and the fulfillment of God's design became the focus of humanist inquiry.

Glossary

canto one of the main divisions of a long poem

excommunication ecclesiastical censure that excludes the individual from receiving the sacraments

grace the free, unearned favor of God

heresy the denial of the revealed truths or orthodox doctrine by a baptized member of the Church; an opinion or doctrine contrary to Church dogma

interdict the excommunication of an entire city, district, or state

memento mori (Latin, "remember death") a warning of the closeness of death and the need to prepare for one's own death

miracle play a type of medieval play that dramatized the lives of, and especially the miracles performed by, Christ, the Virgin Mary, or the saints

morality play a type of medieval play that dramatized moral themes, such as the conflict between good and evil

mystery play a type of medieval play originating in church liturgy and dramatizing biblical history from the fall of Satan to the Last Judgment

pageant a roofed wagon-stage on which medieval plays and spectacles were performed

sacrament a sacred rite or pledge; in medieval Christianity, a visible sign (instituted by Jesus Christ) of God's grace

Chapter

13

The Medieval Synthesis in the Arts

ca. 1000–1300

"That which is united in splendor, radiates in splendor
And the magnificent work inundated with the new light shines."
Abbot Suger

Figure 13.1 South rose and lancets, thirteenth century. Chartres Cathedral. One of the three great rose windows at Chartres cathedral, the south rose centers on the image of Christ, surrounded by symbols of the evangelists, censing angels, and the elders of the Apocalypse. In the lancet windows, Mary and the Christ Child stand between four Old Testament prophets who carry on their shoulders the four evangelists, visually representing the idea that Jesus had come to fulfill the Hebrew Law (Matthew 5:17). The donors are shown kneeling at the base of the five lancets.

LOOKING AHEAD

If the Catholic Church was the major source of moral and spiritual instruction, it was also the patron and wellspring of artistic creativity. Its great monastic complexes, majestic cathedrals, painted altarpieces, illuminated manuscripts, and liturgical music all reflect the irrepressible vitality of an age of faith. While each of these genres retained its distinctive quality, each contributed to a grand synthesis, the all-embracing "whole" of Christian belief and worship. As with Dante's *Commedia* and Aquinas' *Summa*, the enterprise of synthesis involved the reconciliation of many diverse components. It drew inspiration from the idea of God as Master Architect (see Figure 12.1). If the macrocosm (the lesser universe) was designed by God so that no part stands independent of the whole, then the microcosm (the lesser universe of the Christian on earth) must mirror that design. The medieval architect, artist, and composer served the Christian community by recreating the majesty of God's plan. While operating to point the way to salvation, their creations worked to unite the temporal and divine realms.

The Romanesque Church

After the year 1000, devout Christians, who had expected the return of Jesus at the end of the millennium, reconciled themselves to the advent of a new age. The Benedictine abbey of Cluny in southeastern France launched a movement for monastic revitalization that witnessed—within a period of 150 years—the construction of more than 1000 monasteries and abbey churches throughout Western Europe. The new churches, most of which were modeled on Cluny itself, enshrined relics brought back from the Holy Land by the Crusaders or collected locally. Such relics—the remains of saints and martyrs, a piece of the Cross on which Jesus was crucified, and the like—became objects of holy veneration. They were housed in ornamented containers, or **reliquaries**, some in the shape of the body part they held. The reliquary statue pictured in Figure **13.2** held the cranium of the child martyr and favorite local saint of Conques. On feast days, the image, sheathed in thin sheets of gold and semiprecious stones, was carried through the streets in sacred procession. The monastic churches that housed the holy relics of saints and martyrs attracted thousands of Christian pilgrims. Some traveled to the shrine to seek pardon for sins or pay homage to a particular saint. Suppliants afflicted with blindness, leprosy, and other illnesses often slept near the saint's tomb in hope of a healing vision or a miraculous cure.

There were four major pilgrimage routes that linked the cities of France with the favorite shrine of Christian pilgrims: the cathedral of Santiago de Compostela in northwestern Spain (Map **13.1**). Santiago—that is, Saint

James Major (brother of Saint John the Evangelist)—was said to have brought Christianity to Spain. Martyred upon his return to Judea, his body was miraculously recovered in the early ninth century and buried at Compostela, where repeated miracles made his shrine a major pilgrimage center. Along the roads that carried pilgrims from Paris across to the Pyrenees, old churches were rebuilt and new churches erected, prompting one eleventh-century chronicler to observe, "The whole world seems to have shaken off her slumber, cast off her old rags, and clothed herself in a white mantle of new churches."

Like the Crusades, the pilgrimage was an expression of increased mobility and economic revitalization (see chapter 11). Since pilgrims, like modern tourists, constituted a major source of revenue for European towns and churches, parishes competed for them by enlarging church interiors and by increasing the number of reliquary chapels. The practical requirement for additional space in which to house these relics safely and make them accessible to

Figure 13.2 Reliquary statue of Sainte Foy, Conques, France, late tenth–eleventh century. Gold and gemstones over a wooden core, height 33½ in.

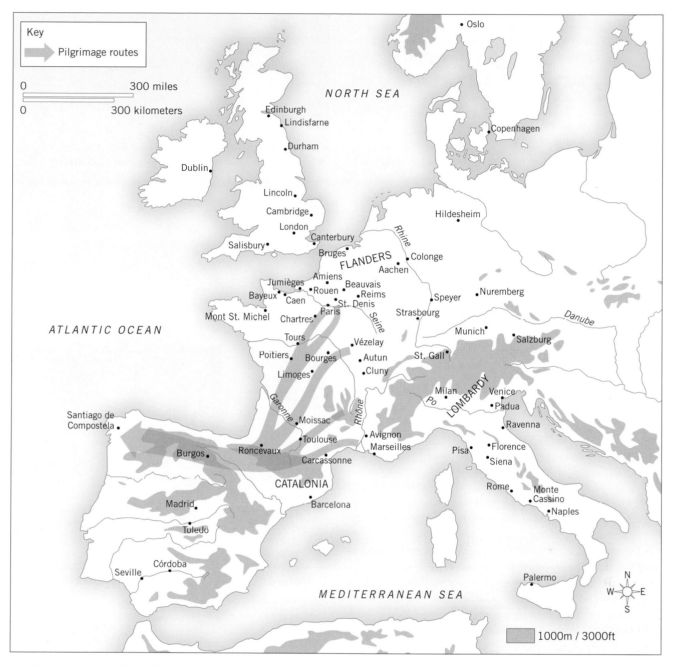

Map 13.1 Romanesque and Gothic Sites in Western Europe, ca. 1000–1300.

Christian pilgrims determined the plan of the pilgrimage church. To provide additional space for shrines, architects enlarged the eastern end of the church to include a number of radiating chapels. They also extended the side aisles around the transept and behind the apse to form an ambulatory (walkway). The ambulatory allowed lay visitors to move freely into the chapels without disturbing the monks at the main altar (Figure **13.3**). In the Early Christian church (see Figure 9.8), as in the Carolingian abbey (see Figure 11.12), the width of the nave was limited by the size and availability of roofing timber, and the wooden super-structure itself was highly susceptible to fire. The use of cut stone as the primary vaulting medium provided a solution to both of these problems. Indeed, the medieval architect's return to stone barrel and groin vaults of the kinds first used by the Romans (see chapter 6) inaugurated the *Romanesque style*.

Romanesque architects employed round arches and a uniform system of stone vaults in the upper zones of the nave and side aisles. While the floor plan of the typical Romanesque church followed the Latin cross design of Early Christian and Carolingian churches, the new system of stone vaulting allowed medieval architects to build on a grander scale than ever before. In the construction of these new, all-stone structures, the Normans led the way. The technical superiority of Norman stonemasons, apparent in their castles (see Figure 11.16), is reflected in the abbey churches at Caen and Jumièges in northwestern France. At the abbey of Jumièges, consecrated in 1067 in the presence of William the Conqueror, little remains other than the

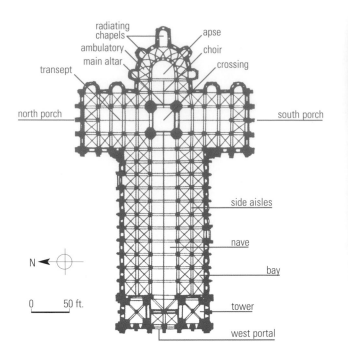

Figure 13.3 Plan of Saint-Sernin, Toulouse.

The diagram labels include: radiating chapels, apse, ambulatory, choir, main altar, crossing, transept, north porch, south porch, side aisles, nave, bay, tower, west portal. Scale: 0 — 50 ft.

Figure 13.4 West façade of the abbey of Jumièges, on the lower Seine near Rouen, France, 1037–1067. Height of towers 141 ft.

Figure 13.5 Saint-Sernin, Toulouse, France, ca. 1080–1120 (tower enlarged in the thirteenth century).

westwork (west façade), with its 141-foot-high twin towers (Figure **13.4**). This austere entrance portal, with its **tripartite** (three-part) division and three round arches, captures the geometric simplicity and rugged severity typical of the Romanesque style in France and England. It also anticipates some of the main features of medieval church architecture: massive towers pointed heavenward and made the church visible from great distances; stone portals separated the secular from the divine realm and dramatized the entrance door as the gateway to salvation.

The church of Saint-Sernin at Toulouse, on the southernmost pilgrimage route to Compostela, is one of the largest of the French pilgrimage churches (Figure **13.5**). Constructed of magnificent pink granite, Saint-Sernin's spacious nave is covered by a barrel vault divided by ornamental transverse arches (Figure **13.6**). Thick stone walls and heavy piers carry the weight of the vault and provide lateral (sideways) support (see Figure 13.18). Since window openings might have weakened the walls that buttressed the barrel vault, the architects of Saint-Sernin eliminated the clerestory. Beneath the vaults over the double side-aisles, a gallery that served weary pilgrims as a place of overnight refuge provided additional lateral buttressing.

The formal design of Saint-Sernin follows rational and harmonious principles: the square represented by the crossing of the nave and transept is the module for the organization of the building and its parts (see Figure 13.3). Each nave **bay** (vaulted compartment) equals one-half the module, while each side-aisle bay equals one-fourth of the module. Clarity of design is also visible in the ways in which the exterior reflects the geometry of the interior: at the east end of the church, for instance, five reliquary chapels protrude uniformly from the ambulatory, while at the crossing of the nave and transept, a tower (enlarged in the thirteenth century) rises as both a belfry

and a beacon to approaching pilgrims (see Figure 13.5). Massive and stately in its exterior, dignified and somber in its interior, Saint-Sernin conveys the effect of a monumental spiritual fortress.

Romanesque architects experimented with a wide assortment of regional variation in stone vaulting techniques. At the pilgrimage church of Sainte Madeleine (Mary Magdalene) at Vézelay in France—the site from which the Second Crusade was launched—the nave was covered with groin vaults separated by pronounced transverse arches. The concentration of weight along the arches, along with lighter masonry, allowed the architect to enlarge the width of the nave to 90 feet and to include a clerestory that admitted light into the dark interior (Figure **13.7**). The alternating light and dark stone **voussoirs** (wedges) in the arches of this dramatic interior indicate the influence of Muslim architecture (see Figure 10.10) on the development of the Romanesque church.

Figure 13.7 (below) Nave of Sainte Madeleine, Vézelay, France, ca. 1104–1132. Width 90 ft.

Romanesque Sculpture

Pilgrimage churches of the eleventh and twelfth centuries heralded the revival of monumental stone sculpture—a medium that, for the most part, had been abandoned since Roman antiquity. Scenes from the Old and New Testaments—carved in high relief and brightly painted—usually appeared on the entrance portals of the church, as well as in the capitals of columns throughout the basilica and its cloister. The entrance portal, normally located at the west end of the church, marked the dividing point between the earthly city and the City of God. Passage through the portal marked the beginning of the symbolic journey from sin (darkness/west) to salvation (light/east). As they passed beneath the elaborately carved west portal of the church of Saint Lazarus at Autun in France, medieval Christians were powerfully reminded of the inevitability of sin, death, and judgment. The forbidding image of Christ as Judge greeted them from the center of the **tympanum** (the semicircular space within the arch of the portal) just above their heads (Figures **13.8**, **13.9**). Framed by a **mandorla** (an almond-shaped halo) that surrounds his body, Jesus displays

Figure 13.8 GISLEBERTUS, *Last Judgment*, ca. 1130–1135. West tympanum, Autun Cathedral, France.

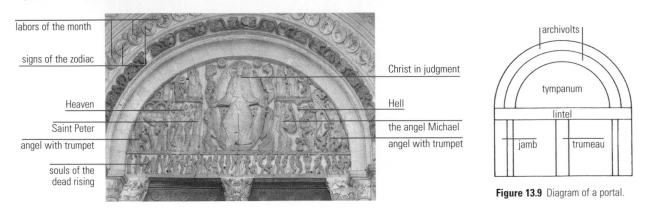

labors of the month

signs of the zodiac

Heaven

Saint Peter

angel with trumpet

souls of the
dead rising

Christ in judgment

Hell

the angel Michael

angel with trumpet

archivolts

tympanum

lintel

jamb   trumeau

Figure 13.9 Diagram of a portal.

Figure 13.10 GISLEBERTUS, detail of *Last Judgment*, ca. 1130–1135. Autun Cathedral, France.

his wounds and points to the realms of the afterlife: Heaven (on his right) and Hell (on his left). Surrounding the awesome Christ, flamelike saints and angels await the souls of the resurrected. Saint Michael weighs a soul in order to determine its eternal destiny, a motif that recalls late Egyptian art (see Figure 2.14), while a wraithlike devil tries to tip the scales in his own favor (Figure **13.10**).

In the **lintel** (the horizontal band below the tympanum), the resurrected are pictured rising from their graves. Just beneath the mouth of Hell, a pair of disembodied claws clutch at the damned, who cower in anticipation of eternal punishment. The **archivolts** that frame the tympanum hold roundels with signs of the zodiac and depictions of the labors of the months, symbols of the calendar year and the passage of time between the First and Second Coming of Christ. Like a medieval morality play, the tympanum at Autun served as a *memento mori*, reminding Christians of the inevitability of death and judgment. Indeed, beneath his signature, the artist Gislebertus added the warning, "Let this terror frighten those bound by earthly sin."

Among the most intriguing examples of Romanesque sculpture are those that adorn the capitals of columns in churches and cloisters. These so-called **historiated capitals** feature narrative scenes depicting the life of Christ. One of the largest extant groups of historiated capitals comes from the west porch of the pilgrimage church of Saint Benoît-sur-Loire in France, which housed the relics of Saint Benedict. In *The Flight to Egypt*, a moon-faced

Mary sits awkwardly upon a toylike donkey led by a bearded Joseph (Figure **13.11**). The six-pointed star above Mary's right shoulder and the naively shortened figures—altered to fit into the shape of the capital—give the scene a whimsical quality. Romanesque artisans plumbed their imaginations to generate the legions of fantastic beasts and hybrid demons that embellish church portals and capitals. The popularity of such imagery moved some medieval

Figure 13.11 *The Flight to Egypt*, late eleventh century. Capital, Saint Benoît-sur-Loire, France.

MAKING CONNECTIONS

Figure 13.12 *Jeremiah the Prophet*, early twelfth century. Trumeau of south portal, Saint Pierre, Moissac, France. The placement of this figure is symbolic. It illustrates the Christian claim that Old Testament prophets "supported" New Testament revelation.

Figure 13.13 *Capture and Flagellation of Christ*, from the Psalter of Saint Swithin, ca. 1250. The gestures and facial expressions of the figures in these scenes are exaggerated to emphasize contrasting states of arrogance and humility.

Romanesque sculpture shares with Romanesque painting a distinctive style marked by abstract stylization and linear movement. In carved Romanesque portals, as in painted illustrations for all types of religious and secular manuscripts, the figures are lively and elongated; they bend and twist, as if animated by the restless energy of the age—an age of pilgrimage and crusades. The carved sculptures at the abbey church of Saint Pierre at Moissac, France (Figure **13.12**), are similar to the painted illustrations for the Psalter

of Saint Swithin (Figure **13.13**): both feature thin, dancelike figures, their bodies defined by rhythmic, concentric folds of drapery that emphasize movement. At Moissac, the Hebrew prophet Jeremiah stretches like taffy to conform to the shape of the **trumeau** (the central post supporting the superstructure). Both sculpture and painting preserve the graphic features of early medieval metalwork techniques (see chapter 11), as well as the decorative draftsmanship of Byzantine and Islamic art.

churchmen to debate whether the visual arts inspired or distracted the faithful from contemplation and prayer. Nevertheless, the fusion of dogma and fantasy that characterizes so much Romanesque sculpture must have made a tremendous impact on the great percentage of people who could neither read nor write.

The Gothic Cathedral

Seventeenth-century Neoclassicists coined the term "Gothic" to condemn a style they judged to be a "rude and barbarous" alternative to the Classical style. But modern critics have recognized the *Gothic style* as a sophisticated and majestic expression of the age of faith.

The Gothic style was born in northern France and spread quickly throughout medieval Europe. In France alone, eighty Gothic cathedrals and nearly 500 cathedral-class churches were constructed between 1170 and 1270. Like all Christian churches, the Gothic cathedral was a sanctuary for the celebration of the Mass. But, reflecting a shift of intellectual life from the monastery to the town, the Gothic cathedral was also the administrative seat (*cathedra*) of a bishop, the site of ecclesiastical authority, and an educational center—a fount of theological doctrine and divine precept. The Gothic cathedral honored one or more saints, including and especially the Virgin Mary—the principal intercessor between God and the Christian believer. Indeed, most of the prominent churches of the Middle Ages were dedicated to Notre Dame ("Our Lady"). On a symbolic level, the church was both the Heavenly Jerusalem (the City of God) and a model of the Virgin as Womb of Christ and Queen of Heaven. In the cathedral, the medieval synthesis was realized: sculpture appeared in its portals, capitals, and choir screens; stained glass diffused divine light through its windows; painted altarpieces embellished its chapels; religious drama was enacted both within its walls and outside its doors; liturgical music filled its choirs.

Finally, the Gothic cathedral, often large enough to hold the entire population of a town, was the municipal center of gravity. If the Romanesque church constituted a rural retreat for monastics and pilgrims, the Gothic cathedral served as the focal point for an urban community. Physically dominating the town, its spires soaring above the houses and shops below (Figure **13.14**), the cathedral attracted civic events, public festivals, and even local business. The construction of the cathedral was usually a town effort, supported by the funds and labors of local citizens and guild members, including stonemasons (Figure **13.15**), carpenters, metalworkers, and glaziers.

In contrast with the Romanesque church, which drew on Greco-Roman principles and building techniques, Gothic architecture represented a clear break with the Classical past. Unlike the Classical temple, which seemed to hug the earth, the Gothic cathedral soared heavenward. It rejected the static, rationalized purity of the Classical canon in favor of a dynamic system of thrusts and counterthrusts; and it infused form with symbolic meaning.

The definitive features of the Gothic style were first assembled in a monastic church just outside the gates of

Figure 13.14 Chartres Cathedral, France, begun 1194. This aerial view shows the south porch of the cathedral, which was added in the thirteenth century. The double sets of flying buttresses at the west end of the building are also visible.

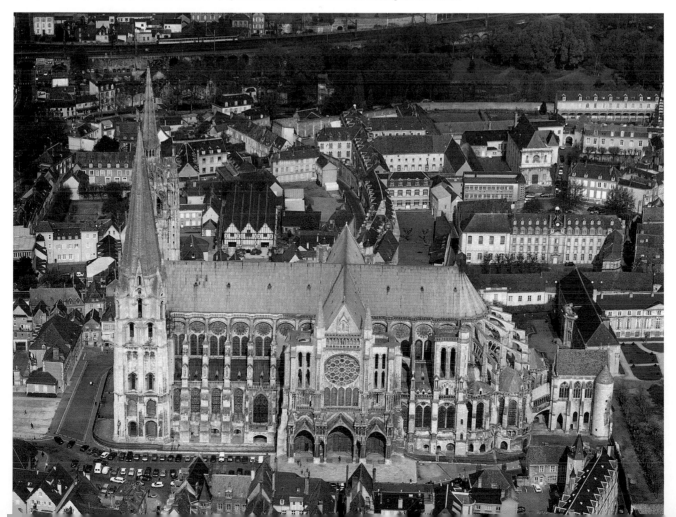

Figure 13.15 *Thirteenth-Century Masons*, French miniature from an Old Testament building scene, ca. 1240. 15⅓ × 11⅞ in. Stones, shaped by the two men (bottom right), are lifted by a hoisting engine powered by the treadwheel on the left. The man climbing the ladder carries mortar on his back.

Paris: the abbey church of Saint-Denis—the church that held the relics of the patron saint of France and, for centuries, the burial place of French royalty. Between 1122 and 1144, Abbot Suger (1085–1151), a personal friend and adviser of the French kings Louis VI and VII, enlarged and remodeled the old Carolingian structure. Suger's designs

Figure 13.16 Choir and ambulatory of the abbey church of Saint-Denis, France, 1140–1144. The wooden church pews shown in photographs of medieval churches are modern additions. In the High Middle Ages, as the liturgy expanded in length and complexity, benches and stalls for members of the choir came into use in the area behind the altar; but parishioners normally stood in the nave before the altar during the Mass.

for the east end of the church called for a combination of three architectural innovations that had been employed only occasionally or experimentally: the pointed arch, the rib vault, and stained glass windows. The result was a spacious choir and ambulatory, free of heavy stone supports and flooded with light (Figure **13.16**).

While Gothic cathedrals followed Saint-Denis in adopting a new look, their floor plan—the Latin cross—remained basically the same as that of the Romanesque church; only the transept might be moved further west to create a larger choir area (Figure **13.17**). The ingenious combination of rib vault and pointed arch, however, had a major impact on the size and elevation of Gothic structures. Stone ribs replaced the heavy stone masonry of Romanesque vaults, and pointed arches raised these vaults to new heights. Whereas the rounded vaults of the Romanesque church demanded extensive lateral buttressing, the steeply pointed arches of the Gothic period, which directed weight downward, required only the combination of slender vertical piers and thin lateral ("flying") buttresses (Figures **13.18**, **13.19**). In place of masonry, broad areas of glass filled the interstices of this "cage" of stone. The nave wall consisted of an arcade of pier bundles that swept from floor to ceiling, an ornamental **triforium** gallery (the arcaded passage between the nave arcade and the clerestory), and a large clerestory

Figure 13.17 Floor plan of Chartres Cathedral.

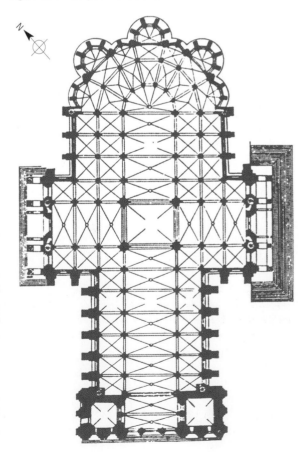

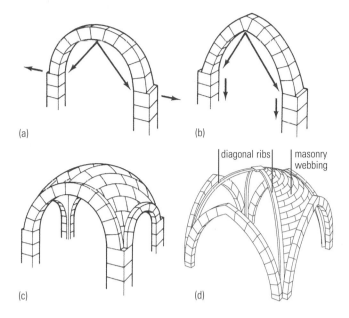

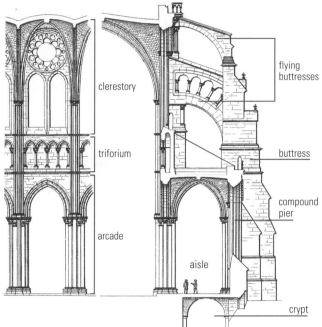

Figure 13.18 Round and pointed arches and vaults. The round arch (a) spreads the load laterally, while the pointed arch (b) thrusts its load more directly toward the ground. The pointed arch can rise to any height while the height of the semi-circular arch is governed by the space it spans. Round arches create a dome-shaped vault (c). The Gothic rib vault (d) permits a lighter and more flexible building system with larger wall openings that may accommodate windows.

Figure 13.19 Elevations and sections of Chartres Cathedral nave.

Figure 13.20 Nave facing east, Chartres Cathedral. Nave completed in 1220. Height of nave 122 ft.

consisting of **rose** (from the French *roue*, "wheel") and **lancet** (vertically pointed) windows (see Figure 13.19). Above the clerestory hung elegant canopies of **quadripartite** (four-part; Figure **13.20**, also frontispiece) or **sexpartite** (six-part) rib vaults. Lighter and more airy than Romanesque churches, Gothic interiors seem to expand and unfold in vertical space. The pointed arch, the rib vault, and stained glass windows, along with the flying buttress (first used at the cathedral of Notre Dame in Paris around 1170), became the fundamental ingredients of the Gothic style.

Medieval towns competed with one another in the grandeur of their cathedrals: at Chartres, a town located 50 miles southwest of Paris (see Map 13.1), the nave of the cathedral rose to a height of 122 feet (Figure **13.21**; see also Figures 13.14, 13.20); architects at Amiens took the space from the floor to the apex of the vault to a breathtaking 144 feet. At Beauvais, the 157-foot vault of the choir (the equivalent of a fourteen-story high-rise) collapsed twelve years after its completion and had to be reconstructed over a period of forty years. These major enterprises in engineering design and craftsmanship often took decades to build, and many were never finished. In contrast to the Romanesque church, with its well-defined cubic volumes and its simple geometric harmonies, the Gothic cathedral was an intricate web of stone, a dynamic network of open and closed spaces that evoked a sense of unbounded extension. Despite its visual complexity, however, the Gothic interior obeyed a set of proportional principles aimed at achieving harmonious design: at Chartres, for instance, the height of the clerestory and the height of the nave arcade

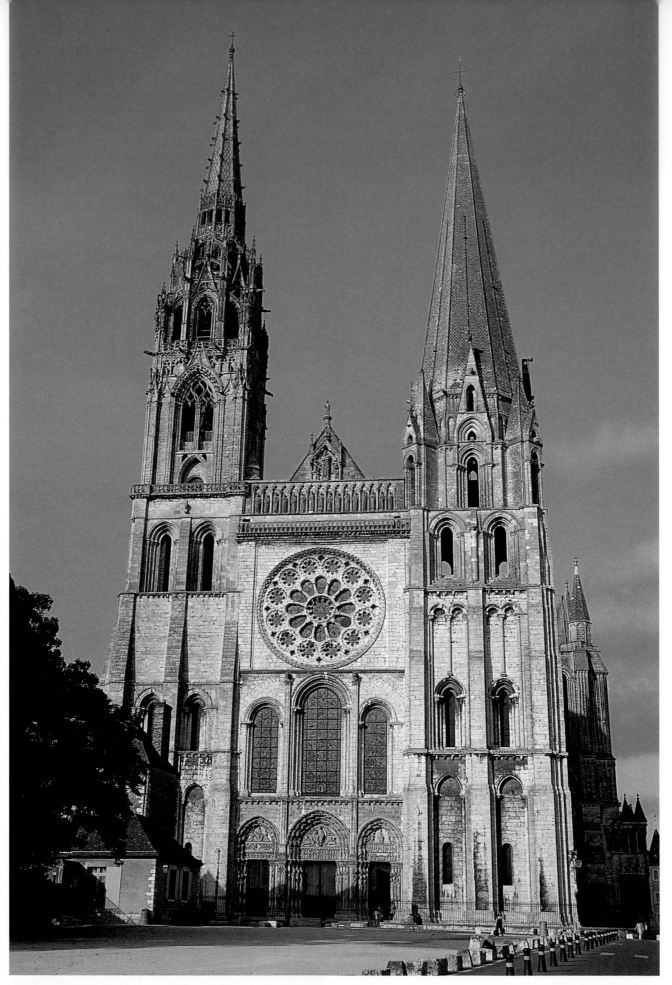

Figure 13.21 West façade of Chartres Cathedral, lower parts 1134–1150, mainly after 1194.

are each exactly three times the height of the triforium (see Figure 13.20). At the cathedral of Notre Dame in Paris, these interior sections are mirrored in the three-story elevation of the façade: the height of the nave arcade corresponds to that of the west portals; the triforium arcade is echoed in the rows of saints standing above those portals; and the clerestory is marked by a majestic rose window (Figure 13.22).

Gothic architects embellished the structural extremities of the cathedral with stone **crockets** (stylized leaves) and **finials** (crowning ornamental details). At the upper portions of the building, **gargoyles**—waterspouts in the form of grotesque figures or hybrid beasts—were believed to ward off evil (Figure 13.23). During the thirteenth century and thereafter, cathedrals increased in structural and ornamental complexity. Flying buttresses became ornate stone wings terminating in minichapels that housed individual statues of saints and martyrs. Crockets and finials sprouted in greater numbers from gables and spires, and sculptural details became more numerous. But, like an Aquinan proposition, the final design represents the reconciliation of all individual parts into a majestic and harmonious synthesis.

Figure 13.22 West façade of Notre Dame, Paris, ca. 1200–1250.

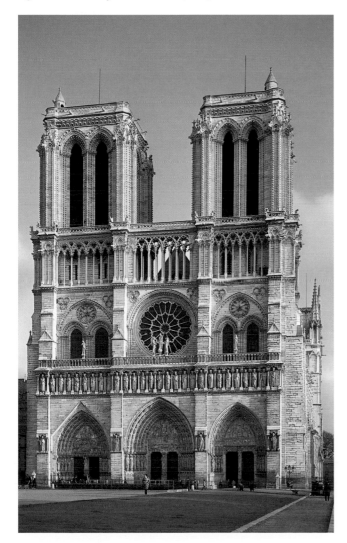

Figure 13.23 Grotesques and a gargoyle waterspout on a tower terrace of Notre Dame, Paris, as restored in the nineteenth century.

Gothic Sculpture

The sculpture of the Gothic cathedral was an exhaustive compendium of Old and New Testament history, Classical and Christian precepts, and secular legend and lore. The sculptural program of the cathedral—that is, the totality of its carved representations—conveyed Christian doctrine and liturgy in terms that were meaningful to both scholars and laity. Learned churchmen might glean from

Science and Technology	
1122	Abbot Suger combines pointed arches and rib vaults in remodeling the abbey church of Saint-Denis
ca. 1175	flying buttresses are first used in the cathedral of Notre Dame in Paris
ca. 1225	Villard de Honnecourt (French) begins a sketchbook of architectural plans, elevations, and engineering devices
1291	Venetian glassmakers produce the first clear (as opposed to colored) glass

Figure 13.24 Royal Portal, west façade, Chartres Cathedral, ca. 1140–1150.

these images a profound symbolic message, while less educated Christians might see in them a history of their faith and a mirror of daily experience. Designed to be "read" by the laity, the Gothic façade was both a "bible in stone" and an encyclopedia of the religious and secular life of an age of faith.

In the sculpture of the cathedral, as in the stained glass windows, the Virgin Mary holds a prominent place. This is especially so at Chartres Cathedral, which, from earliest times, had housed the tunic that the Virgin Mary was said to have worn at the birth of Jesus. When, in 1194, the tunic survived the devastating fire that destroyed most of the old cathedral, it was taken as a miracle indicating the Virgin's desire to see her shrine gloriously rebuilt. Financial contributions for its reconstruction poured in from all of Christendom. Chartres' west portal, which survived the fire, is called the Royal Portal for its jamb figures of the kings and queens of the Old Testament (Figure **13.24**). Its central tympanum features Christ in Majesty. Rigidly posed, he is flanked by symbols of the four evangelists and framed in the archivolts by the Elders of the Apocalypse. In the lintel below, the apostles are ordered into formal groups of threes.

On the right tympanum, the Mother of God is pictured as the Seat of Wisdom and honored as the Queen of the Liberal Arts (Figure **13.25**). Enthroned above two registers showing scenes from the youth of Christ, she is framed by archivolts that include allegorical representations of the trivium and the quadrivium (see chapter 12). Each of the disciplines is accompanied by the appropriate historical authority. On the lower right, for instance, the allegorical figure of Music, holding on her lap a **psaltery** (a stringed instrument), strikes a set of bells. Below her Pythagoras (celebrated for having discovered the numerical relation between the length of strings and musical tones), is shown hunched over his lap desk.

On cathedral façades, the Virgin Mary appears frequently as Mother of God and Queen of Heaven. The central trumeau of the west portal at Notre Dame in Paris shows the regal Mary carrying the Christ Child (Figure **13.28**). Beneath her feet is an image of the fallen Eve, standing alongside Adam in the Garden of Eden. The conjunction of Mary and Eve alluded to the popular medieval idea that Mary was the "new Eve," who brought salvation as a remedy for the sentence of death resulting from the disobedience of the "old Eve."

The thousands of individually carved figures on the façades of the cathedrals at Chartres, Paris, Amiens, and elsewhere required the labor of many sculptors working over long periods of time. Often, a single façade reflects a

Figure 13.25 *Scenes from the Life of the Virgin Mary*, between 1145 and 1170. Right tympanum of the Royal Portal, west façade, Chartres Cathedral.

angels

angels

Mary as the seat of wisdom

presentation of Jesus in the Temple

Music (liberal arts)

Gemini (zodiac)

annunciation

annunciation to the shepherds

visitation

Pythagoras

Pisces (zodiac)

nativity

MAKING CONNECTIONS

Figure 13.26 *Isis and Horus Enthroned*, Middle Egyptian, fourth century C.E. Limestone, height 35 in.

From the earliest years of its establishment as a religion, Christianity exalted the Virgin Mary as an object of veneration. Long revered as "the second Eve," Mary was honored as the woman who redeemed humankind from damnation and death, the twin consequences of the first Eve's disobedience. The image of Mary as a paragon of virtue and chastity constituted an ideal feminine type not unlike that held by Isis in the ancient world (Figure **13.26**). The great cathedrals, most of which were dedicated to the Virgin, portrayed her as Mother of God, Bride of Christ, and Queen of Heaven. Enthroned alongside Jesus—often no smaller in size—she appears as co-equal in authority. During the twelfth century, as emphasis came to be placed on the humanity of Jesus, Mary was depicted as the suffering mother and compassionate intercessor, her praises recounted in literature and song. As legends of her miracles proliferated, the cult of the Virgin inspired worship at

Figure 13.27 *Yolande de Soissons Kneeling before a Statue of the Virgin and Child*, from Psalter and Book of Hours, northern France, ca. 1290.

shrines in her honor (Figure **13.27**) and special prayers of supplication. Increasingly, images of Mary and depictions of her life came to adorn church portals, stained glass windows, altarpieces, and illuminated manuscripts.

variety of styles, the efforts of different workshops and different eras. The present cathedral at Chartres, at least the fifth on that site, was the product of numerous building campaigns. The Royal Portal retains the linear severity of the Romanesque style (see Figure 13.24), while the figures on its north and south portals, added in the early thirteenth century, seem to detach themselves from the stone frame. Like the sculptures on the west façade of Notre

Dame, they are weighty and lifelike (see Figure 13.28). Their robes reflect the movements of their bodies, and their gestures are varied and subtle. Clearly, between the eleventh and thirteen centuries, medieval sculpture moved in the direction of heightened Realism. This trend accompanied a proliferation of religious imagery and architectural detail that turned some Late Gothic church façades into encyclopedias in stone.

Figure 13.28 *Virgin and Child* (above) and *Temptation of Adam and Eve* (below), thirteenth century. Central trumeau of the west portal, Notre Dame, Paris.

Stained Glass

Stained glass was to the Gothic cathedral what mosaics were to the Early Christian church: a source of religious edification, a medium of divine light, and a delight to the eye. Produced on the site of the cathedral by a process of mixing metal oxides into molten glass, colored sheets of glass were cut into fragments to fit preconceived designs. They were then fixed within lead bands, bound by a grid of iron bars, and set into stone **mullions** (vertical frames). Imprisoned in this lacelike armature, the glass vibrated with color, sparkling in response to the changing natural light and casting rainbows of color that seemed to dissolve the stone walls. The faithful of Christendom regarded the cathedral windows as precious objects—glass tapestries that clothed the House of God with radiant light. They especially treasured the windows at Chartres, with their rich blues, which, in contrast to other colors, required a cobalt oxide that came from regions far beyond France. Legend had it that Abbot Suger, the first churchman to exploit the aesthetic potential of stained glass, produced blue glass by grinding up sapphires—a story that, although untrue, reflects the popular equation of precious gems with sacred glass.

Suger exalted stained glass as a medium that filtered divine revelation. To the medieval mind, light was a symbol of Jesus, who had proclaimed to his apostles, "I am the light of the world" (John 8:12). Drawing on this mystical bond between Jesus and light, Suger identified the *lux nova* ("new light") of the Gothic church as the symbolic equivalent of God and the windows as mediators of God's love. But for Suger, light—especially as it passed through the stained glass windows of the church—also signified the sublime knowledge that accompanied the progressive purification of the ascending human spirit (compare Canto 33 of Dante's "Paradiso," Reading 12.4). Suger's mystical interpretation of light, inspired by his reading of Neoplatonic treatises (see chapter 8), sustained his belief that contemplation of the "many-colored gems" of church glass could transport the Christian from "the slime of this earth" to "the purity of heaven." On the wall of the ambulatory at Saint-Denis, Abbot Suger had these words inscribed: "That which is united in splendor, radiates in splendor/And the magnificent work inundated with the new light shines."

The light symbolism that Suger embraced was as distinctive to medieval sermons and treatises as it was to the everyday liturgy of the Church. It permeates the writings of Hildegard of Bingen (see Reading 12.1), who referred to God as "the Living Light," and it is the principal theme in Saint Ambrose's sixth-century song of praise, the "Ancient Morning Hymn" (see Reading 9.2).

The Windows at Chartres

The late twelfth and early thirteenth centuries were, without doubt, the golden age of stained glass. At Chartres, the 175 surviving glass panels with representations of more than 4000 figures comprise a cosmic narrative of humankind's religious and secular history. Chartres' windows, which were removed for safekeeping during World War II and thereafter returned to their original positions, follow a carefully organized theological program designed, as Abbot Suger explained, "to show simple folk . . . what they ought to believe." In one of Chartres' oldest windows, whose vibrant combination of reds and blues inspired the title *Notre Dame de la Belle Verrière* ("Our Lady of the Beautiful Glass"), the Virgin appears in her dual role as Mother of God and Queen of Heaven (Figure **13.29**). Holding the Christ Child on her lap and immediately adjacent to her womb, she also becomes the Seat of Wisdom.

In the lancet windows below the rose of the south transept wall (see Figure 13.1), Mary and the Christ Child are flanked by four Old Testament prophets who carry on their shoulders the four evangelists, a symbolic rendering of the Christian belief that the Old Dispensation (the

Figure 13.29 *Notre Dame de la Belle Verrière* ("Our Lady of the Beautiful Glass"), twelfth century. Stained glass. Chartres Cathedral.

Figure 13.30 *Sculptors and Masons at Work,* Chartres Cathedral, ca. 1220. Local artisans assisted in the building of Chartres Cathedral. At the left, masons cut and finish stone; at the right, sculptors put the finishing touches on statues for the cathedral portals.

Figure 13.31 Sainte Chapelle, Paris, from the southwest, 1245–1248.

Hebrew Law) upheld the New Dispensation (the Gospels; compare Figure 13.12). Often, the colors chosen for parts of the design carry symbolic value. For instance, in scenes of the Passion from the west-central lancet window, the cross carried by Jesus is green—the color of vegetation—symbolizing rebirth and regeneration.

Many of Chartres' windows were donated by members of the nobility, who are frequently shown kneeling in prayer (see Figure 13.1). The activities of bakers, butchers, stonemasons, and other laborers appear among the windows commemorating the patron saints of the guilds (Figure 13.30).

Sainte Chapelle: Medieval "Jewelbox"

The art of stained glass reached its height in Sainte Chapelle, the small palace chapel commissioned for the Ile de France by King Louis IX ("Saint Louis") (Figure 13.31). Executed between 1245 and 1248, the chapel was designed to hold the Crown of Thorns, a prized relic that Christian Crusaders claimed to have recovered along with other symbols of Christ's Passion. The lower level of the chapel is richly painted with frescoes that imitate the canopy of Heaven, while the upper level consists almost entirely of 49-foot-high lancet windows dominated by ruby red and purplish blue glass (Figure 13.32). More than a thousand individual stories are depicted in the windows that make up two-thirds of the upper chapel walls. In its vast iconographic program and its dazzling, ethereal effect, this medieval "jewelbox" is the crowning example of French Gothic art.

Figure 13.32 Upper chapel of Sainte Chapelle, Paris. Height of lancet windows 49 ft.

Medieval Painting

Responsive to the combined influence of Germanic, Islamic, and Byzantine art, medieval artists cultivated a taste for decorative abstraction through line. In fresco, manuscript illumination, and panel painting, line worked to flatten form, eliminate space, and enhance the iconic nature of the image. The artist who painted the *Crucifixion and Deposition of Christ* for the Psalter of Blanche of Castile (the mother of Saint Louis) recreates the geometric compositions and strong, simple colors of stained glass windows (Figure 13.33). To the right and left of the two interlocked roundels are depicted the Church (representing the New

Dispensation) and the Synagogue (representing the Old Dispensation). Book illuminators might make use of pattern books filled with stock representations of standard historical and religious subjects, a practice that encouraged stylistic conservatism. Nevertheless, in the execution of thousands of miniatures and marginal illustrations for a wide variety of secular and religious manuscripts, the imagination of medieval artists seems unbounded.

The preparation of medieval manuscripts was a time-consuming and expensive enterprise, usually shared by many different workers. The production of a bible might require the slaughter of some 200 sheep or calves, whose hides were then scraped, bleached, and carefully processed

Figure 13.33 *Crucifixion and Deposition of Christ with the Church and the Synagogue,* from the Psalter of Blanche of Castile, ca. 1235.

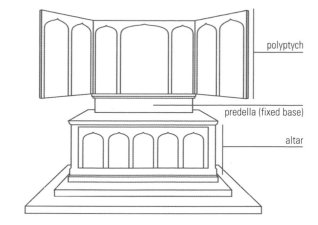

Figure 13.34 Diagram of an altar and altarpieces. The medieval altarpiece was a devotional object set on or behind an altar. Two hinged panels made up a **diptych**; three a **triptych**; and many panels (seen here) a **polyptych**.

before becoming the folded sheets of parchment (or, if derived from calves, vellum) that made up the book itself. Gold was used lavishly to "illuminate" the images, while rich colors, such as the blue used in Figure 13.33, might come from places as far away as Afghanistan, hence the name "ultramarine" ("beyond the sea") to designate a shade of blue.

Some of the finest examples of medieval painting appear in the form of altarpieces installed on or behind chapel altars dedicated to the Virgin or one of the saints (Figure **13.34**). The typical Gothic altarpiece consisted of a wooden panel or group of panels coated with **gesso** (a chalky white plaster), on which figures were painted in **tempera** (a powdered pigment that produces dry, flat surface colors), and embellished with gold leaf that reflected the light of altar candles. The object of devotional prayer, the altarpiece usually displayed scenes from the life of Jesus, the Virgin Mary, or a favorite saint or martyr. A late thirteenth-century altarpiece by the Florentine painter Cimabue (1240–1302) shows the Virgin and Child elevated on a monumental seat that is both a throne and a tower (Figure **13.35**). Angels throng around the throne, while, beneath the Virgin's feet, four Hebrew prophets display scrolls predicting the coming of Jesus. To symbolize their lesser importance, angels and prophets are pictured considerably smaller than the enthroned Mary. Such

Figure 13.35 CIMABUE, *Madonna Enthroned,* ca. 1280–1290. Tempera on wood, 12 ft. 7½ in. × 7 ft. 4 in.

hierarchic grading, while typical of medieval art, also characterized Egyptian and Byzantine compositions.

Cimabue's lavishly gilded devotional image has a schematic elegance: line elicits the sharp, metallic folds of the Virgin's dark blue mantle, the crisp wings of the angels, the chiseled features of the Christ Child, and the decorative surface of the throne. The figure of the Virgin combines the hypnotic grandeur of the Byzantine icon and the weightless, hieratic clarity of Gislebertus' Christ in Majesty at Autun (see Figure 13.8). Although Cimabue's Virgin is more humanized than either of these, she is every bit as regal.

Medieval altarpieces integrated the ornamental vocabulary of Gothic architecture and the bright colors of stained glass windows. The Sienese painter Simone Martini (1284–1344) made brilliant use of Gothic architectural motifs in his *Annunciation* altarpiece of 1333 (Figure **13.36**). The frame of the altarpiece consists of elegant Gothic spires and heavily gilded **ogee** arches (pointed arches with S-shaped curves near the apex) sprouting finials and crockets. Set on a gold leaf ground, the petulant Virgin, the angel Annunciate, and the vase of lilies (symbolizing Mary's purity) seem suspended in time and space. Martini's composition depends on a refined play of lines: the graceful curves of the Angel Gabriel's wings are echoed in his fluttering vestments, in the contours of the Virgin's body as she shrinks from the angel's greeting, and in the folds of her mantle, the pigment for which was ground from semiprecious lapis lazuli.

Medieval Music

Early Medieval Music and Liturgical Drama

The major musical developments of the Early Middle Ages, like those in architecture, came out of the monasteries. In Charlemagne's time, monastic reforms in church liturgy and in sacred music accompanied the renaissance in the visual arts. Early church music took the form of unaccompanied monophonic chant (see chapter 9), a solemn sound that inspired one medieval monk to write in the margin of his songbook, "The tedious plainsong grates my tender ears." Perhaps to remedy such complaints, the monks at Saint-Gall enlarged the range of expression of the classical Gregorian chant by adding **antiphons**, or verses sung as responses to the religious text. Carolingian monks also embellished plainsong with the **trope**, an addition of music or words to the established liturgical chant. Thus, "Lord, have mercy upon us" became "Lord, omnipotent Father, God, Creator of all, have mercy upon us." A special kind of trope, called a **sequence**, added words to the long, melismatic passages—such as the alleluias and amens—that occurred at the end of each part of the Mass (Figure **13.37**).

By the tenth century, singers began to divide among themselves the parts of the liturgy for Christmas and Easter, now embellished by tropes and sequences. As more and more dramatic incidents were added to the texts for these Masses, full-fledged music-drama emerged. Eventually, liturgical plays broke away from the liturgy and were performed in the intervals between the parts of the Mass. Such was the case with the twelfth-century *Play of Daniel*, whose dramatic "action" brought to life episodes

from the Book of Daniel (in the Hebrew Bible) that Christians took to prophesy the birth of the Messiah—a story appropriate to the Christmas season.

By the twelfth century, spoken dialogue and possibly musical instruments were introduced. At the monastery of the German abbess, Hildegard of Bingen, Benedictine nuns may have performed her *Ordo virtutum* (see chapter 12). In this music-drama, the earliest known morality play in Western history, the Virtues contest with the Devil for the Soul of the Christian. The Devil's lines are spoken, not sung, consistent with Hildegard's belief that satanic evil was excluded from knowing music's harmony and order. Hildegard's most important musical compositions, however, were liturgical. Her monophonic hymns and antiphons in honor of the saints, performed as part of the Divine Office, are exercises in musical meditation. Some offer praise for womankind and for the virgin saints, while others such as the chant *O Successores* celebrate the holy confessors—Christ's "successors," who hear confession and give absolution.

Medieval Musical Notation

Musical notation was invented in the monasteries. As with Romanesque architecture, so with medieval musical theory and practice, Benedictine monks at Cluny and

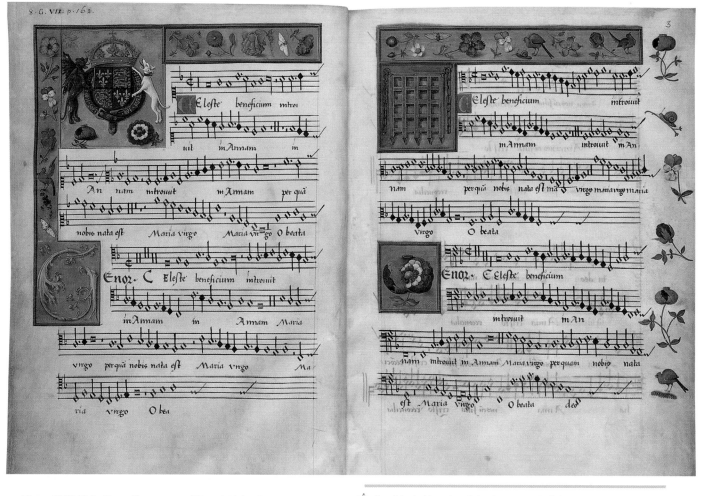

Figure 13.37 Mainz Troper (Sequences and Tropes), Mainz, Germany, ca. 970.

See Music Listening Selections at end of chapter.

elsewhere were especially influential. During the eleventh century, they devised the first efficient Western system of musical notation, thus facilitating the performance and transmission of liturgical music. They arranged the tones of the commonly used scale in progression from A through G and developed a formal system of notating pitch. The Italian Benedictine Guido of Arezzo (ca. 990–ca. 1050) introduced a staff of colored lines (yellow for C, red for F, etc.) on which he registered neumes—notational signs traditionally written above the words to indicate tonal ascent or descent (see chapter 9). Guido's system established a precise means of indicating shifts in pitch. Instead of relying on memory alone, singers could consult songbooks inscribed with both words and music. Such advances anticipated the kinds of compositional complexity represented by medieval polyphony.

Medieval Polyphony

Although our knowledge of early medieval music is sparse, there is reason to believe that, even before the year 1000, choristers were experimenting with multiple lines of music as an alternative to the monophonic style of Gregorian chant. **Polyphony** (music consisting of two or more lines of melody) was a Western invention; it did not make its appearance in Asia until modern times. The earliest polyphonic compositions consisted of Gregorian melodies sung in two parts simultaneously, with both voices moving note-for-note in parallel motion (parallel **organum**), or with a second voice moving in contrary motion (free organum), perhaps also adding many notes to the individual syllables of the text (melismatic organum). Consistent with rules of harmony derived from antiquity, and with the different ranges of the voice, the second musical part was usually pitched a fourth or a fifth above or below the first, creating a pure, hollow sound.

Throughout the High Middle Ages, northern France—and the city of Paris in particular—was the center of polyphonic composition. From the same area that produced the Gothic cathedral came a new musical style that featured several lines of melody arranged in counterpoised rhythms. The foremost Parisian composer was Pérotin (ca. 1160–1240). A member of the Notre Dame School, Pérotin enhanced the splendor of the Christian Mass by writing three- and four-part polyphonic compositions based on Gregorian chant. Pérotin's music usually consisted of a principal voice or "tenor" (from the Latin tenere, meaning "to hold") that sang the chant or "fixed song" (Latin, cantus firmus) and one or more voices that moved in shorter phrases and usually faster tempos. The combination of two or three related but independent voices, a musical technique called counterpoint, enlivened late twelfth- and thirteenth-century music. Indeed, the process of vertical superimposition of voice on voice enhanced sonority and augmented the melodic complexity of medieval music

much in the way that the thrusts and counterthrusts of the Gothic structure enriched its visual texture.

As medieval polyphony encouraged the addition of voices and voice parts, the choir areas of Gothic cathedrals were enlarged to accommodate more singers. Performed within the acoustically resonant bodies of such cathedrals as Notre Dame in Paris, the polyphonic Mass produced an aural effect as resplendent as the multicolored light that shimmered throughout the interior. Like the cathedral itself, the polyphonic Mass was a masterful synthesis of carefully arranged parts—a synthesis achieved in *time* rather than in *space*.

The "Dies Irae"

One of the best examples of the medieval synthesis, particularly as it served the Christian immortality ideology, is the "Dies irae" ("Day of Wrath"). The fifty-seven-line hymn, which originated among the Franciscans during the thirteenth century, was added to the Roman Catholic **requiem** (the Mass for the Dead) and quickly became a standard part of the Christian funeral service. Invoking a powerful vision of the end of time, the "Dies irae" is the musical counterpart of the apocalyptic sermons and Last Judgment portals that issued solemn warnings of final doom. The hymn opens with the words:

> Day of Wrath! O day of mourning!
> See fulfilled the prophets' warning,
> Heaven and earth in ashes burning!

But, as with most examples of apocalyptic art, including Dante's *Commedia*, the hymn holds out hope for absolution and deliverance:

> With Thy favored sheep, oh, place me!
> Nor among the goats abase me,
> But to Thy right hand upraise me.
>
> While the Wicked are confounded,
> Doomed to flames of woe unbounded,
> Call me, with Thy saints surrounded.

Like so many other forms of medieval expression, the "Dies irae" brings into vivid contrast the eternal destinies of sinners and saints. In later centuries, it inspired the powerful requiem settings of Mozart, Berlioz, and Verdi, and its music remains a familiar symbol of death and damnation.

The Motet

The thirteenth century also witnessed the invention of a new religious musical genre, the **motet**—a short, polyphonic choral composition based on a sacred text. Performed both inside and outside the church, it was the most popular kind of medieval religious song. Like the trope, the motet (from the French *mot*, meaning "word") developed from the practice of adding words to the melismatic parts of a melody. Medieval motets usually juxtaposed two or more uncomplicated themes, each with its own lyrics and metrical pattern, in a manner that was lilting and lively. Motets designed to be sung outside

---

See Music Listening Selections at end of chapter.

Figure 13.38 *Music and Her Attendants*, from **BOETHIUS**, *De Arithmetica*, fourteenth century. Holding a portable pipe organ, the allegorical figure of Music is surrounded by an ensemble of court musicians.

the church often borrowed secular tunes with vernacular words. A three-part motet might combine a love song in the vernacular, a well-known hymn of praise to the Virgin, and a Latin liturgical text in the *cantus firmus*. Thirteenth-century motets were thus polytextual as well as polyphonic and polyrhythmic. A stock of melodies (like the stock of images in medieval pattern books) was available to musicians for use in secular and sacred songs, and the same one might serve both types of song. Subtle forms of Symbolism occurred in many medieval motets, as for instance where a popular song celebrating spring might be used to refer to the Resurrection of Jesus, the awakening of romantic love, or both.

Instrumental Music

Musical instruments first appeared in religious music not for the purpose of accompanying songs, as with *troubadour* poems and folk epics, but to substitute for the human voice in polyphonic compositions. Medieval music depended on **timbre** (tone color) rather than volume for its effect, and most medieval instruments produced sounds that were gentle and thin by comparison with their modern (not to mention electronically amplified) counterparts. Medieval string instruments included the harp, the psaltery, and the lute (all three are plucked), and bowed fiddles such as the vielle and the rebec (Figure **13.38**). Wind instruments included portable pipe organs, recorders, and bagpipes. Percussion was produced by chimes, cymbals, bells, tambourines, and drums. Instrumental music performed without voices accompanied medieval dancing. Percussion instruments established the basic rhythms for a wide variety of high-spirited dances, including the estampie, a popular round dance consisting of short, repeated phrases.

See Music Listening Selections at end of chapter.

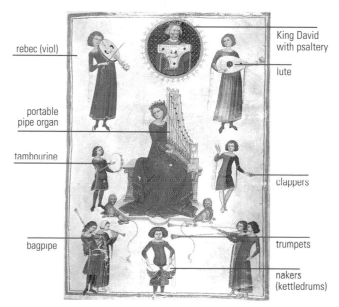

rebec (viol)

King David with psaltery

lute

portable pipe organ

tambourine

clappers

bagpipe

trumpets

nakers (kettledrums)

LOOKING BACK

The Romanesque Church

- After the year 1000, Romanesque pilgrimage churches were constructed in great numbers throughout Western Europe. Their stone portals and capitals displayed Christian themes of redemption and salvation.
- Largely rural, the churches were gathering points for pilgrims who traveled to visit the holy relics of saints and martyrs enshrined in church chapels.
- Since pilgrims constituted a major source of revenue for European towns and churches, parishes competed for them by enlarging church interiors. They revived the systems of stone vaulting used by the Romans. Built on a Latin cross plan, the Romanesque church features round arches and thick barrel and groin vaults.
- The Romanesque style, characterized by lively linearity and vivid imagination, is apparent in the stone sculpture of entrance portals and historiated capitals, as well as in illuminated manuscripts.

The Gothic Cathedral

- The Gothic cathedral was the focus and glory of the medieval town. First developed in the region of Paris, the cathedral was an ingenious synthesis of three structural elements: rib vaults, pointed arches, and flying buttresses.
- Often large enough to hold the entire population of a town, the Gothic cathedral was the center of the urban community. It attracted civic events, public festivals, theatrical performances, and local business.
- The great cathedrals, most of which were dedicated to the Virgin, portrayed her as Mother of God, Bride of Christ, and Queen of Heaven. The image of Mary as a paragon of virtue and chastity constituted an ideal feminine type.
- The medieval cathedral represents the point of synthesis at which all of the arts—visual, literary, and musical—served a common, unified purpose.

Gothic Sculpture

- The sculpture of the Gothic cathedral was an exhaustive compendium of Old and New Testament history, Classical and Christian precepts, and secular legend and lore. The totality of its carved representations conveyed doctrine in terms that were meaningful to scholars and laity alike.
- During the thirteenth century, figural representation became more detailed and lifelike. Figures assume natural poses, and

cease to conform to the architectural framework. The trend toward greater realism in Gothic sculpture accompanied the proliferation of religious imagery and architectural details.

Stained Glass

- Stained glass was a source of religious edification and a delight to the eye. Following Abbot Suger, the faithful Christian regarded cathedral windows as glass tapestries that served the House of God by filtering the light of divine truth.
- The windows at Chartres Cathedral and at Sainte Chapelle in Paris constitute the high point of medieval stained glass ornamentation.

Medieval Painting

- Responsive to the combined influence of Germanic, Islamic, and Byzantine arts, medieval painting styles were generally abstract and symbolic; they reveal an expressive linearity, the use of bright colors, and a decorative treatment of form.
- Thousands of medieval manuscripts were handwritten and richly illuminated during the Middle Ages. Their production was time-consuming, despite the fact that book illuminators often used pattern books with stock representations of historical and religious subjects.
- Installed on or behind the chapel altar, the medieval altarpiece featured an image of the Virgin and/or the saints as objects of devotional prayer. Lavishly gilded, medieval Italian altarpieces reveal a humanized Byzantine style.

Medieval Music

- As with the visual arts, the music of the Middle Ages was closely related to religious ritual. In Carolingian times, tropes and sequences came to embellish Christian chant, a process that led to the birth of liturgical drama.
- In the eleventh century, Benedictine monks devised a system of musical notation that facilitated performance and made possible the accurate transmission of music from generation to generation.
- Medieval polyphony, consisting of multiple, independent lines of melody, introduced a new richness to both religious and secular music. Polyphonic religious compositions known as motets often integrated vernacular texts and secular melodies.
- A combination of many medieval instruments provided music for dance and secular entertainments.

CD One Selection 7 Medieval liturgical drama, *The Play of Daniel*, "Ad honorem tui, Christe," "Ecce sunt ante faciem tuam".

CD One Selection 8 Hildegard of Bingen, *O Successores* (Your Successors), ca. 1150.

CD One Selection 9 Two examples of early medieval polyphony: parallel organum, "Rex caeli, Domine," excerpt; melismatic organum, "Alleluia, Justus ut palma," ca. 900–1150; excerpts.

CD One Selection 10 Pérotin, three-part organum, "Alleluya" (Nativitas), twelfth century.

CD One Selection 11 Anonymous, Motet, "En non Diu! Quant voi; Eius in Oriente," thirteenth century, excerpt.

CD One Selection 12 French dance, "Estampie," thirteenth century.

Glossary

antiphon a verse sung in response to the text

archivolt a molded or decorated band around an arch or forming an archlike frame for an opening (see Figure 13.9)

bay a regularly repeated spatial unit of a building; in medieval architecture, a vaulted compartment

counterpoint a musical technique that involves two or more independent melodies; the term is often used interchangeably with "polyphony"

diptych a two-paneled painting

crocket a stylized leaf used as a terminal ornament

finial an ornament, usually pointed and foliated, that tops a spire or pinnacle

gargoyle a waterspout usually carved in the form of a grotesque figure

gesso a chalky white plaster used to prepare the surface of a panel for painting

historiated capital the uppermost member of a column, ornamented with figural scenes

lancet a narrow window topped with a pointed arch

lintel a horizontal beam or stone that spans an opening (see Figure 13.9)

mandorla a halo that surrounds the entire figure

motet a short, polyphonic religious composition based on a sacred text

mullion the slender, vertical pier dividing the parts of a window, door, or screen

ogee a pointed arch with an S-shaped curve on each side

organum the general name for the oldest form of polyphony: In *parallel organum*, the two voices move exactly parallel to one another; in *free organum* the second voice moves in contrary motion; *melismatic organum* involves the use of multiple notes for the individual syllables of the text

polyphony (Greek, "many voices") a musical texture consisting of two or more lines of melody that are of equal importance

polyptych a multi-paneled painting

psaltery a stringed instrument consisting of a flat soundboard and strings that are plucked

quadripartite consisting of or divided into four parts

reliquary a container for a sacred relic or relics

requiem a Mass for the Dead; a solemn chant to honor the dead

rose (from the French *roue*, "wheel") a large circular window with stained glass and stone tracery

sequence a special kind of trope consisting of words added to the melismatic passages of Gregorian chant

sexpartite consisting of or divided into six parts

tempera a powdered pigment that produces dry, flat colors

timbre tone color; the distinctive tone or quality of sound made by a voice or a musical instrument

triforium in a medieval church, the shallow arcaded passageway above the nave and below the clerestory (see Figure 13.19)

tripartite consisting of or divided into three parts

triptych a three-paneled painting

trope an addition of words, music, or both to Gregorian chant

trumeau the pillar that supports the superstructure of a portal (see Figure 13.9)

tympanum the semicircular space enclosed by the lintel over a doorway and the arch above it (see Figure 13.9)

voussoir (French, "wedge") a wedge-shaped block or unit in an arch or vault

westwork (from the German, *Westwerk*) the elaborate west end of a Carolingian or Romanesque church

Chapter

14

The World Beyond the West: India, China, and Japan

ca. 500–1300

"Heaven is my father and earth is my mother, and even such a small creature as I finds an intimate place in their midst."
Zhang Zai

Figure 14.1 *Shiva Nataraja, Lord of the Dance*, from southern India, Chola period, eleventh century. Bronze, height 5 ft. Surrounded by a ring of fire, Shiva dances the eternal rhythms of the universe: birth, death, and rebirth.

LOOKING AHEAD

Western students often overlook the fact that Europe—home of the culture that is most familiar to them—occupies only a tiny area at the far western end of the vast continental landmass of Asia. At the eastern end of that landmass lie two geographic and cultural giants, India and China, and the small but mighty Japan. During the European Middle Ages, East and West had little contact with each other, apart from periodic exchanges of goods and technology facilitated by Muslim intermediaries.

Between 500 and 1300 C.E., India produced some of the finest Sanskrit literature ever written. Hindu temple architecture and sculpture reached new levels of imagination and complexity, and Indian music flourished. In China, during roughly the same period, the Tang and Song dynasties fostered a golden age in poetry and painting. The Chinese surpassed the rest of the world in technological invention and led global production in fine pottery and textiles. Medieval Japan originated the world's oldest prose fiction, as well as a unique form of theatrical performance known as Nō drama. In both secular and religious art, the Japanese cultivated a style governed by elegance and artless simplicity. A brief examination of the artistic record of these three civilizations puts our study of the medieval era in global perspective.

India

Although the term "medieval" does not apply to the history of India in the Western sense of an interlude between Classical and early modern times, scholars have used that term to designate the era between the end of the Gupta dynasty (ca. 500) and the Mongol invasion of India in the fourteenth century—a thousand-year period that roughly approximates the Western Middle Ages. The dissolution of the Gupta Empire at the hands of Central Asian Huns, an event that paralleled the fall of Rome in the West and the collapse of the Han Empire in China, destroyed the remains of South Asia's greatest culture. Following this event, amidst widespread political turmoil and anarchy, India reverted to a conglomeration of fragmented, rival local kingdoms dominated by a warrior caste (not unlike the feudal aristocracy of medieval Europe). Ruling hereditary chiefs or *rajputs* ("sons of kings") followed a code of chivalry that set them apart from the lower classes.

The caste system (see chapter 3), which had been practiced in India for many centuries, worked to enforce the distance between rulers and the ruled. And as groups were subdivided according to occupation and social status, caste distinctions became more rigid and increasingly fragmented. Extended families of the same caste were ruled by the eldest male, who might take a number of wives. Children

were betrothed early in life and women's duties—to tend the household and raise children (preferably sons)—were carefully prescribed. In a society where males were masters, a favorite Hindu proverb ran, "A woman is never fit for independence." The devotion of the upper-caste Hindu woman to her husband was dramatically expressed in *sati*, a custom by which the wife threw herself on her mate's funeral pyre.

Early in the eighth century, Arab Muslims entered India and began to convert the native population to Islam. Muslim authority took hold in northern India, and Muslims rose to power as members of the ruling caste. During the tenth century, the invasions of Turkish Muslims brought further chaos to India, resulting in the capture of Delhi (Map **14.1**) in 1192 and the destruction of the Buddhist university of Nalanda in the following year. Muslim armies destroyed vast numbers of Hindu and Buddhist religious statues, prohibited by Islamic law. Islam ultimately supplanted Hinduism and Buddhism in the Indus valley (modern Pakistan) and in Bengal (modern Bangladesh). Elsewhere, however, the native traditions of India itself prevailed. Indeed, most of India—especially the extreme south, which held out against the Muslims until the fourteenth century—remained profoundly devoted to the Hindu faith. Today, approximately 85 percent of India's population is Hindu. Buddhism, on the other hand, would virtually disappear from India by the thirteenth century.

Map 14.1 India in the Eleventh Century.

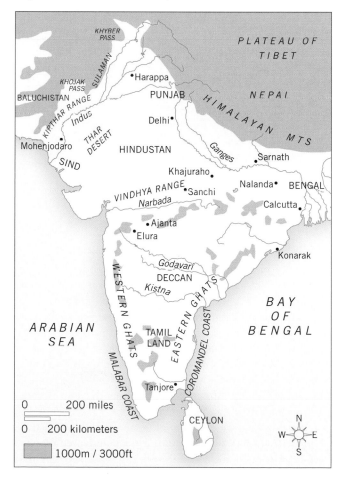

Figure 14.2 *Standing Vishnu*, from southern India, Chola period, tenth century. Bronze, with greenish blue patination, height 33¾ in. Icons of Vishnu often resemble those of the Buddha, who is accepted by Hindus as an avatar of Vishnu.

Hinduism

Unique in having no historical founder, Hinduism teaches that all individual aspects of being belong to the same divine substance: the impersonal, all-pervading Absolute Spirit known as Brahman. Pantheistic Hinduism, as defined in the principal religious writings, the *Upanishads* and the *Bhagavad-Gita* (see chapter 3), would seem to be contradicted by the sheer numbers of Hindu gods and goddesses worshiped in India. The growing devotion to the gods that took place between the fifteenth and fourteenth centuries was the result of a process of **syncretism** by which Hinduism accommodated a wide variety of local and regional deities, along with India's ancient nature gods and mythological beings. Although the worship of many gods suggests that

Hindus are polytheistic, in reality, India's gods are perceived as the facets of a diamond: they exist as individual aspects of the One, more specifically, as **avatars** ("incarnations") of Brahman. Much in the way that Christians regard Jesus as the incarnate form of God, Hindus believe that the avatars of Brahman assume various names and forms, even those of animals. They freely honor the Buddha and Jesus as human forms of the Absolute Spirit.

In that Hinduism embraces a multitude of sects, there exists no monolithic Hindu authority (comparable, for instance, to the Church in the Christian West), nor is there a prescribed or uniform liturgy. Hinduism encourages its devotees to seek union with Brahman in their own fashion, or in the fashion taught by their *guru* (spiritual guide), placing a fundamental faith in the concept that there are infinite ways of reaching the godhead.

Hindu devotional practice involves visiting the shrine of the god, and offering prayers, flowers, or food. Gazing at the god's image is essential: Hinduism holds that the god is present in its representation. Thus, visual contact with an image of the deity is a form of direct contact with the divine; this they call *darshan* (literally, "seeing and being seen by the god"). The very act of beholding the image is an act of worship and an expression of intense personal devotion by which divine blessings are received.

Out of the host of deities that characterized Hindu worship in medieval India, three principal gods dominate: Brahma, Vishnu, and Shiva. Hindus associate this "trinity" with the three main expressions of Brahmanic power: creation, preservation, and destruction. They honor Brahma—his name is the masculine form of Brahman—as the creator of the world. They prize Vishnu (identified with the sun in ancient Vedic hymns) as the preserver god. Hindu mythology recounts Vishnu's appearance on earth in nine different incarnations, including that of Krishna, the hero-god of the *Mahabharata* (see chapter 3). The conically crowned Vishnu pictured in Figure **14.2** holds in his upper right hand a flaming solar disk; his upper left hand displays a conch shell, a reminder of his association with the primeval ocean, but also a symbol of the ancient war trumpet used by Vishnu to terrorize his enemies. With his lower right hand, he makes the *mudra* of protection (see Figure 9.25), while his lower left hand points to the earth and the sacred lotus, symbol of the cosmic womb. Ritual icons like this one, cast in bronze by the lost-wax method (see Figure 0.18), are among the finest freestanding figural sculptures executed since Golden Age Greece. Produced in large numbers in tenth-century Tamil Nadu in south India, bronze effigies of the god were often bedecked with flowers and carried in public processions. (Note the rings at the four corners of the base of the *Standing Vishnu* in Figure 14.2, which once held poles for transporting the statue.) As a ninth-century Tamil poet explained, "The god comes within everyone's reach."

The third god of the trinity, Shiva, is the Hindu lord of regeneration. A god of destruction and creation, of disease and death, and of sexuality and rebirth, Shiva embodies the dynamic rhythms of the universe. While often shown in a dual male and female aspect, Shiva is most commonly portrayed as Lord of the Dance, an image that evokes the Hindu notion of time. Unlike the Western view of time, which is linear and progressive, the Hindu perception of time is cyclical; it resembles an ever-turning cosmic wheel. The four-armed figure of Shiva as Lord of the Dance is one of medieval India's most famous Hindu icons (see Figure 14.1)—so popular, in fact, that Tamil sculptors cast multiple editions of the image. Framed in a celestial ring of fire, Shiva enacts the dance of creation and destruction, the cosmic cycle of birth and death. His serpentine body bends at the neck, waist, and knees in accordance with specific and prescribed dance movements. Every part of the statue has symbolic meaning: Shiva's earrings are mismatched to represent the male/female duality. One right hand holds a small drum, the symbol of creation; a second right hand (the arm wreathed by a snake, ancient symbol of regeneration) forms the *mudra* meaning protection; one left hand holds a flame, the symbol of destruction; the second left hand points toward Shiva's feet, the left "released" from worldliness, the right one crushing a demon-dwarf that symbolizes egotism and ignorance. Utterly peaceful in countenance, Shiva embodies the five activities of the godhead: creation, protection, destruction, release from destiny, and enlightenment. By these activities, the god dances the universe in and out of existence.

Indian Religious Literature

Medieval Indian literature drew heavily on the mythology and legends of early Hinduism as found in the Vedic hymns and in India's two great epics, the *Mahabharata* and the *Ramayana* (see chapter 3). This body of classic Indian literature was recorded in Sanskrit, the language of India's educated classes. Serving much the same purpose that Latin served in the medieval West, Sanskrit functioned for centuries as a cohesive force amidst India's diverse regional vernacular dialects.

Among the most popular forms of Hindu literature are the *Puranas* (Sanskrit, "old stories"), a collection of eighteen religious books that preserve the myths and legends of the Hindu gods. Transmitted orally for centuries, they were not written down until well after 500 C.E. Many of the tales in the *Puranas* illustrate the special powers of Vishnu and Shiva or their avatars. In the *Vishnu Purana*, for instance, Krishna (the eighth and most venerated incarnation of Vishnu), is pictured as the "cosmic lover" who courts his devotees with sensual abandon, seducing them to become one with the divinity. Over the next five centuries, as the devotional aspects of Hinduism came to overshadow the metaphysical aspects of the faith, Krishna became increasingly humanized. His seduction of Radha, his principal consort, became the focus of religious poems, the most notable of which is the twelfth-century *Gita Govinda*, written by Jayadeva (fl. 1200). This epic poem, which holds an important place in Indian devotional music and art, tells of the enduring romance between Govinda (Krishna) and Radha, the most enticing of his 16,000 wives and lovers (Figure 14.3).

Figure 14.3 Page from *Gita Govinda*, "Krishna and Radha with their Confidantes," India, ca. 1635–40. Ink and opaque watercolor on paper, 10¼ × 8⅜ in. Krishna (his name means "dark" or "dark blue") declares his love for Radha, symbol of human longing for the divine. Her servants are shown on the right; below is a garden bower set with refreshment.

In both the *Puranas* and the *Gita*, intense earthly passion serves as a metaphor for the Self (Atman) seeking union with the Absolute (Brahman). Unlike the medieval Christian condemnation of erotic sensuality, Hinduism values the physical union of male and female as symbolic of the eternal mingling of flesh and spirit, a state of spiritual unity that would lead believers out of the cycle of reincarnation. The *Upanishads* make clear the analogy:

> In the embrace of his beloved a man forgets the whole world—everything both within and without. In the same manner, he who embraces the Self knows neither within nor without.

In the following passage from the *Vishnu Purana*, Krishna's cajoling and sensuous courtship, culminating in the circle of the dance, symbolizes the god's love for the human soul and the soul's unswerving attraction to the One.

READING 14.1 From the *Vishnu Purana*
(recorded after 500)

. . . [Krishna], observing the clear sky, bright with the autumnal   1
moon, and the air perfumed with the fragrance of the wild
water-lily, in whose buds the clustering bees were murmuring
their songs, felt inclined to join with the milkmaids [Gopis] in
sport. . . .
    Then Madhava [Krishna], coming amongst them, conciliated
some with soft speeches, some with gentle looks; and some he

took by the hand: and the illustrious deity sported with them in the stations of the dance. As each of the milkmaids, however, attempted to keep in one place, close to the side of Krishna, the circle of the dance could not be constructed; and he, therefore, took each by the hand, and when their eyelids were shut by the effects of such touch, the circle was formed. Then proceeded the dance, to the music of their clashing bracelets, and songs that celebrated, in suitable strain, the charms of the autumnal season. Krishna sang of the moon of autumn—a mine of gentle radiance; but the nymphs repeated the praises of Krishna alone. At times, one of them, wearied by the revolving dance, threw her arms, ornamented with tinkling bracelets, round the neck of the destroyer of Madhu [Krishna]; another, skilled in the art of singing his praises, embraced him. The drops of perspiration from the arms of Hari [Krishna] were like fertilizing rain, which produced a crop of down upon the temples of the milkmaids. Krishna sang the strain that was appropriate to the dance. The milkmaids repeatedly exclaimed "Bravo, Krishna!" to his song. When leading, they followed him; when returning they encountered him; and whether he went forwards or backwards, they ever attended on his steps. Whilst frolicking thus, they considered every instant without him a myriad of years; and prohibited (in vain) by husbands, fathers, brothers, they went forth at night to sport with Krishna, the object of their affection.

   Thus, the illimitable being, the benevolent remover of all imperfections, assumed the character of a youth among the females of the herdsmen of [the district of] Vraja; pervading their natures and that of their lords by his own essence, all-diffusive like the wind. For even as the elements of ether, fire, earth, water, and air are comprehended in all creatures, so also is he everywhere present, and in all . . .

Q How do "seduction" and "the dance" function as metaphors of Hindu spirituality?

Indian Poetry

If the religious literature of India is sensuous in nature, so too is the secular literature, much of which is devoted to physical pleasure. Sanskrit lyric poetry is the most erotic of all world literatures. Unlike the poetry of other ancient cultures, that of India was meant to be spoken, not sung. On the other hand, Sanskrit poetry shares with most ancient Greek and Latin verse a lack of rhyme. It makes use of such literary devices as **alliteration** (the repetition of initial sounds in successive words, as in "panting and pale") and **assonance** (similarity between vowel sounds, as in "lake" and "fate").

   In Sanskrit verse, implication and innuendo are more important than direct statement or assertion. The multiplicity of synonyms in Sanskrit permits a wide range of meanings, puns, and verbal play. And although this wealth of synonyms and near-synonyms contributes to the richness of Indian poetry, it makes English translation quite difficult. For example, there are some fifty expressions in Sanskrit for "lotus"; in English there is but one. Sanskrit poets employ a large number of stock similes: the lady's face is like the moon, her eyes resemble lotuses, and so on.

Classical rules of style dictate that every poem must exhibit a single characteristic sentiment, such as anger, courage, wonder, or passion. Grief, however—the emotion humans seek to avoid—may not dominate any poem or play.

   A great flowering of Indian literature occurred between the fourth and tenth centuries, but it was not until the eleventh century and thereafter that the renowned anthologies of Sanskrit poetry appeared. One of the most honored of these collections, an anthology of 1739 verses dating from between 700 and 1050, was compiled by the late eleventh-century Buddhist monk Vidyakara. It is entitled *The Treasury of Well-Turned Verse*. As with most Indian anthologies, poems on the subject of love outnumber those in any other category, and many of the love lyrics feature details of physical passion. As suggested by the selection that follows, Indian poetry is more frank and erotic than ancient or medieval European love poetry and less concerned with the romantic aspects of courtship than most Islamic verse.

READING 14.2 From *The Treasury of Well-Turned Verse* (ca. 1050)

"When we have loved, my love"

When we have loved, my love,
Panting and pale from love,
Then from your cheeks my love,
Scent of the sweat I love:
And when our bodies love
Now to relax in love
After the stress of love,
Ever still more I love
Our mingled breath of love.

"When he desired to see her breast"

When he desired to see her breast
She clasped him tight in an embrace;
And when he wished to kiss her lip
She used cosmetics on her face.
She held his hand quite firmly pressed
Between her thighs in desperate grip;
   Nor yielded to his caress,
   Yet kept alive his wantonness.

"If my absent bride were but a pond"

If my absent bride were but a pond,
her eyes the water lilies and her face the lotus,
her brows the rippling waves, her arms the lotus stems;
then might I dive into the water of her loveliness
and cool of limb escape the mortal pain
exacted by the flaming fire of love.

Q How do these poems compare with similar expressions of love in Egypt (Reading 2.2), Greece (Reading 5.2), and Rome (Reading 6.6)?

Indian Architecture

Hinduism generated some of the finest works of art and architecture in India's long history. Buddhist imagery influenced the style of medieval Hindu art, and Buddhist rock-cut temples and shrines provided models for Hindu architects. Between the sixth and fourteenth centuries, Hindus built thousands of temple-shrines to honor Vishnu and Shiva. These structures varied in shape from region to region, but generally they took the shape of a mound (often square or rectangular) topped with lofty towers or spires. Such structures were built of stone or brick with iron dowels frequently substituting for mortar. As with the early Buddhist *stupa* (see Figure 9.20), the Hindu temple symbolized the sacred mountain. Some temples were even painted white to resemble the snowy peaks of the Himalayas.

The Buddhist *stupa* was invariably a solid mound; however, the Hindu temple, more akin to the *chaitya* hall (see Figures 9.22, 9.23), encloses a series of interior spaces leading to a shrine—the dwelling place of the god on earth. Devotees enter the temple by way of an ornate porch or series of porches, each porch having its own roof and spire. Beyond these areas lies a large hall, and, finally, the dim, womblike sanctuary that enshrines the cult image of the god. The Hindu temple does not serve as a place for congregational worship (as does the medieval church); rather, its basic function is as a place of private, individual devotion, a place in which the devotee may visit and make offerings to the god. Often the focus of pilgrimage, at particular times of the year it hosts religious festivals specific to the god (or gods) to which it is dedicated. The design of the Hindu temple is based on the cosmic mandala (the diagrammatic map of the universe) and governed by divine numerology. The sacred space at the center is the primordial Brahman; the surrounding squares correspond to gods, whose roles in this context are as guardians of the Absolute Spirit. Although the Hindu temple and the Gothic cathedral were very different in terms of design and building function, both signified the profoundly human impulse to forge a link between heaven and earth and between matter and spirit.

The Kandariya Mahadeo temple in Khajuraho is but one of twenty-five remaining Hindu temple-shrines that rise like cosmic mountains out of the dusty plains of central north India (see Map 14.1). Dedicated in the early eleventh century to the god Shiva, the temple rests on a high masonry terrace and is entered through an elevated porch (Figures **14.4**, **14.5**). Like most Indian temples, Kandariya Mahadeo consists of a series of extensively ornamented horizontal cornices that ascend in narrowing diameter to their lotus-shaped peaks. At each tier of the beehivelike tower is a row of high-relief sculptures: human beings and animals drawn from India's great epics appear at the lower levels, while divine nymphs and celestial deities adorn the upper sections. The ornamental ensemble comprises a total of some 600 figures (Figure **14.6**).

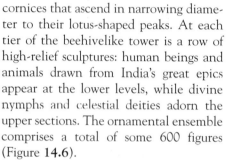

Figure 14.6 Sculpted figures on the Kandariya Mahadeo temple, Khajuraho.

Figure 14.4 Kandariya Mahadeo temple, Khajuraho, India, ca. 1000. Stone, height approx. 102 ft.

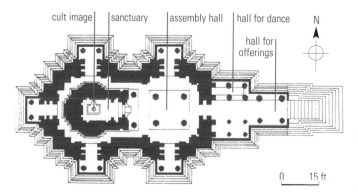

cult image | sanctuary | assembly hall | hall for dance

hall for offerings

N

0   15 ft

Figure 14.5 Plan of Kandariya Mahadeo temple, Khajuraho.

Like the Gothic cathedral, the Hindu temple was a kind of "bible" in stone. Yet no two artistic enterprises could have been further apart: whereas the medieval Church discouraged the depiction of nudity as suggestive of sexual pleasure and sinfulness, Hinduism exalted the representation of the human body as symbolic of abundance, prosperity, and regeneration. The sinuous nudes that animate the surface of the Kandariya Mahadeo temple assume languid, erotic poses. Deeply carved, and endowed with supple limbs and swelling breasts and buttocks, their bodies signify the divine attributes of life-breath and "fullness." The loving couples (known as **mithunas**)—men and women locked in passionate embrace (Figure **14.7**)—call to mind the imagery of the dance in the *Vishnu Purana*. They symbolize the interdependence of male and female forces in the universe, and the ultimate union of human and divine love.

Indian Music and Dance

The music of India is inseparable from religious practice. A single musical tradition—one that goes back some 3000 years—dominates both secular and religious music. In ancient times, India developed a system of music characterized by specific melodic sequences (**ragas**) and rhythms (**talas**). The centuries have produced thousands of *ragas*, sixty of which remain in standard use; nine are considered primary. Each *raga* consists of a series of seven basic tones arranged in a specific order. The performer may improvise on a chosen *raga* in any manner and at any length. As with the Greek modes, each of the basic Indian *ragas* is associated with a different emotion, mood, or time of day. A famous Indian anecdote tells how a sixteenth-century court musician, entertaining at midday, once sang a night *raga* so beautiful that darkness instantly fell where he stood. Governing the rhythmic pattern of an Indian musical composition is the *tala*, which, in union with the *raga*, shapes the mood of the piece. Indian music divides the octave into twenty-two principal tones and many more microtones, all of which are treated equally. There is, therefore, no tonal center and no harmony in traditional Indian music. Rather, the character of a musical composition depends on the choice of the *raga* and on its exposition. A typical *raga* opens with a slow portion that establishes a particular mood, moves into a second portion that explores rhythmic variations, and closes with rapid, complex, and often syncopated improvisations that culminate in a frenzied finale.

India developed a broad range of stringed instruments that were either bowed or plucked. The most popular of these was the **sitar**, a long-necked stringed instrument with a gourd resonator, which came into use during the thirteenth century (Figure **14.8**). Related to the kithara, an instrument used in ancient Greece (see chapter 5), the sitar provided a distinctive rhythmic "drone," while its strings were plucked for melody. Accompanied by flutes,

Figure 14.7 *Mithuna* couple, from Orissa, India, twelfth to thirteenth centuries. Stone, height 6 ft.

🎼 See Music Listening Selections at end of chapter.

Figure 14.8 Ravi Shankar playing the sitar (right); the other musicians play the tabla (hand drums) and a tamboura (plucked string instrument).

drums, bells, and horns, sitar players were fond of improvising patterns of notes in quick succession against a resonating bass sound.

The Sanskrit word for music (*sangeeta*) means both "sound" and "rhythm," suggesting that the music of India, like that of most ancient cultures, was inseparable from the art of the dance. Indian dance, like the *raga* that accompanied it, set a mood or told a story by way of rigidly observed steps and hand gestures (*mudra*). India trained professional dancers to achieve difficult leg and foot positions, some of which may be seen on the façades of Indian temples (see Figure 14.5). Each of some thirty traditional dances requires a combination of complex body positions, of which there are more than a hundred. The close relationship among the arts of medieval India provides something of a parallel with the achievement of the medieval synthesis in the West. On the other hand, the sensual character of the arts of India distinguishes them sharply from those of Christian Europe.

Science and Technology

499	Indian mathematicians complete a compilation of known mathematical and astronomical principles
ca. 600	the decimal system is in use in India
876	the symbol for "zero" is first used in India

China

Nowhere else in the world has a single cultural tradition dominated so consistently over so long a period as in China. When European merchants visited China in the thirteenth century, the Chinese had already enjoyed 1700 years of civilization. China's agrarian landmass, rich in vast mineral, vegetable, and animal resources, readily supported a large and self-sufficient population, the majority of which constituted a massive land-bound peasantry. Despite internal shifts of power and repeated attacks from its northern nomadic neighbors, China experienced a single form of government—imperial monarchy—and a large degree of political order until the invasion of the Mongols in the thirteenth century. Even after the establishment of Mongol rule under Kublai Khan (1215–1294), the governmental bureaucracy on which China had long depended remained intact, and Chinese culture continued to flourish. The wealth and splendor of early fourteenth-century China inspired the awe and admiration of Western visitors, such as the famous Venetian merchant-adventurer Marco Polo (1254–1324). Indeed, in the two centuries prior to Europe's rise to economic dominion (but especially between 1250 and 1350), China was "the most extensive, populous, and technologically advanced region of the medieval world."

China in the Tang Era

Tang China (618–907) was a unified, centralized state that had no equal in Asia or the West. In contrast with India, class distinctions in China were flexible and allowed a fair degree of social mobility: thanks to the imperial meritocratic system, even commoners could rise to become members of the ruling elite. Nevertheless, as in all Asian and European civilizations of premodern times, the great masses of Chinese peasants had no voice in political matters.

Under the rule of the Tang emperors, China experienced a flowering of culture that was unmatched anywhere in the world. Often called the greatest dynasty in Chinese history, the Tang brought unity and wealth to a vast Chinese empire (Map 14.2). Tang emperors perpetuated the economic policies of their immediate predecessors, but they employed their vast powers to achieve a remarkable series of reforms. They completed the Grand Canal connecting the lower valley of the Yellow River to the eastern banks of the Yangzi, a project that facilitated shipping and promoted internal cohesion and wealth. They initiated a full census of the population (some four centuries before a similar survey was undertaken in Norman England), which was repeated every three years. They also humanized the penal code and tried to guarantee farmlands to the peasants. They stimulated agricultural production, encouraged silk production (Figure 14.9) and the flourishing silk trade, launched a tax reform that based assessments on units of land rather than agricultural output, and they commuted payments from goods to coins.

The Tang Empire dwarfed the Carolingian Empire in the West not only in terms of its geographic size and population but also with respect to its intellectual and educational accomplishments. Tang bureaucrats, steeped in Confucian traditions and rigorously trained in the literary classics, were members of an intellectual elite that rose to service on the basis of merit. Beginning in the seventh century (but rooted in a long tradition of leadership

Science and Technology

700	the Chinese perfect the making of porcelain, which reaches Europe as "china"
725	the Chinese build a water clock with a regulating device anticipating mechanical clocks
748	the first printed newspaper appears in Beijing
868	the *Diamond Sutra*, the first known printed book, is produced in China

based on education and ability), every government official was subject to a rigorous civil service examination. A young man gained a political position by passing three levels of examinations (district, provincial, and national) that tested his familiarity with the Chinese classics as well as his grasp of contemporary political issues. For lower-ranking positions, candidates took exams in law, mathematics, and calligraphy. As in the Islamic world and the Christian West, higher education in China required close familiarity with the basic religious and philosophical texts. But because Chinese characters changed very little over the centuries, students could read 1500-year-old texts as easily as they could read contemporary ones. Chinese classics were thus accessible to Chinese scholars in a way that the Greco-Roman classics were not accessible to Western scholars. Training for the arduous civil service examinations required a great degree of memorization and a thorough knowledge of the Chinese literary tradition, but originality was also important: candidates had to prove accomplishment in the writing of prose and poetry, as well as in the analysis of administrative policy. Strict standards

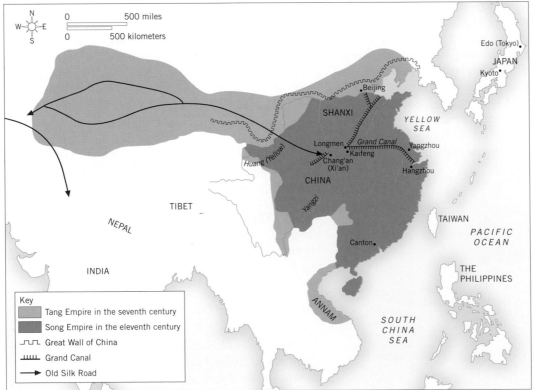

Map 14.2 East Asia, ca. 600–1300.

Figure 14.9 Attributed to the Song emperor **HUIZONG** (reigned 1101–1125), but probably by court academician, after a lost painting by Zhang Xuan (fl. 713–741), *Women Combing Silk*, detail of *Court Ladies Preparing Newly Woven Silk*, Northern Song dynasty, early twelfth century. Ink, color, and gold on silk handscroll, height 14½ in., length 4 ft. 9¼ in.

applied to grading, and candidates who failed the exams (only 1 to 10 percent passed the first level) could take them over and over, even into their middle and old age.

During the seventh century, the imperial college in the capital city of Chang'an (present-day Xi'an) prepared some 3000 men for the civil service examinations. (As in the West, women were excluded from education in colleges and universities.) Such scholar officials constituted China's highest social class. And while the vast population of Chinese peasants lived in relative ignorance and poverty, the aristocratic bureaucracy of the Tang generally enjoyed lives of wealth and position (Figure 14.10). Nowhere else in the world (except perhaps ninth-century Baghdad) was such prestige attached to scholarship and

Figure 14.10 Attributed to **GU HONGZHONG**, detail of *Night Revels of Han Xizai*, ca. twelfth-century copy of a tenth-century composition. Ink and color on silk handscroll, 11¼ in. × 11 ft. 1 in. The tenth-century emperor Li Yu, angry with one of his officials who had been lax in attending court, is said to have assigned the artist to spy on him at the all-night parties in his private quarters. The courtier's misdeeds apparently continued even after the "evidence" was brought before the emperor. On the left, a young girl plays a pipa, the Chinese equivalent of the lute.

intellectual achievement. Despite instances in which family connections influenced political position, the imperial examination system remained the main route to official status in China well into the twentieth century.

A less enlightened Chinese practice survived into the modern period: the binding of women's feet. From earliest times, Chinese women participated in agricultural activities as well as in the manufacture of silk (see Figure 14.9); many were trained in dance and musical performance (see Figure 14.10). In the early 900s, however, as women seem to have assumed a more ornamental role in Chinese society, footbinding became common among the upper classes. To indicate that their female offspring were exempt from common labor, prosperous urban families bound the feet of their infant daughters—a practice that broke the arch and dwarfed the foot to half its normal growth. Footbinding, a cruel means of signifying social status, persisted into the early twentieth century.

Confucianism

During the Tang Era, Confucianism remained China's foremost moral philosophy. Confucian teachings encouraged social harmony and respect for the ruling monarch, whom the Chinese called the "Son of Heaven." While Tang rulers drew on Buddhism and Daoism to legitimize their office, political counsel remained Confucian. Confucian culture held firmly to a secular ethic that emphasized proper conduct (*li*) and the sanctity of human life on earth. These tenets challenged neither the popular worship of Chinese nature deities, nor the ancient rites that honored the souls of the dead. Confucian ideals of order, harmony, and filial duty were easily reconciled with holistic Daoism. Tolerant of all religions, the Chinese never engaged in religious wars or massive crusades of the kind that disrupted both Christian and Islamic civilizations.

Buddhism

The Tang Era was the golden age of Chinese Buddhism. Buddhist monasteries flourished and Buddhist sects proliferated. These sects emphasized various aspects of the Buddha's teachings or practices, the first of which was meditation. The image of the Buddhist **luohan** (or *arhat*, "worthy one"), transfixed in a state of deep meditation (Figure **14.11**), became a popular model of self-control and selflessness—an ideal type not unlike the Christian saint.

The most famous of Tang China's Buddhist sects was the Pure Land sect, presided over by Amitabha, the Buddha of Infinite Light. In the Mahayana tradition, this sect emphasized faith (and the repeated invocation of the Buddha's name) as a means of achieving rebirth in the Pure Land, or Paradise. Simply uttering his name many times a day assured the faithful of salvation. Followers of Amithaba were assisted by the *bodhisattva* of mercy known as Guanyin (Figure **14.12**).

Chan Buddhism ("Zen" in Japan) became equally influential. Rejecting other popular practices, such as the study of Scriptures or the performance of meritorious deeds, it held meditation as the sole means of achieving enlightenment—deliverance in a sudden illuminating flash.

Figure 14.11 *Luohan*, China, tenth to thirteenth centuries. Pottery with three-color glaze, height 3 ft. 10½ in.

Figure 14.12 *Guanyin*, tenth to early twelfth century. Wood with painted decoration, height 7 ft 11 in. Brightly painted and gilded, this Chinese wood-carved *bodhisattva* wears sumptuous robes, a profusion of jewels, and an ornate headdress. Guanyin is equally popular in Japan, where he is known as "Kannon."

While Confucianism was generally tolerant of popular religious practice, it disapproved of Buddhist celibacy, which contravened the Confucian esteem for family. The vast wealth and political influence accumulated by the Buddhist community and the loss of large numbers of talented men to Buddhism moved some emperors to restrict the number of Buddhist monasteries and to limit the ordination of new monks and nuns. This culminated in a brief but catastrophic ban of the religion in the year 845; Buddhist temples and monasteries were closed, and monks and nuns were forced to return to the population at large. The ban, however, was short in duration; and the vigor of Buddhist religion became ever more evident in subsequent years.

China in the Song Era

After a brief period of political turmoil resulting from the collapse of the Tang dynasty and attacks by nomadic tribes, the Song dynasty (960–1279) reestablished a unified Chinese empire. Although its territory was much reduced compared to that of the Tang Empire, and it had powerful and land-hungry neighbors to the north and west, the Song nevertheless is a period of great advancement both in terms of culture and technology. The three centuries of Song rule corresponded roughly to the golden age of Muslim learning, the waning of the Abbasid Empire and the era of Norman domination in Europe (see chapters 10, 11).

The Song Era enjoyed population growth, agricultural productivity, and vigorous commercial trade centering on the exportation of tea, silk, and ceramics. China's new economic prosperity caused a population shift from the countryside to the city, where social mobility was on the rise. The imperial capitals of Kaifeng and Hangzhou (see Map 14.2), with populations of over one million people, boasted a variety of restaurants, teahouses, temples, gardens, and shops, including bookstores and pet shops (Figure **14.13**). Chinese cities were larger and more populous than those in the West and city dwellers enjoyed conditions of safety that are enviable even today—in Hangzhou, the streets were patrolled at night, and bridges and canals were guarded and fitted with balustrades to prevent drunken revelers from falling into the water.

Given the constant threat posed by their northern neighbors, a ready army was a necessity. Mercenaries, however, characterize the military of the Song state. Where medieval Islam and the feudal West prized heroism and the art of war, the Chinese despised military life. A Chinese proverb warned that just as good steel should not be made into common nails, good men should not become soldiers. Chinese poets frequently lamented the disruption of family life as soldiers left home to defend remote regions of the Empire. In combat, the Chinese generally preferred starving out their enemies to confronting them in battle. The peaceful nature of the Chinese impressed their first Western visitors: arriving in China a half century after the end of the Song Era, Marco Polo observed with some astonishment that no one carried arms. Well into the twentieth century, China espoused the notion of cosmic harmony best expressed in the writings of the Neo-Confucian philosopher Zhang Zai (1020–1077):

> Heaven is my father and earth is my mother, and even such a small creature as I finds an intimate place in their midst. Therefore that which extends throughout the universe I regard as my body and that which directs the universe I consider as my nature. All people are my brothers and sisters, and all things are my companions.

Confucian, Dao, and Buddhist practices continued to flourish during the Song Era. It was at this time that the image and person of the *bodhisattva* of compassion, Guanyin, became feminized (see Figure 14.12). This beloved icon, like that of the Virgin Mary in medieval Christendom, embodied the loving, forgiving aspect of devotional faith.

Technology in the Tang and Song Eras

Chinese civilization is exceptional in the extraordinary number of its technological inventions, many of which came into use elsewhere in the world only long after their utilization in China. A case in point is printing, which originated in ninth-century China but was not perfected in the West until the fifteenth century. The earliest printed document, the *Diamond Sutra*, dated 868, is a Buddhist text produced from large woodcut blocks (Figure **14.14**). In the mid-eleventh century, the Chinese invented movable type and, by the end of the century, the entire body of Buddhist and Confucian classics, including the commentaries, were available in printed editions. One such classic (a required text for civil service candidates) was *The Book of Songs*, a

Figure 14.13 ZHANG ZEDUAN, detail from *Life Along the River on the Eve of the Qing Ming Festival,* late eleventh to early twelfth century. Handscroll, ink on silk.

Figure 14.14 The *Diamond Sutra*, the world's earliest printed book, dated 868. 6 ft. × 30 in. In 1900, the *Diamond Sutra* was found along with hundreds of other scrolls sealed in a Chinese cave. It records the Buddha's teachings on the nature of perception.

Science and Technology

1000	the magnetic needle compass is developed in China
1009	the Chinese first use coal as fuel
ca. 1040	three varieties of gunpowder are described by Zeng Kongliang
1041	movable type is utilized in China

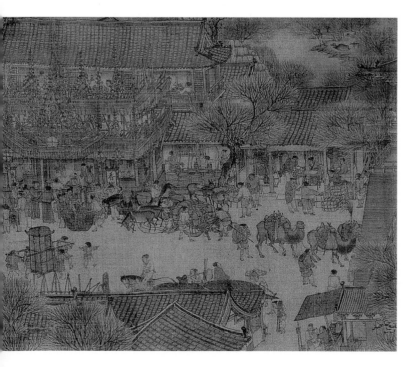

venerable collection of over 300 poems dating from the first millennium B.C.E. By the twelfth century, the Chinese were also printing paper money—a practice that inevitably gave rise to the "profession" of counterfeiting. Although in China movable type did not inspire a revolution in the communication of ideas (as it would in Renaissance Europe), it encouraged literacy, fostered scholarship, and facilitated the preservation of the Chinese classics.

Chinese technology often involved the intelligent application of natural principles to produce labor-saving devices. Examples include the water mill (devised to grind tea leaves and to provide power to run machinery), the wheelbarrow (used in China from at least the third century but not found in Europe until more than ten centuries later), and the stern-post rudder and magnetic compass (Song inventions that facilitated maritime trade). The latter two devices had revolutionary consequences for Western Europeans, who used them to inaugurate an age of exploration and discovery (see chapter 18). Gunpowder, invented by the Chinese as early as the seventh century and used in firework displays, was employed (in the form of fire-arrow incendiary devices) for military purposes in the mid-tenth century, but arrived in the West only in the fourteenth century. Other contrivances, such as the abacus and the hydromechanical clock, and such processes as iron casting (used for armaments, for suspension bridges, and for the construction of some Tang and Song pagodas) were unknown in the West for centuries or were invented independently of Chinese prototypes. Not until the eighteenth century, for instance, did Western Europeans master the

Science and Technology

1045	Su Song builds a giant water clock and mechanical armillary sphere
1100	the Chinese use coke in iron smelting
1145	illustrations of the internal organs and circulatory vessels are published in China
1221	the Chinese devise shrapnel bombs with gunpowder

technique of steel casting, which had been in use in China since the sixth century C.E.

Some of China's most important technological contributions, such as the foot stirrup (in use well before the fifth century) and gunpowder, improved China's ability to withstand the attacks of Huns, Turks, and other tribal peoples who repeatedly attacked China's northern frontiers. In the West, however, these devices had revolutionary results: the former ushered in the military aspect of medieval feudalism; and the latter ultimately undermined siege warfare and inaugurated modern forms of combat. While thirteenth-century China was far ahead of the medieval West in science and technology, its wealth in manpower—a population of some hundred million people—may have made industrial technology unnecessary.

In addition to their ingenuity in engineering and metallurgy, the Chinese advanced the practice of medicine. From the eleventh century on, they used vaccination to prevent diseases, thus establishing the science of immunology. Their understanding of human anatomy and the theory that illness derives from an imbalance of *qi* (life energy) gave rise to acupuncture—the practice of applying needles to specific parts of the body to regulate and restore proper energy flow. Chinese medical encyclopedias dating from the twelfth century were far in advance of any produced in the medieval West. In both India and China, the belief in the unity of mind and body encouraged healing practices (such as meditation and yoga) that have met with an enthusiastic reception in the West only in recent decades.

Chinese Literature

Chinese literature owes little to other cultures. It reflects at every turn a high regard for native traditions and for the concepts of universal harmony expressed in Confucian and Daoist thought. Philosophic in nature, it is, however, markedly free of religious sentiment. Even between the fifth and ninth centuries, when Buddhism was at its height, Chinese literature was largely secular, hence quite different from most of the writings of medieval Europe and the rest of Asia.

The Tang and Song Eras saw the production of a wide variety of literary genres, including treatises on history, geography, religion, economics, and architecture; monographs on botany and zoology; essays on administrative and governmental affairs; drama, fiction, and lyric poetry. Experts in the art of compiling information, the Chinese produced a vast assortment of encyclopedias, manuals of

divination and ritual, ethical discourses, and anthologies based on the teachings of Confucius and others. Like the medieval Scholastics in the West, Chinese scholars esteemed their classical past, but, unlike the Europeans, they acknowledged no conflict between (and therefore no need to reconcile) faith and reason.

During the twelfth and thirteenth centuries, in Song urban centers, storytelling flourished, and popular theater arose in the form of dramatic performance. Popular genres included comedy, historical plays, and tales of everyday life—many of which featured love stories. As dramatists began to adapt literary plots to music, **opera** (musical drama) became the fashionable entertainment among ordinary townspeople and at the imperial court. The first Chinese **novels**—products of a long tradition of oral narrative—also appeared during the twelfth century, their themes focusing on the adventures of contemporary heroes.

The novel, however, was not original to China. Rather, it was a product of the aristocratic and feudal culture of medieval Japan (discussed later in this chapter). In China, early fiction reached a high point with the monumental historical novel entitled *Three Kingdoms* (attributed to the fourteenth-century playwright Luo Guanzhong). This 1000-page work, filled with hundreds of characters and lengthy descriptions of martial prowess, brings alive the turbulent era (220–280) that followed the breakup of the Han dynasty.

Chinese Music and Poetry

To the Chinese, music functioned to imitate and sustain the harmony of nature. Both Daoists and Confucians regarded music as an expression of cosmic order, and Daoists even made distinctions between *yin* and *yang* notes. Like most of the music of the ancient world, that of China was monophonic, but it assumed a unique timbre produced by nasal tones that were often high in pitch and subtle in inflection. The sliding nasal tones that typify Chinese music resemble those of the zither. Frequently used for Buddhist chant (see chapter 9), the zither was the favorite Chinese instrument, and musical notation to guide the performer was devised as early as the second century B.C.E. Chinese instrumental ensembles included the zither, the *pipa* (a short-necked lute) and a variety of flutes, bells, and chimes (see Figure 14.10).

The most popular Chinese musical genre was the solo song, performed with or without instrumental accompaniment. A close kinship between Chinese music and speech was enforced by the unique nature of the Chinese language. Consisting of some 50,000 characters, spoken Chinese demands subtle intonations: the pitch or tonal level at which any word is pronounced gives it its meaning. A single word, depending on how it is uttered, may have more than a hundred meanings. In this sense, all communication in the Chinese language is musical—a phenomenon that has particular importance for Chinese poetry.

See Music Listening Selections at end of chapter.

Chinese poetry is a kind of vocal music: a line of spoken poetry is—like music—essentially a series of tones that rise and fall in various rhythms. Moreover, since Chinese is a monosyllabic language with few word endings, rhyme is common to speech. All Chinese verse is rhymed, often in long runs that are almost impossible to imitate in English. Equally difficult to capture in translation are the extraordinary kinds of condensation and innuendo that most characterize Chinese verse.

During the Tang Era, China produced some of the most beautiful poetry in world literature. The poems of the eighth and ninth centuries—an era referred to as the golden age of Chinese poetry—resemble diary entries that record the intimate experience of everyday life. Unlike the poetry of India, Chinese lyrics are rarely sensuous or erotic and only infrequently attentive to either physical affection or romantic love. Restrained and sophisticated, the poetry of the Tang period was written by scholar-poets (the so-called *literati*) who considered verse-making, along with calligraphy and painting, the mark of educational and intellectual refinement. From earliest times, nature and natural imagery played a large part in Chinese verse. Tang poets continued this long tradition: their poems are filled with the meditative spirit of Daoism and a sense of oneness with nature.

Two of the greatest poets of the Tang period, Li Bo (ca. 700–762) and Du Fu (712–770), belonged to the group of cultivated individuals who made up China's cultural elite. Although Li Bo was not a scholar-official, as was his friend Du Fu, he was familiar with the Chinese classics. Both Li Bo and Du Fu were members of the Eight Immortals of the Wine Cup, an informal association of poets who celebrated the kinship of ink and drink and the value of inebriation to poetic inspiration. Du Fu, often regarded as China's greatest poet, wrote some 1400 poems, many of which are autobiographical reflections that impart genuine emotion and humor. In contrast, the ninth-century poet Bo Zhuyi, who headed the Tang Bureau of War, brought to his poems a note of cynicism and worldliness that is particularly typical of the late Tang period and that of the succeeding Song. Like most of the poets of his time, he was a statesman, a calligrapher, an aesthetician, and a moralist. He thus epitomized the ideal well-rounded individual long before that concept became important in Renaissance Europe.

READING 14.3 Poems of the Tang and Song Eras
(750–900)

Li Bo's "Watching the Mount Lushan Waterfall"

Incense-Burner Peak shimmers in the sun,   1
Purple mist slowly rising.
A flying stream, seen from below,
Hangs like clouds down the crag.
The waterfall pours itself   5
Three thousand feet straight down,
Roaring like the Milky Way
Tumbling from high heaven.

Li Bo's "Zhuang Zhou and the Butterfly"

Zhuang Zhou[1] in dream became a butterfly,   1
And the butterfly became Zhuang Zhou at waking.
Which was the real—the butterfly or the man?
Who can tell the end of the endless changes of things?
The water that flows into the depth of the distant sea   5
Returns anon to the shallows of a transparent stream.
The man, raising melons outside the green gate of the city,
Was once the Prince of the East Hill,[2]
So must rank and riches vanish.
You know it, still you toil and toil,—What for?   10

Du Fu's "Spring Rain"

Oh lovely spring rain!   1
You come at the right time, in the right season.
Riding the night winds you creep in,
Quietly wetting the world.
Roads are dark, clouds are darker.   5
Only a light on a boat, gleaming.
And in the morning the city is drunk with red flowers,
Cluster after cluster, moist, glistening.

Du Fu's "Farewell Once More"
(To my friend Yan at Feng Ji Station)

Here we part.   1
You go off in the distance,
And once more the forested mountains
Are empty, unfriendly.
What holiday will see us   5
Drunk together again?
Last night we walked
Arm in arm in the moonlight,
Singing sentimental ballads
Along the banks of the river.   10
Your honor outlasts three emperors.
I go back to my lonely house by the river,
Mute, friendless, feeding the crumbling years.

Bo Zhuyi's "On His Baldness"

At dawn I sighed to see my hairs fall;   1
At dusk I sighed to see my hairs fall.
For I dreaded the time when the last lock should go . . .
They are all gone and I do not mind at all!
I have done with that cumbrous washing and getting dry;   5
My tiresome comb forever is laid aside.
Best of all, when the weather is hot and wet,
To have no topknot weighing down on one's head!
I put aside my dusty conical cap;
And loose my collar fringe,   10
In a silver jar I have stored a cold stream;

---

[1] A fourth-century follower of Lao Zi (see chapter 3), whose writings describe how, in a dream, he became a butterfly.

[2] The marquis of Dongling, a third-century-B.C.E. official, lost his exalted position at court after the fall of the Qin dynasty, and retired to grow melons outside of the city of Chang'an.

On my bald pate I trickle a ladle-full.
Like one baptized with the Water of Buddha's Law,
I sit and receive this cool, cleansing joy.
Now I know why the priest who seeks repose   15
Frees his heart by first shaving his head.

Bo Zhuyi's "Madly Singing in the Mountains"

There is no one among men that has not a special failing: 1
And my failing consists in writing verses.
I have broken away from the thousand ties of life:
But this infirmity still remains behind.
Each time that I look at a fine landscape: 5
Each time that I meet a loved friend,
I raise my voice and recite a stanza of poetry
And am glad as though a god had crossed my path.
Ever since the day I was banished to Xunyang
Half my time I have lived among the hills.   10
And often, when I have finished a new poem,
Alone I climb the road to the Eastern Rock.
I lean my body on the banks of white stone:
I pull down with my hands a green cassia[1] branch.
My mad singing startles the valleys and hills: 15
The apes and birds all come to peep.
Fearing to become a laughing-stock to the world,
I choose a place that is unfrequented by men.

Q What themes dominate these six poems?

Q How do these poems differ from those of
       medieval India (Reading 14.2)?

Chinese Landscape Painting

During the Tang Era, figural subjects dominated Chinese art (see Figure 14.9), but by the tenth century, landscape painting became the favorite genre. The Chinese, and especially the literati of Song China, referred to landscape paintings as wordless poems and poems as formless paintings; such metaphors reflect the intimate relationship between painting and poetry in Chinese art. In subjects dealing with the natural landscape, both Chinese paintings and Chinese poems evoke a mood rather than provide a

literal, objective description of reality. Chinese landscapes work to convey a spirit of harmony between heaven and earth. This cosmic approach to nature, fundamental to Confucianism, Daoism, and Buddhism, asks the beholder to contemplate, rather than simply to view the painted image. It requires that we integrate multiple viewpoints, shifting between foreground, middleground, and background in ways that resemble the mental shifts employed in reading lines of verse.

Chinese paintings generally assume one of three basic formats: the handscroll, the hanging scroll, or the album leaf (often used as a fan). Between 1 and 40 feet long, the handscroll is viewed continuously from right to left (Figure **14.15**). Like a poem, the visual "action" unfolds in time. An object of lingering contemplation and delight, such a scroll would have been unrolled privately and read, one section at a time. The hanging scroll, on the other hand, is vertical in format and is meant to be read from the bottom up—from earth to heaven, so to speak (see Figure 14.16). The third format, the album leaf, usually belongs to a book that combines poems and paintings in a sequence. Both leaves and scrolls are made of silk or paper and ornamented with ink or thin washes of paint applied in monochrome or in muted colors. An interesting Chinese practice is the addition of the seals or signatures of collectors who have owned the work of art. These appear along with occasional marginal comments or brief poems inspired by the visual image. The poem may serve as an extension of the content of the work of art. Transmitted from generation to generation, the Chinese painting, then, is a repository of the personal expressions of both artist and art lover.

By comparison with the art of the medieval West, much of which is religious in subject matter, Chinese painting draws on everyday human activities. Yet, Chinese artists rarely glorify human accomplishments. Their landscapes often dwarf the figures so that human occupations seem mundane and incidental.

A *Solitary Temple Amid Clearing Peaks*, attributed to Li Cheng (active 940–967), is meditative in mood and subtle in composition (Figure **14.16**). There is no single viewpoint from which to observe the mountains, trees, waters, and human habitations. Rather, we perceive the whole from what one eleventh-century Chinese art critic called the "angle of totality." We look down upon some elements, such as the rooftops, and up to others, such as the tree tops.

---

[1] A tree whose bark is used as a source of cinnamon.

Figure 14.15 MI YOUREN, *Cloudy Mountains*, 1130. Ink, white lead, and slight touches of color on silk handscroll, 13 ft. 6 in. × 6 ft. 3 in. Mountains, Chinese symbols of immortality, were often described as living organisms that issued the life force (*qi*) in the form of cloud vapor.

The lofty mountains and gentle waterfalls seem protective of the infinitely smaller images of temples, houses, and people. Misty areas provide transition between foreground, middleground, and background, but each plane—even the background—is delineated with identical precision. Chinese painting displays a remarkable economy of line and color—that is, a memorable image is achieved by means of a limited number of brushstrokes and tones. Li Cheng fulfilled the primary aim of the Chinese landscape painter (as defined by Song critics): to capture the whole universe within a few inches of space.

More intimate in detail but equally subtle in its organization of positive and negative space, *Apricot Blossoms* by Ma Yuan reflects the Song taste for decorative works featuring floral motifs (Figure **14.17**). Refined nature studies like this one, executed in ink and color on silk, dwell on a single element in nature (the "broken branch") rather than the expansive landscape. The couplet at the right (added by the Empress Yang (1162–1232) extends the "message" of the image as fragile, elegant, fleeting:

Figure 14.16 (above) Attributed to **LI CHENG**, *A Solitary Temple Amid Clearing Peaks*, Northern Song dynasty, ca. 950. Ink and slight color on silk hanging scroll, 3 ft. 8 in. × 22 in.

Meeting the wind, they offer their artful charm;
Moist with dew, they boast their pink beauty.

The earliest treatises on Chinese painting appeared in the Song Era. They describe the integration of complementary pictorial elements: dark and light shapes, bold and muted strokes, dense and sparse textures, large and small forms, and positive and negative shapes, each pair interacting in imitation of the *yin/yang* principle that underlies cosmic wholeness. Specific

Figure 14.17 (left) **MA YUAN**, *Apricot Blossoms*, Song dynasty. Fan mounted as an album leaf, ink and color on silk, 10 × 10¾ in.

brushstrokes, each bearing an individual name, are prescribed for depicting different natural phenomena: pine needles, rocks, mountains, and so forth. A form of calligraphy, the artist's brushstrokes are the "bones" of Chinese painting. Economy of line and color, gestural expressiveness, and spontaneity are hallmarks of the finest Chinese paintings, as they are of the best Chinese poems. Tradition rather than originality was prized: artists freely copied the works of the masters honoring their forebears by "quoting" from their poems or paintings.

Chinese Crafts

From earliest times, the Chinese excelled in the production of ceramic wares. They manufactured fine terracotta and earthenware objects for everyday use and for burial in the tombs of the dead (see chapter 7). During the Tang Era, Chinese craftspeople produced thousands of realistic clay images: a terracotta court dancer wears an elegant dress with long sleeves designed to sway with her body movements (Figure **14.18**). Other female figures are shown playing polo or performing on musical instruments—evidence of the wide range of activities enjoyed by aristocratic women. Representations of horsemen and horses—the treasured animals of China—appear in great numbers in Tang graves (as they had in the tombs of earlier dynasties, see Figure 7.5). Such figures were usually cast from molds, assembled in sections, and glazed with green, yellow, and brown colors (Figure **14.19**).

Tang and Song craftspeople perfected various types of stoneware, the finest of which was **porcelain**—a hard, translucent ceramic fired at extremely high heat. Glazed with delicate colors, and impervious to water, porcelain vessels display a level of sophistication that is not merely technical; their elegant shapes, based on natural forms, such as lotus blossoms and buds, are marvels of calculated simplicity in formal design (Figure **14.20**). Describing the magnificent porcelain vessels of the Tang Era, a ninth-century merchant marveled that one could see the sparkle of water through Chinese bowls that were "as fine as glass." International trade featuring porcelain did not begin, however, until the Song Era. Exported along with silk, lacquerware, and carved ivory, porcelain became one of the most sought-after of Chinese luxury goods— indeed, it was so popular that Westerners still refer to dishes and plates as "china." Classic porcelains reflect the refinement of age-old traditions: their shapes often drew inspiration from those conceived by early bronze workers of the Shang Era (see chapter 3), while the cool blues and yellowish greens of the finest Chinese porcelains recall the color and texture of Chinese jades. Still other types, such as the cobalt blue and white porcelains that influenced Islamic art, originated in the thirteenth century.

The somber restraint of Chinese pottery stands in sharp contrast to the ornate richness of Chinese metal-

Figure 14.18 *Standing Court Lady*, Tang dynasty, mid-seventh century. Pottery with painted decoration, height 15⅛ in. Filled with pottery figures like this one, showing a court dancer, Tang graves provide a record of the various roles played by women in Chinese society.

Figure 14.19 *Horse and Rider*, Tang dynasty, early eighth century. Pottery with three-color glaze and painted decoration, height 15 in.

Figure 14.20 Ru ware, bowl in the shape of a lotus, Northern Song dynasty, twelfth century. Porcelain, height 4 in.

work, inlaid wood, carved lacquers, and textiles. Weavers of the Song Era produced exquisite silks embroidered to imitate flower-and-bird-paintings. Luxury silks and Chinese embroideries were so highly valued that they were often buried, along with fine ceramics and gold and silver objects, in the graves of wealthy Asians found along the Silk Road, that 8000-mile trade route from Constantinople on the Black Sea to Chang'an on the Pacific Ocean.

Chinese Architecture

Chinese architects embraced a building system that reflected the practice of *feng shui* (see chapter 7) and the ancient Daoist quest for harmony with nature. Structures were emphatically horizontal—built to hug the earth. Whole towns and individual buildings were laid out according to a cosmic axis that ran from north to south. Celestial symbolism governed design: for instance, four doors represented the seasons, eight windows signified the winds, and twelve halls stood for the months in the year. House doors faced the "good" southerly direction of the summer sun, and rear walls were closed to the cold north, homeland of the barbarian hordes that threatened China throughout its history. Chinese residences were normally self-enclosed and looked inward to courtyards or gardens.

In the Tang Era, the classical period of Chinese architecture, Buddhist temple complexes attracted scores of pilgrims. The complex featured a hall for the veneration of the Buddha-image, and a multiroofed pagoda (see chapter 9), erected over Buddhist relics. Temples and shrines were constructed of wood, a building material that was plentiful in China and one that was highly valued for its natural beauty. Chinese architectural ingenuity lay in the invention of a unique timber frame that—in place of walls—bore the entire weight of the roof while making the structure earthquake-resistant (Figure **14.21**). Perfected during the Tang Era, the Chinese system of vaulting consisted of an intricate series of wooden cantilevers (horizontal brackets extending beyond the vertical supports) that provided support for centrally pitched, shingled, or glazed-tile roofs. By the tenth century, the aesthetics of wood construction were firmly established and, during the following century, scholars enshrined these principles in China's first manual on architecture. Because wooden buildings were highly vulnerable to fire—almost all examples of early Chinese shrines had been destroyed by the end of the first millennium—Chinese architects began to build in brick and in cast iron. Regardless of medium, however, Chinese pagodas, temples, and domestic structures, with their projecting upturned eaves, became models of elegant design. The many magnificent pagodas found in Japan (see Figure 14.21) and Southeast Asia, testify to China's influence in disseminating an architectural style dependent on the wooden cantilever.

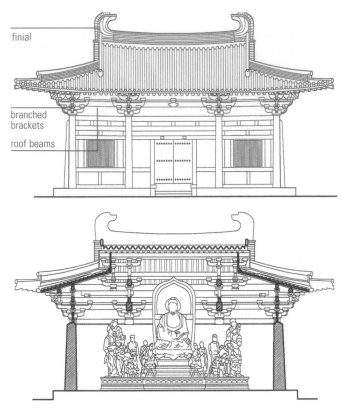

Figure 14.21 Elevation and transverse section through the main hall of Nanchan Monastery, Shanxi Province, 782. In one of China's earliest surviving wooden Buddhist temple halls, architects used layered (or branched) brackets to support the roof beams. The cantilevered brackets allow the roof to overhang the exterior, thus giving the building a sense of lightness and grace, while affording protection from foul weather.

Japan

Buddhism entered Japan from China by way of Korea in the early sixth century, bringing in its wake a restructuring of the government on Chinese imperial models. Japan's elite embraced all things Chinese: the Chinese system of writing, record keeping, and governing, as well as the fundamentals of Chinese art and architecture. By the eighth century, Japan had absorbed both Buddhism and Chinese culture. For roughly four centuries (794–1185), Japan enjoyed a cultural golden age centered on the imperial capital of Heian (modern Kyoto), from which came Japan's first wholly original literature and a set of aesthetic norms that left a permanent mark on Japanese culture.

It was Japan that introduced to world literature the prose form known as the novel. *The Tale of Genji* (ca. 1004), a Japanese classic, tells the story of the "shining prince" of the Heian court. Because the novel exposes the inner life of Genji and other characters, it has been called the world's first psychological novel. However, it also paints a detailed picture of Japanese life within a small segment of the population: the aristocracy. The men and women of this class prized elegant clothes (women usually wore five to twelve layers of silk robes), refined manners, and poetic versatility: inability to compose the appropriate on-the-spot poem was considered a serious social deficiency.

The Heian aristocracy regarded as essential education in the Confucian classics and the cultivation of dance, music, and fine calligraphy—in all, a set of values that prefigured by some five hundred years the Renaissance ideal of the well-rounded courtier.

The author of *The Tale of Genji*, Murasaki Shikibu (978–1016), was one of a group of outstanding female writers and a member of Heian court society. Upper-class women like Murasaki were prized in East Asian literary history: their fame in writing polished intimate prose was so great that one tenth-century male diarist pretended his work had been penned by a woman. Their achievement is all the more remarkable in that (like their Chinese counterparts) they were excluded from the world of scholarly education and, hence, from training in written Chinese. Nevertheless, using a system of phonetic symbols derived from Chinese characters, these women produced the outstanding monuments of medieval Japanese prose.

The Tale of Genji—in English translation some six volumes long—cannot be represented adequately here. But it is possible to gain insight into both the talents of Murasaki Shikibu and the character of the Heian court by means of a brief look at her *Diary*. Written between the years 1008 and 1010, it reveals her keen eye for visual detail evident in this vivid description of court attire:

> . . . the older women wore plain jackets in yellow-green or dark red, each with five damask cuffs. The brightness of the wave pattern printed on their trains caught the eye, and their waistlines too were heavily embroidered. They had white robes lined with dark red in either three or five layers but of plain silk. The younger women wore jackets with five cuffs of various colors, white on the outside with dark red on yellow-green, white with just one green lining, and pale red shading to dark red with one white layer interposed; they were all arranged most intelligently.

Beyond its importance as a historical record, Murasaki's *Diary* is significant as an exercise in self-analysis. Not an autobiography, it is, rather, a series of reminiscences, anecdotes, and experiences. Nevertheless, it documents the author's quest to understand her role as a writer and her place in the highly artificial imperial court. As such, the *Diary* displays a dimension of self-consciousness that has long been considered an exclusively Western phenomenon.

READING 14.4 From *The Diary of Lady Murasaki*
(ca. 1000)

The wife of the Governor of Tanba is known to everyone in the service of Her Majesty and His Excellency as Masahira Emon. She may not be a genius but she has great poise and does not feel that she has to compose a poem on everything she sees, merely because she is a poet. From what I have seen, her work is most accomplished, even her occasional verse. People who think so much of themselves that they will, at the drop of a hat, compose   1 lame verses that only just hang together, or produce the most pretentious compositions imaginable, are quite odious and rather pathetic.

Sei Shōnagon,[1] for instance, was dreadfully conceited. She thought herself so clever and littered her writings with Chinese characters; but if you examined her closely, they left a great deal to be desired. Those who think of themselves as being superior to everyone else in this way will inevitably suffer and come to a bad end, and people who have become so precious that they go out of their way to try and be sensitive in the most unpromising situations, are bound to look ridiculous and superficial. How can the future turn out well for them?

Thus do I criticize others from various angles—but here is one who has survived this far without having achieved anything of note. I have nothing in particular to look forward to in the future that might afford me the slightest consolation, but I am not the kind of person to abandon herself completely to despair. And yet, by the same token, I cannot entirely rid myself of such feelings. On autumn evenings, which positively encourage nostalgia, when I go out to sit on the veranda and gaze, I seem to be always conjuring up visions of the past—"and did they praise the beauty of this moon of yore?" Knowing full well that I am inviting the kind of misfortune one should avoid, I become uneasy and move inside a little, while still, of course, continuing to recall the past.

And when I play my koto[2] rather badly to myself in the cool breeze of the evening, I worry lest someone might hear me and recognize how I am just "adding to the sadness of it all";[3] how vain and sad of me. So now both my instruments, the one with thirteen strings and the one with six, stand in a miserable, sotty little closet still ready-strung. Through neglect—I forgot, for example, to ask that the bridges be removed on rainy days—they have accumulated dust and lean against a cupboard. Two biwa[4] stand on either side, their necks jammed between the cupboard and the pillar.

There is also a pair of larger cupboards crammed to bursting point. One is full of old poems and tales that have become the home for countless insects which scatter in such an unpleasant manner that no one cares to look at them any more; the other is full of Chinese books that have lain unattended ever since he who carefully collected them passed away. Whenever my loneliness threatens to overwhelm me, I take out one or two of them to look at; but my women gather together behind my back. "It's because she goes on like this that she is so miserable. What kind of lady is it who reads Chinese books?" they whisper. "In the past it was not even the done thing to read sutras!"[5] "Yes," I feel like replying, "but I've never met anyone who lived longer just because they believed in superstitions!" But that would be thoughtless of me. There is some truth in what they say.

Each one of us is quite different. Some are confident, open and forthcoming. Others are born pessimists, amused by nothing, the kind who search through old letters, carry out penances, intone sutras without end, and clack their beads, all of which makes one feel uncomfortable. So I hesitate to do even those things I should be able to do quite freely, only too aware of my own servants' prying eyes. How much more so at court, where I have many things I would like to say but always think the better of it,

because there would be no point in explaining to people who would never understand. I cannot be bothered to discuss matters in front of those women who continually carp and are so full of themselves: it would only cause trouble. It is so rare to find someone of true understanding; for the most part they judge purely by their own standards and ignore everyone else.

So all they see of me is a façade. There are times when I am forced to sit with them and on such occasions I simply ignore their petty criticisms, not because I am particularly shy but because I consider it pointless. As a result, they now look upon me as a dullard.

"Well, we never expected this!" they all say. "No one liked her. They all said she was pretentious, awkward, difficult to approach, prickly, too fond of her tales, haughty, pronen to versifying, disdainful, cantankerous and scornful; but when you meet her, she is strangely meek, a completely different person altogether!"

How embarrassing! Do they really look upon me as such a dull thing, I wonder? But I am what I am. Her Majesty has also remarked more than once that she had thought I was not the kind of person with whom she could ever relax, but that I have now become closer to her than any of the others. I am so perverse and standoffish. If only I can avoid putting off those for whom I have a genuine regard.

To be pleasant, gentle, calm and self-possessed: this is the basis of good taste and charm in a woman. No matter how amorous or passionate you may be, as long as you are straightforward and refrain from causing others embarrassment, no one will mind.

But women who are too vain and act pretentiously, to the extent that they make others feel uncomfortable, will themselves become the object of attention; and once that happens, people will always find fault with whatever they say or do: whether it be how they enter a room, how they sit down, how they stand up or how they take their leave. Those who end up contradicting themselves and those who disparage their companions are also carefully watched and listened to all the more. As long as you are free from such faults, people will surely refrain from listening to tittle-tattle and will want to show you sympathy, if only for the sake of politeness.

I am of the opinion that when you intentionally cause hurt to another, or indeed if you do ill through mere thoughtless behaviour, you fully deserve to be censured in public. Some people are so good-natured that they can still care for those who despise them, but I myself find it very difficult. Did the Buddha himself in all his

---

[1] Female writer (ca. 968–1025) famous for her *Pillow Book*, a long collection of notes, stories, and descriptions of everyday life among members of the Heian upper class.

[2] A Japanese musical instrument of the zither family.

[3] A reference to Poem 985 in the Kokinshū by Yoshimine no Munesada (Bishop Henjō): "While on his way to Nara he heard a woman playing a *koto* in a dilapidated house. He wrote this poem and sent it in: *It seemed to be a dwelling where you might expect someone dejected to be living; and now I hear the sound of a* koto *that adds to the sadness of it all.*"

[4] A short-necked lute, similar to the Chinese *pipa*.

[5] Buddhist discourses (see chapter 8).

compassion ever preach that one should simply ignore those who slander the Three Treasures?[6] How in this sullied world of ours can those who are hard done by be expected not to reciprocate in kind? And yet people react in very different ways. **110**

Some glare at each other face to face and fling abuse in an attempt to gain the upper hand; others hide their true intent and appear quite friendly on the surface—thus are true natures revealed.

Q **What does this reading reveal about the court culture of medieval Japan, and about the role of women in that culture?**

---

[6] The Three Treasures without which the teachings would not survive were the Buddha himself, the Buddhist Law, and the community of monks who preserved that law. Slander of these three treasures was one of the gravest offences.

Buddhism in Japan

As Buddhism spread throughout Japan, it inspired the construction of hundreds of shrines and temples, the oldest of which are found just outside Japan's early capital city of Nara. The site of the oldest wooden buildings in the world, this eighth-century temple complex at Yakushiji with its graceful five-storied pagoda (Figure **14.22**) preserves the timber style that originated in China. The Buddhism that arrived in sixth-century Japan was of the Mahayana variety (see chapter 8). It coexisted with Japan's native Shinto religion, which venerated the divinity of the emperor as well as the host of local and nature spirits of the countryside. The two faiths, Buddhism and Shintoism, formed a vigorous amalgam that accommodated many local beliefs and practices. The aspiration of the Buddhist faithful to be reborn in a Buddhist paradise proving very popular in Japan, the Pure Land sect venerated Amitabha (known in Japanese as Amida).

Figure 14.22 East pagoda of Yakushiji, Nara, Japan, ca. 720.

Figure 14.23 *Kichijoten*, Late Heian period, late twelfth century. Painted wood, height 35½ in. Associated with the virtues of prosperity, the plump goddess stands on a lotus, an emblem of purity and gentleness. Her right hand makes the *mudra* of reassurance and protection.

True to Mahayana Buddhism's practice across Asia, its sects in Japan assimilated the divine beings of India and China, honoring them in paintings and sculptures often based on Korean or Indian prototypes. Kichijoten, for instance, a Buddhist deity of Indian derivation, is represented in a richly polychromed wooden statue of the Late Heian period (Figure **14.23**). The popular goddess of abundance and good fortune, she is shown dressed in the elegant robes and jewelry of a Heian aristocrat.

MAKING CONNECTIONS

Figure 14.24 MATTHEW PARIS, *Vassal Paying Homage to His Lord*, from the Westminster Psalter, ca. 1250. The chain mail shown here consisted of thousands of individually joined metal links. By the fourteenth century, plate mail came to replace chain mail.

Though not identical with European feudalism, the Japanese feudal system flourished between the ninth and twelfth centuries—the age of medieval warfare in the West (Figure **14.24**). As with Western feudalism, skilled warriors, known in Japan as *samurai* (literally, "those who serve"), held land in return for military service to local landlords. The strength of the Japanese clan depended on the allegiance of the *samurai*.

Outfitted with warhorses and elaborate armor (Figure **14.25**), and trained in the arts of archery and swordsmanship, *samurai* clans competed for position and power. Their code of honor, known as *bushido* ("the way of the warrior"), exalted fierce loyalty to one's overlord, selflessness in battle, and a disdain for death. The code called for ritual suicide, usually by disembowelment, if the *samurai* fell into dishonor. Not surprisingly, the sword was the distinctive symbol of this warrior class.

Figure 14.25 Yoshihisa Matahachiro's Suit of Armor. Muromachi period, ca. 1550. Steel, blackened and gold-lacquered; flame-colored silk braid, gilt bronze, stenciled deerskin, bear pelt, and gilt wood; approx. height 5 ft. 6 in., approx. weight 48 lb. Japanese armor was made of iron, plated with lacquer to protect against the rain. In contrast with the rigidity of European plate armor, *samurai* armor was notable for its flexibility.

The Age of the *Samurai*:
The Kamakura Shogunate (1185–1333)

Toward the mid-twelfth century, Heian authority gave way to a powerful group of local clans that competed for political and military preeminence. Two in particular—the Taira and the Minamoto—engaged in outright war, fought by the military nobility known as **samurai** (see Box opposite). When the civil wars came to an end in 1192, the generals of the Minamoto clan became the rulers of Japan. They established the seat of their government at Kamakura, near modern Tokyo. Minamoto no Yoritomo (1147–1199) adopted the title of *shogun* ("general-in-chief") and set up a form of military dictatorship that ruled in the emperor's name. The events of the turbulent Kamakura era were recorded in the Japanese war epic known as the *Heiji Monogatari Emaki* (*Tale of the Heiji Rebellion*), a thirteenth-century picture-scroll version of which shows the Minamoto attack on the palace at Kyoto and the capture of the Taira clan leader (Figure **14.26**). Read from right to left, the visual narrative, enlivened by realistic details, is accompanied by written portions of the epic.

In the domain of sculpture, the Japanese were master woodcarvers. During the Kamakura Era they cultivated a style of intense pictorial Realism. The late twelfth-century sculptor Jokei executed a series of painted wood temple guardians that reveal the Japanese fascination with the human figure in violent action (Figure **14.27**). These superhuman sentinels, with their taut muscles and their grimacing faces, direct their wrath toward those who would oppose the Buddhist law. By means of exaggeration and forthright detail, Jokei achieved a balletic union of martial-arts grace and *samurai* fierceness. The Kamakura shogunate remained the source of Japanese government only until 1333, but the values of the *samurai* prevailed well into modern times.

Figure 14.26 Attributed to SUMIYOSHI KEION *Heiji Monogatari Emaki (Tale of the Heiji Rebellion)*. Picture-scroll, 13th century, detail. Colored ink on paper. Reminiscent of the Bayeux Tapestry (see Figures 11.1 and 11.17), this illustrated handscroll commemorates an important chapter in Japanese national history.

drum), the play explored a given story to expose its underlying meaning.

Nō plays—still flourishing in modern-day Japan—are performed on a square wooden stage that opens to the audience on three sides and is connected by a raised passageway to an offstage dressing room. Though roofed, the stage holds almost no scenery and that which does appear serves a symbolic function. As in ancient Greek drama, all roles are played by men. A chorus that sits at the side of the stage expresses the thoughts of the actors. Elegant costumes and masks, often magnificently carved and painted (Figure **14.28**), may be used to represent individual characters. This mask of a young woman reveals the classic Heian preference for the white-powdered face, plucked eyebrows, and blackened teeth—marks of high fashion among medieval Japanese females. A single program of Nō drama (which lasts some six hours) consists of a group of plays, with a selection from each of the play-types, such as god-plays, warrior-plays, and women-plays. Comic interludes are provided between them to lighten the serious mood.

The formalities of Nō drama were not set down until the early fifteenth century, when the playwright and actor Zeami Motokiyo (1363–1443) wrote an instructional manual for Nō actors. Zeami's manual, the *Kadensho*, prescribes demanding training exercises for the aspiring actor; it also analyzes the philosophic and aesthetic purposes of Nō theater. In the excerpt that follows, certain hallmarks of Japanese culture emerge, including a high regard for beauty of effect and a melancholic sensitivity to the pathos of human life.

Figure 14.27 JOKEI, *Kongorikishi*, Kamakura period, ca. 1288. Painted wood, height 5 ft. 4 in.

Nō Drama

Nō drama, the oldest form of Japanese theater, evolved from performances in dance, song, and mime popular in the Heian Era and possibly even earlier. Like Greek drama, the Nō play treats serious themes drawn from a legacy of history and literature. Just as Sophocles recounted the history of Thebes, so Nō playwrights recalled the civil wars of the *samurai*. They also drew on episodes from *The Tale of Genji*. Nō drama, however, was little concerned with character development or the realistic reenactment of actual events. Rather, by means of a rigidly formalized text, gestures, dance, and music (usually performed on flute and

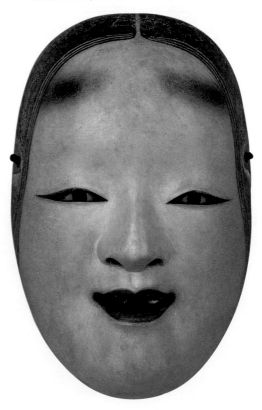

Figure 14.28 *Ko-omote* Nō mask, Ashikaga period, fifteenth century. Painted wood, height approx. 10 in.

READING 14.5 From Zeami's *Kadensho* (ca. 1400)

Sometimes spectators of the Nō say, "The moments of 'no-action' are the most enjoyable." This is an art which the actor keeps secret. Dancing and singing, movements and the different types of miming are all acts performed by the body. Moments of "no-action" occur in between. When we examine why such moments without actions are enjoyable, we find that it is due to the underlying spiritual strength of the actor which unremittingly holds the attention. He does not relax the tension when the dancing or singing come to an end or at intervals between the dialogue and the different types of miming, but maintains an unwavering inner strength. This feeling of inner strength will faintly reveal itself and bring enjoyment. However, it is undesirable for the actor to permit this inner strength to become obvious to the audience. If it is obvious, it becomes an act, and is no longer "no-action." The actions before and after an interval of "no-action" must be linked by entering the state of mindlessness in which one conceals even from oneself one's intent. This, then, is the faculty of moving audiences, by linking all the artistic powers with one mind.

      Life and death, past and present—
      Marionettes on a toy stage.
      When the strings are broken,
      Behold the broken pieces.

This is a metaphor describing human life as it transmigrates between life and death. Marionettes on a stage appear to move in various ways, but in fact it is not they who really move—they are manipulated by strings. When these strings are broken, the marionettes fall and are dashed to pieces. In the art of the Nō too, the different sorts of miming are artificial things. What holds the parts together is the mind. This mind must not be disclosed to the audience. If it is seen, it is just as if a marionette's strings were visible. The mind must be made the strings which hold together all the powers of the arts. If this is done the actor's talent will endure. This resolution must not be confined to the times when the actor is appearing on the stage. Day or night, wherever he may be, whatever he may be doing, he should not forget this resolution, but should make it his constant guide, uniting all his powers. If he unremittingly works at this his talent will steadily grow. This article is the most secret of the secret teachings. . . .

Q What is "no-action"? How does it serve Nō theater?

Chronology

India:
550–1192	era of regional states
1192	Muslim conquest of Delhi

China:
618–907	Tang dynasty
960–1279	Song dynasty

Japan:
794–1185	Heian Era
1185–1333	Kamakura shogunate

LOOKING BACK

India

- Following the collapse of the Gupta Empire, local kingdoms competed for power in India. In the early eighth century, Arab Muslims entered India and began to convert members of the native population to Islam. By the early twelfth century, the Muslims had become the ruling caste.
- Nevertheless, Hinduism prevailed as the dominant faith in most of India, ultimately overshadowing Buddhism, which virtually disappeared by the thirteenth century.
- Hinduism developed a growing devotion to the many gods and goddesses of Vedic mythology. The three principal gods, Brahma, Vishnu, and Shiva, were regarded as avatars of the regenerative Brahmanic powers of creation, preservation, and destruction. Bronze images of the gods were central to devotional practice, which involved viewing the image as a form of contact with the god.
- Popular Indian religious literature, the *Puranas*, drew heavily on the mythology and legends of early Hinduism as found in the Vedic hymns and in India's great epics, the *Mahabharata* and the *Ramayana*.
- Sensuality is a key feature of India's vast body of Sanskrit poetry.
- Modeled on Buddhist *chaitya* halls, Hindu temples honoring the gods rose like stone mountains across India. Like the medieval cathedrals, these temples were adorned with hundreds of high-relief sculptures; but unlike medieval religious statuary, the

Hindu figures—mostly nude and locked in erotic embrace—are symbols of the union of human and divine love.

- A single musical tradition dominates secular and religious music in India. Prescribed melodic sequences (*ragas*) and rhythmic patterns (*talas*) are associated with specific moods and emotions. Similarly, the art of dance prescribes specific gestures and steps that signify distinct states of mind.

China

- Ruled by the Tang dynasty, China was a unified, centralized state without equal in Asia or the West. Steeped in Confucian tradition and trained in the literary classics, its administrators were members of an intellectual elite.
- The Tang Era, a golden age of Chinese Buddhism, saw the proliferation of Buddhist monasteries and sects that encouraged the popularity of Buddhist statuary. Buddhist temples and shrines made use of earthquake-resistant, wooden cantilevers that supported elegant pitched roofs.
- The Song Era, which followed upon the collapse of the Tang, was a period of population growth, agricultural productivity, and vigorous commercial trade centering on the exportation of tea, silk, and ceramics.
- Chinese technology often involved the intelligent application of natural principles to produce labor-saving devices. Their inventions include the water mill, the wheelbarrow, the foot stirrup, steel casting, gunpowder, movable type, and the stern-post rudder.
- Chinese literature and music are closely related. Musical drama (or opera) and prose fiction were popular. Tang and Song

scholar-poets (*literati*) left hundreds of lyrics that are refined in style and filled with human emotion.

- The Chinese invented the genre of landscape painting: on silk scrolls and album leaves, master calligraphers created cosmic views of natural surroundings whose majesty dwarfed the presence of human beings
- Silk and porcelain, traded with other luxury goods along the Silk Road, brought wealth and prestige to China.

Japan

- By the eighth century, Japan had absorbed the Buddhist faith, and the Chinese system of writing, governing, and record keeping, as well as the fundamentals of Chinese art and architecture.
- Japan introduced the first novel to world literature. Written by Murasaki Shikibu, *The Tale of Genji* tells the story of the "shining prince" of the Heian court. Because the novel exposes the inner life of its protagonist, it has also been called the world's first psychological novel.
- Buddhism and Shintoism formed an amalgam that accommodated Japan's local beliefs and practices. Mahayana Buddhist sects embraced Indian and East Asian deities and temple guardians, whom they represented in realistically carved and painted wooden sculptures.
- The *samurai* culture that began with the Kamakura shogunate belonged to a feudal tradition that produced magnificent weapons, armor, and palace portraits.
- The Japanese preference for refined form and beauty of effect is illustrated in the visual arts, in literature, and (perhaps most distinctively) in Nō theater, the classic drama of Japan.

Music Listening Selections

CD One Selection 13 Indian music, *Thumri*, played on the sitar by Ravi Shankar.

CD One Selection 14 Chinese music: Cantonese music drama for male solo, zither, and other instruments, "Ngoh wai heng kong" ("I'm Mad About You").

Glossary

alliteration a literary device involving the repetition of initial sounds in successive or closely associated words or syllables

assonance a literary device involving a similarity in sound between vowels followed by different consonants

avatar (Sanskrit, "incarnation") the incarnation of a Hindu deity

luohan (Chinese, "worthy one")

a term for enlightened being, portrayed as a sage or mystic

mithuna the Hindu representation of a male and a female locked in passionate embrace

novel an extended fictional prose narrative

opera a drama set to music and making use of vocal pieces with orchestral accompaniment

pipa a short-necked lute

porcelain a hard, translucent ceramic ware made from clay fired at high heat

raga a mode or melodic form in Hindu music; a specific combination of notes associated with a particular mood or atmosphere

samurai (Japanese "those who serve") the warrior nobility of medieval Japan

sitar a long-necked stringed instrument popular in Indian music

syncretism the effort or tendency to combine or reconcile differing beliefs

tala a set rhythmic formula in Hindu music

Picture Credits

The author and publishers wish to thank the following for permission to use copyright material. Every effort has been made to trace or contact copyright holders, but if notified of any omissions, Laurence King Publishing would be pleased to insert the appropriate acknowledgement in any subsequent edition of this publication.

Chapter 8

Figure:

8.1 Mausoleo di Galla Placidia, Ravenna, Italy/ Giraudon/ The Bridgeman Art Library.
8.2 Staatliche Museen, Berlin.
8.3 Metropolitan Museum of Art. Gift of Mr. and Mrs. Klaus G. Perls, 1997. 145.3.
8.4 © 1990, Photo Scala, Florence—courtesy of the Ministero Beni e Att. Culturali.
8.5 The Cleveland Museum of Art. Leonard Hanna, Jr. Bequest. CMA 61.418.
8.6 Courtesy Museum of Fine Arts, Boston. Helen and Alice Colburn Fund. Photograph © 2006 Museum of Fine Arts, Boston.

Chapter 9

9.1 © 1990 Photo Scala, Florence, Courtesy of the Ministero Beni e Attività Culturali.
9.2 Sant'Apollinare in Classe, Ravenna, Italy. Alinari, Florence.
9.4 © 1990, Photo Scala, Florence.
9.5 Pontificia Commissione per l'Archeologia Cristiana, Rome.
9.6 Vatican Museums, Rome.
9.7 © 1990, Photo Scala, Florence—courtesy of the Ministero Beni e Att. Culturali.
9.9 © Canali Photobank, Capriolo (BS) Italy.
9.10 © 1990, Photo Scala, Florence.
9.12 Sonia Halliday Photographs.
9.13 © AKG Images/Erich Lessing.
9.15 Art Archive, London.
9.16 © 1990, Photo Scala, Florence.
9.17 © Cameraphoto Arte, Venice.
9.18 © Cameraphoto Arte, Venice.
9.20 © 1990, Photo Scala, Florence.
9.21 Photo: Douglas Dickins, London.
9.22 Government of India, Archeological Survey of India.
9.24 Courtesy of the Freer Gallery of Art, Smithsonian Institution, Washington, D.C. 49.9.
9.26 © Classic Image / Alamy.
9.28 © the Huntington Archive, Columbus, Ohio.
9.29 Werner Forman Archive, London.
9.30 The Nelson-Atkins Museum of Art, Kansas City, Missouri. Purchase: Nelson Trust.
9.31 The Metropolitan Museum of Art, Rogers Fund, 1938 (38.158.1a-n). Photograph by Schechter Lee. Image © The Metropolitan Museum of Art

Chapter 10

10.1 © Achim Bednorz.
10.2 AP Photo/Amr Nabil
10.3 The Nelson-Atkins Museum of Art, Kansas City, Missouri. Purchase: Nelson Trust.
10.4 Bibliothèque Nationale, Paris. MS Arabe 5847, fol. 105.

10.5 The Metropolitan Museum of Art, New York. Cora Timken Burnett Collection of Persian Miniatures and Other Persian Art Objects. Bequest of Cora Timken Burnett, 1956. 57.51.21.
10.6 British Museum, London.
10.7 The Metropolitan Museum of Art, New York. Rogers Fund.
10.8 The Metropolitan Museum of Art, New York. 39.20.
10.10 AKG Images / A. F. Kersting.
10.11 Photo: Spectrum Picture Library, London.
10.12 The Metropolitan Museum of Art, New York. Rogers Fund, 1965.
10.14 El Escorial de Santa Maria, MS E-Eb-1-2, f.162.

Chapter 11

11.1 The Art Archive / Musée de la Tapisserie Bayeux / Gianni Dagli Orti.
11.2 British Museum, London.
11.3 From Richard Phipps and Richard Wink, Introduction to the Gallery. Copyright © 1987 Wm. C. Brown Publishers, Dubuque, Iowa. All rights reserved. Reprinted by permission.
11.4 © The Trustees of the British Museum.
11.5 Trinity College Dublin/Bridgeman Art Library.
11.6 National Museum of Ireland, Dublin.
11.7 Achim Bednorz.
11.8 © RMN / Réunion des Musées Nationaux.
11.10 Bibliothèque Nationale, Paris, MS Lat. 9428, f.71v.
11.11 © The J. Pierpont Morgan Library, New York. Art Resource, NY.
11.12 Monastery Library of Saint-Gall, Switzerland.
11.13 Reproduced by permission of the British Library, London.
11.14 The Metropolitan Museum of Art, New York. Gift of J. Pierpont Morgan, 1917.
11.15 Photo: Skyscan Balloon Photography.
11.17 Town of Bayeux, France. Photo: By special permission of the City of Bayeux.
11.19 Reproduced by permission of the British Library, London, Add. MS 42130, f.172.
11.20 El Escorial de Santa Maria, Spain. Ms. E-Eb-1-2, f. 162.
11.21 © The J. Pierpont Morgan Library, New York, 1990, MS 806, f.166. Art Resource, NY.
11.22 University Library, Heidelberg, Germany, Codex pal. germ. 848, f.249v. Rheinisches Köln Bildarchiv, Cologne, Germany.
11.23 Editions Maillart.
11.24 Universitätsbibliothek, Heidelberg, Germany, MS Pal. germ. 848, f.64. Rheinisches Köln Bildarchiv, Cologne, Germany.

Chapter 12

12.1 Austrian National Library/Picture Archive, Vienna, Cod. 2554, fol 1v.
12.2 Rheinisches Bildarchiv, MS 13 321, Wiesbaden Codex B, folio 1.
12.3 Photo: De Jongh, Lausanne. © Musée de l'Elysée, Lausanne, Switzerland.
12.4 Reproduced by permission of the British Library, London, MS Cotton Nero, C.IV, f.39.
12.5 Alinari, Florence.
12.8 Louvre, Paris. Photo: Roger Viollet, Paris.
12.9 Photo: Dagli Orti, Paris.
12.10 State Museum, Berlin. Preussischer Kulturbesitz, Kupferstichkabinett. Photo: Bildarchiv Preussischer Kulturbesitz, Berlin.

Chapter 13

13.1 Photo: © Sonia Halliday, Western Turville, UK.
13.2 © Paul M. R. Maeyaert, Belgium.
13.4 Photo: Serge Chirol, Paris.
13.5 Photo: Yan, Toulouse.
13.6 Photo: Serge Chirol, Paris.
13.7 © Paul M. R. Maeyaert, Belgium.
13.8 © Paul M. R. Maeyaert.
13.10 © RMN/Bulloz, Paris.
13.11 Photo: James Austin, Cambridge, U.K.
13.12 Photo © Adrian Fletcher, www.paradoxplace.com.
13.13 Reproduced by permission of the British Library, London.
13.14 Sonia Halliday Photographs.
13.15 © The J. Pierpont Morgan Library, New York, 1991, MS 638 f.3. Art Resource, NY.
13.16 © Paul M. R. Maeyaert, Belgium.
13.20 Bob Burch/Bruce Coleman Inc.
13.21 John Elk III, Oakland, California.
13.22 AKG Images / A. F. Kersting.
13.23 © 1996 Photo Scala, Florence.
13.25 Photo: © James Austin, London.
13.26 Staatliche Museen, Berlin.
13.27 The Pierpont Morgan Library NY. Art Resource, NY.
13.28 © RMN/Bulloz.
13.29 Photo: Sonia Halliday, Weston Turville, U.K.
13.30 Sonia Halliday Photographs.
13.31 AKG Images / A. F. Kersting.
13.32 Sonia Halliday Photographs.
13.33 Bibliothèque de l'Arsenal, Paris. MS 1186, f.24.
13.35 Uffizi Gallery, Florence. © Studio Fotografico Quattrone, Florence.
13.36 Uffizi Gallery, Florence. © 2002, Photo Scala, Florence—courtesy of the Ministero Beni e Att. Culturali.
13.37 British Library. MS 19768, ff.10v-11.
13.38 © 1990, Photo Scala, Florence—courtesy of the Ministero Beni e Att. Culturali.

Chapter 14

14.1 Rijksmuseum, Amsterdam (AK-MAK-187).
14.2 The Metropolitan Museum of Art, New York. Purchase 1962. Gift of Mr. and Mrs. John D. Rockefeller.
14.3 Metropolitan Museum of Art, Gift of Cynthian Hazen Olsky 1985 (1985.398.12). Image © The Metropolitan Museum of Art.
14.4 AKG Images / A. F. Kersting.
14.6 AKG Images/Jean-Louis Nou.
14.7 The Metropolitan Museum of Art, New York. Florence Waterbury Fund, 1970.
14.8 Photo: © Silverstone/Magnum Photos, Inc.
14.9 Courtesy Museum of Fine Arts, Boston. Special Chinese and Japanese Fund. Photograph © 2006 Museum of Fine Arts, Boston.
14.10 The Palace Museum, Beijing.
14.11 The Nelson-Atkins Museum of Art, Kansas City, Missouri. Purchase: Nelson Trust.
14.12 The Nelson-Atkins Museum of Art, Kansas City, Missouri. Purchase: Nelson Trust. Photo: Jamison Miller.
14.13 Collection of the Palace Museum, Beijing.
14.14 Reproduced by courtesy of the British Library, London. Department of Oriental Manuscripts and Books.
14.15 The Cleveland Museum of Art. Purchase from the J. H. Wade Fund.

14.16 The Nelson-Atkins Museum of Art, Kansas City, Missouri. Purchase: Nelson Trust. 47–71.

14.17 National Palace Museum, Taipei.

14.19 The Metropolitan Museum of Art, New York. Rogers Fund, 1954. 54.169.

14.20 National Palace Museum, Taiwan.

14.22 Robert Harding World Images, London.

14.23 Joruriji, Kyoto.

14.24 Reproduced by the permission of the British Library, London.

14.25 Metropolitan Museum of Art, Rogers Fund 1904 (04.4.2) Image © The Metropolitan Museum of Art.

14.26 Photograph © 2009 Museum of Fine Arts, Boston. Fenollosa-Weld Collection 11.4000.

14.27 Kofukuji, Nara, Japan.

14.28 Kongoh Family Collection, Tokyo.

Literary Credits

The author and publishers wish to thank the following for permission to use copyright material. Every effort has been made to trace or contact copyright holders, but if notified of any omissions or errors, Laurence King Publishing would be pleased to insert the appropriate acknowledgement in any subsequent edition of this publication.

Chapter 8

READING

8.1 (p. 3): Apuleius, from *Apuleius: Volume II*, translated by Arthur Hanson (Harvard University Press, 1989). The Loeb Classical Library.

8.2 (p. 6): From "Sermon on the Mount" from *The Jerusalem Bible,* edited by Alexander Jones (Doubleday/Darton, Longman & Todd, 1966), copyright © 1966 by Darton, Longman & Todd, Ltd. and Doubleday, a division of Random House, Inc. Used by permission of Doubleday, a division of Random House, Inc.

8.3 (p. 8): From "Paul's Epistle to the Church in Rome" from *The Jerusalem Bible*, edited by Alexander Jones (Doubleday/Darton, Longman & Todd, 1966).

8.4A (p. 12), **8.4B** (p. 13): Lin Yutang, from Buddha's "Sermon at Benares" and "Sermon on Abuse" from *The Wisdom of China and India* (Random House, 1970), copyright 1942 and renewed 1970 by Random House, Inc. Reprinted by permission of Richard Ming Lai and Hsiang Ju Lin.

Chapter 9

9.1 (p. 18): From "The Nicene Creed" from *Documents of the Christian Church*, edited by Henry Bettenson (Oxford University Press, 1963).

9.3 (p. 19): Saint Augustine, from *Confessions of St. Augustine*, translated by Rex Warner (Dutton Signet, 1991), copyright © 1963 by Rex Warner, renewed © by F. C. Warner. Used by permission of Dutton Signet, a division of Penguin Group Group (USA) Inc.

9.4 (p. 21): Saint Augustine, from "City of God Against the Pagans" from *St. Augustine: Volume IV*, translated by Phil Levine (Harvard University Press, 1966). Loeb Classical Library Volume 414.

Chapter 10

10.1 (p. 48): From *The Qur'an*, translated by M. A. S. Haleem (Oxford University Press, 2004).

10.2 (p. 55): From Tarafa, "Praise for His Camel", Al-Asmai, "Romance of Antar", Ibn Zaydun "Two Fragments" and Ibn Abra, "The Beauty Spot" from *Anthology of Islamic Literature from the Rise of Islam to the Modern World*, edited by James Kritzeck (Henry Holt, 1964), © 1964 by James Kritzeck. Reprinted by permission of the publisher.

10.3 (p. 56): Rumi, "The Man of God" and "Empty the Glass of Your Desire" from *Love is a Stranger*, translated by Kabir Edmund Helminski (Threshold Books, 1993). Reprinted by permission of the publisher.

10.4 (p. 60): "Prince Behram and the Princess Al-Datma" from *Arabian Nights*, translated by Jack Zipes (Dutton Signet, 1991), copyright © 1991 by Jack Zipes. Used by permission of Dutton Signet, a division of Penguin Group (USA) Inc.

Chapter 11

11.1 (p. 70): From *Beowulf*, translated by Burton Raffel (Dutton Signet, 1963), copyright © 1963, renewed © 1991 by Burton Raffel. Used by permission of Dutton Signet, a division of Penguin Group (USA) Inc.

11.2 (p. 78): From *The Song of Roland*, translated by Patricia Terry (Prentice-Hall, 1965), © 1965.

11.3 (p. 86): Chrétien de Troyes, from *Lancelot*, translated by W. W. Comfort (Everyman, 1970).

11.4 (p. 90): Troubadour poems from *The Troubadours and Their World*, translated by Jack Lindsay (Frederick Muller, 1976). Reprinted by permission of David Higham Associates.

Chapter 12

12.4 (p. 106): Dante, from The Divine Comedy, translated by John Ciardi (W. W. Norton, 1970), copright 1954, 1957, 1959, 1960, 1961, 1965, 1967, 1970 by the Ciardi Family Publishing Trust.

12.5 (p. 111): Saint Francis, "The Canticle of Brother Sun" from *Francis and Clare: The Complete Works*, translation and introduction by Regis J. Armstrong and Ignatius C. Brady (Paulist Press, 1982), copyright © 1982 by Paulist Press, Inc., New York/Mahwah, NJ. Reprinted by permission of the publisher, www.paulistpress.com.

12.6 (p. 115): Thomas Aquinas, from "Summa Theologica" from *Basic Writings of Saint Thomas Aquinas*, edited by Anton C. Pegis (Hackett Publishing Company, 1997). Reprinted by permission of the publisher.

Chapter14

14.2 (p. 148): Vidyakara, "From the swaying of their equal commerce", "When his eyes seek out her breast" and "If my absent bride were but a pond" from *An Anthology of Sanskrit Court Poetry*, translated by Daniel H. Ingalls (Harvard University Press, 1988). Harvard Oriental Series, 44; © 1988 by the President and Fellows of Harvard College.

14.3 (p. 159): Li Bo, "Watching the Mount Lushan Waterfall" from *Gems of Chinese Poetry*, translated by Ding Zuxin and Burton Raffel (University of Liaoning Press, 1987). Reprinted by permission of Ding Zuxin; Du Fu, "Spring Rain" and "Farewell Once More" from *One Hundred Poems from the Chinese*, edited by Kenneth Rexroth (New Directions, 1971), © 1971 by Kenneth Rexroth.

14.4 (p. 164): Murasaki Shikibu, from *The Diary of Lady Murasaki*, translated an introduced by Richard Bowring (Penguin Classics, 2005), copyright © Richard Bowring, 1996, 2005. Reprinted by permission of the translator.

14.5 (p. 171): Zeami Motokiyo, from "Kadensho" from *Sources of Japanese Tradition*, edited by William Theodore de Bary (Columbia University Press, 1958), © Columbia University Press. Reprinted by permission of the publisher.

13.30

chatras 35–6, 43

chi rho 22, 30, **9.2**, **9.3**

Children's Crusade (1212) 85

China 52, 53, 54, 145, 172, **Map 14.2**

  architecture 39, 163

  Buddhism/Buddhist art and architecture 2, 14,
    39, 41, 154–5, 156, 158, 160, 163, **9.28**

  ceramics 162, 163, **14.18–14.20**

  education 152–4

  landscape painting 160–2

  literature 158

  medicine 158

  music 41, 154, 158, 162, **14.10**

  poetry 156, 157, 158–60

  technology 145, 156–8

  see also trade

chivalry 77, 89, 93

Chola dynasty

  images of Vishnu 146, **14.2**

  Shiva Nataraja, Lord of the Dance 147, **14.1**

Chrétien de Troyes: *Lancelot* 86–9 (quoted), **11.21**

Christ as Good Shepherd (catacomb fresco) 23, **9.5**

Christ Teaching the Apostles... (mosaic) 28, **9.10**

Christianity, early 2, 5–10, 13, 17–22, 46, 50, 51,
  56, 68, 72, 111, **Map 11.1**

  architecture 26–8

  art 22–6

  music 19, 33–4

  sculpture 23, 24, **9.6**

  and symbolism 22–6, 36, **13.1**

  see also iconography/icons; mosaics; Orthodox
    Christianity; Roman Catholic Church

Cimabue: *Madonna Enthroned* 137–8, **13.35**

circumference of earth 52, 54

City of God, The (Augustine) 21–2 (quoted), 99

clerestory windows 26, 126–7, **9.8**, **13.19**

cloisonné enamelwork 71, 75, 93, **11.2**, **11.3**

Cloudy Mountains (Mi Youren) 160, **14.15**

Cluny, abbey of 118, 139–40

coal 86, 157

Commedia Divina see Divine Comedy

common law 70, 93

compasses, magnetic 86, 157

Confessions (Augustine) 19–21 (quoted)

Confucianism 152, 154, 155, 156, 158, 160, 164

Constantine, Emperor 10, 13, 17, 22

Constantinople 17, 30, 51, 85, 110

  Hagia Sophia 28–30, **9.11–9.14**

constitutional monarchy 91

Córdoba, Spain 45, 53, 64, 65

  Great Mosque 61, **10.1**, **10.9**, **10.10**

counterpoint 140, 143

courtly love 86

crenellations 81, 93

crockets 129, 138, 143

crossbows 83

crosses

  Latin 24, 26, 28, 43, 119, 126, **9.3**

  Greek 26, 28, 43, 75, **9.3**, **9.11**

Crucifixion and Deposition of Christ (psalter illus.)
  136, **13.33**

Crucifixion, Santa Sabina, Rome 5, 23, **8.4**

Crusades 68, 78, 84–5, 86, 95, 114, 118, 121, 124,
  135, 154, **Map 11.3**, **11.20**

Curia Regis 81

Cybele, cult of 2, 3

D

Damascus, Syria 51, 52

dance 52, 56, 124, 141, 147, 151, 154, 162, 164,
  170, **14.1**, **14.18**

Dante Alighieri: *Divine Comedy* 103–5, 106–10
  (quoted), 118, 140, **12.5–12.8**

Dante and His Poem (Domenico di Michelino)
  12.5

Daoism 14, 39, 154, 156, 158, 160, 163

Dark Ages 68

Dead Sea Scrolls 5

Delhi, India 145

dervishes 56, 63, **10.7**

dharma 11, 34

Dia, Countess of ("Beatriz") 90–1 (quoted)

Diamond Sutra 152, 156, **14.14**

Diaspora 4, 14

"Dies Irae" 140 (quoted)

Diocletian, Emperor 17

Dionysius Exiguus 18

Dionysus, cult of 3

Dioscorides: *Materia Medica* **10.5**

diptychs 24, 43, 143, **13.34**

dits 92

Divine Comedy (Dante) 103–5, 106–10 (quoted),
  118, 140, **12.5–12.8**

Diwan (Book of Poems) (Hafiz) **10.7**

dogma 17, 18, 43, 50

Dome of the Rock, Jerusalem 62, **10.11**

Domenico di Michelino: *Dante and His Poem* **12.5**

domes 62, 74, **10.11**

  pendentive 28, 43, **9.14**

Domesday Book 81

Dominic, Saint 112

Dominican order 112, 114

Dover Castle, Kent, England 81, **11.15**

drama

  Chinese 158

  Japanese 145, 170–1, **14.28**

  liturgical 139

  see also miracle plays; morality plays; mystery
    plays

Du Fu 159

  "Farewell Once More" 159 (quoted)

  "Spring Rain" 159 (quoted)

E

ecumenism 17, 43

education

  Chinese 152–4

  Islamic 50, 52, 53

  monastic 18

  see also universities

Egypt 2, 3, 18, 26, 51, 52, 53, **11.20**

embroidery 163

Empress as Donor with Attendants, The (relief) 39,
  9.30

enamel, cloisonné 71, 75, 93, **11.2**, **11.3**

England 85, 91

  Cambridge 112

  Dover Castle, Kent 81, **11.15**

  Oxford 112

  Sutton Hoo 71, 72, **11.2**, **11.4**

Enlightenment (Gandharan frieze) 37, **9.24**

epics 69–71, 147 *see also Song of Roland; Divine
  Comedy*

equestrian sculpture (Charlemagne) 74, **11.8**

Essenes 5, 6, 18

estampie 141

Everyman 99–103(quoted), 105

excommunication 110, 111, 116

Ezra 4

F

fabliaux 92

fealty 69, 93

feng shui 163

feudalism 68, 69, 76–8, 80, 82–3, 85, 89, 93, 145,
  168

  literature 78–80

fiefs 77, 93

finials 129, 138, 143

Five Pillars, The (Islam) 46, 47, 66

Flight to Egypt, The (sculpture) 123, **13.11**

footbinding, Chinese 154

frame tale 58, 66

Francis, Saint 111, **12.9**

  The Canticle of Brother Sun 111–12 (quoted)

Franciscan order 111, 112, 140

Franks 68, 69, 70

  Song of Roland 69, 70, 78–80 (quoted), 81, 82

*French knights under Louis IX besieging Damietta,
  Egypt* (ms. illus.) **11.20**

frescoes 135, 136, **12.9**

  Ajanta, India 38, **9.27**

  catacombs 23, **9.4**, **9.5**

  Islamic 62

G

Gabriel, Angel 46, 138

Galen 54

galleries 26, **9.8**

  triforium 126, 129, 143, **13.19**

Gandhara, India 37

  Enlightenment 37, **9.24**

  Seated Buddha **8.5**

  Standing Bodhisattva **8.6**

gardens, Islamic 63

gargoyles 129, 143, **13.23**

Germanic tribes 10, 68–9

  art 71–2

  law 69

  literature 69–70

gesso 137, 143

gilding 62, 66

Giotto: *Sermon to the Birds* 111, **12.9**

Gislebertus: *Last Judgement* 122–3, 138, **13.8**,
  13.10

Gita Govinda (Jayadeva) 147, **14.3**

glass, Venetian 129

God as Architect of the Universe (ms. illus.) 95, 118,
  12.1

Golden Ass, The (Apuleius) 3 (quoted)

Good Shepherd, The (marble) 23, **9.6**

Good Shepherd, The (mosaic) **8.1**

Gospel of Judas 9

Gospels, the 5, 9, 22

  Lindau 75–6, **11.11**

  non-canonical 9

  Saint Matthew 6–9 (quoted), **11.5**